'A Nation of Beg

'A NATION OF BEGGARS'?

*Priests, People, and Politics
in Famine Ireland,
1846–1852*

DONAL A. KERR

'We are still struggling with famine and fever, and what is more than
both, the demoralization of our people consequent on the system of
relief that this incapable Government has inflicted on the country.
Every feeling of decent spirit . . . has vanished, and instead there is
created . . . a Nation of Beggars.'

*Archbishop Slattery of Cashel to Laurence Renehan, president of
Maynooth College, June 1847*

CLARENDON PRESS · OXFORD

Oxford University Press, Great Clarendon Street, Oxford OX2 6DP

Oxford New York
Athens Auckland Bangkok Bogota Bombay
Buenos Aires Calcutta Cape Town Dar es Salaam
Delhi Florence Hong Kong Istanbul Karachi
Kuala Lumpur Madras Madrid Melbourne
Mexico City Nairobi Paris Singapore
Taipei Tokyo Toronto Warsaw
and associated companies in
Berlin Ibadan

Oxford is a registered trade mark of Oxford University Press

Published in the United States
by Oxford University Press Inc., New York

British Library Cataloguing in Publication Data
Data available

Library of Congress Cataloging in Publication Data
Kerr, Donal, 1927– .
A nation of beggars? : priests, people, and politics in famine
Ireland, 1847–1852 / Donal A. Kerr.
p. cm.
Includes bibliographical references.
1. Ireland—Politics and government—1837–1901. 2. Church and
state—Ireland—History—19th century. 3. Protestants—Ireland—
History—19th century. 4. Catholics—Ireland—History—19th
century. 5. Violence—Ireland—History—19th century. 6. Famines—
Ireland—History—19th century. 7. Ireland—Church history—19th
century. 8. Russell, John Russell, Earl, 1792–1878. I. Title.
DA955.K47 1994 941.5081—dc20 94–13314
ISBN 0–19–820050–1
ISBN 0–19–8207379 (pbk)

Printed in Great Britain
on acid-free paper by
Biddles Ltd., Guildford & King's Lynn

*To peace-makers and relief workers
and for Kevin B. Nowlan and my family*

Acknowledgements

It is a pleasure to acknowledge my indebtedness to many individuals and institutions. To Professor Kevin B. Nowlan I am particularly indebted for his initial encouragement, continuous support, and helpful advice on all occasions. Among many scholars from whose advice I have greatly benefited, I would like to mention Professor Thomas O'Neill, Professor Emmet Larkin, Dr John Prest, Dr William Vaughan, Dr Cormac Ó Gráda, Dr Michael Hurst, Dr Maurice R. O'Connell, David Sheehy, Dr Ambrose Macaulay, Revd Dr Martin Coen, and the late Dr Mary Purcell. I also have a special debt of thanks to Professor Derek Beales, Dr Chris Woods, Dr Sheridan Gilley, Dr Douglas Leighton, Dr Angus Macintyre, Dr Margaret O'Callaghan, and Tony Hepburn, who read the typescript in whole or in part, for many useful suggestions.

Much unpublished material has been generously placed at my disposal. I am greatly indebted to Dr Kieran O'Shea and Dr Mark Tierney O.S.B. for providing copies of two interesting clerical diaries. I have benefited from the unpublished work of Dr Peter Gray, Dr Jacinta Prunty, Dr Austin Bourke, Dr Peter O'Dwyer, Bob Cullen and Gerry Martin. Dr Francis McKiernan, bishop of Kilmore, showed continuing interest in the work and, together with Dr Dan Galogly, provided valuable information on the clergy of the diocese of Kilmore.

I would like to express my thanks to the librarians, archivists, and staff of the following libraries, record offices, and archives: Russell Library and John Paul II Library at St Patrick's College, Maynooth and to Penny Woods in particular; the Bodleian, Oxford; Cambridge University Library; Dublin Diocesan Archives; National Library of Ireland; Archives of Saint Vincent de Paul; the Rare Books Department of Trinity College Dublin; Cashel Diocesan Archives; Kilmore Diocesan Archives, Dublin; Leeds Diocesan Archives; Department of Paleography and Diplomatic, University of Durham; Public Record Office, London; Congregation of Propaganda Fide, Rome; Irish College, Rome; St Paul-outside-the-walls, Rome, and Arundel Castle.

For permission to cite from the Clarendon Papers I am indebted to the Earl of Clarendon. For permission to use the cartoon from *Punch* on the cover I am indebted to the Board of Trinity College Dublin. I wish to thank, also, the Presentation Sisters, the Christian Brothers, and the Capuchin Fathers for furnishing useful information on relief work during the Famine by their communities.

Revd Larry Duffy, Revd James O'Brien, Revd Joseph Murphy and Ursula ní Dhálaigh read the proofs and made many useful suggestions. I am indebted to Paddy Pender and the computer staff at Maynooth College for help with word-processing. I wish to express my gratitude to the Master and Fellows of Jesus College, Oxford, and the Master and Fellows of Sidney Sussex College, Cambridge; the Principal and Fellows of St John's College, Oxford; to the Revd Chaplain, Dr John Osman, Fisher House, Cambridge; and to the Marist communities at Monteverde and Milltown. Finally, I wish to thank the staff of the Oxford University Press for their interest, advice, and unfailing courtesy.

Donal A. Kerr
Saint Patrick's College, Maynooth,
Saint Patrick's Day 1994

Contents

Abbreviations

CDA	Cashel Diocesan Archives
ClDA	Clogher Diocesan Archives
DDA	Dublin Diocesan Archives
ICA	Archives of the Pontifical Irish College, Rome
KDA	Kilmore Diocesan Archives
KrDA	Kerry Diocesan Archives
LDA	Leeds Diocesan Archives
MCA	Maynooth College Archives
NLI	National Library of Ireland
PFA	Archives of the Congregation of Propaganda Fide
PRO	Public Record Office
StPA	Archives of Saint Paul-Outside-the-Walls, Rome
UD	University of Durham

TABLE 1. The Irish Bishops, 1846–1852

PROVINCE OF ARMAGH	Date of accession	PROVINCE OF DUBLIN	Date of accession
Ardagh and Clonmaćnois		*Dublin*	
William Crolly	1835	Daniel Murray	1823
Paul Cullen	1849	Paul Cullen	1852
Joseph Dixon	1852	*Ferns*	
Ardagh		James Keating	1819
William O'Higgins	1829	Myles Murphy	1849
John Kilduff	1852	*Kildare and Leighlin*	
Clogher		Francis Haly	1838
Charles McNally	1844	*Ossory*	
Derry		Edward Walsh	1846
John MacLaughlin	1840	PROVINCE OF TUAM	
(Edward Maginn)[a]		*Tuam*	
Francis Kelly[b]		John MacHale	1834
Down and Connor		(trs. from Killala)	
Cornelius Denvir	1835	*Achonry*	
Dromore		Patrick MacNicholas	1818
Michael Blake	1833	Patrick Durcan	1852
Kilmore		*Clonfert*	
James Browne	1829	Thomas Coen	1831
Meath		John Derry	1847
John Cantwell	1830	*Elphin*	
Raphoe		George Joseph Plunket	
Patrick McGettigan	1820	Browne (trs. from	
		Galway)	1844

PROVINCE OF CASHEL

Cashel and Emly
Michael Slattery   1834

Ardfert (Kerry)
Cornelius Egan   1824

Cloyne and Ross
Bartholomew Crotty   1833
David Walsh   1847
Timothy Murphy   1849

Cork
John Murphy   1815
William Delany   1847

Killaloe
Patrick Kennedy   1836
David Vaughan   1851

Limerick
John Ryan   1828

Ross[c]
William Keane   1850

Waterford and Lismore
Nicholas Foran   1837

Galway
Laurence O'Donnell   1844

Killala
Francis O'Finan   1835
Thomas Feeny (appointed Administrator in 1839)   1848

Kilmacduagh and Kilfenora
Edward French   1825
Patrick Fallon   1852

Notes:

[a] MacLaughlin fell ill and in 1845 Maginn was provided as coadjutor with the right of succession, but died in 1849.

[b] Kelly was appointed coadjutor in 1849 and succeeded in 1864 on the death of MacLaughlin.

[c] Ross was separated from Cloyne by papal brief, 17 Dec. 1850.

TABLE 2. The Catholic Church in Ireland in 1847

Dioceses	Parish priests	Curates	Churches	Convents of nuns	Monasteries or Christian schools	Regular clergy	Catholic Population (1834)
Archd. Armagh	50	64	126	2	—	10	309,564
Derry	37	57	70	—	—	—	196,614
Clogher	36	54	78	—	—	—	260,241
Raphoe	25	30	48	—	—	—	145,385
Down and Connor	32	25	82	—	—	—	154,029
Kilmore	40	47	90	—	—	—	240,593
Ardagh	38	50	68	—	1	4	195,056
Meath	66	71	142	4	—	16	377,562
Dromore	16	23	39	1	—	—	76,275
Total in Armagh	340	421	743	7	1	30	1,955,319
Archd. Dublin	46	130	122	26	2	83	391,006
Kildare and Leighlin	45	72	112	11	1	10	290,038
Ossory	34	60	94	3	—	15	209,848
Ferns	37	59	100	6	—	15	172,789
Total in Dublin	162	321	428	46	3	123	1,063,681

Archd. Cashel and Emly	44	59	90	2	4	10	296,667
Cork	31	46	84	7	2	22	303,984
Killaloe	51	65	120	2	2	3	359,585
Kerry	43	44	93	8	2	2	297,131
Limerick	42	60	84	3	4	12	246,302
Waterford	36	70	76	10	4	14	253,091
Cloyne and Ross	48	90	113	—	2	2	436,627
Total in Cashel	295	434	660	32	20	65	2,193,387
Archd. Tuam	52	62	113	3	8	6	411,467
Clonfert	20	18	44	1	—	14	119,082
Achonry	22	23	44	—	—	—	108,835
Elphin	41	51	81	—	—	4	309,761
Kilmacduagh and Kilfenora[a]	18	11	36	1	2	—	81,642
Galway	13	8	16	5	—	14	56,503
Killala	20	13	40	—	—	—	136,383
Total in Tuam	186	186	374	10	10	38	1,223,673
GRAND TOTAL	983	1,362	2,205	95	34	256	6,436,060

Sources: W. J. Battersby, *The Complete Catholic Directory* (1848), 340; *Public Instruction Report* (1835).
[a] Kilfenora, though united to Kilmacduagh in 1750, was part of the province of Cashel.

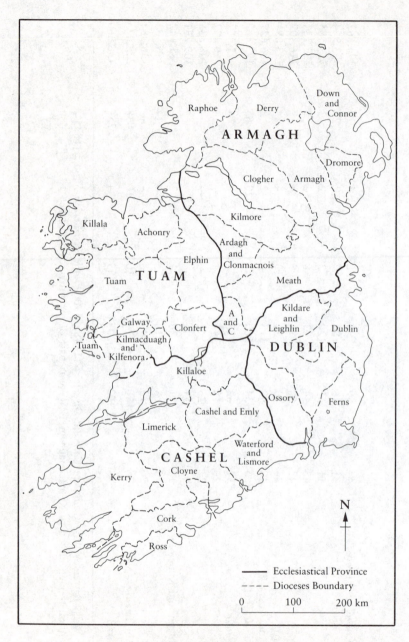

Irish Roman Catholic Ecclesiastical
Provinces and Dioceses

1

Lord John Russell and the Irish Catholic Church: Problems and Plans

'John and I, too, looked beyond [the Corn Laws crisis] to . . . a golden age for Ireland.'

(Lady Russell to Lord Melgund, c.Jan. 1846)

'Ireland will be the chief difficulty of the Whigs.'

(Lincoln to Peel, 13 Aug. 1846)

'Once at least in every generation the question, "What is to be done with Ireland?", rises to perplex the councils and trouble the conscience of the British nation', wrote John Stuart Mill in 1868.[1] This was certainly true of the 1840s, one of the most fateful decades in Irish history, when, faced with a frightening mass agitation for the repeal of the legislative union between Britain and Ireland, and then with unprecedented famine, Conservative and Whig governments wrestled with the problem. William Pitt the younger's plan of a United Kingdom of Great Britain and Ireland, whatever the immediate causes that impelled him to propose it, was a bold attempt to solve the problem by absorbing the smaller kingdom into the larger one. Irish Catholic leaders, gentry and bishops, hoped, and were encouraged to hope, that the Act of Union of 1801, by changing the context from the narrow ground of Ireland to the broader one of the United Kingdom, would provide the framework within which a solution to the Irish Catholic problem could be achieved. They were to be disappointed. Pitt, after his first attempt had been blocked by George III, abandoned Catholic emancipation, and for twenty years the 'Catholic question' remained unsolved. It was only in the 1820s, when Daniel O'Connell mobilized the whole Catholic community, that the Tory

---

[1] John Stuart Mill, 'England and Ireland 1868', in J. M. Robson (ed.), *Essays on England, Ireland and the Empire* (1992), 507.

government of the Duke of Wellington and Robert Peel gave way and brought in the Relief Act of 1829, or 'emancipation' as it was generally called. Yet despite the hopes of many statesmen, emancipation had not really resolved the wider question of Irish Catholics and the British state. Emancipation was certainly a psychological boost to Irish Catholics but, under O'Connell's leadership, instead of accepting it as a final settlement of their claims, they pressed for further concessions. Since they constituted between a quarter and a third of the citizens of the United Kingdom, what were concerned statesmen to do with this huge minority? How were they to reconcile to Great Britain some six and a half million people who had stubbornly insisted on remaining Catholic and Irish?

The long rule of the Tories finally ended in 1830 and for the next eleven years, with the exception of the short interlude of Peel's administration from December 1834 to April 1835, the Whigs were in power. The Whig administration, especially Lord Melbourne's second ministry from 1835 to 1841, was a period of modest reforms, impartial administration, and harmonious relations between the Irish Catholics and the government.[2] With the fall of the Whigs and the return to power of Peel and the Conservatives in 1841, O'Connell launched his movement for the repeal of the legislative union with Britain. The success of the Repeal movement startled the government, but when Peel banned the monster meeting organized for Clontarf in October 1843 he effectively halted the agitation. Peel, however, under pressure from the repeal agitation and Whig criticism, offered concessions to Catholics. He passed a Bequests Act, which facilitated private endowment of the Catholic Church, an increased grant to St Patrick's College, Maynooth, and a Colleges Act which set up three Queen's Colleges for the further education of, in the first place, Catholics, but also Presbyterians. The Maynooth Grant, however, split his party.[3] When, six months later, he proposed the repeal of the Corn Laws, the split deepened and his government fell in June 1846. In his place came Lord John Russell with his own plans for tackling the Irish problem.

That problem had become more acute than when the Act of Union brought a large mass of new citizens into what had been a

---

[2] A. Macintyre, *The Liberator: Daniel O'Connell and the Irish Party, 1830–1847* (1965).

[3] Peel had trebled the grant to Maynooth, and allotted a sum for buildings and repairs. The monies were to come from the consolidated fund.

union of England, Wales, and Scotland. The 1820s and 1830s had seen a sharpening of old religious antagonisms and an increase in the size of the population. Every English visitor to Ireland and many foreign ones, struck by the appalling poverty and the religious divide, recognized the existence of a major problem and, from Sydney Smith, the witty divine, to Thomas Carlyle the writer and from Alexis de Tocqueville the historian in 1835 to Adolphe Perraud (later a cardinal) in 1860, each, together with a host of politicians, produced his own solution. Apart from a score of coercion acts, the first half of the century saw over a hundred official inquiries into the state of Ireland. A critic justly observed that these inquiries were 'packed with opinions, based overwhelmingly on local circumstances, virtually useless as guides to policymaking', yet they afforded overwhelming evidence of the seriously disturbed condition of the country and forced government to recognize the magnitude of the problem.[4]

Three remarkable debates in the space of less than a year manifested the urgency of the matter. At the three-day debate of Dublin Corporation in February and March 1843 the Irish leader, O'Connell, argued powerfully, yet with moderation, that the only satisfactory solution was the repeal of the Union and the re-establishment of a separate kingdom united to Britain by the crown. This speech was the launching-pad for a dynamic agitation for repeal as O'Connell, sweeping triumphantly from monster meeting to monster meeting, riveted the attention of Ireland, Britain, and western Europe on his spectacular campaign. In July the prime minister, Peel, reflecting the alarmed yet determined attitude of the Tory government, rejected repeal as 'tantamount to a dismemberment of the empire.'[5] In February 1844, the leader of the opposition, Lord John Russell, provoked the most comprehensive debate yet on Ireland, thrusting it squarely into the centre of British politics. In the course of this nine-day debate, Russell insisted that major concessions were the only way forward.[6] After that marathon debate the well-informed observer Charles Greville, clerk to the privy council, believed that he detected a turning point in English views on Ireland:

[4] J. Lee, *The Modernisation of Irish Society* (1973), 22.
[5] *Hansard*, cxxxvi. 997, 11 July 1843.
[6] Ibid. lxxii. 684, 13 Feb. 1844.

It is difficult to meet any one in or out of Parliament who does not admit
that *something must be done* and the whole of the minority of 226, with
no inconsiderable portion of the majority . . . appeared . . . impressed with
the necessity of laying the foundation of a real and permanent union
between the two countries. Much difference of opinion prevails as
to . . . what the people of England could be brought to consent, and what
the people of Ireland could be content to receive. But . . . [all] admit that
the Catholics must be satisfied.[7]

If 'something must be done' and the Union were to become 'a
real and permanent union', legitimate Irish demands would have
to be accommodated, as legitimate Scottish demands had been
accommodated at the time of the union of England and Scotland.
Greville's observation of the difficulty in reconciling what the people
of England could be brought to consent to offer and what the
people of Ireland could be content to receive was the nub of any
administration's difficulty. Furthermore, politicians could reach no
agreement in either their analyses or their remedies. For some it
was mainly a question of law and order, for others a problem of
social disruption, for others the baneful effects of popery and
priestly domination. Disraeli expressed well the perplexity of statesmen faced with the Irish problem: 'One says it was a physical
question; another, a spiritual one. . . . It was the Pope one day,
potatoes the next.' In a clever phrase he gave his own summary:
'a starving population, an absentee aristocracy and an alien Church
and the weakest executive in the world.'[8] Disraeli's comment was
not so wide of the mark. Justice, land, and religion constituted the
hydra of the Irish problem. Justice was unequally enforced by
Orange magistrates or thwarted by the peasantry. Land was neglected by absentee or rack-renting landlords, while improving
and consolidating landlords faced rural violence. Religion divided
where it should have united.

The religious question was for most observers the important
element in the problem. Ireland had three major religious groups:
the Catholics, forming some 81 per cent of the population, the
Anglicans (members of the Established Church of England and
Ireland) about 10 per cent, and the Dissenters (mainly Presbyterians)

[7] C. C. F. Greville, *Past and Present Policy of England towards Ireland* (1845),
pp. vi–vii; id., *The Greville Memoirs: A Journal of the Reign of Queen Victoria*,
ed. H. Reeve (1903), 17 Feb. 1844, v. 162–3.

[8] *Hansard*, lxxii. 1016, 16 Feb. 1844.

the other 9 per cent. For Catholics, who were mostly at the bottom of the social ladder, with many living at subsistence level, the well-endowed Established Church constituted a double grievance, financial and psychological. Tocqueville and his friend and companion, Gustave de Beaumont, reflecting on their visits to Ireland, concluded that the solution of the religious question was the real test for British statesmen.[9] How to achieve it, in the face of a hostile and powerful Protestant minority in Ireland and an equally hostile majority in Britain, was the problem. Religious zeal had remained strong throughout the United Kingdom. For most British people—including those of English and Scottish stock in Ireland—the heritage of the Reformation was inextricably linked to England's free institutions, its rejection of despotic power, its glorious past, and its modern enterprise. Most Irish people had remained loyal to Catholicism, and the collective memory of religious persecution promoted their ethnic consciousness. In the clash between these two identities lay the great tragedy of Anglo-Irish relations in the nineteenth century. Two peoples, among the most religious in western Europe—the one zealously Protestant, the other zealously Catholic—were bound together by links that were rooted in history and geography, colonization and emigration, yet antagonistic on grounds where religion and politics intertwined. Sir George Cornewall Lewis explained his view to his brother-in-law and close friend, Lord Clarendon, in 1848:

Ireland is the great question and the great difficulty. The state of things there is not sound, and . . . it will never be, so long as the Catholic and Protestant Churches remain in their present state. However, it is impossible to enjoy the luxury of religious bigotry, and at the same time to have a united and prosperous people. The present condition of Ireland is the price which England pays for her Protestant zeal—which, be it observed, has not made a single conversion to Protestantism, or in any way weakened the Catholic clergy.[10]

---

[9] G. de Beaumont, *L'Irlande sociale, politique et religieuse*, 2 vols. (7th edn., 1863); A. de Tocqueville, *Journey in Ireland, July–August, 1835*, ed. E. Larkin (1990).

[10] Lewis to Clarendon, 11 Apr. 1848, Clarendon Papers, c. 530. Sir George Cornewall Lewis (1806–63), assistant commissioner to inquire into the condition of the poor in Ireland (1833) and into the state of religious and other instruction (1834). Wrote *On Local Disturbances in Ireland and on the Irish Church Question* (1836). He was married to Clarendon's sister Theresa, and Clarendon corresponded regularly with both of them.

Lewis spoke out of knowledge of the subject for, making use of his work on commissions investigating the state of Ireland, he had produced an important study on Irish disturbances and the Church question.[11] His remark highlighted the dilemma of liberal statesmen: if British statesmen rejected repeal of the Union out of hand they still faced the challenge of how to achieve this ideal of 'a united and prosperous people'. The independent-minded radical, John Arthur Roebuck, stated bluntly the options: 'are we to govern Ireland as a conquered country by means of the garrison we have placed there in the Protestants of Ireland; or are we to govern it . . . in the spirit which teaches us . . . how the welfare of the millions may be secured by an upright and virtuous administration of affairs?' A type of social élitism, however, prevailed in the attitudes of most statesmen, which made them believe that the Irish, whether by nature, habit, or religion, were in some way inferior and not yet fit for full citizenship. Whether through lack of sympathy, hostility, or the priority they accorded to home affairs, few prime ministers exerted themselves sufficiently and continuously over the Irish problem. Pitt abandoned it when it proved too hot to handle; Spencer Perceval, prime minister from 1809 to 1812, opposed all concessions to Catholics; Lord Liverpool, who succeeded him, allowed the Catholic question to fester for fifteen years. To their credit, Peel, challenged by O'Connell's agitations, addressed the problem pragmatically in the 1840s, and Gladstone, shaken by the Fenian rebellion, faced up to it more comprehensively. Both Peel and Gladstone, however, were following in the footsteps of Russell who was the first major political leader to make the solution of the Irish problem a priority. Russell saw his mission as completing the work Pitt had begun but not finished—the task of integrating Catholic Ireland into the Union; for, although it was never articulated in so many words, it was the Union that was on trial in the nineteenth century, no matter what government was in power. More than any other prime minister before him, Russell combined the vision and the will to make the Union a reality. His plan would not appeal later on to 'advanced' Irish nationalists, for it was one of assimilation, a solution dear to liberals; but it had at least the merit of wanting to give Irish Catholics equal treatment.[12]

[11] Lewis, *On Local Disturbances.*
[12] The standard life of Russell, J. Prest, *Lord John Russell* (1972), is particularly good on his Irish policies.

Russell's interest in Ireland had party and family roots. It was at Edmund Burke's urging that the Whigs had become interested in Irish reforms, and the advent to power in 1782 of the Marquis of Rockingham as prime minister and Charles James Fox as foreign secretary enabled Henry Grattan to achieve legislative independence for the Dublin parliament. Ireland retained a special place in the political programme of the Foxite Whigs.[13] They embraced Catholic emancipation as part of their political *raison d'être* and considered Irish tenants as the victims of landlord exploitation. Russell's father, the 6th duke of Bedford, and his uncle had been enthusiastic colleagues of Fox: Russell was brought up to venerate Fox and later wrote his biography. In 1806 the Ministry of All the Talents was formed with Fox as foreign secretary, and Bedford was appointed lord lieutenant of Ireland. Bedford brought John to Dublin to stay at the viceregal lodge in the summer of that year, and from him Russell had learned of the distressed state of Ireland and of the complexities of governing that country riven by division. Years later he quoted with pleasure a letter from his father who claimed:

I think I am not mistaken ... when I say that I ... conciliated the affections and obtained the confidence of the Irish people, that throughout the whole of my administration I ... proceeded upon the broad Principle that all governments are made for the happiness of the many, and not for the benefit of the few; that I consequently set my face against a system of exclusion ... and endeavoured to dispense the blessings of a mild and conciliatory Government to all sects.[14]

Bedford's conciliatory attitude towards Irish Catholics had been partly responsible for the collapse of the Ministry of All the Talents and the beginning of the long reign of the Tories between 1807 and 1830, during which time the Catholic question had festered. Bedford's eldest son William also espoused the Irish cause, and told John in 1826: 'It is Ireland, suffering, ill-used Ireland—the gratitude of millions, the applause of the world would attend the Man who would rescue this poor Country.'[15] Part of Russell's

---

[13] P. H. Gray, 'British Politics and the Irish Land Question, 1843–1850' (Ph.D. thesis, 1992), fos. 15–16.

[14] Rollo Russell (ed.), *Early Correspondence of Lord John Russell, 1805–1840* (1913), i. 144–6. See also Prest, *Russell*, 9.

[15] S. Walpole, *The Life of Lord John Russell* (1889), i. 132.

lifelong ambition was to be himself that man. Already at that time he was one of a number of young Whigs anxious to rejuvenate the party and, by the late 1820s, he was emerging as one of the Whigs' foremost leaders pressing forward the great issues of the day: the removal of discriminatory tests for Nonconformists and Catholics and the reform of parliament. By 1833 he had become involved in Irish matters and had announced his commitment to achieving 'justice for Ireland'.

If Russell, in the tradition of Burke and Fox, made 'justice for Ireland' a priority, yet in his own make-up there were also factors that limited his understanding of Irish Catholics. He was a religious man, but he opposed much of what he saw as the multiplication of creeds, dogmas, and ceremonies. He disliked clergy, and Lady Russell wrote of him that 'he looked forward to the day when there would be no priests, or rather when every man would be a priest, and all superstitious notions—such as is implied in the notion that only a clergyman ought to perform certain offices of religion—should be cast aside by Christian men forever.'[16] He was proud of the Whig sentiments of his forebears of the sixteenth and seventeenth century and wrote the life of William, Lord Russell, the Whig martyr, executed for plotting to exclude James II from the throne. His novella, *The Nun of Arrouca*, and his play, *Don Carlos*, were attacks on aspects of Catholicism he disliked, and later, in his *Recollections*, he again revealed his distaste for Catholicism.[17] O'Connell, who had worked with him and supported his return to power, commented sharply: 'I know him well. He has a thorough, contemptuous, Whig hatred of the Irish. He has a strong and, I believe, a conscientious abhorrence of Popery everywhere, but, I believe, particularly of Irish Popery'.[18]

Yet if Russell shared the English dislike of Catholicism, he possessed to a high degree the Whig insistence on liberty and justice. His sympathy for Irish Catholics was genuine, if somewhat removed from the reality of the peasant's plight. The Irish poet Thomas Moore, whose romantic melodies on Ireland's tragic history

[16] Ibid. ii. 469. See O. Chadwick, *The Victorian Church* (1966), i. 233–4; Prest, *Russell*, 79–80.

[17] R. Brent, *Liberal Anglican Politics: Whiggery, Religion, and Reform 1830–1841* (1987), 58–9.

[18] O'Connell to Charles Buller, 9 Jan. 1844, M. R. O'Connell (ed.), *The Correspondence of Daniel O'Connell* (1972–80), vii. 237.

were all the rage in liberal salons in London, was his lifelong
friend, and Moore's passionate lyric, 'The Irish Peasant to his
Mistress', depicting the loyalty of the Irish peasant to the Catholic
Church, wronged and scorned by its privileged rival, was known
to him. He was delighted when one of Moore's poems gave 'all
Orangemen the jaundice with spleen'.[19] In 1832 he told the poet:
'I enter into your Irish rebel sentiments and I wish I knew what
to do to help your country; but as I do not know, it is no use
going on with smooth words, as O'Connell told me.'[20] O'Connell's
criticism, however, led Russell to make one important decision.
To remedy his lack of knowledge Russell decided to visit Ireland
in 1833 and pressed Moore to accompany him. 'You may be as
patriotic as you please ... about the "First Flower of the Earth",'
he told Moore, 'you being a rebel may somewhat atone for my
being a cabinet minister.' Moore could not come. Russell spent
seven weeks in Ireland and, although his trip was typical enough
of a touring liberal-minded aristocrat, few other nineteenth-
century ministers undertook such a fact-finding mission. The impressions it left on the young politician helped to shape his Irish
policies over the next twenty years.[21]

Packing as much as he could into his whistle-stop tour, he met
a cross-section of influential Irish people. He stayed with the
Duncannons at Bessborough and with Lord Fortescue in Waterford. He travelled south to Cork, which was mainly Catholic,
and north to Belfast, which was mainly Presbyterian. He visited
Dublin Castle and Maynooth College, two different centres of
influence in Irish life; he spoke to army officers and priests, to
archbishops and landlords, to bankers in Dublin and repealers in
Belfast, to O'Connell and the duke of Leinster. During the penin-
sular war, he had lived in Spain with Lord Holland, nephew and
admirer of Charles James Fox, and he found Ireland, which in
1833 was in the throes of the tithe war, 'resembles nothing so
much as Spain in 1810, in the occupation of the French'. He dined
with officers of the guard and recorded that 'the general tone of
the officers, who had been serving in the cavalry, was that of pity
for the peasantry, and dislike of the gentry'. His own sympathies

[19] Prest, *Russell*, 55.
[20] Russell to Moore, 9 Dec. 1832, Russell Papers, PRO 30/22/1C.
[21] Prest, *Russell*, 60–2.

lay in the same direction. 'Poor people,' he wrote in his diary, 'alternately the anvil and the hammer of others.' Yet it is doubtful if he ever spoke to one of them, and certainly he had not the first-hand knowledge of them of O'Connell, or even Bessborough. The scandal of an over-wealthy Protestant Church, paid for by the Catholic poor, who also had to support their own Church, hit him forcibly when he went to stay with the duke of Leinster at Carton, near Maynooth. There were few enough Anglicans in that parish of Maynooth but, as he noted: 'in the next parish [Taghadoe] there are only five Protestants including the Duke of Leinster . . . yet . . . they have built a new church. The First Fruits paid for it.' He believed that 'these five Protestants can, on average, have not attended divine service three years before to [*sic*] 33 [1833]'. In contrast, the Church of the majority remained poor and totally dependent on the voluntary support of its people. His own con-clusion, and his hosts shared his view, was that something would have to be done for that Church. 'It must come to this,' he mused, 'the Catholic Clergy must be paid, and paid out of the revenues of the [Protestant] Church, which are ample for that purpose.'[22] All three religions in Ireland should be endowed to establish equality among them. On the question of law and order, he identified the partiality of the magistrates as the problem. The Orange magis-tracy in the north and the repeal agitators in the south should be put down. Finally, on the land question, he favoured state purchase of encumbered estates, a radical measure by the standards of the time. His itinerary and comments show that the knowledge of the country he acquired was patchy and superficial, but he had al-ready sketched here the Irish policies he would try to implement over the next quarter of a century.[23]

It was precisely on an Irish issue that Russell, in May 1834, took his major political stand within his party, braving the dis-pleasure of the prime minister Earl Grey, and setting himself in opposition to colleagues of the calibre of Lord Stanley and Sir James Graham. On that occasion when, as Stanley's scribbled note to Graham remarked, 'Johnny had upset the coach', Russell declared in parliament that the revenues of the Church of Ireland were

---

[22] Lord John Russell's diary, 6, 7, 8, 9, 16 Sept. 1833, Ogden MSS, University College London, MS 84; see also Walpole, *Life*, i. 197.

[23] Prest, *Russell*, 61–2.

larger than necessary and that the surplus should be appropriated for Irish education and other purposes. Even if it meant separation from his political and personal friends, he would 'at whatever cost, do what he considered his bounden duty; namely, do justice to Ireland'.[24] When, in April 1835, Russell's resolution supporting appropriation of Church funds forced Peel, thrice defeated, to resign, and he became home secretary in the new Whig government, a delighted O'Connell, echoing Russell's words, announced that 'a new era opens for Ireland—an administration is formed, pledged . . . to justice for Ireland'.[25] This period marks the beginnings of a fruitful but complex relationship between Russell and O'Connell, who promised his support to the Whigs in the agreement known as the Lichfield House compact. The Tory-dominated House of Lords blocked much of the Irish reform legislation, but, by working through the administration in Dublin, or Irish government as it was generally called, and in particular Thomas Drummond, the zealous reforming under-secretary, Russell succeeded in making the administration more acceptable to Irish Catholics. '[E]very precedent on the file was a model for partiality', Russell claimed, 'the clerks were familiar with nothing but Protestant ascendancy and Catholic degradation' before the Whigs took office; now for the first time since the seventeenth century a Catholic was appointed attorney-general and other Catholics received public office.[26] In parliament, Russell defended Drummond, condemned Orange rule, and rejected coercion as a remedy for Ireland's problems. This Whig government was the most equitable administration Irish Catholics had experienced, and Archbishop Daniel Murray of Dublin confessed that for the first time Catholics believed they were being fairly treated. Russell was in opposition from 1841 to 1846 and, alarmed at the discontent in Ireland, he concluded that the Tory government was ruining the good relations he had established. 'Peel and the good government of Ireland', he complained, 'appears to be a contradiction in terms.' In February 1844 he had initiated the great debate on Ireland. Russell took for granted the superiority of the British constitution and, as a liberal Whig, he was convinced that integration and assimilation

---

[24] *Hansard*, xxiii. 666, 6 May 1834.
[25] R. B. O'Brien, *Fifty Years of Concessions to Ireland* (1883), i. 497.
[26] *Hansard*, lxxii. 684, 15 Feb. 1844. See Prest, *Russell*, 194.

into the mainstream of English life was the most beneficial policy for Ireland. The union of the two countries was, he believed, the best hope for Irish distress, and when the first signs of what became the Great Famine had begun to ravage Ireland he told the people of Glasgow: 'I consider that the Union was but a parchment and an unsubstantial union, if Ireland is not to be treated, in the hour of difficulty and distress, as an integral part of the United Kingdom.'[27] Ireland's distress, he was convinced, could be England's opportunity to prove once and for all to Irish people that the two islands formed but one undivided realm and that Ireland, in its need, could count on the full support of the richer and more powerful sister island. During the debate on the Irish Coercion bill he cited with approval Shakespeare's words in *Romeo and Juliet*:

> Famine is in thy cheeks,
> Need and oppression starveth in thine eyes,
> Upon thy back hangs ragged misery.
> The world is not thy friend, nor the world's law;
> The world affords no law to make thee rich:
> Then be not poor, but break it.[28]

His dream for Ireland, he told the House of Commons, was to bring in 'a large and comprehensive scheme of measures' which would lay the foundation of future peace and, 'upon that account, and upon that account only', he regretted his inability to form a government in December 1845.[29] This dream was shared by Lady Russell, who wrote at this time that 'John and I, too, looked beyond that [the crisis over the Corn Laws] to a better H'se of Commons, and a golden age for Ireland'.[30] In April 1846 when some Whigs were suggesting a coalition with protectionists, Russell reaffirmed his determination to grant Irish Catholics equal opportunities and fair government:

[27] Cited in J. O'Rourke, *The History of the Great Irish Famine of 1847 with notices of earlier Irish Famines* (3rd edn., 1902), 149.

[28] *Hansard*, lxxxvii. 508, 15 June 1846. The citation, from Act v, Sc. i, is inaccurate.

[29] Ibid. lxxxiii. 109, 22 Jan. 1846.

[30] Lady Russell to Melgund (n.d.), Minto Papers, National Library of Scotland, cited in F. A. Dreyer, 'The Whigs and the Political Crisis of 1845', *English Historical Review*, 80 (1965), 530. Gray, 'British Politics', fo. 150. Melgund was Lord Minto's son.

I should not like to embark in a Government which rested on the support of any extreme party . . . liberal protectionists must sincerely consider whether they can bear to see franchises, equal to those of Englishmen, bestowed on Irishmen, offices given to Catholics as well as to Protestants, the Irish landlord compelled to act fairly by his tenants, crime put down by vigilance and exertion rather than by shutting up honest people all night; and, when measures of severity are necessary, taking care to give the soothing as well as the drastic medicine.[31]

Russell finally came to power on issues closely connected with Ireland and her problems—the repeal of the Corn Laws and an Irish Coercion bill. Peel's decision to repeal the Corn Laws had infuriated a majority of his party, the Protectionists, and on 25 June 1846, in what Wellington described as the 'blackguard combination', they joined the Whigs and the O'Connellite Irish to throw out the Coercion bill. Two days later Peel resigned and the Whigs came into power. Some contemporaries thought Russell opportunistic in using the Irish Coercion bill to turn Peel out of office, and Lord Morpeth suspected that it betrayed a grasping desire for political power.[32] Certainly Russell possessed the politician's passion for power and harboured, moreover, a sharp jealousy of his rival, Peel, whom he regarded as stealing his political clothes. There were, however, other reasons that justified Russell's action.[33] His 'delight that the regeneration of Ireland' had been reserved for him, as he told Clarendon, showed that he still nurtured his vision of a 'Golden Age for Ireland'.[34] The time was ripe. No longer, as in 1835, had he to face the obstinate opposition of a relatively united Tory party, for Peel and Graham were now converted to a policy of concessions to Ireland. Russell could also count on the support of O'Connell who, frustrated by his lack of progress on repeal, welcomed Russell's return to power, convinced that Catholics could expect a better deal and a fairer share in public office. For the first time in his life, Russell, now head of a government of his own choosing, was in a position where he could

---

[31] Russell to Duncannon, 11 Apr. 1846, Russell Papers, PRO 30/22/5A, fos. 184–5.

[32] George Howard Morpeth (1802–64), viscount and 7th earl of Carlisle (succ. 1848); chief secretary for Ireland (1835–41), when he enthusiastically backed Russell and Drummond; first commissioner of woods and forests (1846–52).

[33] Prest, *Russell*, 215–18.

[34] Clarendon to Bedford, 23 Feb. 1849, Clarendon Papers, Box 80.

make a reality of his vision of a golden age. As he drew up the list
of members of the Irish administration over the next few weeks he
appeared set fair to carry out his long-proclaimed wish for the
'regeneration of Ireland'. The government lacked a clear majority
in parliament, but that weakness was compensated for by the
reluctance of any party, after the overthrow of Peel, to bring down
a second government.

The Church question was central to his schemes. Equality for
Catholics, he told Macvey Napier, editor of the Whig journal, the
Edinburgh Review, earlier, could not remain in the statute book
but would have to be applied in daily life:

unless the promises of equal rights and full participation in the benefits
of the constitution are fairly kept; unless Catholics are chosen for office
as well as eligible; unless distinction in Parliament and at the Bar are
made the roads to the Privy Council and the Bench for Catholics as well
as Protestants—in deed as well as in law—it is impossible to expect that
any measures, the wisest that could be framed, can have a healing effect.[35]

Russell's great plan, without which, he said, 'everything else
would be lame and imperfect', was to conciliate Irish Catholics by
improving the state of their Church and by according it rights, ana-
logous, if not actually equal to, those of the Established Church.[36]
This work is a study of his effort to implement his policies and the
dynamic of the relations between his government and the Catholic
Church at a time of social upheaval. The state of the Irish Catholic
Church at the outbreak of the Famine must be considered.[37] A
proper assessment of a religious body should give precedence to
the devotional life of its faithful. Since Russell, however, directed
his efforts towards winning over the leaders of the Church, who,
he believed, held a pivotal role in Irish society, this study devotes
more attention to them and to the public and political face of the

[35] Russell to Napier, 1 Dec. 1843, cited in S. L. Levy, *Nassau W. Senior, 1790–
1864: Critical Essayist, Classical Economist, and Adviser of Governments* (1970),
138. Macvey Napier (1776–1847), had been editor of the *Edinburgh Review* since
1829.
[36] Russell to Clarendon, 28 Feb. 1849, Clarendon Papers, Box 26; Prest, *Russell*,
292.
[37] Apart from the accounts given in such works as those of Kevin Nowlan and
John Prest in the 1960s, little has been written about the religious aspect of
Russell's policy. K. B. Nowlan, *The Politics of Repeal: A Study in the Relations
between Great Britain and Ireland, 1841–50* (1965); Prest, *Russell*.

Church.[38] All accounts of pre-Famine Ireland agree about, if some exaggerate, the prominent position occupied by the Catholic Church.[39] This prominence was in part a reflection of the fact that Catholics formed four-fifths of the population and were strongly attached to their faith. After his visit to Ireland in 1830 Count Charles de Montalembert wrote (in 1831) to the Liberal Catholic paper *L'Avenir* that he could not conceive of anything more worthy of respect than the faith of the Irish people. Two other well-informed and perceptive French visitors, Alexis de Tocqueville and Gustave de Beaumont, formed the same conclusions.[40] Johann Kohl, a German Lutheran, commented that 'the Irish are the most genuine Roman Catholics in the world'; James Johnson, a widely travelled physician, remarked that '[in] no country have I ever observed the *people* more zealous and sincere in their religious devotions than the Catholics of Ireland.'[41] Visitors' impressions find general confirmation in the reports of bishops to Rome, parish clergy to bishops, and priests' diaries.[42] British politicians gener-

---

[38] Discussion of the devotional and spiritual life has been deferred to the final chapter of this volume.

[39] S. J. Connolly, *Religion and Society in Nineteenth Century Ireland* (1985) provides an excellent survey of writings up to 1985. Among many publications since then, mention should be made of the recent volumes in Emmet Larkin's monumental history of the Catholic Church in the nineteenth century, chapters in W. E. Vaughan (ed.), *A New History of Ireland*, v: *Ireland under the Union, I, 1801–70* (1989), and, for local Church history, I. Murphy, *The Diocese of Killaloe, 1800–1850* (1992).

[40] C. de Montalembert, *L'Avenir*, 18 Jan. 1831; Tocqueville, *Journey in Ireland*, 7, 9–13; de Beaumont, *L'Irlande sociale, politique et religieuse*, ii. 36–9, 47.

[41] J. G. Kohl, *Ireland: Dublin, the Shannon, Limerick* . . . (1844), 413; J. Johnson, *A Tour in Ireland, with Meditations and Reflexions* (1844), 120. Similar comments were made by William Thackeray in 1843 and by Édouard Déchy, a French traveller, in 1846.

[42] For a fuller treatment of this subject see D. A. Kerr, *Peel, Priests, and Politics: Sir Robert Peel's Administration and the Roman Catholic Church in Ireland, 1841–1846* (1982), 1–67. Among the valuable recent studies of the Church during the nineteenth century, see D. W. Miller, 'Irish Catholicism and the Great Famine', *Journal of Social History*, 9/1 (1975), 81–98; E. Larkin, *The Making of the Roman Catholic Church in Ireland 1850–1860* (1980); id., *The Historical Dimensions of Irish Catholicism* (1981); id., *The Consolidation of the Roman Catholic Church in Ireland, 1860–1870* (1987); S. J. Connolly, *Priests and People in Pre-Famine Ireland, 1780–1845* (1982); id., *Religion and Society in Nineteenth-Century Ireland* (1985); J. O'Shea, *Priests, Politics and Society in Post-Famine Ireland: A Study of County Tipperary, 1850–1891* (1983), 13–51; D. Keenan, *The Catholic Church in Nineteenth-Century Ireland: A Sociological Study* (1983); K. T. Hoppen, *Elections, Politics, and Society in Ireland 1832–1885* (1984), 171–256; id., *Ireland*

ally assumed that the Church was dominated by the priests and, in 1844, Nassau Senior, the Whig *laissez-faire* economist, accused them of a kind of spiritual intimidation, claiming that they were 'armed with such all-powerful weapons as confession, penance and absolution'.[43] There is no evidence for this claim but, as synodal decrees and episcopal condemnations reveal, there were denunciations from the altar and domineering on the part of some priests. The basis for the clergy's influence, however, lay in the manner in which the clergy saw their mission; priests and bishops were convinced that to them was entrusted the responsibility for the eternal welfare of their 'flock', a claim accepted by the laity, and this conviction of the importance of their role could give rise to an intolerant or arrogant attitude if it was not tempered by experience or Christian humility. Of equal importance was the clergy's responsiveness to the laity's feeling. Right through the century the clergy showed themselves unwilling to carry out any Roman decision which they thought would jeopardize the people's attachment to their Church and to themselves as its ministers. Tocqueville and Beaumont believed that the major cause of the priests' influence was this attachment of the people to a religion in which the priest's role was central; religious persecution had, furthermore, forged close links between them. The practice of celebrating the sacraments in private houses, or 'stations' as they were called, maintained this close relationship. There were other reasons for the predominant role of the clergy. The Catholic Church was strongly hierarchical, and Catholic ecclesiology did not accord the role to the laity that was common in many Protestant Churches. The Catholic gentry— tiny in number as against the total Catholic population—did not wield the same power in the Church as they did in England. The clergy, too, were often the best-educated people in the parish, and it was natural that the faithful accepted their guidance even outside

since 1800: Conflict and Conformity (1989), 60–80, 143–69; P. Corish, *The Irish Catholic Experience: A Historical Survey* (1985), 151–258; T. G. McGrath, 'The Tridentine Evolution of Modern Irish Catholicism: A Re-examination of the "Devotional Revolution" Thesis', in R. O. Muirí (ed.), *Irish Church History Today: Cumann Seanchais Ard Mhaca, Seminar 10 March 1990* (1991); Murphy, *Killaloe*. The diary of John O'Sullivan, parish priest of Kenmare (1839–74), in the Kerry Diocesan Archives is a rich source of information on clerical life in Co. Kerry. Also of interest is the diary of Thomas O'Carroll (1810–65), curate in Clonoulty, Co. Tipperary (1846–52).

[43] Nassau Senior, 'Ireland in 1843', *Edinburgh Review*, 79 (1844), 215.

the strictly religious sphere. Where money and politics were concerned, however, the laity maintained their independence and were
content to be led only where they wanted to go.

The thousand or so parish priests, together with their assistants
or curates, who numbered about 1,400, represented the Church at
local level. The curates, who were dependent on the parish priests
for their meagre salary, were badly off and, in the 1830s, the
bishops had intervened to improve their lot. The parish priests,
whose income varied from diocese to diocese and from parish to
parish, although not rich, in general lived in modest comfort, as
the diary of Archdeacon John O'Sullivan, Parish priest of Kenmare,
County Kerry, and other sources indicate.[44] They depended on the
faithful for their upkeep, but a number of them kept farms and
a few were chaplains in asylums or poorhouses. The priests possessed a considerable amount of independence, although the bishops were gradually gaining control of them. Besides the diocesan
or parish clergy, there were a few hundred regular or order clergy.
The older orders had not recovered from their decline in the eighteenth century and numbered no more than a few hundred, mainly
friars and nuns: Franciscans, Dominicans, Carmelites, or Augustinians, some Jesuits, and the recently re-established Cistercian
monks. Over the previous fifty years new religious congregations
had sprung up; most had engaged in providing schools, while
others had visited the poor or established hospitals and orphanages. Nano Nagle, Catherine McAulay, Frances Ball, and Mary
Aikenhead had founded congregations of sisters, and Ignatius Rice
a congregation of teaching brothers.[45] Their work was a revitaliz-
ing force in the Church, but they were few in number and mostly
confined to the cities and towns.

In the decades after Waterloo the Irish Church shared in the
general renewal and buoyancy of the Catholic Church throughout
Europe. New and more independent-minded leaders had emerged
—James Warren Doyle, bishop of Kildare and Leighlin, and John
MacHale, a professor in Maynooth College—who had spiritedly

---

[44] Diary of John O'Sullivan, parish priest of Kenmare (1839–74), KrDA. O'Shea,
Priests, Politics and Society, 20–1.

[45] Technically the new communities were 'religious congregations' and the term
'religious order' is reserved for the monks, friars, and canons regular. The generic
term 'order' is used here to denote both the older and the more recent communities
of men and women who took religious vows.

defended the Church in a way that had not been heard in public since the seventeenth century. O'Connell's successful campaign for emancipation had given a psychological boost to Catholics, and a series of concessions ranging from the national education system of 1831 and the commutation of tithes in 1838 to the increased Maynooth Grant in 1845 had followed. Within the Church, too, the bishops, led by Archbishops Troy and Murray in Dublin and Doyle in Kildare and Leighlin, had been carrying out a programme aimed at reforming and reorganizing the Church, and had held a series of reforming synods in the 1830s. This period witnessed an ambitious programme of church-building as the bishops sought to provide badly needed accommodation for worshippers. They also set up diocesan centres in the main towns in their sees, where they built a cathedral, a residence, and a seminary.

In public affairs, the uneasy relationship between the state and the Catholic Church in Ireland had centuries-old roots. The state recognized the Anglican Church as the Church of the nation, and regarded the Catholic Church, with its allegiance to Rome, as potentially and often actually disloyal. For its part, the Catholic Church had regarded England as a persecuting state and its Church as heretical. With the final defeat of the Stuarts, however, it had accepted the Hanoverian monarch and, shortly before the accession of George III in 1760, began to offer prayers for his welfare. At the time of the American War of Independence, the state began to dismantle its penal system and at the same time sought some control over the Catholic Church. This came to a head in the aftermath of the 1798 rebellion. In the belief that complete emancipation would come, the bishops accepted a government scheme that involved the incorporation of the Church into the constitution through the nomination of the bishops and the paying of the clergy. To Catholic dismay Pitt, faced with Protestant opposition and the refusal of George III to accept emancipation, abandoned the project. Circumstances were never as favourable again. In the long and crucial controversy over the appointment of bishops, or 'veto' as it was called, bishops first and then the clergy and laity vehemently opposed giving the government any control.[46]

[46] On the key issue of the veto, see C. D. Leighton, 'Gallicanism and the Veto Controversy: Church, State and Catholic Community in early Nineteenth-Century Ireland', in R. V. Comerford, M. Cullen, J. Hill, and C. Lennon (eds.), *Religion, Conflict and Coexistence in Ireland* (1990), 135–58.

If the government had failed to gain control over the Irish Church, Rome's control over it was patchy. Under the pope, the Irish Church was responsible to the Sacred Congregation of Propaganda Fide, the Congregation, or department, with responsibility for Churches in countries where the government was not Catholic. Propaganda, however, interfered in the running of the Irish Church only in important matters or when appeal was made to it. In the controversy over the appointment of bishops, the bishops, clergy, and laity had resisted pressure from Propaganda and Pius VII to accept the veto. Ireland was distant and, because Rome had no resident nuncio to keep it informed, it did not understand the Irish situation and remained wary about intervening. In 1826 Thomas Wyse, a lieutenant of O'Connell, reported: 'I have heard Pope Pius VII state in a conference which I had with him that he found more difficulty in governing the Church of Ireland [the Catholic Church] from its refractory disposition than all the rest of the Churches put together.'[47]

The Irish Church was in an unusual position. On the one hand, it was, and regarded itself as, a marginalized majority excluded from power and privilege, disliked and disdained by the Protestant establishment in Church and state. Its faithful, for the most part poor and ill-educated and often exposed to the zealous efforts of a vigorous Protestant crusade, lacked adequate churches and schools. With a hostile local Protestant ascendancy in every position of influence, its priests felt they were members of a poor, persecuted Church, a sentiment that recurred often in the bishops' correspondence. Yet it enjoyed remarkable freedom. The state did not nominate its bishops, pay its clergy, or regulate its seminaries; Rome was distant and intervened only rarely even in the selection of bishops. This remarkable independence meant that the Irish Church approximated, in the eyes of European Liberal Catholics, to the ideal of 'a free Church in a free state'. On the other hand, its critics saw it as insufficiently accountable. In 1825 the British minister plenipotentiary to Florence, Lord Burghersh, reported to Canning, with what accuracy it is difficult to know:

it [the Curia] would be anxious to bring it [the Irish Church] to a more orderly conduct both as regards the British Government and its own

---

[47] Cited in J. A. Reynolds, *The Catholic Emancipation Crisis in Ireland* (1954), 50.

authority. . . . They [the Curia] conceive that to have the whole body of the clergy of 5 or 6 millions of people totally separated in interest, and without connection with, or control from the Ruling Power must be calculated to render the people under the spiritual charge of this powerful Body bad subjects.[48]

Nowhere was the freedom of action enjoyed by the Irish Church more manifest than when the twenty-seven bishops assembled in Archbishop Murray's Dublin residence for their annual meeting. Rome, fearing Gallicanism, was wary of regular and unsupervised meetings of national hierarchies. National governments throughout Europe, fearing ecclesiastical power blocs, were also wary. French bishops, under the watchful eye of the *préfet*, were not permitted to leave their dioceses to consult fellow bishops. Irish bishops, however, living under the more liberal British institutions, could meet as often as it suited them without let or hindrance. They had begun to meet as a body in the 1790s and, from 1820 or earlier, held regular annual meetings where they discussed matters of common policy, especially pastoral matters, and harmonized their reform measures. The meetings helped to give some official standing to the infrequent contact of the Church with the state, for the bishops used the occasion to wait on the lord lieutenant and present a memorial of their grievances: penal laws against the regular clergy, Catholic soldiers, and their families, educational matters, marriage laws, or the needs of the poor and famine-stricken.[49] The meetings gave the hierarchy cohesion, strength, and influence in their role as leaders of the Catholic community and in the wider world of national affairs as they presented a united front to their clergy, the faithful, and the government.

In the formulation of the Church's policy towards the state, the archbishops played the leading role. The archbishops of Armagh, Cashel, Dublin, and Tuam were also metropolitans of the ecclesiastical provinces of the same names. The provinces of Cashel and Tuam corresponded to the secular provinces of Munster and Connacht, but Armagh, in addition to Ulster, took in part of north Leinster, leaving Dublin with the major part of that

[48] John Fane, Lord Burghersh, to George Canning, 2 Apr. 1825, PRO, FO 79/44, cited in J. Broderick, *The Holy See and the Repeal Movement 1829–1847* (1951), 68.

[49] S. Cannon, 'Irish Episcopal Meetings, 1788–1822', *Annuarium Historiae Conciliorum*, 13 (1981), 270–421.

province. The archbishops had precedence, but no authority, over the other twenty-three bishops, each of whom was independent in his own see and responsible directly to the Holy See. The nominal head of the Irish Church was William Crolly (1780–1849), archbishop of Armagh, and primate of all Ireland. Crolly, who was from County Down, had been bishop of Down and Connor, where his disposition towards Protestants had gained him their sympathy in Belfast. A tendency to change his mind, however, weakened the confidence of his fellow bishops in his leadership. Bishop Kinsella of Ossory complained of the recurrent 'wavering of our brother of Armagh', and Fr. William Yore, a Dublin vicar-general, called him the 'unsteady Pilot' at the head of the Church.[50] The archbishop of Cashel, Michael Slattery (1783–1857), came of well-to-do farming stock in Tipperary and was the only member of the hierarchy to have a degree from Dublin University. Although he was in poor health and introspective, his position, ability, and businesslike habits gave him considerable influence on the affairs of the Church. Daniel Murray (1768–1852), the archbishop of Dublin, was the most influential of the bishops.[51] Murray had trained at the Irish College at Salamanca where he was ordained in 1790. During the 1798 rebellion he barely escaped being slaughtered with his congregation in his church in Arklow by the Antrim militia. The horrors of the period had left an indelible mark on him. Murray had been consecrated coadjutor archbishop to the ageing Archbishop Thomas Troy of Dublin in 1809 and had long years of distinguished service to his credit. He had been chosen by the bishops to represent them at Rome on the difficult question of the veto. It was when Murray was effectively running the diocese that the bishops' meetings became annual events. Murray was bishop of the richest diocese in the country with a Catholic population of 400,000 and, since Dublin was the seat of government, it was he whom government normally consulted. He had accomplished much. To provide schools and hospitals and to take care of the poor he invited the Christian Brothers into his diocese, took the initiative in founding the Sisters of Loreto and the Sisters of Charity, and helped in establishing the Sisters of

---

[50] G. Crolly, *The Life of the Most Rev. Dr Crolly* (1851); Eliot to Graham, 16 Oct. 1844; Yore to Slattery, 13 Nov. 1845, Slattery Papers, CDA.
[51] For a brief sketch of Murray and the other bishops, see Kerr, *Peel*, 6–27.

Mercy. In 1846 his diocese was well served by three hundred parish clergy (including fifty regular clergy), twenty-six convents of nuns, Catholic hospitals, orphanages, and schools. Murray, essentially a pastoral bishop, was a prudent churchman, with a realistic grasp of the practicalities of politics, well liked for his mild manner and personal goodness. His willingness to co-operate with the government aroused the suspicion of some of his fellow bishops and priests.

Different in almost every way was the charismatic archbishop of Tuam, John MacHale (1791–1881).[52] Like Murray, MacHale was marked by the rebellion of 1798, but in a completely different way. As a child he was aware, and perhaps had been present, when the parish priest, Andrew Conroy, was summarily hanged in Castlebar for allegedly harbouring some French officers, and he had been present when Conroy's sorrowing parishioners buried him in the churchyard at Addergoole.[53] MacHale was highly intelligent and courageous and already in 1820, while lecturing in theology in Maynooth College, he had challenged abuses in the educational system and the Bible Societies. After becoming archbishop of Tuam in 1834, his attacks on the government increased in virulence and he remained a thorn in the side of all administrations during his long life. His intractability intimidated and irritated some of his fellow bishops. 'The sole obstacle to perfect harmony in the episcopal body', complained Paul Cullen, archbishop of Armagh, in 1854, 'is Monsignor, the archbishop of Tuam, who cannot resign himself to thinking like his colleagues, and who even changes his own opinions when they come to be adopted by others, so as to remain always in opposition.'[54] Yet he was a natural leader, well loved by the poor of his diocese, whose cause he championed in innumerable public letters. The suffering

---

[52] B. O'Reilly, *John MacHale, Archbishop of Tuam: His Life, Times and Correspondence*, 2 vols. (1890); U. J. Bourke, *The Life and Times of the Most Rev. John MacHale, Archbishop of Tuam and Metropolitan* (1928); N. Costello, *John MacHale, Archbishop of Tuam* (1939); Á. Ní Cheannain (ed.), *Leon an Iarthair: Aistí ar Sheán Mac Héil, Ardeaspag Thuama, 1834–1881* (1982).

[53] E. McHale, 'John MacHale, 1791–1881', in Ní Cheannain (ed.), *Leon*, 88–9. Castlebar, Co. Mayo, was the scene of the most important victory of the French and Irish in 1798.

[54] Cullen to Propaganda, 26 May 1854, *Acta* (1854), vol. 218, fo. 336, PFA. Paul Cullen (1803–78); rector of the Irish College, Rome (1832–49), archbishop of Armagh (1849–52), archbishop of Dublin (1852–78), cardinal (1866).

and deprivations he witnessed in Tuam, the largest and one of the poorest dioceses in Ireland, where many lived constantly on the fringe of starvation, account, in part, for the severity of his criticism of the existing order. Despite his strongly expressed views, he retained the support of many bishops and clergy.[55] He was also a cultural nationalist deeply interested in the Irish language, which he wrote with vigour.

None of the other bishops exercised the same influence as the four archbishops, but collectively they had worked well together. Their public influence had increased, in part because of O'Connell's successful effort to involve them in public affairs and in part because of the government's willingness to negotiate with them and receive their memorial after their annual meeting.[56] The training of priests inculcated the peaceful role of preaching the gospel and administering the sacraments, loyalty to the state, and the promotion of peace among the faithful, and so it might be expected that the Irish Catholic clergy would not become entangled in policies of which government did not approve. In many countries in the nineteenth century, however, government and clergy were at odds over state policies and Ireland, where the Catholic Church had come through centuries of either persecution or discrimination from a Protestant state, was no exception. In common with the Catholic Church throughout post-Napoleonic Europe, the Irish Church was anti-revolutionary and the clergy exercised a moderating influence on its members. Yet, in the 1820s, Bishops Doyle and MacHale had joined O'Connell in demanding with increasing boldness civil rights for Catholics as British subjects, and the clergy co-operated enthusiastically with O'Connell in his campaign for emancipation. Once they had become involved, their efforts to withdraw from politics proved ineffective. First the tithe war in the 1830s and later the enormous enthusiasm O'Connell generated in his agitation for the repeal of the Union had kept them involved. By the 1840s most of the bishops and priests, with a few exceptions, notably Archbishop Murray of Dublin and Archbishop Crolly of Armagh, had been persuaded to support O'Connell's campaign

---

[55] M. A. G. Ó Tuathaigh, 'Seán Mac Héil, Ardeaspag agus Conspóidí: Athbhreithniú', in Ní Cheannain, *Leon*, 73–87.
[56] O. MacDonagh, 'The Politicization of the Irish Catholic Bishops, 1800–1850', *Historical Journal*, 18 (1974), 37–53.

and justified their support on the grounds that it channelled popular discontent away from rural violence to a constitutional campaign for redress of grievances. The clergy regarded overtures from the government with the suspicion of a colonized people, and their special fear was that close co-operation with the government would alienate their faithful, with whose aspirations they often sympathised. A majority of the bishops had welcomed Peel's conciliatory policies, in particular the Maynooth Grant. When Russell came to power bishops and clergy, taking their line from O'Connell, were, with few exceptions, well disposed towards his government and aware of his record in Melbourne's administration.

Even before Russell entered office, suggestions on how to resolve the Irish problem flowed in to him. One of the most interesting was that made by Richard More O'Ferrall, a wealthy Catholic landowner from County Kildare and one of the leading Irish Whigs. O'Ferrall thought that the only basis for solving the Irish problem was for the two parties to adopt a bipartite policy on Ireland. 'If it were possible for your Lordship', he told Russell, 'to have the same understanding with Sir Robert Peel on Irish policy that you have on commercial policy and the same singleness of purpose in carrying it out, I would entertain for the first time in my life a confident hope of the regeneration of this country.' More O'Ferrall believed that the twin objects 'of the new policy' should be equality for the Catholic Church and the improvement of the relationship between landlord and tenant.[57] Since changes on the English political scene proved a major obstacle in the way of a consistent approach to Irish problems, O'Ferrall's plan, by removing the Irish question from the realms of party politics, could have made a major contribution towards resolving it. With O'Connell, Lord George Bentinck, leader of the Protectionists, and Peel well disposed, this suggestion of a bipartite approach was well timed. O'Ferrall's ingenious suggestion was not taken up; it was too much to ask of Russell, who considered himself the pioneer of Irish reforms, to share the credit for Irish reform with Peel as he had previously been forced to share the credit for the Maynooth Grant. In any case, the constraints of party loyalties would have made it difficult.

Early in July 1846 Russell announced his government, whose

[57] More O'Ferrall to O'Connell, 17 Mar. 1846, Russell Papers, PRO 30/22/5A.

composition was to prove of great significance for his Irish policy.[58] Two leading members, Lord Palmerston and Lord Lansdowne, were Irish landlords. Though in Irish affairs Lansdowne was conservative, Russell had to depend on him for support in his difficulties with Palmerston. Lord Morpeth, who had been chief secretary for Ireland from 1835 to 1841, was most interested in Irish affairs, but Russell, who considered his abilities limited, appointed him commissioner of woods and forests. Among the other ministers who would be most involved in Irish affairs were Sir George Grey, who proved a capable home secretary, and Charles Wood, who as a tight-fisted, if not always efficient, chancellor of the exchequer, was determined to spend as little money as possible on Ireland. Russell made the remark in parliament that there were too many people in the cabinet 'connected by family entirely with land', and, as John Prest points out, much the most significant thing about the cabinet was that it was a cabinet of landowners, and not least the owners of land in Ireland. Although this was true of most nineteenth-century governments, Russell had perhaps more than most: Palmerston, Lansdowne, Clanricarde, and Bessborough.[59] The other important feature of the cabinet, that emerged only with time, was Russell's difficulty in dominating it in the way that Peel had dominated his ministry.

Russell's Irish appointments, however, gave satisfaction to Irish Catholics and augured well for a fairer deal for Ireland. The repeal magistrates, dismissed by Peel in 1843, were restored to office. O'Connell's son, Morgan, his son-in-law, Charles O'Connell, and his lifelong friend and aide, Patrick Vincent Fitzpatrick, all received government appointments. Thomas Wyse was appointed secretary for the board of control, O'Conor Don became lord of the treasury, and Richard Lalor Sheil master of the mint. More O'Ferrall became governor of Malta. David Richard Pigot, a friend of O'Connell became chief baron of the exchequer in Ireland. All

[58] For a full discussion of its composition see Prest, *Russell*, 223–32. Boyd Hilton, *The Age of Atonement: The Influence of Evangelicalism on Social and Economic Thought 1785–1865* (1988) has uncovered a new dimension to the religious motivation of many of the political leaders. See also P. Mandler, *Aristocratic Government in the Age of Reform: Whigs and Liberals 1830–1852* (1990), 236–74. Gray, 'British Politics', applies Mandler's analysis of the ideas of the Whig-Liberal politicians to the Irish situation and clarifies the attitude of cabinet ministers to Irish relief (fos. 11–20, 154–9).

[59] Prest, *Russell*, 231, 237–8.

those appointments were Catholics. Within the government, another Catholic, James Henry Monahan, became solicitor general. Of potentially greater significance, Thomas Redington, a Catholic landowner from County Galway, received Drummond's old position of under-secretary, the highest post in government occupied by any Catholic since the seventeenth century.[60] The under-secretary had charge of the Dublin administration during the frequent absences of the chief secretary in London and, as Drummond had demonstrated during the Melbourne administration, his role could be the key one in the Irish government. While O'Connell congratulated Pigot for obtaining Redington's appointment, he expressed serious reservations about his attitude towards the bishops. 'The Peel Ministry', he told Pigot, 'flattered themselves, not entirely without reason, that they had *a party* in the Irish Episcopacy. Now Redington must necessarily lean in favour of those who were considered "the party" and distinctly against the wishes of the great majority of the Bishops.'[61] O'Connell's assessment was right, for Redington never built up a proper working relationship with the majority of the bishops. For a while rumours circulated that Russell might go further and appoint an Irish Catholic as chief secretary and Sheil, and probably More O'Ferrall, would have welcomed the position. Russell, however, decided to appoint Henry Labouchere, president of the Board of Trade in an earlier ministry, who knew little about Ireland.[62] The appointment of the earl of Bessborough as lord lieutenant (or viceroy, a frequently used alternative) set the seal on the liberal intentions of Russell's Irish government.[63] John William Ponsonby, earl Bessborough, a resident, reforming landowner, for long the Whigs' main contact with the Irish party, had played a major role in bringing about the Lichfield House compact between O'Connell and the Whigs

[60] Sir Thomas Nicholas Redington (1815–62), Liberal MP for Dundalk (1837–52); knighted (1849). Clarendon thought him 'the most honourable and loyal person possible', Clarendon to Russell, 10, 15 Nov. 1850, Clarendon Papers, Letterbook 6. Young Irelanders called him 'the Knight of the Carpet bag' for using documents found in Smith O'Brien's bag, while Orangemen described him as 'the rascally rebel'.

[61] O'Connell to Pigot, 8 July 1846, O'Connell, *Correspondence*, viii. 62–3.

[62] Sheil to Russell, 20 June 1846, Russell Papers, PRO 30/22/5A; Labouchere to Russell, 21 June 1846, ibid.

[63] John William Ponsonby (1787–1847), Viscount Duncannon and Earl Bessborough.

in 1835. He was on good terms with O'Connell and his appointment was popular in Ireland. The stage was set for Russell's Irish reforms.

That Russell was more committed than many of his party to liberal reforms for Ireland emerges from his rejection of recommendations made by Nassau Senior, who saw himself as one of the Whigs' experts on Irish affairs. Senior had published some substantive and semi-official articles in the Whig *Edinburgh Review*. These articles, particularly a lengthy one on 'Ireland in 1843' which appeared in January 1844, were seen as a type of 'party manifesto', since they were written in concert with the principal Whig statesmen.[64] Russell showed himself sensitive to Irish Catholic feeling by endeavouring to get Senior to tone down the antipathy in his writings. As the Whigs came into government, Senior drafted an article on the 'Proposals for Extending the Irish Poor Law', but Russell sharply rebuked his authoritarian views:

To hold out that franchises and rights are mere obsolete phrases, that Ireland would do better under a despotism than with a free government; that liberty is to be granted to that country only as a melancholy necessity—these are doctrines which I believe to be as false as preposterous and which, I am sure, would be injurious as political doctrines.

Such policies, he believed, stood 'in contradiction to what all Whigs maintained from 1796 to 1846, and what Sir Robert Peel has adopted in 1846 [and] would do infinite mischief in Ireland while they can give no satisfaction in England'.[65] Although unprepared to do more than sketch the outline, his overall plan, as it emerged in his correspondence, was a bold one. 'Good landlords, good priests and good magistrates', he told Clarendon, were Ireland's real needs.[66] The twin pillars of Irish society—the landed class and the Church—were to undergo radical change. The landlords, Russell was convinced, bore most blame, for they had criminally neglected their duty, merely collecting rents and returning nothing to the country; they were responsible for the permanent warfare between themselves and the tenants. The remedy was the

[64] Levy, *Nassau Senior*, 132–43. The articles were 'Mendicancy in Ireland'; 'Ireland in 1843'; 'Proposals for Extending the Irish Poor Law'; 'Relief of Irish Distress in 1847 and 1848'.

[65] N. W. Senior, 'Relief of Irish Distress', *Edinburgh Review*, 89 (1849), 189–266. Russell to Napier, 8 Sept. 1846, cited in Levy, *Nassau Senior*, 141–3.

[66] Russell to Clarendon, 8 Feb. 1848, Clarendon Papers, Box 43.

sale of land in smaller lots and the replacement of absentee and bankrupt Protestant landlords by resident Catholic proprietors. As for the Church, Russell was more cautious. Nevertheless, he was convinced that the Church of Ireland had failed in its mission to establish itself as a truly national Church and thus to fulfil its role of civilizing and assimilating the Irish people. By becoming the privileged religion of an élite minority, it created a sense of injustice among the majority and brought division where it should have brought stability. He hoped that by bringing the Catholic Church into the establishment the parsons ministering to the few would be joined by the priests serving the masses. Although he does not say it explicitly, what he envisaged was a type of Catholic parson and Catholic squire, more in sympathy with the Catholic peasantry, which would restore the balance in society and help the government to stabilize, civilize, and modernize Ireland and assimilate it to English norms.[67] The other components of his plans were less innovatory. Impartiality in the execution of justice was a basic necessity, and in the first Young Ireland trials he warned Clarendon against any attempt to pack the jury. The final step in assimilation would be the abolition of the lord lieutenancy and its replacement by a secretary of state. In this way, the complete and harmonious assimilation of Ireland into the United Kingdom would be accomplished. Russell never fully worked out this generalized plan, but the Encumbered Estates Act, the plan to salary the priests and provide glebes, and the bill to abolish the lord lieutenancy, were his attempt to implement it.[68]

When he came to power Russell resolved to move prudently on the Church question. In March Lord Grey, one of Russell's ablest colleagues, identifying the scandal of Ireland as the contrast between the splendid riches of the Established Church and the poverty of the Church of the great majority, demanded that 'The superfluous prosperity of the Protestant Church . . . be diverted to the purpose of religious instruction of such a character, and reaching them through such a channel, that the Roman Catholics would

---

[67] Bessborough to Russell, 3 Nov., 22 Dec. 1846, Russell Papers, PRO 30/22/5G; Russell to Bessborough, 28 Feb. 1847, Russell Papers, PRO 30/22/6B; Russell to Clarendon, 13, 18 Dec. 1847, Clarendon Papers, Box 43.

[68] See Prest, *Russell*, 236. The most complete discussion of the Whigs and the land question is Gray, 'British Politics', fos. 150–242.

consent to avail themselves of it.'[69] Russell feared that to do so
would be to return to the sterile appropriation debate of the 1830s,
and he admitted to Lord Aberdeen, who had been foreign secretary in Peel's administration, that the times would not allow for
any experiments with the Established Church, an attitude supported
by O'Connell, who warned Bessborough against Grey's suggested
course of action.[70] Again, immediately after the formation of the
new government, when Thomas Duncombe, the radical member
for Finsbury, raised the question of reforming the Irish Church,
Russell replied that while he retained his opinions of Catholic
endowment, he did not think that he should urge them at the
present moment, for 'the social grievances of Ireland were the
most pressing evil the Legislature had to deal with'.[71] Russell's
assessment was realistic. Important though the religious question
was for a lasting solution to the Irish problem, the distress caused
by the Famine was more urgent and pushed long-term plans into
the background. The first nine months of Russell's administration
saw more deaths than in any similar period before or since in the
history of Ireland and brought about social changes of lasting
significance. That terrible winter of 'Black '47', as it came to be
known, impinged deeply on the state and its relations with the
Catholic Church.

[69] *Hansard*, lxxxiv. 1367, 23 Mar. 1846. Henry Grey (1802–94), 3rd Earl Grey,
secretary for war and colonies in Russell's 1846 cabinet.
[70] Prince Albert memorandum, 10 Apr. 1846, Royal Archives, C 24, 27, cited
in Prest, *Russell*, 213; Bessborough to Russell, 11 Sept. 1846, Russell Papers,
30/22/5C.
[71] *Hansard*, lxxxvii. 1181, 16 July 1846.

2

The Hecatomb and the Church's Silence?

'How could they save the Hecatomb sacrificed at Bantry? . . . If they raise their voice against oppression they run the risk of being accused of exciting to murder.'

(Fr. James Maher to a Dublin paper, 4 Dec. 1847)

'My heart shudders', wrote Peter Ward, a Connemara priest, at the height of the Famine, 'when I hear the cry, "Here is a corpse", "Here is a corpse", "Here are three corpses half-devoured by wild beasts".'[1] Thus wrote a priest in 1847, and his experience was relived by relief workers and priests throughout most of Ireland. What had happened to reduce the country to such a state?[2]

It was at the end of June 1845 that Belgian journals reported a potato blight which Abbé Edouard van den Hecke, grand vicar to the bishop of Versailles, in *L'Organe des Flandres* correctly diagnosed as a fungus. The blight caused extensive damage in Belgium, the Netherlands, north-east France, and Switzerland. It also affected parts of England. Ireland, however, was the great source of concern for, although a potato failure might cause hardship elsewhere, in Ireland it would be a major calamity. Out of a population of 8 million, 3.3 million Irish lived exclusively on the potato, and for 4.7 million it was the predominant item of diet.[3] By September the blight had come to Ireland, but the dreaded

---

[1] *Tablet*, 22 Apr. 1848.

[2] In Irish historiography the Famine itself and famine relief have aroused renewed interest and are the subject of some excellent writing, published and unpublished. A. Bourke, 'The Visitation of God'? The Potato and the Great Irish Famine, ed. J. Hill and C. Ó Gráda (1993), a major contribution to studies on the Famine, contains an excellent bibliography. See, too, C. Ó Gráda, ' "For Irishmen to Forget?", Recent Research on the Great Irish Famine', in A. Häkkinen (ed.), *Just a Sack of Potatoes? Crisis Experiences in European Societies Past and Present* (1992), 17–52.

[3] Bourke, *Visitation of God?*, 140–9.

calamity did not follow. The loss of the crop was substantial—40 per cent—but because of a high yield the crop was only from 25 per cent to 33 per cent below normal. Of equal importance in preventing a catastrophe were Peel's decisive measures of establishing public works to provide employment and importing Indian corn for sale at cost price.[4] As a result there was no widespread starvation during the winter of 1845–6. After Peel fell from power and was succeeded by Russell, blight struck again. This time the crop failure was calamitous—five-sixths of the total. Although the need was many times greater, government aid was less, for Russell abandoned Peel's policy of buying and importing grain.[5] Private enterprise and Peel's impressive initiative had coped in 1845–6; Russell hoped that private enterprise would cope with little or no government assistance in 1846–7.[6] Apart from his belief in classical economics with its emphasis on the market, of which many of his own supporters were proponents, Russell wanted permanent improvements for Ireland. British taxpayers' money could not be wasted for a second year running in doling out immense sums from an impoverished treasury to relieve the apparently chronic distress of the Irish peasant. Russell's decision was to have devastating consequences.

The total failure of the potato resulted in death on a massive scale through hunger, disease, and exposure during the following winter. The suffering was extreme for, despite Bessborough's strenuous exertions, the government's relief proved totally inadequate. Although by the standards of the time there had been a major outlay of public money, the relief schemes were overwhelmed by the scale of the disaster. The soup kitchens, Russell's tardy but most effective measure, were not in operation until the end of March or later. During that long and bitter winter of 1846–7

---

[4] J. S. Donnelly, 'Famine and Government Response, 1845–6', in W. E. Vaughan (ed.), *A New History of Ireland*, v: *Ireland under the Union, I, 1801–70* (1989), 282–4.

[5] The Whig government's policies towards land and famine relief have been the subject of two major doctoral theses: R. J. Montagu, 'Relief and Reconstruction in Ireland, 1845–9: A Study in Public Policy during the Great Famine' (D.Phil. thesis, 1976), and, more recently, P. H. Gray's 'British Politics and the Irish Land Question, 1843–1850' (Ph.D. thesis, 1992), which breaks new ground on this central question.

[6] Although it has been contrasted unfavourably with Peel's action, it is important to record that the Peelites offered no opposition to Russell's bill and almost certainly approved of it. Gray, 'British Politics', fos. 131–2, 245–6.

hundreds of thousands of peasants died. The appalling scale of deaths through starvation and fever in Skibbereen, County Cork, were highlighted in the *Illustrated London News*, but similar horrors were repeated all over the west of Ireland, dispelling any lingering doubt as to the extent of the catastrophe. As Russell admitted, it was a famine of the thirteenth century acting upon a population of the nineteenth. A world was disappearing as a whole class of people perished or emigrated, and what was once one of the most densely populated areas in Europe saw farms, hamlets, and villages abandoned. Over a period of six months a change had taken place that no government would have deemed possible. The scale of the catastrophe was so great that people were only dimly aware of what was happening. On the local clergy, who lived in the midst of the suffering people, the death of so many of their parishioners was bound to have a profound impact.

The scarcity of surviving autobiographical material makes it difficult to appraise the involvement of the clergy in famine relief and the impact of the catastrophe on the morale and faith of both clergy and people. The scarcity may be due to Irish indifference towards keeping diaries, or because the Famine was an experience that few Irish people wished to recall. What do survive, however, from as early as the winter of 1845, are many letters written by priests commenting on the Famine in their area. Together with their public statements, those letters provide an insight into clerical feelings and reactions to the Famine and famine relief during the period.

At the outset of Famine in 1845, Archbishop Murray decided to investigate for himself the alarming rumours of a major failure of the potato crop. He turned for information to the priests of the outlying parishes of his diocese for reports, which were probably more reliable than the police reports arriving at Dublin Castle. Priest after priest reported the gravity of the situation. The first report was not untypical of the others, and came from Balbriggan, County Dublin, where John Smyth, the parish priest, reported that 'there is not at this *moment*, more than a fourth of the potato safe from disease' and that the same was true of all north County Dublin. In his own area, much of the existing crop had been sold to the starch millers, leaving the cottiers in want. 'What then', he asked, 'is to become of them or where will they get the money to buy meal for their famishing families? Their only recourse will be the poor-houses; and oh, what a blessing that we have even that, to fall back on.'[7] Smyth's anguished question was to be heard over and over again during the next four years and the poor-house was to figure prominently, if rarely so favourably, in countless letters from his brother priests up and down the country. The eastern part of the country, including Dublin and Wicklow, where most of Murray's diocese was located, was the area first hit in 1845, but before that winter was out clergy throughout the country became aware of the gravity of the situation. Cornelius Egan, bishop of Kerry, in thanking the Maynooth professors who had sent £25 for relief in Brosna near Castleisland, County Kerry, described 'the emaciated countenances, the sunken eyes, the faltering steps of those who last year were young and athletic, but now exhibit the appearances of old age'.[8]

When the blight returned with renewed intensity at the beginning of August 1846 alarm set in among the clergy. Father Mathew, the respected temperance leader, wrote anxiously to Trevelyan to warn him of extensive crop failure. While travelling from Dublin to Cork he beheld the potatoes with all the luxuriance of an abundant harvest, but on his return trip they had withered into 'one wide waste of putrefying vegetation'. The wretched people were wringing their hands and wailing bitterly at being left food-less.[9] MacHale, who had visited extensive areas in the west, testified that the potato stalks had decayed and that even apparently healthy roots were 'in a state of rapid decomposition'.[10] The quiet-spoken Murray, worried at what he saw of the crop while travelling from Dublin to Rahan, Queen's County, voiced his concern that the poor would not get through the coming winter and, in biblical terms, expressed both fear and hope:

It is a singular thing that the hawthorn berries have not made their appearance at all this year though formerly they used to load their bushes. What will next be struck at? Our atmosphere seems to be undergoing some extraordinary change, and perhaps these are only premonitory symptoms of something more alarming. We have heard of old of a seven years famine, and we should not forget that with all our agricultural

---

[7] J. Smyth to Murray, 28 Nov. 1845, Murray Papers, DDA.
[8] Egan to Renehan, 22 Apr. 1846, Renehan Papers, MCA.
[9] Mathew to Trevelyan, 7 Aug. 1846, Fr. Augustin, cited in [Hayden], *Footprints of Father Theobald, O.F.M. CAP: Apostle of Temperance* (1947), 402–3.
[10] MacHale to Russell, 1 Aug. 1846, *Freeman's Journal*, 5 Aug. 1846.

improvements we are not yet independent of Providence. Hitherto, Sir Robert has been our Joseph.[11]

What is striking in these comments, and in the response of most clergy to the recurrence of famine, was the confident reliance on the government that they revealed. As Murray noted, Peel had proved himself a bountiful Joseph and the clergy expected that Russell, the champion of justice for Ireland, would prove a second Joseph. 'For heaven's sake', Slattery wrote to Bessborough imploring him to speed up relief, 'let the public works begin.'[12] 'Your Lordship', wrote MacHale to Russell, 'has now a great destiny to fulfil,—the rescuing of an entire people from the jaws of famine.'[13] O'Connell, too, made an urgent appeal to Russell, warning him of 'the frightful state of Famine, by which the people of that County [Cork] are, not merely menaced, but actually engulphed'.[14] By September frightful accounts of impending starvation poured in from all over Ireland—from Cork, Belfast, Mayo, and Dublin— and the *Nation* was not exaggerating when it complained that 'the cry of starvation reverberates through the land'.[15] Even then the clergy counselled calm. When 10,000 Mayo peasants marched into Castlebar to protest that 'there is not a stone of sound potatoes among the whole of us' the curate, Fr. James M'Manus, told them that 'the Ministers of the Crown were a humane and good government'. He reminded the people 'that Lord John Russell, than whom no better man lived, had declared "that no person in Ireland should die while England had the means to prevent it"'.[16] Thomas O'Carroll, the curate in Clonoulty, County Tipperary, recorded in his diary how he and his parish priest took action to prevent trouble in their parish. The local constable told him of 'an inflammatory notice posted on the chapel gate, calling on the people to assemble on the Fair Green . . . to devise some means to keep themselves from starvation'. The constable told him that he was afraid to pull it down, so O'Carroll tore it down himself.

[11] Murray to Hamilton, 15 Aug. 1846, Hamilton Papers, P1/35/1(182), DDA. Murray often stayed with friends at Rahan.

[12] Slattery to Bessborough, 21 Oct. 1846, Slattery Papers, CDA.

[13] MacHale to Russell, 15 Dec. 1847, cited in B. O'Reilly, *John MacHale, Archbishop of Tuam: his Life, Times and Correspondence* (1890), ii. 37.

[14] O'Connell to Russell, 12 Aug. 1846, Russell Papers, PRO 30/22/5B, fos. 345/6.

[15] *Nation*, 26 Sept. 1846.   [16] *Tablet*, 5 Sept. 1846.

Despite his action parties went from house to house requiring the labourers to attend the meeting and two hundred came. When the parish priest, John Mackey, persuaded them to disperse, O'Carroll commented wryly:

It is well for those folk who take such a delight in calumniating the Catholic priesthood that we still retain so much influence over the people— it is generally exerted for their protection and I have known several instances where the lives of oppressive landlords have been saved by our interference.[17]

A month later at Carrigtoohill, County Cork, when a notice calling a meeting to demand that public work pay be raised to one shilling and sixpence a day was posted on the chapel doors, 'the clergy from the altars . . . adjured their flock not to attend, and the meeting failed'.[18] In Coolock, a few miles from the centre of Dublin, labourers met to complain of want of food and, while the curate spoke in favour of a society for the protection of the labouring classes, he used his influence to persuade them 'to separate peacefully and pay the strictest obedience to the law'.[19] At O'Briensbridge in County Clare, on 8 October, a boat laden with corn was forced to turn back, despite its police escort; only the arrival of Daniel Vaughan, parish priest of Killaloe, prevented the mill being burned down.[20] An immense body of starving and angry peasants marched into Macroom, west Cork, and gathered outside the workhouse seeking work and food. What was to become of their wives and children 12 or 13 miles off, who could not come to the workhouse for a meal, they demanded.[21] Despite the presence of soldiers and armed police, a riot was avoided, it was alleged, only by the influence of the parish priest, Thomas Lee. Food riots did break out in Youghal in east Cork, and in Croom, County Limerick, people stopped three loads of corn. Only after the entreaties of the local curate, James Enright, did they let them through.[22] In taking this line, the clergy believed they were being faithful to the role of 'ministers of peace' and following, too, the

[17] Diary of Revd Thomas O'Carroll, 13, 15 Sept. 1846, CDA. Thomas O'Carroll (1810–65), trained for priesthood at Irish College, Paris; professor at Thurles College (1838–42, 1852–5); curate at Clonoulty (1846–52); parish priest at Clonoulty (1855–65).

[18] *Tablet*, 10 Oct. 1846.   [19] Ibid. 11 Nov. 1846.

[20] I. Murphy, *The Diocese of Killaloe, 1800–1850* (1992), 210.

[21] *Nation*, 10 Oct. 1846.   [22] Ibid. 17 Oct. 1846.

advice of O'Connell and his son, John, who still trusted in the government. The Repeal Association committee issued an address signed by John as chairman declaring that:

The government is doing all that in them lies to supply for this most sudden and utter destruction of your food . . . remember what your religion teaches and commands—PATIENCE, PEACE, AVOIDANCE OF CRIME, CONFIDENCE IN ALMIGHTY GOD, AND RESIGNATION TO HIS HOLY WILL.[23]

That winter of 1846 was bitterly cold and set in as early as October. Relief was disappointingly slow in coming. From Swinford in County Mayo, Bernard Durcan complained that seven-eighths of the people would starve unless it arrived.[24] Desperately anxious to prevent rioting and lawlessness, many clergy now found their efforts unavailing. From County Roscommon came reports of 'starving peasants killing sheep and black cattle of the rich farmers'.[25] Early in December five or six thousand starving peasants marched into Listowel, County Kerry, shouting 'Bread or Blood!' Despite the pleas of the parish priest, Jeremiah Mahoney, they refused to disperse. Exhausted from his exertions Mahoney collapsed in a faint; at this the local people protested that they [the peasants] might be the cause of the priest's death, and the starving peasants dispersed.[26] The clergy's efforts to keep the people peaceful reveal that the perception, not uncommon in England, of the priest as one seeking 'some cry wherewith to excite the people' is difficult to substantiate.[27]

The false security induced by the previous year's successful relief work meant that at first the clergy, in common with most responsible citizens, believed that it was sufficient to alert the government and it would take the necessary measures. Scores of priests wrote to the Dublin government explaining the situation and appealing for help. Meetings at which clergy of all denominations were represented met to voice public alarm at the growing disaster. Delegations, which normally included the local priest, travelled to Dublin or crossed to London to put the case of the starving to the

---

[23] Ibid. 10 Oct. 1846. According to O. MacDonagh, *O'Connell: The Life of Daniel O'Connell, 1775–1848* (1991), 585, this statement was issued against John O'Connell's, and probably O'Connell's, own better judgement.
[24] *Nation*, 19 Nov. 1846.   [25] Ibid. 5 Dec. 1846.   [26] Ibid.
[27] Clarendon to Russell, 12 July 1847, Clarendon Papers, Letterbook 1.

lord lieutenant or the prime minister. MacHale wrote a stream of open letters to Russell begging for immediate action.

How the government would react became clear from the reception Sir Randolph Routh, the commissary-general, accorded to a delegation from Achill. The delegation explained to Routh that, because the merchants charged high prices, the people could not buy the corn, and they asked him to sell food at a lower price. His reply was that 'it was essential to the success of commerce that the mercantile interest should not be interfered with'. Astounded, Fr. Monahan, the leader of the delegation, reminded him that in the previous year the government had sold at a cheaper rate in order to keep down the market price. Routh agreed, but regretted it as a bad decision for it gave bad habits to the people; the government, he affirmed, was now determined not to interfere with the merchants but to act in accordance with the enlightened principles of political economy. Monahan said he could not understand why, at such a crisis as this, the government should be fettered by notions of political economy; political economy might be very well in its way but the people of Achill knew nothing about it. Routh replied that there was nothing more essential to the welfare of a country than a strict adherence to the principles of free trade, and begged to assure the reverend gentleman that, had he carefully read and studied Edmund Burke, his illustrious countryman, he would agree that it was essential to the success of any measure of relief that the strict rules of political economy should be steadily attended to.[28]

This remarkable interview reveals the policy of the government in the starkest light. Routh, however, was merely following the line taken by Russell in London, who regaled delegations who had crossed the Irish sea to put the case of the starving peasants with chapters from Adam Smith's *Wealth of Nations*.[29] The government was not prepared to interfere with the ordinary market forces. Furthermore, many British politicians felt Ireland should stand on its own feet and not depend on the government.[30] To those who saw people wasting away with hunger and who had confidently

---

[28] *Nation*, 17 Oct. 1846. The work referred to was Burke's *Thoughts and Details on Scarcity originally presented to ... William Pitt in the month of November 1795.*

[29] *Nation*, 20, 27 Feb. 1847.

[30] C. Trevelyan, 'The Irish Crisis', *Edinburgh Review*, 87 (1848), 316–20.

pinned their hope on the government, this *laissez-faire* attitude brought incredulous dismay; without government intervention and control of prices the outlook was grim. From Clifden in County Galway Fr. William Flannelly, denouncing 'the slowness and the bungling of officials and the greed of the merchants and hucksters', complained that, since the relief committees were forbidden to sell at less than market prices, they were clearly intended to protect the exorbitant famine prices charged by merchants.[31] At a meeting held in the Music Hall in Dublin the Revd David Creighton, a Presbyterian minister, seconded a motion by Murray, criticizing the government 'who allowed the poor to perish sooner than interfere with the interests of the general trader'.[32]

The new year brought no relief and the priests became increasingly alarmed. To Thomas Synnott, who worked with Murray in the distribution of relief, John Madden, parish priest of Roscommon, disclosed the growing desperation. 'My House', he said, 'is surrounded by them [the poor] . . . calling for Work or Food . . . We are doing what we can to distribute Soup. What can we do? The Applicants are so numerous; our means so limited.'[33] One of the most effective appeals came from the Revd John Fitzpatrick, whose description of the appalling conditions in his parish of Skibbereen shocked readers in many countries, for his appeals were published in Irish, English, and French papers. The *Freeman's Journal* reported that humane people throughout the Empire 'had their feelings sharpened by the daily horrors of Skibbereen, and remitted directly to the district either through the clergy or through respectable citizens in Cork'.[34]

A grim function the priests now found thrust upon them was ensuring that the dead were buried in coffins. People dreaded that they or their relations should be buried without a coffin, and it often fell to the priest to procure coffins, to coffin the dead, and to bury, Tobias-like, the victims of pestilence.[35] Archdeacon John

---

[31] *Nation*, 5 Dec. 1846.   [32] Ibid. 23 Dec. 1846.

[33] Madden to Synnott, 5 Feb. 1847, Murray Papers, DDA. Thomas Lambert Synnott (1810–97), high constable and billet master for the city of Dublin (1842–8); secretary of Mansion House Committee (1845) and India Relief Fund (1846); governor of Grangegorman Female Prison (1849–65). B. Cullen, 'Thomas L. Synnott, Famine Relief Secretary and Dublin Prison Governor', unpub. study.

[34] *Freeman's Journal*, 9 Jan., 17, 18 Feb. 1847; *Tablet*, 6 Feb. 1847; *Le Correspondant*, xvii. 622, 25 Feb. 1847.

[35] MacHale to Russell, 29 Nov. 1847, cited in O'Reilly, *MacHale*, ii. 64.

O'Sullivan, parish priest of Kenmare, County Kerry, recorded that there was 'nothing more usual than to find four or five bodies on the street every morning. They would remain so and in their homes unburied, had we not employed three men to go about and convey them to the graveyard.'[36] Joseph Kirwan, parish priest of Oughterard, County Galway, and later first president of Queen's College, Galway, frequently coffined the dead himself.[37] 'They are lying out in the fields', wrote McNally, 'and the people are so terrified that none but the clergy can be induced to approach. I yesterday sent a coffin out for a poor creature who died in a field of fever and have just heard that no one could be prevailed to put the body in it.'[38] 'I had,' Thomas Quinn, parish priest of Inagh and Kilnamona in County Clare, told the poor law inspectors, 'together with my curate, Revd Mr Reid, to convey by torchlight two successive nights, the remains of two persons who were abandoned by their own immediate family and friends.'[39] Peter Ward, parish priest of Aughagower, County Mayo, told Murray of poor people 'banished from a crowded poor-house, to die on the roads and buried without coffins everywhere as the living are not able to carry their remains to the Grave Yard'.[40] In Crookhaven, County Cork, the parish priest Laurence O'Sullivan, reported that 'Of the hundreds that are borne to the grave yard not more than one half are enclosed in coffins, the remaining portion are wrapped in straw and borne upon a door—the bearers being the only funeral attendants.'[41]

The bishops were shaken by the distress. Their private correspondence with Dr Laurence Renehan, the president of Maynooth College, shows how Church leaders in the three provinces most affected assessed the situation in early 1847. From Carrickmacross, in County Monaghan, Charles MacNally, bishop of Clogher, gave a grim picture of what was becoming a daily scene.

[36] O'Sullivan, diary, 18 May 1847, KrDA. John O'Sullivan (1806–74), parish priest of Kenmare and Archdeacon of Aghadoe (1839–74).

[37] Joseph W. Kirwan (d. 1848), vicar-general to the Bishop of Galway; parish priest of Oughterard (1827); first president of Queen's College, Galway (1847–8).

[38] MacNally to Renehan, 9 Mar. 1847, Renehan Papers, MCA.

[39] Cited in Murphy, *Killaloe*, 221.

[40] Ward to Murray, 14 Apr. 1848, Murray Papers, 32/4/73, DDA.

[41] *Nation*, 13 Feb. 1847.

It would be impossible to give an idea of the deplorable state of our poor people. In this neighbourhood fever and famine are making frightful ravages among them. . . . Fourteen deaths in this parish on yesterday were reported to me last night. It is wonderful how the clergy can bear their unceasing labours attending on the sick and dying.[42]

A sense of hopelessness in the face of so great a calamity is evident in the letters of Dr French, bishop of Kilmacduagh in Connacht, who wrote that 'we are so overpowered with the distress of the multitudes. May God relieve them—the clergy and bishops of Ireland never experienced such times!!'[43]

From Thurles, in the heartland of Munster, Slattery described the situation:

The distress of the People is every day increasing and persons, who three months ago were able to do without assistance, are now run out and are seeking relief. For some weeks past the deaths in this Parish alone average from 15 to 20 every week exclusive of the Poor house where on some days there have been 10 and 12 dead together. . . . It is undeniable that those public works are objectionable and tended much to demoralize our people, but at the same time they were the means of keeping them alive, although they barely did the same.[44]

Appalled at the inadequate relief and what he called 'the Extermination going on under the protection of the law', Slattery prayed: 'Oh, that I . . . could fly from this wretched country into some solitude where I might . . . die in peace.'[45] When his oldest friend, Bishop Murphy of Cork, had died, Slattery predicted that his own time would soon come, for his soul was 'sorrowful unto death and I think those happy who are released from the calamities that have befallen our unhappy Country'.[46] The frightful strain was telling on more than the archbishop. In the privacy of his diary the tireless John O'Sullivan, archdeacon of the diocese of Kerry, admitted he often thought of fleeing the country 'rather than see with my eyes and hear with my ears the melancholy spectacle and dismal wailing of the gaunt spectres that persecute and crowd about me from morning until night imploring for some assistance'.[47]

[42] MacNally to Renehan, 9 Mar. 1847, Renehan Papers, MCA.
[43] French to Renehan, ibid.
[44] Slattery to Renehan, 25 Feb. 1847, Renehan Papers, MCA.
[45] Slattery to Murray, 5 Feb. 1847, Murray Papers, DDA.
[46] Slattery to Renehan, 3 Apr. 1847, Renehan Papers, MCA.
[47] John O'Sullivan, diary, 18 May 1847, KrDA.

One priest, Francis Keogh, parish priest of Kildacomogue, Castlebar, did flee from the scene. He had come under fearful pressure from his starving people, who claimed that neighbouring parishes had received relief, though they had not. In a letter begging for money to purchase seed, he explained to Murray that his unfortunate parishioners, reduced to extremities, 'seeing their neighbours *favoured* with the assistance of the . . . relief committee, felt jealous with me for not having procured them the same advantages'.[48] He finally sought refuge in his native parish of Menlo, County Galway, with John Noone the parish priest, who commented that 'it is out of the frying pan into the fire to come here but . . . we must console each other.'[49] Whether other priests became so disheartened as Keogh it is impossible to guess, but such reactions raise the question of the psychological cost of those years on both clergy and people. Slattery was horrified by the Famine's demoralizing effects on the people:

We are still struggling with famine and fever, and what is more than both, the demoralization of our people consequent on the system of relief that this incapable Government has inflicted on the country. Every feeling of decent spirit and of truth has vanished, and instead there is created for us a cringing lying population, a Nation of Beggars. It would actually make one's blood run cold to be an eyewitness of what we are obliged to submit to, the able bodied obliged to leave their work and the youth their schools and spend their time congregated about the gate of a Soup Kitchen where their scanty rations are doled out, mixed up with all manner of persons good and bad.[50]

For some the continuing catastrophe brought forth courage, but for others it was a severe test. Although McNally praised the faith of the clergy in his diocese, Count Strzelecki suggested that some priests were shaken in their faith as the disaster dragged on.[51] They were overstretched. They worked 'like tigers' in the relief work, wrote begging letters and attended sessions and meetings, travelled long journeys on delegations. All this was in addition to their main work of bringing the sick and dying the consolation of

---

[48] J. Keogh to Synnott, 3 July 1847, Murray Papers, DDA.
[49] J. Noone to Synnott, 3 July 1847, Murray Papers, DDA.
[50] Slattery to Renehan, June 1847, Renehan Papers, MCA.
[51] *Report and Minutes of Evidence of the Select Committee, Lords, on Irish Poor Laws*, PP 1849, xvi. 979–80, 4 May 1849. Count Paul Edmunde de Strzelecki (1797–1873) agent for the British Association's relief scheme.

the rites of the Church.[52] The account by Hugh Quigley, curate in Killaloe, County Clare, of his daily life at the height of the Famine merits citing at length:

We rise at four o'clock ... when not obliged to attend a night call, and to proceed on horseback a distance of from four to seven miles to hold stations of Confession for the convenience of the poor country people, who ... flock in thousands ... to prepare themselves for the death they look to as inevitable. At these stations we have to remain up to five o'clock, p.m. administering both consolation and instruction to the famishing thousands. ... The confessions are often interrupted by calls to the dying, and generally, on our way home, we have to ... administer the last rites ... to one or more fever patients. Arrived at home, we have scarcely seated ourselves to a little dinner, when we are interrupted by groans and sobs of several persons at the door, crying out, 'I am starving', 'if you do not help me I must die'; and 'I wish I was dead' etc. ... In truth the Priest must either harden his heart against the cry of misery, or deprive himself of his usual nourishment to keep victims from falling at his door. After dinner—or, perhaps before it is half over—the Priest is again surrounded by several persons, calling on him to come in haste— that their parents, or brothers, or wives, or children, are 'just departing'. The Priest is again obliged to mount his jaded pony, and endeavour to keep pace with the peasant who trots before him as a guide, through glen and ravine, and over precipice, to his infected hut. ... The Curate has most commonly to say two Masses ... at different chapels; and ... to preach patience and resignation to the people, to endeavour to prevent them rising *en masse* and plundering and murdering their landlords. This gives but a faint idea of the life of a Priest here, leaving scarcely any time for prayer or meditation.[53]

Dramatic though this description was, it is corroborated by other accounts.[54] All, officials and relief workers, who visited the famine-stricken poor, risked catching the dreaded famine fever.[55] This danger was particularly great for priests administering the last rites to the sick and dying and for medical staff coming into

[52] T. P. O'Neill, 'The Catholic Clergy and the Great Famine', *Reportorium Novum* (1956), i. 461–9.

[53] Hugh Quigley, *Tablet*, 19 June 1847, cited in Murphy, *Killaloe*, 222–3. Quigley was curate in Killaloe parish.

[54] Murphy, *Killaloe*, 222–3.

[55] W. P. MacArthur, 'Medical History of the Famine', in R. D. Edwards and T. D. Williams (eds.), *The Great Famine* (1956), 281.

close physical contact with them.[56] Of the sixty-four priests in the diocese of Kilmore in Ulster, seven died in 1846–7. From Kinsale in County Cork Denis Murphy, the vicar forane, told Cullen that 'the mortality among priests is beyond conception. We have buried seven or eight priests since the bishop's death.'[57] In the west the mortality was also high—the issue of the *Nation* for 14 August announced the deaths from fever of Patrick O'Gorman, parish priest of Clare and Killoon, County Clare, Martin Loftus, chancellor of the Tuam diocese, and John Moloney, aged 33. Of the latter two it was explicitly noted that they contracted the disease 'in the discharge of their duty'.[58] In the diocese of Killaloe a further five died, one of cholera and four of famine-related disease in 1847–8.[59] Already by July, the *Nation* had listed twenty-seven clergymen who had fallen victim to the Famine, of whom eighteen were Catholic and nine Protestant.[60] At the end of the year, the *Catholic Directory* gave a more complete list, and for the month of May alone listed eighteen priests who had died from fever.[61] Some forty priests died in the course of that year.[62] Among the more eminent to die in Dublin was Fr. Luigi Gentili, who contracted fever while hearing confessions.[63] In the six years from 1847 to 1852 the deaths occurred of eight bishops, some at least from famine fever. The spring of 1849 was to see an unusually high mortality among the bishops—Walsh of Cloyne, Maginn of Derry, and Crolly of Armagh. Browne of Kilmore caught famine-related fever but recovered.[64]

Used as they were to rural distress, Black '47 appalled the clergy. Their horror at the terrible scenes they were witnessing was com-

---

[56] P. Froggart, 'The Response of the Medical Profession to the Great Famine', in E. M. Crawford (ed.), *Famine: The Irish Experience, 900–1900: Subsistence Crises and Famines in Ireland* (1989), 134–57.

[57] Murphy to Cullen, 18 June 1847, Cullen Papers, ICA. Bishop Murphy had died on 1 Apr. 1847. Vicar forane is the senior priest in a deanery and is the equivalent of a rural dean.

[58] *Nation*, 14 Aug. 1847.   [59] Murphy, *Killaloe*, 221–2.

[60] *Nation*, 17 July 1847. A leading historian of the Famine estimated that: 'In 1847 at least thirty-six priests died of fever, sixteen of them during the month of May.' O'Neill, 'The Catholic Clergy and the Great Famine', 463.

[61] W. J. Battersby, *The Complete Catholic Directory, 1848*, 342.

[62] O'Neill, 'The Catholic Clergy and the Great Famine', 463.

[63] D. Gwynn, *Father Luigi Gentili and his Mission (1835–1848)* (1951), 256–7.

[64] T. P. Cunningham, 'The Great Famine in County Cavan', *Breifne, journal of Cumann Seanchais Bhreifne* [Breifne Historical Society], 2 (1965), 427.

bined with a feeling of frustration at their own helplessness. Frantically they appealed for help, hoping that if the suffering of the people were known relief would surely come.[65] 'How I wish the real sufferings of the people could reach the ears of the rich of this life', wrote Flannelly from Clifden.[66] Yet government aid was inadequate and too late for many. The multitude, Fr. Patrick Byrne from Gort, County Galway, recorded, was 'dying a slow but *dire death*'. Their complaints were not directed against the people but at the merchants who charged high prices, the delays and inadequacy of relief, and the overcrowded, fever-infested poor-houses.

The 'Gregory clause' in the Poor Relief Act of 1847 had barred public relief to anyone holding more than a quarter-acre of land.[67] By the end of 1847, Thomas Timblin, parish priest of Ballisakeery, County Mayo, lamenting that 'hundreds of *my poor parishioners must necessarily perish*' revealed that, besides famine and fever, there was a new threat—death through exposure:

they must as a sine qua non Condition give up not only the possessions of their small patches of land but also level their cabins, thereby leaving themselves no other shelter than that of gathering the former roofing of their cabins and placing them on the ditches, there to perish not by hunger alone but by cold.[68]

The clause made it easier for landlords to clear the land and the cabins had to be levelled lest the evicted tenants returned. The results were appalling. 'Ballintubber is *gone*, alas!', lamented its parish priest, James Browne. 'My fine virtuous, holy people have been starved to death. The Landlords of all sects and creeds have conspired for their destruction—the Catholic Landlords the most cruelly disposed. *We* are *ourselves* nearly reduced to the level of our people.'[69] The dreadful living conditions forced on those evicted were vividly portrayed by James Dwyer, parish priest of Lackagh, Claregalway, County Galway. He told of the awful circumstances

[65] This conclusion emerges from the consideration of a substantial number of the clergy's letters; those exchanged with Renehan, Synnott, and Murray provide a better indication of their feelings than the begging letters they sent to the Dublin administration.

[66] Flannelly to Synnott, 27 June 1848, Murray Papers, DDA.

[67] The clause was so called because it was an amendment introduced by William Henry Gregory, member for the City of Dublin.

[68] Thomas Timblin to Synnott, 26 Jan. 1848, ibid.

[69] Browne to Murray, 19 Apr. 1848, Murray Papers, DDA.

of the sick he visited, who were 'dying on the road side or under the bridges or in sheds where a few sticks are erected for their reception, to be visited by myself who am doomed frequently to crawl *on my knees* into the abode of death'.[70]

The situation was as bad in parts of Ulster. Thomas Brady, of Drung near Cavan, complained that

In this parish . . . there are fifty farms vacant, two hundred human beings sent adrift in an inclement weather to beg or die. . . . As I meet them on the highways, livid corpses raised from the grave, I can but give a faint idea of their wretched appearance . . . wishing for the happy release of death. . . . The landlords exterminate right and left.[71]

John McCullagh, parish priest of Spiddal, County Galway, revealed that 'the Priest is called on every other day to attend from two to five dying persons where more than fifty houses were tumbled down last winter, the persecuted starving outcasts living in ditches or in sheds'.[72]

Edward Waldron from Ballinrobe, County Mayo, could not restrain his indignation at the inhumanity he witnessed:

We had the last visit from the Sheriff here two days before *Christmas-day*, with horse and foot soldiers and a posse of men well paid . . . for evicting the starving tenants and tumbling houses. These poor evicted people (forty eight families) are wandering about at present as there was no room for them in the Work house and if you were to see where some of them slept at night! I can only say that it was not fit for pigs. Man made to God's image and likeness to be thus treated by fellow man, the same by nature but that birth and fortune has made a distinction!![73]

There was also a feeling that, although some of the upper classes were generous, on the whole they did not make sufficient effort. Many landlords spent considerable sums on relief. Lord Dufferin contributed £1,000 anonymously for relief at Skibbereen and the final report of the Dublin General Relief Committee praised individual members (Lords Cloncurry and Dufferin, Richard Devereux of Wexford, and Errington of Kingstown).[74] That report went

---

[70] J. Dwyer to Synnott, 27 Apr. 1848, ibid.
[71] *Freeman's Journal*, 3 Mar. 1848.
[72] McCullagh to Synnott, 22 Apr. 1848, Murray Papers, DDA.
[73] E. Waldron to Synnott, 31 Dec. 1848, ibid.
[74] Russell placed too much blame on the landlords.

on to mention the 'unparalleled benevolence of the people of Dublin'.[75]

This 'unparalleled benevolence' brings up the question of private relief. The most important was that of the British Association for the Relief of Extreme Distress in Ireland and Scotland, founded on 1 January 1847 by Stephen Spring Rice, Baron Lionel de Rothschild, Thomas Baring, Jonathan Pim, and others to help those who were 'beyond the reach of the government'. Torn between exasperation at the ingratitude of the Irish and their incomprehensible behaviour, on the one hand, and pity for the victims, on the other, the British public responded generously. Queen Victoria gave £2,000 and the Duke of Devonshire, Baron Rothschild, the king of Hanover, and the Queen Dowager gave £1,000 each. Other organizations, such as the Dublin-based General Central Relief Committee and the Irish Relief Association, raised significant sums.[76] Religious bodies, too, made an admirable contribution. The practical, sustained, and well-organized relief operation of the Society of Friends was highly successful and drew well-merited praise.[77] Apart from taking part in the work of those relief agencies, was any relief organized by the Catholic Church? There is no mention of it in works on the Famine, although since the victims were mainly Catholic it might have been expected that their Church would have exerted herself on their behalf. An examination of this aspect of the Church's reaction to the Famine is now necessary.[78]

[75] *Report of the Proceedings of the General Famine Relief Committee of the Royal Exchange from 3 May to 3 September 1849* (1849), 1–4.

[76] The General Central Relief Committee distributed £84,000 and the Irish Relief Association £42,000. Other organizations which contributed sums from £4,000 to £20,000 were the Indian Relief Fund, the National Club, London, the Ladies Relief Association, the Ladies Industrial Society, the Wesleyan Methodist Relief Fund, London, the Evangelical Society, London, the Baptist Relief Fund, the Belfast Ladies Association, and the Belfast Industrial Association for Connaught. W. P. O'Brien, *The Great Famine in Ireland and a Retrospect of the Fifty Years 1845–92* (1896), 156–206; J. O'Rourke, *The History of the Great Irish Famine*, 3rd edn. (1902) 508–13.

[77] T. P. O'Neill, 'The Society of Friends and the Great Famine', *Studies*, 39 (1950) 203–13. The Central Relief Committee of the Society of Friends was formed after a meeting in Dublin on 13 Nov. 1846.

[78] O'Neill, 'The Catholic Clergy and the Great Famine', is an excellent general survey. Valuable local studies are M. Coen, 'Gleanings—The Famine in Galway', *Connaught Tribune*, 14, 21, 28 Mar., 4, 11, 18, 25 Apr., 9, 16 May 1975; D. Sheehy, 'Archbishop Murray of Dublin and the Great Famine in Mayo', *Cathair na Mart, journal of the Westport Historical Society*, 11 (1991), 118–28; Murphy, *Killaloe*.

In assessing the attitude of the Church to the Famine, the mentality of the age has to be taken into account. The period was an intensely religious one, and Catholic Ireland no less than Protestant England perceived calamities in religious categories. Irish bishops like Murray and Slattery, no less than English statesmen like Graham and Ashley, saw the Famine as a visitation from God, a punishment for sin, a humbling of pride, and a call to repentance. As during previous famines, again and again the priests invoked the example of the Old Testament—Jeremiah, Jonah, and Job—and urged the people to prayer and penance. Yet they were not fatalistic or moralizing, but saw suffering as redemptive. Murray invited the suffering to 'Look upon Jesus . . . who having joy before him, endured the cross' and reminded them that 'the sufferings of the present time bear no proportion to the glory to come.'[79] To the better-off, the clergy represented it as an urgent call to share their bread with the hungry. Bishop Kennedy of Killaloe, at a meeting of magistrates and clergy in County Clare, asked 'what was the language of Scripture on the subject—"If any man sees his brother or sister suffer want and shut up his bowels of compassion from him, how dwelleth the love of God in him?"'[80]

The clergy, however, also took an active part in famine relief. From the beginning of the relief operations, priest and parson sat on the same relief boards, and Catholic bishops and Protestant landlords worked together to help the starving.[81] The *Freeman's Journal*, remarking on 'the perfect harmony which distinguishes the ministers of religion of all classes', commented:

The Catholic and Protestant clergymen vie with one another in acts of benevolence. They are the most active members of relief committees— they confer together, remonstrate together, evoke together the aid of a dilatory government, and condemn together its vicious and dilatory refusals.[82]

Clergy of the Established Church threw themselves wholeheartedly into the work of relief and Joseph Bewley, one of the joint secretaries of the Society of Friends Committee, assured the Select

[79] *Sermons of the late Most Revd Daniel Murray, Archbishop of Dublin*, (1859), i. 248.
[80] *Limerick and Clare Examiner*, 28 Oct. 1846, cited in Murphy, *Killaloe*, 211–12.
[81] O'Carroll, diary, 6, 10, 14, 21 Dec. 1847. In Cavan Lord Farnham and Bishop Browne worked together for famine victims, and this was not uncommon.
[82] *Freeman's Journal*, 11 Jan. 1847.

Committee on Irish Poor Laws that they 'found none more efficient than the Protestant Clergy: the means they possessed in the
aid of their wives and daughters, of attending to the wants of the
poor, rendered their services very valuable'.[83] Their stipends, being
primarily charges on the rent, were regularly paid. The Catholic
clergy, too, Bewley told the Poor Law Committee, 'were . . .
exceedingly useful' pointing out, however, that they had not the
advantage of the help of wives and daughters like the Anglican
clergy.[84] Their duties in bringing the sacraments or last rites to the
sick and dying, although revealing to them the extent of the misery,
often left them with less time for ordinary relief work. Father John
Fitzpatrick reported from Skibbereen that, although his two extra
curates devoted their entire time to the sick and dying, they could
scarcely afford them the last rites, while from Balla, County Mayo,
the parish priest, Martin Browne, grieved that his curates were
'toil worn in ministering to the starving poor'.[85] When the curates,
who outnumbered the parish priests and constituted the younger
and more active section of the clergy, were excluded from the
relief committees, the veteran Irish Whig and reforming landowner,
Lord Monteagle, protested to Bessborough: 'You also exclude all
the Roman Catholic curates. Without them, and here they are
labouring like tigers for us working day and night, we could not
move a stroke.'[86]

The priests were not wealthy and the Famine had seen a sharp
decrease in the offerings of the faithful on which they depended.
They were able, however, to do considerable relief work for they
were in receipt of substantial sums of money. Some of this money
came from the British Association, the Central Relief Committee,
and the Society of Friends. The Irish Church, however, through its
overseas network, managed to generate a substantial flow of relief
money from all over the Catholic world. This largely unknown

[83] *Select Committee, Lords, on Irish Poor Laws*, PP 1849, xvi. 979–80, 4 May
1849.
[84] Ibid.
[85] *Freeman's Journal*, 18 Feb. 1847; ibid. 13 Feb. 1847.
[86] Monteagle to Bessborough, 1 Oct. 1846, Monteagle Papers, 13,396, NLI. The
attempt to exclude them was Trevelyan's. There were approximately 1,385 curates
and 1,008 parish priests in Ireland in 1845. Thomas Spring-Rice, first baron
Monteagle of Brandon in Co. Kerry (1790–1866); chancellor of the exchequer in
Melbourne's second administration (1835–9).

Catholic relief work was instrumental in keeping many thousands alive during the worst periods of the Famine.[87]

At first some priests gave from their own monies as for instance Dean Nolan, parish priest of Gowran, County Kilkenny, who gave £50 for relief in his parish, and the parish priest of Killeshan, Queen's County, James Maher, the uncle of Paul Cullen, rector of the Irish College in Rome, who sold his horse and gig to raise money. Soon, however, they had to appeal for outside help. Relief money came directly from individuals or groups, but from January 1847 on much of it came directly to Archbishop Murray, who was among the first to organize widespread voluntary aid. Though he was now 80 years of age, his activity was remarkable.[88] Later, he brought in Thomas Synnott, who had experience in relief work, to help him with the distribution and correspondence. Synnott's efficiency won him praise from many priests. Martin Browne, parish priest of Balla, told him: 'your untiring exertions have contributed under Heaven to save the lives of thousands.'[89] Generally, Murray and Synnott distributed the monies directly to the priests and religious for distribution—a more expeditious and less wasteful manner than government relief. As Bishop O'Donnell of Galway pointed out, the advantage of dividing the relief monies among the parish priests was that they would know the most needy cases in their own parishes.[90]

From the beginning of the Famine Murray was active in providing relief to country districts in his diocese, and by early 1847 he was sending monies to badly distressed areas in Cork and in Roscommon.[91] Among the earliest recorded gifts he received for relief were ten guineas from two English Protestant lawyers in Lichfield.[92] His extensive network of charitable and often well-to-do friends came to his aid. In January 1847 Lady Lucy Foley, the widowed aunt of the Duke of Leinster, sent Murray £100 from Marseilles

---

[87] The account given here is incomplete due to the imperfect nature of the evidence available.

[88] Priests from all the worst-affected areas sang his praises as again and again he came to their aid. James White of Dromore West, Kilmacshalgan, called him 'the Angelical Primate'. Another priest referred to him as the 'good, zealous and Patriarchal Bishop'. J. White to Synnott, 5 Mar. 1849, Murray Papers, DDA.

[89] Browne to Synnott, 13 Mar. 1849, Murray Papers, DDA.

[90] O'Donnell to Murray, 13 Apr. 1848, ibid.

[91] J. Madden to Murray, 5 Feb. 1847, ibid.; P. Sheehy to Murray, 27 Mar. 1847, ibid.

[92] J. Kirk, St Cross Lichfield, to Murray, 11 Jan. 1847, ibid.

and Mary Leonora Sheil from London sent him a similar amount.[93] He attended relief meetings, encouraged subscriptions, and looked after the distribution of relief funds that came to him from all over Europe, and from as far away as America, Africa, and Australia. The work of other bishops is less well documented, but it is recorded that MacHale spent ten hours a day organizing the distribution of relief and Browne of Kilmore worked side by side with Lord Farnham in relief work.[94] Maynooth College was sheltered from the effects of the distress by Peel's munificent Maynooth Grant, but Renehan (the president), the staff, and the students contributed generously.[95] Local initiative was important. In Kenmare, County Kerry, the enterprising Archdeacon O'Sullivan, at his own risk, imported food, sold it at cost price, then used the money to import again and recommence the process; thus he managed to distribute cheaply £30,000-worth of food. He told the select committee: 'I felt that it was an unusual business for a person in my sphere of life to turn flour merchant, but still someone must have done it at the time.'[96] Others, like Vaughan in Killaloe, County Clare, bought potatoes which they cut up for seed and distributed free.[97]

Despite their small numbers, the religious orders—priests, religious brothers, and nuns—made an impressive contribution.[98] Father Mathew pleaded the cause of the famine victims with

---

[93] Coutts to Murray, 7 Jan. 1847, ibid.

[94] U. J. Bourke, *The Life and Times of the Most Rev. John MacHale, Archbishop of Tuam and Metropolitan* (1882), 146.

[95] *Tablet*, 12 May 1849; a list in Murray's handwriting gives the staff as contributing £120, the senior students £30, and the other students £76. Murray Papers, DDA. The professor of Irish, James Tully, the bursar Thomas Farrelly, and the physics professor, Nicholas Callan, were singled out by Bishop Derry for their generosity. Nicholas Callan (1799–1864), inventor of the induction coil.

[96] *Select Committee, Lords, on Irish Poor Laws, PP* 1849, xvi. 211, 16 Mar. 1849; O'Sullivan, diary, 5 June 1845, KrDA. Later he had £600-worth of food sent to Kenmare on the government steamer, the *Zephyr*. O'Sullivan went to see Trevelyan, with whom he dined and lodged, and recorded that 'the last expression of Mr Trevelyan . . . was a request I would write to him as often as my good sense would say I ought' (diary, 18 May 1847). 'Through my English acquaintance I have been able to collect £80', he noted on 18 May 1847. As early as 1845 he had been providing relief with money and food received or begged from the British Association, the Society of Friends, and the Treasury.

[97] Murphy, *Killaloe*, 210.

[98] The records of religious congregations for the period are scanty and in some places non-existent.

Redington, Clarendon, Trevelyan, Routh, and with Cardinal Acton in Rome, and used his many contacts in England and America to help him set up a soup-kitchen in Cork.[99] The Dublin Carmelite, John Spratt, organized an interdenominational relief committee in which it was laid down that 'to perpetuate the kind feeling now so liberally evinced in favour of our starving people by those of every class and creed, in the distribution of Relief there shall be no Religious distinction whatever'.[100] The abbot of the Cistercian abbey of Mount Melleray, County Waterford, gave a graphic picture of the situation in Waterford:

even in this isolated place, on a most ungrateful and profitless mountain, we relieve from eighty to a hundred wandering poor daily, besides thirty three families around us ranging from four to ten in each, who are our regular weekly pensioners and whom we have, under God, saved from hopeless starvation. To have been enabled to do even this little for the sons and daughters of God, is a luxury beyond the banquet of kings.[101]

Convents everywhere provided meals and, in particular, breakfasts for the children.[102] John Leonard, superior of the Christian Brothers in Peacock Lane, Cork city, told his confrères: 'We must feed the children we have before taught, and to do this let us first begin with ourselves and make some sacrifices for their sakes.' Thanks to 'the charity of our friends in England', they were able to give one meal a day to four hundred children.[103] In England Frederick Lucas, editor of the *Tablet*, shocked by the reports from Ireland, used his journal to launch and sustain a significant fundraising campaign mainly among English Catholics who, he

[99] [Hayden], *Footprints*, 392–426.

[100] *Freeman's Journal*, 1 Jan. 1847. John Spratt (1797–1871), provincial superior of the Irish Carmelite Fathers; founded an asylum for the blind and a night refuge, and organized a temperance movement.

[101] *Tablet*, 30 Jan. 1847.

[102] Among those convents that were active in providing relief were: the Presentation Sisters in Tuam; the Sisters of Mercy at Tuam, Co. Galway, Westport, Co. Sligo, Birr, King's County, and Charleville, Co. Cork; the Ursuline Sisters in Elphin; the Sacred Heart Sisters in Roscrea; the Sisters of Charity in Oranmore, Galway; the Poor Clares in Newry and Loughrea; the Carmelite Nuns in Loughrea; the Dominican Sisters in Athenry; the Dominican Friars at the Claddagh of Galway; the Christian Brothers; and the Patrician Brothers.

[103] John B. Leonard to Lucas, *Tablet*, 20 Jan. 1849; Paul O'Connor to Lucas, ibid. 9 Mar. 1849.

complained, were not doing enough for the famine victims.[104] Another great organizer of relief was Bishop John Briggs, vicar apostolic or bishop of the Yorkshire district, who issued a pastoral to all his churches pleading for prayers and, from January to Easter of 1847, had a weekly relief collection taken up.[105] Briggs's episcopal colleagues, Thomas Griffiths and Francis Mostyn, vicars-apostolic of the London district and the northern district respectively, followed his example.[106] The Rosminian missioners in England, Luigi Gentili and Dominic Barberi (an Italian Passionist preacher, who had received Newman into the Roman Church in 1845), also raised relief.[107]

Relief for disaster was normally left to national governments, but famine-stricken Ireland was helped by many countries. An important factor was the sympathetic interest in Ireland which O'Connell's astonishing career had aroused. This was particularly true of European countries with which Ireland had long-established links. Important, too, in Rome and France was the activity of Irish people living there. In Rome, the students and staff of the Irish College did without their dinner to raise money. The rector, Paul Cullen, apart from appeals to his family to give all they could to the starving, threw open the Irish College in Rome to receive gifts of money, jewellery, and paintings.[108] The leader of the Liberal Catholics, Padre Gioacchino Ventura, who had great influence with the liberal new pope, Pius IX, and was an ardent admirer of O'Connell, threw in his weight behind relief measures.[109] Ventura

---

[104] *Tablet*, 26 Dec. 1846. Frederick Lucas (1812–55), a Quaker who converted to Catholicism in 1839; founded the *Tablet* (1840); transferred to Dublin (1849); supported Tenant League; MP for Meath (1852). Lucas apparently sent the sums collected directly to the bishops, clergy, and convents of the area; MacHale to Lucas, *Freeman's Journal*, 19 Jan. 1847.

[105] *Tablet*, 23 Jan. 1847.

[106] Ibid. 19 Jan. 1847; *Freeman's Journal*, 7 Jan. 1847. A list (early 1847?) in Murray's handwriting shows that he received £2,000 from Griffiths. This is the largest single sum on that list. Griffiths sent further sums later.

[107] Antonio Serbati-Rosmini, founder of the Rosminians, and Giovanni Pagani, their vice-provincial for England, raised large sums of money in northern Italy for famine relief. Count Mellerio of Milan gave £150, the archbishop of Vercelli £200, and the professors at the University of Turin a further contribution. A. Rosmini to G. B. Pagani, 31 Dec. 1846, ICA; Gwynn, *Father Luigi Gentili and his Mission* (1951), 213–14; C. L. Leetham, *Luigi Gentili: a Sower for the Second Spring* (1965), 267; A. Wilson, *Blessed Dominic Barberi: Supernaturalized Briton* (1967), 341–2.

[108] Cullen to Meyler, 13 Feb. 1847, Murray Papers, DDA.

[109] Ventura also collected for relief. N. N. Roman Citizen to G. Ventura, 26 Jan. 1847, Cullen Papers, ICA, new collection.

or Cullen may well have approached the pope, for Pius IX, shocked by news of the Famine, sent 1,000 Roman dollars to the Irish bishops in January 1847, an example followed by Cardinal Fransoni, secretary to the Congregation of Propaganda, and secretary to the Congregation of the Index.[110] Pius also organized a triduum of prayer in Sant'Andrea della Valle. On the first day Ventura preached in Italian, Cullen preached in English on the second day, and on the third day the bishop of Montreal, where so many famine refugees were arriving, preached in French.[111] In March, distressed at the continuing bad news, Pius took the unusual, if not unprecedented, step of issuing an encyclical appealing to the whole Catholic world on behalf of the famine victims.[112] Bishops everywhere were asked to appoint three days for public prayers and 'to exercise your charity in exhorting your people to contribute towards the relief of the Irish people'.[113]

The response to the pope's appeal was striking: bishops throughout Europe made appeals for the Irish victims, many setting aside their Lenten collections for that purpose.[114] Even before

---

[110] Murray noted that the 'munificent gift' forwarded by Fransoni amounted, 'after deducting discount' to £762. 6s. 8d., Murray to Cullen, 24 Mar. 1847, Murray Papers, DDA.

[111] G. Martina, *Pio IX, 1846–1850* (1974), 122.

[112] Cullen to Murray, 28 Feb. 1847, Murray Papers, DDA.

[113] Pius IX, encyclical letter, 25 Mar. 1847, ibid.

[114] Cardinal Curoli, archbishop of Rieti and Loreto, set aside the Lenten alms in his two dioceses for Ireland, Count Valerio of Parma sent a small sum, and an Irish priest wrote from Naples to say that they were organizing a collection. The archbishop of Turin, Luigi Franzoni, raised £890 and the bishop of Acqui £2,600. One of the most interesting was the subscription from the small and poor diocese of Ivrea. Earlier the bishop of Ivrea, Monsignor Morenzo, had sent money through the Paris committee. Now in June he sent a further 4,000 francs and recounted the devotion still very much alive in his diocese to an Irish bishop, Blessed Taddeo Macher (Blessed Thaddeus McCarthy), who had died at Ivrea in 1492. Moreno to Murray, 13, 23 June 1847, Murray Papers, DDA. Mac Suibhne, *Paul Cullen and his Contemporaries, with their Letters,* 5 vols. (1961–77), ii. 25. Two Italians made an unusual gift-offering to Archbishop Giovanni Brunelli, the secretary to the Congregation of Propaganda—2,000 cubic palms of marble! S. Maura to Brunelli, 26 Jan. 1847, Cullen Papers, ICA, new collection. The bishop of Casino sent his contribution to Father Bernard Smith, later vice-rector of the Irish College. Segretario dell'Indice [T. Degola] to Cullen, 28 Jan. 1847; Count Valerio to Cullen, 13 Feb. 1847, Cullen Papers, ICA; Cardinal Bishop of Loreto to Cullen, 14 Feb. 1847, ibid.; Cardinal Bishop of Ancona to Cullen, 15 Feb. 1847, ibid.; Cardinal Bishop of Rieti to Cullen, 7 Mar. 1847, ibid.; Cardinal Bishop of Terni to Cullen, 8 Mar. 1847, ibid.; Cardinal Bishop of Osimo to Cullen, n.d., ibid.

the pope's appeal was issued, French bishops and organizations were organizing relief. French sympathy had historical and religious roots for 'L'Irlande catholique' was often seen as 'la Pologne de l'ouest'. This sympathy had taken deeper root over the previous twenty years because the movements for Catholic emancipation and repeal had caught the imagination of Catholic Europe, particularly France. In February a number of French Catholics had requested the pope to issue a general appeal to bishops everywhere to make a combined effort for the famine-stricken Irish, a plea that may also have influenced Pius IX. In May, a committee, which included Baron de Schauenberg, the Comtes Montalembert and de Mérode, and the Vicomtes de Falloux and d'Harcourt, was established to co-ordinate aid to the Irish, 'a people to which France is bound by so many memories', and they expressed the hope that the committee would include men of all political persuasions and social positions.[115] Montalembert had first-hand knowledge of Irish famine for he had organized subscriptions through Lamennais's Liberal Catholic paper, *L'Avenir*, for the victims of the distress in Connacht in 1831 and had maintained a lively interest in Irish affairs.

All three leading Catholic papers—Louis Veuillot's ultramontane *L'Univers*, the Liberal Catholic *Le Correspondant*, and the moderately ultramontane *L'Ami de la Religion*—carried reports of the continuing disaster and frequent appeals for subscriptions. When Pius IX launched his appeal, French bishops reprinted it, many of them commenting critically on Russell's apparent failure to cope adequately with the Famine and on England's Irish policies in general.[116] Thus the Cardinal de Bonald, archbishop of Lyons, whose proud title was 'Primat des Gaules', in a passionate appeal for help for Ireland, wrote to his people in terms that would do justice to the Young Irelanders of the *Nation*:

If unjust prejudices have prevented that unfortunate island [Ireland] from enjoying the liberty which would restore life to her; if, . . . that Catholic nation is kept in a humiliating state of minority by a sister-island, which prevents her from enjoying her most legitimate rights, then let us at least console her heart by our most tender compassion . . .[117]

---

[115] *L'Ami de la Religion*, 10 June 1847.
[116] Ibid. 23 Sept. 1847.   [117] Ibid. 7 Aug. 1847.

While the collections were taking place, the dying O'Connell arrived in Paris on 26 March to be greeted by Archbishop Affre and Liberal and Ultramontane Catholics alike. In their name Montalembert read an address naming him not only '*the Man of one Nation*' but 'the Man of all *Christendom*'. When he died six weeks later panegyrics preached on him in Genoa, Paris, and Rome highlighted the suffering in Ireland. Ventura's great two-day funeral oration in June 1847 in the popular church of Sant'Andrea della Valle eulogized O'Connell for reconciling religion with liberty. Pius IX had carefully studied the text prior to its delivery and approved of it.[118] In appealing for help for the famine victims Bishop Gaston de Bonnechose of Carcassonne said their alms would be offerings on the tomb of the great O'Connell, the hero of Christianity, the new Judas Maccabeus, who bravely defended the rights of a people for long wrongfully oppressed, and who died gloriously for religion and liberty.[119]

The bishops' appeals were successful. Already by July 1847 large sums had poured in: the diocese of Strasbourg headed the first list with 23,365 francs.[120] Individual priests and laity also were moved to collect for the relief of the famine victims. By August 1847 the fortnightly review *Le Correspondant* reported that 'in the midst of the unceasing and frightful misery in our countryside, the appeals made by our bishops have yielded more than 300,000 francs.'[121] One body whose important relief work spanned Ireland and France was the Society of Saint Vincent de Paul, which Frédéric Ozanam, the Liberal Catholic, had founded in 1833.[122] In 1844 an Irish branch, which included John O'Connell, O'Connell's son and political heir, and Charles Gavan Duffy, one of the leaders of

---

[118] E. Costa, 'Da O'Connell a Pio IX: Un Capitolo del Cristianesimo Sociale del P. Gioacchino Ventura (1847)', in L. Morabito (ed.), *Daniel O'Connell: Atti del Convegno di Studi nel 140° Anniversario della Morte* (1990), 113–15. G. Ventura, *The Funeral Oration on Daniel O'Connell Delivered at Rome on the 28th June, 1847, . . .* (1847).

[119] *L'Ami de la Religion*, 7 Aug. 1847.

[120] There were approximately 25 francs to £1.

[121] *Le Correspondant*, xix. 461, 10 Aug. 1847. Although the report was concerned solely with Ireland, the comment on the bishops' collection indicates that some of the 300,000 francs may have been destined for the Lebanon.

[122] *Bulletin de la Société de Saint-Vincent-de-Paul*, i, 1848–9 (1854), 103. The Society was active in Italy and Cardinal Tadini informed Murray that the Saint Vincent de Paul Society, which had already sent £5,633 for relief, had collected a further £5,000 since the pope's encyclical was published.

the Young Ireland group and editor of their lively weekly, the
Nation, had been founded, and this branch took on the task of
distributing relief collected by the parent body in France. Its relief
expenditure amounted to some 150,000 francs in 1847 alone.[123]
Belgian Catholics also responded generously; the archbishops of
Malines, Bruges, and Ghent and the bishop of Antwerp all sent
considerable sums. O'Connell's campaigns had impressed many
German states, particularly in the Rhineland and Bavaria; the
archbishops of Augsburg and Trier and the bishops of Aachen,
Bonn, Münster, Paderborn, and Culm raised large sums.[124] From
the Austrian Empire, too, considerable sums were sent to Murray
for the 'relief of Irish Catholics'.[125] Perhaps influenced by his Irish
doctor, Sultan Abd-el-Medjid of Turkey sent a gift of £1,000.[126]

Apart from these European countries, a new source of relief had
opened up. Irishmen had followed the British flag and now from
Australia, Canada, India, South Africa, Newfoundland, and the
West Indies, Irish and English, Protestants and Catholics, sent
relief. Bengal sent £15,000 to the Irish poor and more than half
that amount to the Scottish poor.[127] Irish soldiers serving abroad
were open-handed in helping their fellow Irishmen: in Gibraltar

---

[123] Among the first responses to the Society's appeal was an anonymous dona-
tion of magnificent altar plate and silver table furniture; the donor was Abbé
Dupanloup, a curate at Saint-Roch, later the celebrated bishop of Orleans; S.
Atkinson, *Mary Aikenhead: her Life, her Work, and her Friends . . .* (1879), 364.
There were many instances of people of very modest circumstances sending relief,
among others an anonymous servant from Paris, who from the savings he made,
'sur mes économies', sent 50 francs. 'Un pauvre domestique de France' to Murray,
30 Apr. 1847, Murray Papers, DDA.

[124] One of Murray's lists gives the amount received from Münster as £1,050.
Murray Papers, DDA.

[125] Somerville to Murray, 23 Aug. 1850, ibid.; Redington to Murray, 4 Dec.
1851, ibid.

[126] Address of thanks to the Sultan by the British Association, *Report of the British
Association for the relief of the extreme distress of Ireland and Scotland . . .* (1849),
181–2. O'Neill Daunt relates that a Mr M'Carthy, the son of the Sultan's Irish
doctor, told him that the Sultan offered £10,000 but was deterred by the English
ambassador, as Queen Victoria had only subscribed £1,000. W. J. O'Neill Daunt,
*A Life Spent for Ireland: Selections from the Journal of W. J. O'Neill Daunt
. . .* (1896), 98–9. There is no confirmation for this story. At first the queen subscribed £1,000, but then increased it to £2,000. I am grateful to Dr T. P. O'Neill
for this information.

[127] Carew to Leahy, 1 June 1847, Leahy Papers, CDA. Patrick Joseph Carew
(*c.*1800–55), professor of theology at Maynooth (1828–38); coadjutor to the
vicar-apostolic of Madras (1838); vicar-apostolic of Bengal (1840). Patrick Leahy
(1806–75), president of Thurles College, later archbishop of Cashel (1857–75).

the bishop, Henry Hughes, found the soldiers among the most generous in contributing, and from Bombay Bishop Luigi Fortini told Murray that 'almost all the Irish Catholic soldiers and many other persons have made a collection for the Irish poor'.[128]

Of all countries, the United States was the most generous as state governments, mayors, bishops, priests, and Indians all contributed.[129] One of the earliest to organize was Fr. Thomas O'Flaherty, parish priest of Salem, Massachusetts who, in December 1845, collected over $2,000.[130] The Society of Friends acknowledged that for their own impressive and sustained relief operations, '[t]he chief source whence the means at our disposal were derived, was the munificent bounty of the citizens of the United States', adding that the supplies from America to Ireland 'were on a scale unparalleled in history'.[131] Already in December the Society in New York had set about raising subscriptions 'from the rich . . . through John J. Palmer, President of the Merchants' Bank and [from] the poor through the R.C. Bishop Hughes.'[132] Vice-President George Dallas chaired a meeting in Washington on 9 February 1847, where an appeal was launched to all villages and towns in the country.[133] In the same month the *Freeman's Journal* reported with astonishment that New York had contributed as much as $80,000 (£17,000) and claimed that this was 'about the same sum that has been contributed at home from all the wealthy classes of Ireland to the Central Relief Committee for all Ireland'. Massachusetts' contribution in 1847 reached approximately $350,000.[134] Cities chartered ships to bring food to Ireland—the Irish Relief Committee of Philadelphia sent the *John Walsh* and the *Lydia Anne* to Derry and the *St George* to Cork with supplies. A meeting in Faneuil Hall, Boston, resulted in the dispatch of two warships lent by the government, one the *Jamestown*, manned by

---

[128] Fortini to Murray, 1 May 1847, Murray Papers, DDA; Hughes to Murray, 18 Mar. 1847, ibid.

[129] O'Rourke, *Famine*, 512–13; C. Woodham-Smith, *The Great Hunger: Ireland 1845–9* (1962), 241–6.

[130] H. A. Crosby Forbes and H. Lee, *Massachusetts Help to Ireland during the Great Famine* (1967), 1–3.

[131] O'Rourke, *Famine*, 512.

[132] *Transactions of the Central Relief Committee of the Society of Friends during the Famine in Ireland in 1846 and 1847* (1852), 217–19.

[133] Ibid. 224–6.

[134] Forbes, *Massachusetts*, 58.

volunteers and crammed with 8,000 barrels of flour, and the other, the *Macedonian,* with 550 tons of food.[135]

The Irish bishops played a significant part: Hughes of New York, John Fitzpatrick of Boston (whose diocese subscribed $150,000), William Walsh of Halifax, Nova Scotia, Peter Kenrick of Saint Louis, and Michael Portier of Mobile, kept up a continuous stream of relief for Ireland. Elsewhere, where there were no Irish bishops, from Capetown and Port Elizabeth in South Africa, from Montevideo in Uruguay, and from Caracas in Venezuela Irish priests strained to keep relief monies flowing to Ireland.[136] In Liverpool, Manchester, and Bolton fourteen priests died, thirteen more died in Canada where seventeen nuns also perished.

Cullen and other bishops, critical of the inadequacy of official relief, alleged that the government was annoyed at foreign help for it appeared to reflect on its own willingness or ability to cope with the Irish disaster. The *Revue des Deux Mondes* saw it as a profound embarrassment for England:

English pride has been profoundly hurt on seeing world sympathy directed towards the *sister of England.* The aid coming from the subscriptions opened in France, the United States, in all Europe and all America, have been received as so many humiliations.[137]

This may have been so, yet the government welcomed American aid and undertook to pay the freights of all vessels from the United States carrying food gifts to Ireland, at a cost of £70,000.[138] Foreign aid was smaller far than the amount raised in the United Kingdom. Yet the total of foreign relief was considerable—that from

[135] Woodham-Smith, *Hunger,* 243–5.
[136] G. D. Corcoran to Murray, 6 May 1847, Murray Papers, DDA. Anthony Fahy, the Dominican chaplain to the Irish in Argentina, sent over £600 for relief. From Montevideo, at that time undergoing a siege, James Devlin sent first £151 and later a further sum. Account in Murray's hand of sums from Montevideo, Murray Papers, DDA; Fahy to Murray, 15 June 1847, cited in J. M. Ussher, *Father Fahy: A Biography of Anthony Dominic Fahy, O.P., Irish Missionary in Argentina, 1805–1871* (1951), 59–64; Fahy to Murray, 12 Sept. 1847; bills of exchange, 14 May, 14 June, Murray Papers, DDA. Reverend Anthony Fahy, OP (1805–71), born in Loughrea, Co. Galway; chaplain to the Irish community in Argentina (1844–71). J. Devlin to Murray, 18 June 1847, Murray Papers, DDA. R. Devereux to Murray, 31 May 1847, ibid. From Caracas, Archbishop Rafael de Escaboral sent £116 through the medium of Fr. Lawrence O'Callaghan.
[137] Jean Lemoinne, *Revue des deux mondes,* 67 (1847), 1059–81. The *Revue* was a journal published in France throughout most of the 19th cent.
[138] O'Rourke, *Famine,* 508.

the United States has been estimated at $1,000,000, a sum, moreover, that does not include clothing, nor emigrants' remittances, nor the extensive direct relief given by the Canadians and Americans to the fever-ridden victims arriving at Grosse Isle or New York. To quantify the amounts received by Archbishop Murray and other Catholic bishops is difficult because the records are of a fragmentary nature, but Dr Mary Purcell has estimated the amounts received by Murray at over £150,000.[139] A very approximate figure of the total 'Catholic' relief from outside the United Kingdom would be £400,000. This does not include remittances from emigrants, which were calculated at between £200,000 and £300,000 for 1847 and £460,000 for 1848.[140] Incomplete though it is, this brief listing adds to our knowledge of the involvement of the Church in famine relief. Foreign aid did add up to a significant amount and was an important complement to government and charitable exertions in the United Kingdom. After 1848, when Trevelyan mistakenly announced that the distress was over and the Society of Friends, convinced that relief was far beyond the reach of private exertion, wound down its work, foreign money proved very useful.[141] As much of it was distributed directly to the bishops and priests, it avoided the expense and delays of government schemes.

The part played by the Church from Italy to Belgium in the old world, and from Canada to Australia in the new, showed it at its best in its use of its world-wide organization. It is doubtful if any previous relief activity for disaster or famine had attracted such widespread, almost universal, reaction. The sympathy for Ireland which O'Connell had evoked, and initiatives like those of the Quakers in the United States and Pius IX in Rome, helped produce this exceptional response.[142] Of major importance, too, and of

[139] M. Purcell, 'Sidelights on the Dublin Diocesan Archives', *Archivium Hibernicum*, xxxvi (1981), 49. Calculations by David Sheehy, the archivist of the Dublin Diocesan Archives, and the present author, based on the correspondence in the archives, estimate a minimum of £60,000 or £70,000. This figure does not include the considerable sums that were not channelled through Murray.

[140] O'Rourke, *Famine*, 509.

[141] Pim to Trevelyan, 5 June 1849, *Transactions of the Society of Friends*, 453–4.

[142] For the manner in which O'Connell caught the imagination of the continent, see G. F. Grogan, *The Noblest Agitator: Daniel O'Connell and the German Catholic Movement, 1830–50* (1991); T. D. Williams, 'O'Connell's Impact on Europe', in K. B. Nowlan and M. R. O'Connell (eds.), *Daniel O'Connell: Portrait*

significance for the future, was the Irish diaspora. The Irish abroad, particularly the clergy, mobilized relief. Important though this was in France and Rome, it was far more important in the new countries—the British Empire, the United States, South Africa, South America—where a network of Irish clergy had grown up to cater for the Irish abroad. Jacob Harvey, the New York Quaker who began the American appeal, reported: 'I am proud to say that the Irish in America have always remitted more money, ten times over, than all the other foreigners put together.'[143] It is the first indication of the growing influence of the Irish Church throughout the Empire and in the United States, an influence that manifested itself at the Vatican Council of 1870, where over seventy of the bishops were Irish and a further eighty of Irish descent, amounting to a fifth of the bishops present.[144] The accounts of the Famine helped to focus the emigrants' attention on Ireland and prompted an increasing financial and political involvement in its affairs by Irish emigrants. Before long, Irish bishops and priests abroad, like Jews at a later date, were to use their position as influential members of an international faith to help their countrymen at home. British governments would soon have to take into account the pressure for remedial measures by cardinals and archbishops of New York and Boston, Chicago and Melbourne.[145]

Despite the Church's involvement, the Irish clergy did not escape criticism for their role during the Famine. Some of the complaints centred around the priests' role on the relief committees. Remarking on their great influence in the drawing up of the Relief Officers' lists, Charles Fairfield, chairman of the Kerry union, commented:

I would not apply the word undue to it; for the priests are best acquainted with the destitution and the misery of the country, which sometimes

of a Radical (1984), 100–6; P. Alter, 'O'Connell and German Politics', in M. R. O'Connell (ed.), *Daniel O'Connell: Political Pioneer* (1991), 110–17; L. Morabito (ed.), *Daniel O'Connell: Atti del Convegno.*

[143] Harvey to Jonathan Pim, 28 Dec. 1846, *Transactions of the Society of Friends*, 218. Jonathan Pim and Joseph Bewley were secretaries of the Quakers' Relief Committee in Dublin, and largely responsible for organizing relief.

[144] From the 1830s particularly many Irish priests had gone to work abroad, especially throughout the Empire and in the United States. K. Condon, *The Missionary College of All Hallows, 1842–1891* (1986), 93–122; E. M. Hogan, *The Irish Missionary Movement: A Historical Survey, 1830–1980* (1990), 69–141.

[145] D. A. Kerr, 'Government and Roman Catholics in Ireland', in id. (ed.), *Religion, State and Ethnic Groups* (1992), 296–8.

escapes the observation of others. . . . I have found some occasions where the Roman Catholic clergy interfered very properly, and in other instances where they interfered improperly, but not in many instances.[146]

Captain Douglas Labalmondiere, Poor Law Inspector for the unions of Tuam and Ballinrobe, who had supervised relief administration in Kerry, Mayo, and Galway, was more critical, claiming that some of the clergy's certificates for food were improperly issued. He believed that such conduct should be punishable:

It was stated to me by the Reverend Mr Hughes, Roman Catholic clergyman for Claremorris, two days after I arrived in Ballinrobe Union, in the Board room that he considered it to be 'morally justifiable to give certificates to get the starving creatures meal, without reference to the statements in them being correct'. I took down his words.[147]

Elizabeth Smith of Baltiboys complained that the local priest, Arthur Germaine, parish priest of Blackditches in County Wicklow, not only refused to superintend the stores at Blackditches himself but prevented his two curates from undertaking the care of them. Richard Webb, a Quaker, reported that Tom Welsh, a priest in Erris, County Mayo, was selfish and dishonest and abhorred by his people.[148] These are isolated instances and do not change the overall picture. Those criticisms were of far less significance than a charge made about the same time by the *Nation*, the organ of Young Ireland. In July 1847 it stated:

Independent of their local duties, which they have discharged with a devotion unsurpassed in the annals of martyrdom, have they in their political capacity, as . . . citizens, raised their voices against the murder of their people . . .? Or have they . . . backed the abettors of that infamous policy which gave to the butcher two million of their flock? Have they whispered when they should have denounced, or been silent when they should have thundered?[149]

This was a serious charge. Since many attributed the huge number of deaths to the non-interventionist policy of the government the accusation was that the Church through its silence allowed it to

---

[146] *Select Committee, Lords, on Irish Poor Laws*, PP 1849, xvi. 979–80, 15 Mar. 1849.
[147] Ibid. xvi. 583, 23 Mar. 1849.
[148] Webb to William Todhunter, 16 May 1847, cited in H. E. Hatton, '"The Largest Amount of Good": Quaker Relief in Ireland' (Ph.D. thesis, 1988), fo. 268.
[149] *Nation*, 24 July 1847.

happen. The allegation evoked angry refutations. James Fitzpatrick, parish priest of Castletownroche, wrote:

Did this gentleman ever read any of the thousand letters of the Catholic priesthood, complaining of the murder of their parishioners by starvation? ... The Catholic clergy took every opportunity, publicly and privately, of denouncing the criminal policy of the Whigs, whereby millions starved to death. What more could we do? And after this we are accused of being abettors of murder, and to have stimulated [sic] to crime.[150]

This dilemma of the clergy also angered the fiery Fr. James Maher. 'How could they save the Hecatomb sacrificed at Bantry? ... If they raise their voice against oppression they run the risk of being accused of exciting [sic] to murder.'[151] To describe the famine deaths as a hecatomb or holocaust was typical of Maher's impassioned rhetoric. He had, however, made impassioned appeals for the famine victims and was generous in almsgiving. He bitterly attacked the Anglican Archbishop Whately of Dublin for speaking in the House of Lords against the right to outdoor relief, claiming that 'in the absence of such a right, thousands and tens of thousands have lately died of starvation ... and that other thousands and tens of thousands are sentenced to the same death with all its indescribable horror'.[152] Other priests were also angry, as Clarendon reported:

the priests are everywhere behaving ill and are bitterly hostile to the government whom they accuse of starving the people, etc. nor is it much to be wondered at for they are in great distress and consequently in bad humour, they must have some cry wherewith to excite the people.[153]

MacHale had not been silent. Shocked by Russell's announcement in August 1846 of a switch to a policy of non-intervention, he immediately warned him in prophetic language that 'you might as well at once issue an edict of general starvation ....'.[154] Within weeks he made another appeal contrasting the '£50,000 for a starving people' with 'the £20,000,000 ... to give liberty to negroes

---

[150] Ibid. 28 Aug. 1847.
[151] Maher to a Dublin paper, 4 Dec. 1847, F. Moran (ed.), *The Letters of Rev. James Maher ... on Religious Subjects ...* (1877), p. lxxxi.
[152] Maher to Whately, 8 Apr. 1847, ibid., p. 3.
[153] Clarendon to Russell, 12 July 1847, Clarendon Papers, Letterbook 1.
[154] *Freeman's Journal*, 5 Aug. 1846.

of the West Indies'.[155] By January 1847, as the deaths in Connacht multiplied, his next grim prophecy to Russell was that 'the people's bones, piled into cairns more numerous than the ancient pyramids, shall tell posterity the ghastly triumphs of your brief but disastrous administration'.[156] Although his terrible prophecies were to be fulfilled, MacHale's past record of denunciation of government policies told against him, and he was dismissed as a firebrand. The more circumspect Slattery, while claiming that but for 'the untiring persevering exertions of the Relief Committee in procuring work' Thurles would have been 'a second Skibbereen', had publicly expressed his concern, first at the delays and then, in 1847, at the possible effects of government measures.[157] By June he was expressing to Renehan his abhorrence of the Famine and the famine-fever and 'what is more than both the demoralization of our people consequent on the system of relief that this incapable Government has inflicted on the Country'.[158] In June 1848 he finally came out publicly: 'the distress was such that I could not resist the imposition of my voice on behalf of the Poor of Christ'.[159] Little is known of the protests from Archbishops Crolly and Murray. Murray, apart from distributing aid, attended meetings in Dublin to organize relief and to appeal for swifter government help and distributed the aid from foreign bishops. Ryan of Limerick, while condemning the violence of some tenants, denounced the higher classes for being 'cold and callous to the voice of humanity . . . untouched by the cries of famine and pestilence, the wailings of hunger, the lamentations of women and children'.[160] Bishops up and down the country worked closely with the relief committees, where grievances against the dilatoriness of the government were often voiced. Already in October 1846 Bishop Kennedy made the practical proposal that the only way of preventing starvation was 'by the gentlemen of the country associating themselves for the purchasing up the grain, which was at present being exported in such large quantities out of the country'.[161] Irish-born Bishop

[155] MacHale to Russell, 21 Aug. 1846, O'Reilly, *MacHale*, i. 616.
[156] Letters of John MacHale, cviv. 624; *Freeman's Journal*, 19 Jan. 1847.
[157] Slattery to Russell, 25 Feb. 1847, Renehan Papers, MCA.
[158] Slattery to Renehan, 13 June 1847, ibid.
[159] Slattery to Renehan, 12 June 1848, ibid.
[160] Ryan, as cited in *Hansard*, xcv. 880, 9 Dec. 1847.
[161] *Limerick and Clare Reporter*, 28 Oct. 1846, cited in Murphy, *Killaloe*, 211.

Hughes of New York, in a remarkable lecture delivered in New York on 20 March 1847, analysed and rejected the prevailing system of political economy, whose high priest he saw as Russell. Instead he made a well-reasoned case for state intervention in the Famine. Social economy, he insisted was 'that effort of society . . . to accomplish the welfare of all its members' and since there was, he believed, no general scarcity of food in Ireland, the rights of life were dearer and higher than the rights of property. For Hughes, 'political economy' was the murderer of the Famine-stricken and he castigated Russell for his alleged statement 'that nothing prevented him from employing government vessels to carry bread to a starving people, except his unwillingness to disturb the current of trade'.[162] From October 1847 on, protests began to pour in as bishops and priests remonstrated on the plight of the poor, and the clergy of various dioceses held meetings to publicize the distress of the poor.[163]

This still leaves unanswered the question as to why the bishops made no united protest against the inadequacy of government measures before the autumn of 1847. Fitzpatrick and Maher put their finger on the quandary of the clergy and particularly the bishops. If they remained silent the *Nation* could accuse them of timidity in the face of a national tragedy. If they spoke out, they might foment, or would be accused of fomenting, unrest among the people, as some of the priests were accused of doing. Caught in this dilemma only a few of the bishops spoke out publicly. Bishops of a Church that was merely tolerated, they were cautious to the point of timidity. They had never made a united appeal on a social issue before and in any case, in the early months of the Whig administration, whose return to power O'Connell had endorsed, the hierarchy had every reason to believe that Russell, the champion of justice to Ireland, would prove, in Murray's words, another 'Joseph'. With no particular expertise on political economy they shared the prevalent views which regarded property as sacred and relief as a temporary necessity. Neither they nor the government

---

[162] J. Hughes, *A Lecture on the Antecedent causes of the Irish Famine in 1847*, . . . (1847). John Hughes (1797–1864), born Co. Tyrone; emigrated to United States (1817); bishop of New York (1842); first archbishop (1850); friend of Presidents Polk, Quincy Adams, Abraham Lincoln.
[163] *Catholic Directory 1849*, 10, 20 Oct. 1849.

expected the blight to continue or anticipated a disaster on the scale of Black '47. Their duty, as they perceived it, was to persuade their faithful to pray God's mercy and to persuade the better off to give generously to the victims and to take part in the relief work. Since, at the beginning at least, each bishop experienced the disaster as it occurred in his own diocese, they did not think of the Famine in national terms.

A further important reason why the bishops took no collective action was that they were themselves disunited. Their annual meetings, long a source of unity and strength, had become the occasion for enervating wrangling. The government's education policies were the bone of contention. In 1831 Lord Stanley, chief secretary for Ireland, established the national system of education with the aim of providing a united system of education for all children without interfering with their religion. Unlike those of the Established Church, the Catholic bishops had welcomed the system for, though they would have preferred a completely Catholic system, they realized that this new one, with its safeguards against proselytism, was the most they could expect. Moreover, with the rejection of the system by the Established Church, most of the schools became in fact, Catholic schools. In 1838, however, MacHale had denounced government control over the Board of National Education and what he saw as the latitudinarian content of the textbooks. At a meeting of the bishops in January 1839, sixteen bishops, including Archbishops Crolly, Murray, and Slattery, supported the system, while nine opposed it. Appeals to Rome ended, in 1841, with Propaganda's decision in favour of the majority. The sharpness of the quarrel left deep wounds. Thenceforth the bishops began to take different attitudes towards the government. MacHale and his supporters, who regarded every government initiative with suspicion, were called 'turbulent'. Murray and Crolly tended to trust the government and were in turn decried as 'government, or Dublin Castle, bishops', that is, those who frequented Dublin Castle, the seat and symbol of English rule in Ireland. Throughout the 1840s discord over education simmered on and O'Connell's Repeal movement sparked off another difference. MacHale and his supporters endorsed it enthusiastically, whereas Murray distanced himself publicly from it. A further dispute arose over what attitude the bishops should adopt to Peel's Charitable Bequests bill of 1844, which purported to protect Catholic bequests. Again, Murray's views had prevailed although Slattery, wary of links with the government, had sided with MacHale. The most recent dispute concerned the Queen's Colleges which Peel had decided to establish in Cork, Galway, and Belfast. As in the case of national education, the question turned on the threat they posed to the faith of Catholic students. Unlike other universities in the United Kingdom, with the exception of the recently established London University, the Queen's Colleges were to be neutral as regards religion. Although lecture rooms were assigned for religious instruction and private endowment of theological lectures was encouraged, religion was excluded from the official curriculum of the colleges. Like other attempts to impose secular institutions on Ireland in the nineteenth century, this project was deeply offensive in many quarters. Robert Inglis, MP for Oxford, denounced it as 'a gigantic scheme of Godless Education' and the tag stuck. Daniel O'Connell and most Irish bishops, led by Archbishops Slattery of Cashel and MacHale of Tuam attacked the scheme as likely to subvert the students' faith. Pointing to the example of Trinity College Dublin, which was a Protestant college, they demanded that Catholics, too, be given a denominational college. On the other hand a minority, led by Crolly of Armagh and Murray of Dublin, while preferring that the colleges be Catholic institutions, was prepared to accept them. Both sides appealed to Rome and, in July 1846, the Congregation of Propaganda decided in favour of the majority. The new pope, Pius IX, however, advised by Corboli Bussi, his liberal-minded acting secretary for state, withheld the condemnation.[164] Crolly had come in for severe criticism because in May 1846 he had called a special meeting of the bishops to censure the Colleges bill as 'pregnant with danger to the faith and morals' of youth, and had later come round to support it. This switch of opinion had left a bad impression on some colleagues and one nationalist newspaper, the *Pilot*, had suggested he was mentally unstable. The differing views of the

[164] D. A. Kerr, *Peel, Priests, and Politics* (1982), 58–64, 110–351. The most complete account of the dispute on the national system of education is E. Larkin, 'The Quarrel among the Catholic Hierarchy over the National System of Education in Ireland, 1838–41', in R. B. Browne, J. Roscelli, and R. Loftus (eds.), *The Celtic Cross: Studies in Irish Culture and Literature* (1964), 121–46. Giovanni Corboli Bussi (1813–50), secretary for the Congregation of the Consistory (1845); concluded concordat with Russia (1847); sent by Pius IX on a mission to Charles Albert, king of Sardinia (1848).

bishops were made public and the priests and laity took sides. Well over 80 per cent of the clergy signed and published petitions against the colleges.[165] During 1847, this key question of the Queen's Colleges remained undecided with both sides working hard to press their case. With the bishops so sharply divided and his own authority under challenge, it was difficult for Crolly to lead a united approach to the government on the Famine or any other issue. Nor could Murray provide that leadership.

Other disagreements surfaced. The Board of National Education decreed that all schools receiving building grants should in future be vested in the board. Murray, as often before, attempted to explain away the board's decision as harmless, but at their annual meeting in 1847 the majority of bishops rejected his explanations.[166] Disunity surfaced even on the distribution of relief. Murray and Crolly wanted to hand the monies received from the pope and foreign Catholic bishops to the Relief Committees in Dublin.[167] Murray's reasons, he explained to Cullen, were that if it had been distributed through the Central General Committee, it would have been more creditable to Rome, as having less of an exclusive appearance, and more of the spirit of the Good Samaritan; whereas Protestants were subscribing *immense* sums to be applied principally, indeed almost entirely, for the relief of Catholics.[168] Slattery and MacHale, however, insisted that these monies be sent to the archbishops who would then distribute them directly to the other bishops, a view which Cullen supported. Murray was forced to accept it. Murray's view shows a greater sensitivity towards Protestants. The archbishops of Tuam and Cashel, however, were unwilling that monies expressly donated for the Catholic poor should be handed over to a mixed committee in Dublin, which was removed from the worst incidents of the Famine. The cumulative effect of these differences was to paralyse collective action. Edmund O'Reilly, professor of theology at Maynooth and a reliable witness, told Cullen, in 1844, that 'there are notoriously two parties

---

[165] *Freeman's Journal*, 12 Feb. 1846. This issue contained the names of 1,626 priests, to which should be added the Derry priests who issued a similar petition. The total number was *c.*1,710.

[166] Bishops' resolutions, 23 Oct. 1847, *Catholic Directory 1848*, 245.

[167] Murray to Slattery, 11, 20 Feb. 1847, Slattery Papers, CDA; Crolly to Slattery, 18 Mar. 1847, ibid.

[168] Murray to Cullen, 3 Mar. 1847, copy, Murray Papers, DDA.

3

Recriminations: Viceroy's Memorandum and Bishops' Memorial

'The Irish are essentially a religious people, but of late years religion has . . . been so mixed up with politics that the completely distinctive characters of the two are almost lost sight of.'

(Clarendon's memorandum to Russell, 1 Oct. 1847)

'The sacred and indefeasible rights of life are forgotten amidst the incessant reclamations of the subordinate rights of property . . . Hallowed as are the rights of property those of life are still more sacred.'

(Irish bishops' memorial to Clarendon, 30 Oct. 1847)

By May 1847 the second and most disastrous year of the Famine, with its horrendous death-toll, was over. In that month death had also removed two of Ireland's leading figures from the scene. O'Connell's death in Genoa on 15 May was but one more calamity among so many. His death showed the growing irrelevance of the great Repeal party he had built and which still appeared outwardly strong.[1] On the following day, the popular Bessborough, who had tried as best he could to cope with the disaster, also died. So much had changed since the previous June when O'Connell and, at his behest, the bulk of the political nation, had welcomed the return of the Whigs to power and Russell had dispatched Bessborough to Ireland with glowing words of promise for Ireland's golden age. A power vacuum now existed in Irish political life and Russell looked for a substitute for Bessborough. Morpeth, who had proved a successful chief secretary from 1835 to 1841

[1] The classic account of the Repeal movement during this period is K. B. Nowlan, *The Politics of Repeal: A Study in the Relations between Great Britain and Ireland, 1841–50* (1965). See also his chapter 'The Political Background', in Edwards and Williams (eds.), *The Great Famine* (1956), 131–206.

and knew Ireland well, asked for the lord lieutenancy. Before his death Bessborough had pleaded that a strong man be appointed who did not fear unpopularity, and Russell may have thought that this excluded Morpeth. Russell toyed with the idea of appointing his brother, the duke of Bedford, but decided instead to offer the position to Lord Clarendon, who accepted in the belief that the post was to be abolished in the near future.[2] Although Clarendon described the lord lieutenantship as plunging into 'the Irish Bog', his appointment was probably not as unwelcome to him as he first intimated.[3] The new lord lieutenant was liberal-minded, intelligent, and peace-loving. A good family man, he had great charm of manner and Gladstone recalled that, of his sixty cabinet colleagues, Clarendon was the easiest and the most attractive of the lot.[4] A diplomat, he had negotiated a commercial treaty with France in 1831, and as ambassador in Spain he helped to negotiate a truce between the Carlists and Queen Isabella. As commissioner of customs he had come to Dublin in October 1827 to assist in the fusion of the Irish and English boards of excise and had acquired some knowledge of Irish problems. The then lord lieutenant, Lord Anglesey, had formed a sort of private cabinet which included Villiers (as Clarendon was then), in addition to Anthony Blake and William Henry Curran.[5] Clarendon's sympathies, like Russell's during his visit, had been with the people rather than with the landlords and he had described himself as 'an ardent friend of Ireland'.[6] When, in February 1839, Melbourne had offered him the lord lieutenancy of Ireland O'Connell was delighted:

As to Lord Clarendon, there could not probably be a better man. His opinions are all of the very best and highest excellence. I knew him in

---

[2] George William Frederick Villiers (1800–70), 4th earl of Clarendon (1838); attached to British embassy at St Petersburg (1820); commissioner of customs (1823); ambassador at Madrid (1833–9); lord privy seal (1839–41); president of the board of trade (1846). For Clarendon, see H. E. Maxwell, *The Life and Letters of George William Frederick, Fourth Earl of Clarendon*, 2 vols. (1913); G. J. T. H. Villiers, *A Vanished Victorian, being the Life of George Villiers, Fourth Earl of Clarendon* (1938).

[3] Clarendon to Reeve, 5 Jan. 1847, Clarendon Papers, c. 534.

[4] J. Morley, *The Life of William Ewart Gladstone* (1905), ii. 447.

[5] Lawless, *Personal Recollections of the Life and Times, with Extracts from the Correspondence, of Valentine, Lord Cloncurry* (1849), 332.

[6] George Villiers to Lord Cloncurry, 14 Sept. 1831, cited in Lawless, *Recollections*, 454.

Ireland in the time of Lord Anglesey's first government. He knows Ireland well and understands the Orange faction in all its rascality.[7]

Although Clarendon had refused the position on grounds of inexperience, he valued O'Connell's views on Ireland. In 1844 O'Connell, in response to a request by Charles Buller, the radical leader, drew up a demanding list of conciliatory measures, the main one being a demand for Church reform and equality for the Catholic Church. Clarendon recommended all O'Connell's proposals to Russell, except the one demanding a quintupling of income tax on absentee landlords.[8] Clarendon entered the cabinet in July 1846 as president of the board of trade, and now in May 1847 he arrived in Ireland as lord lieutenant. It has been plausibly suggested that Russell may have thought that by sending Clarendon to Ireland cabinet secrets would be better kept, and, given Clarendon's friendship with John Thadeus Delane, editor of *The Times*, the government might receive a better press for its Irish policy.[9] Clarendon certainly cultivated the press. He corresponded constantly with Henry Reeve, *The Times* journalist, and through him successfully attempted to influence *The Times* to support his administration.[10] He did not hesitate to take an active hand in writing to promote his point of view, and when in Spain he had published an anonymous pamphlet on Spanish policies. Palmerston suspected that he interfered in Spanish politics and had to reprove him for secretly negotiating tariff advantages behind the back of Britain's allies.[11] In Ireland, too, he wrote anonymously to advocate his policies and engaged journalists to do the same.

Occasionally his clandestine methods backfired and he horrified the duke of Bedford, Russell's elder brother, and Greville, with whom he was on close terms, when he disclosed that he ran a spy system.[12] Some of his cabinet colleagues distrusted him and Russell

[7] O'Connell to P. V. Fitzpatrick, 11 Feb. 1839, cited in M. R. O'Connell, *The Correspondence of Daniel O'Connell* (1972–80), vi. 216.

[8] A. Macintyre, *The Liberator: Daniel O'Connell and the Irish Party, 1830–1847* (1965), 279; S. Walpole, *The Life of Lord John Russell* (1889), i. 395–6.

[9] J. Prest, *Lord John Russell* (1972), 253. Clarendon corresponded regularly with Greville, Reeve, and Lewis.

[10] Clarendon often attempted to influence the press; Clarendon to Reeve, 27 Oct. 1850, Clarendon Papers, c. 534; Clarendon to Lewis, 28 Apr. 1850, ibid. c. 532/2; Clarendon to Monteagle, 15 Jan. 1848, Monteagle Papers, NLI.

[11] K. Bourne, *Palmerston: The Early Years, 1784–1841* (1982), 473.

[12] C. C. F. Greville, *The Greville Memoirs: A Journal of the Reign of Queen Victoria*, ed. H. Reeve (1903), 11 June 1848, vi. 76.

told Morpeth, now earl of Carlisle, that he was neither very honest nor very Whig.[13] He was an alarmist and it was with a sense of trepidation that the prime minister opened his letters from Ireland. Supremely confident of English superiority, he was dismissive of other nations, whether Spain or France, Austria or Prussia. 'We are too honest for cooperation with France', he told Reeve shortly before coming to Ireland, 'when we interfere with the affairs of other countries it is with the "bona fide" wish of benefiting them'. He placed Ireland on a level with Spain—its affairs unintelligibly intractable, its people hapless and inefficient. Now he would be in a position to effect some reforms. A few years of resolute government, he promised Lewis, would set matters right. Poised and confident in his manner, he came to Ireland in late May 1847 with high expectations, for, like viceroys before and after him, he aspired to be the administrator who would solve the problems of this restless country. Conscious of the influence of the Catholic Church, he believed that if he could establish good relations with the bishops it would be greatly to the advantage of his administration and he looked forward eagerly to contacting them. His predecessor's popularity with both Whigs and Tories and most of the O'Connellites eased his path, and his first reports were optimistic. 'I have little to say and that little is good', he told Russell after a month's stay, 'I have seen a great number of people and they all speak with more confidence of the future than when I was here before . . . Sir Edward Blakeney says the country is tranquil and if it were not for the harrowing duty of escorting provisions, the troops would have little to do.' Crime had dropped by a third and he saw it as 'satisfactory as showing that when the people have wherewithal to live upon they become orderly and abstain from crime'.[14]

His optimism was to be put to the test by the elections. The weak position of the Whigs in parliament meant that sooner or later they must try to strengthen their position through a general election, and Russell finally called one in August 1847. Although the government supporters gained a majority, the results were

[13] Morpeth Journal, 2 Apr. 1849, Castle Howard MSS, J 19/8/20, cited in Mandler, *Aristocratic Government in the Age of Reform: Whigs and Liberals 1830–1852* (1990), 238. Morpeth became 7th earl of Carlisle in 1848.
[14] Clarendon to Russell, 1 July 1847, Clarendon Papers, Letterbook 1. Sir Edward Blakeney (1778–1868) was commander-in-chief in Ireland (1838–55).

disappointing for Russell. No party had real cause for triumph except the extreme radicals.[15] It also proved a very Protestant election, for Peel's increase of the grant to Maynooth was still a live issue and Protestant societies mounted an effective campaign.[16] If the Peelites lost seats it was, Francis Bonham their election agent told Peel, on the religious issue: 'Maynooth lost us many friends, Free Trade hardly any.'[17] Over 150 members returned, or almost a quarter of the total, were pledged against Catholic endowment.[18] A parliament more sensitive to Protestant feelings had the effect of narrowing Russell's options over concessions to Irish Catholics. In Ireland the Whigs' opportunity to improve their position was better than in Britain for the Tories were divided into Peelites and Protectionists and the Repealers were split into O'Connellites and Young Irelanders. Furthermore, since O'Connell had welcomed the Whigs' accession to power, Clarendon expected the clergy to support the candidates favourable to government. This did not happen, and Clarendon complained to Russell of their conduct. Clarendon accused them of systematically promoting the return to parliament of 'men without principles, station, property or intelligence; the very reverse of what is now the great desideratum for Ireland, viz. representatives who should command respect in England and promote sympathy and good will between the two countries!'[19] Clarendon understood well the incomprehension and irritation that Irish behaviour caused in England and knew that generous support from that country could alone avert the horrors of famine. Certainly the Irish results were a blow to the Whigs, for their number showed a drop from 25 to 17 since the election of 1841. The Conservatives held their own, but the most striking result was the increase in the number of Repealers who, divided and leaderless, nevertheless returned 39 members. Russell, disappointed at the results both in Britain and Ireland, felt caught between the resentment of both sides for 'we have in the opinion of Great Britain done too much for Ireland and have lost the

[15] N. Gash, *Sir Robert Peel* (1972), 625; Prest, *Russell*, 262–3; C. Cooke and B. Keith, *British Historical Facts, 1830–1900* (1984), 139.

[16] Chadwick, *The Victorian Church* (1966), i. 236–7; J. Wolffe, *The Protestant Crusade in Great Britain, 1829–1860* (1991), 220–9.

[17] Bonham to Peel, 2 Aug. 1847, Add. MSS 40599, fo. 122, cited in Gash, *Peel*, 625.

[18] Wolffe, *Protestant Crusade*, 227–8.

[19] Clarendon to Blake, 26 July 1847, Clarendon Papers, Letterbook 1.

elections for doing so. In Ireland the reverse.'[20] 'The Irish', he complained, 'seem always to act in the manner most opposite to that which is usual in other countries. The expenditure of ten millions to save the People from starving has thus raised a bitter spirit of hostility.' His comment reflected the frustration of many in England who believed that, despite their generosity in feeding them, the Irish returned members of parliament hostile to the British connection. The priests were blamed as the architects of the Repeal party's success for they provided encouragement and support for a Repeal Association demoralized by poor leadership, divisions, and diminishing resources.

Yet Clarendon's and Russell's comments need to be critically examined, for the newspaper reports of the election meetings prior to the election present a more complex picture. Some priests played a prominent role in the 1847 election, but the number involved represented a tiny proportion of the clergy. The thrust of the clerical speeches reported in the press reflected the divisions within the 'nationalist' camp, rather than opposition to the government. The efforts of the majority were directed to keeping out candidates who favoured physical force; the clerical supporters of Young Ireland, while more anti-government in tone, concentrated their attack on what they saw as the backsliding of Repeal candidates. Loyalty to O'Connell, for long the hero of the clergy, had become an issue in the election. While O'Connell's son, John, tried to profit from the surge of sympathy following O'Connell's death, the Young Ireland weekly, the *Nation*, published an attack by Fr. John Kenyon on O'Connell calling him unprincipled, a mere time-serving politician, a huckster of expediencies who patronized liars, parasites, and bullies.[21] This savage attack envenomed the election campaign. 'The physical force people never meet', Clarendon sarcastically commented, '... without being waylaid by the moral persuasion party and severely beaten', and priests who supported the Young Irelanders, were insulted and had to be escorted home by the police and their fellow clergy.[22] In Limerick and Cork priests opposed the Young Irelanders, including Smith O'Brien. Even when there was no violence, the reports of the meetings confirm that the

---

[20] Russell to Clarendon, 2 Aug. 1847, ibid., Box 43.
[21] *Nation*, 5 June 1847.
[22] Clarendon to Russell, 17 July 1847, Clarendon Papers, Letterbook 1; *Nation*, 7, 14, 21 Aug. 1847.

clergy were not allowed to monopolize proceedings: the laity were vocal and more numerous. As Clarendon observed, however, since many of them were daily compelled to witness misery they could not relieve and were in personal distress, they were registering a protest against government mishandling of the Famine. Other local and Irish issues, such as a pledge not to seek a position from the government, played a greater part than hostility to either of the two great English parties. It was expecting too much to assume that the clergy would canvass for Whig candidates. Clarendon, fresh from England, where the clergy did not play the same role in elections, oversimplified the priests' motives, exaggerated their electoral influence and, regarding the poor result for the Whigs as a personal blow in his first months in office, he pinned the blame on them. His earlier experience of Ireland had been during the campaign for emancipation when the clergy proved themselves O'Connell's ablest lieutenants, and he saw the priests as the key to political progress—a view reinforced by their overwhelming support for the repeal agitation. Confirmed in this view by the 1847 election campaign, Clarendon now envisaged a two-strand strategy to control their influence: on the international level he would put pressure on the pope, and on the local level he would make friendly contact with the bishops. Internationally circumstances played into his hands. In the autumn of 1847, the new pope, Pius IX, unofficially asked for British support. In response, the government was considering the advisability of sending a government minister to Rome.[23] There could have been no more opportune moment for seeking papal help on Irish Catholic affairs.

As a brief for a government mission to Rome, Clarendon now decided to expound in detail his views on the Irish and their religion. This important memorandum merits close examination for it reveals how the chief governor of the country perceived the Church in October 1847. The Irish, he remarked, were essentially a religious people, but the problem was that religion had become mixed up with politics. The result was that:

the completely distinctive characters of the two are almost lost sight of, and an Irishman loves his religion and the Ministers of his Church, not so much for their own sake and his own spiritual welfare, as because he is deeply impressed with the idea that they are national. Nor is this to be

[23] See below, p. 91.

wondered at if we bear in mind the enormous weight of oppression under which they have for centuries laboured, and the various forms of civil persecution which a steadfast adhesion to their religion has entailed upon the Roman Catholics of Ireland.[24]

The position of the priests was of special interest to him. He believed that they shared the same feelings as the people. 'The spirit of nationality', he claimed, 'burns strongly in an Irishman's breast, and the priests encourage the political feelings with which he regards his religion, not only because they themselves are animated by the same feelings, but because they are thereby able to acquire and maintain influence over their flocks.' Despite his own dislike of Catholicism, he acknowledged that 'as a body there exists not in the world a more exemplary priesthood than that of Ireland, more active, zealous, and indefatigable in the discharge of their onerous duties'. Drawn, however, from the lowest classes of society, he commented, they were animated by their feelings and promoted agitation in order to preserve their influence. As a result, 'instead of being Ministers of peace they are too often the instruments of disorder'. They pandered to the people's worst prejudices and passions. If the priest differed from the people he exposed himself to being called a traitor to his religion and to the penalty of having his chapel deserted. The result was:

The Clergy are thus in fact become the slaves of the people and are compelled, although often with extreme reluctance . . . to obey the mandates of their masters; a system of intimidation is organised from the effects of which the prelates . . . are not exempt. With some few exceptions none have dared to attempt their own emancipation from this thraldom.

For Clarendon, one of these 'effects' proved particularly frustrating because of its effects on relations between government and bishops:

Notwithstanding the acknowledged benefits to religion, to education and to the social interests of the people that would result from a free and friendly intercourse between the government and the Roman Catholic prelates, the latter shrink from such intercourse in the dread of being

---

[24] Clarendon to Russell, 1 Oct. 1847, cited in F. Curato, *Gran Bretagna e Italia nei documenti della missione Minto* (1970), i. 81–5. E. D. Steele, 'Gladstone, Irish Violence, and Conciliation', in A. Cosgrove and D. McCartney (eds.), *Studies in Irish History, presented to R. Dudley Edwards* (1979), 261–3.

denounced as traitors to their religion or according to the common expression, as 'having sold their God', by the young and ardent priests of their respective Dioceses . . .

The resulting impasse, he believed, struck at the root of all social order and improvement. The hierarchy, which in all other countries willingly and usefully co-operated with the constituted authorities, in Ireland stood aloof in almost hostile isolation, the people's power over the priesthood was strengthened, and the impression that the government was the enemy of the national religion confirmed. The pope's help should be sought to change it. The difficulty there, however, was that information on Ireland now reached the pope through 'a perverted channel'—the Irish College in Rome—which 'metamorphosed' the facts. What Clarendon had in mind here was the influence of the rector of the Irish College, Paul Cullen, an ardent O'Connellite nationalist and supporter of MacHale.

Clarendon had worked out a solution. The pope should strictly ban the clergy from any involvement in politics, whether by joining political movements, attending meetings, or subscribing in any way. The use of chapels for political purposes should be prohibited. Any bishop who resisted these orders should be removed from his see. Clarendon had another suggestion. The pope should send an eminent and enlightened ecclesiastic, a stranger to Ireland yet not unacquainted with it, who would promulgate and enforce the papal ban on clerical involvement in politics. The time was ripe, he concluded, for O'Connell was dead and the Famine had awakened people to a new and calmer sense of their interests.

Clarendon had been only four months in Ireland as lord lieutenant, but in drawing up this report he would have had the help of Redington and others and much of his assessment was well founded. The identification which he perceived between religion and nationality existed and was probably increasing. It was also true that the bishops were afraid to contact the government openly lest they be branded as traitors by both nationalists and their own clergy.[25] Clarendon could have included other Irish bishops. The archbishops of Cashel and Tuam, Michael Slattery and John

---

[25] In Dublin Peter Cooper kept a close watch on the activities of his archbishop, Murray, who appears to have contacted the viceroy through intermediaries: Anthony Blake, commissioner for education, and David Richard Pigot, chief baron of the exchequer.

MacHale, bitterly denounced Murray and the other bishops to Rome as 'government, or Castle, bishops'. The key reason here was as much religious as political or economic, for a major concern that surfaced throughout the century in the bishops' correspondence with Rome and between themselves was the fear of alienating the people by appearing to be in collusion with the government.

To assert that the priest was 'powerless in his own proper sphere and vocation' was, however, to overstate the case. The Catholic clergy, because of their total dependence on the offerings of their faithful, were economically more tied than the clergy of the Established Church. On the other hand, the Catholic hierarchical structure, in which the bishops had a direct responsibility for their priests, gave them a certain independence not shared by senior ecclesiastics of the Protestant Churches, particularly the Dissenting Churches, where the laity were more involved and had more influence in the parishes. To some extent the Catholic clergy constituted a separate caste with the autonomy and isolation that this involved, and within this caste the bishops held a powerful position. While priests were loath to go against their people for a combination of motives that were religious, economic, political, and social, the diaries of Archdeacon O'Sullivan and Thomas O'Carroll show them, in general, quite independent.

Clarendon's further comment that the clergy were 'drawn from the lowest classes of society' needs examination.[26] The weight of contemporary evidence from parliamentary papers, observers, and visitors' comments, indicates that the priests did not come from the classes who were lowest in the economic scale. The necessity of a pre-seminary education and the cost of seminary training in Maynooth and elsewhere made it difficult for the children of the poor to enter the priesthood. Although the social origins of the Irish clergy in the nineteenth century still awaits a detailed study, some evidence is available. A valuable recent study of the background of 168 priests ordained for the diocese of Kilmore, between 1830 and 1880, shows that 79 per cent were sons of farmers

---

[26] On this question see K. H. Connell, *Irish Peasant Society: Four Historical Essays* (1968), 125–7; S. J. Connolly, *Priests and People in Pre-Famine Ireland* (1982), 35–44; D. A. Kerr, *Peel, Priests, and Politics* (1982), 238–48; J. O'Shea, *Priests, Politics and Society in Post-Famine Ireland* (1983), 13–14; D. Keenan, *The Catholic Church in Nineteenth-Century Ireland* (1983), 61–6; K. T. Hoppen, *Elections, Politics, and Society in Ireland 1832–1885* (1984), 173–9.

possessing over 15 acres, whereas 93.5 per cent of the farms, in 1841, were under 15 acres. The percentage who came from farms of over 20 acres was 71 per cent, while 20 per cent came from farms of over 50 acres and 9 per cent from various businesses.[27] A similar study for County Tipperary for the period 1850–91 supports this conclusion.[28] Priests were sometimes criticized for being out of sympathy with the labouring or cottier class, since they identified with the better-off farmers from whom they sprang.[29] Clarendon's view of the social origins of the priest, then, needs correction unless 'lowest classes of society' is taken as referring to all the farming community. His view, however, was common to many English people and probably arose from the English perception of the social role of a clergyman in England, the shock at observing the influence and involvement of the Irish priests, and attempts to explain this in social terms.

As for the political views of the clergy it is questionable if, by the autumn of 1847, they had a clear vision of the direction they wanted the political life of the country to follow or if they still believed in the feasibility of repeal. It could be argued that, in the 1847 election, the clergy, by opposing Young Ireland, were keeping alive the constitutionalism of O'Connell's movement and blocking the progress of 'physical force' nationalism. Clanricarde was probably right when he told Clarendon that from his conversations with 'a good many priests and men of middle-class . . . I am now convinced that there are few men of intelligence now in Ireland who imagine a Repeal of the Union practicable', though he did believe that there were some 'who look for a *separation* from England'.[30] The failure and death of O'Connell, the feeling of helplessness in the country when faced with a disaster on the scale of the Famine, had convinced many of the clergy of the futility of the campaign for repeal. Notwithstanding Clarendon's complaints, it was unrealistic to expect the priests to view elections through the eyes of an English Whig; their first concern was the local

[27] D. Galogly, 'Background of Kilmore priests', unpub. paper in author's possession. Dr Galogly bases his findings on F. J. McKiernan, *Diocese of Kilmore: Bishops and Priests, 1136–1988* (1990) and Griffith's valuation lists. The total ordained for that period was 224. The sizes of the farms relate to Cavan and Leitrim, the counties that make up most of the diocese.

[28] O'Shea, *Priests, Politics, and Society*, 307–12.

[29] Ibid. 19–35.

[30] Clanricarde to Clarendon, 16 Aug. 1847, Clarendon Papers, Box 9.

scene. The Famine and its horrors constituted the backdrop to the election while politically the struggle was between those who were loyal to the memory of O'Connell and his constitutional movement and those who were not.

Clarendon's remedies, for the most part, were not new. After the granting of Catholic emancipation Murray had attempted to enforce a ban on clerical political involvement, but, although his plan had received the support of all the bishops, it had become a dead letter. Clarendon's suggestion that the pope send a visitor from Rome was interesting but not taken up. Given the sensitivity of Irish nationalists, lay and clerical, to outside interference, it is doubtful if it would have succeeded.[31]

While Clarendon had an opportunity to request the pope's support for his Irish policies, by July he had to report that he had not met the bishops. Even Murray in Dublin had not contacted him. In particular, he would have liked to meet that key figure among the hierarchy, the redoubtable Archbishop MacHale, whose name was a byword in English political circles but, as he humorously remarked: 'I suppose he would as soon be thinking of calling upon the Beelzebub or the Bishop of Exeter as upon me.'[32] Suddenly, shortly after the pope's request for English assistance, the bishops requested a meeting with the lord lieutenant as early as possible. Clarendon was delighted and determined to spare no effort to win them over. If, in addition to papal support, he could, by his undoubted personal charm and some easy concessions, win the bishops, he might well be on the way to attaining that permanent success he so much wanted to achieve. With repeal collapsing and Ireland more than ever dependent on the British treasury, the opportunity for reconciliation was there. Ireland in her need, Russell had declared, should be treated as an integral part of the United Kingdom. Perhaps the time was at hand.

The reason for the bishops' request was their growing concern at the situation in the country. They realized that voluntary relief, however generous, could not save the hundreds of thousands threatened by starvation. Only the government could do that and, despite a temporary financial crisis of that autumn, the United Kingdom, the richest country in the world, might still manage to

---

[31] A visit similar to that envisaged by Clarendon was undertaken by Monsignor Ignazio Persico at the request of Pope Leo XIII in 1887, but was unsuccessful.

[32] Clarendon to Blake, 26 July 1847, Clarendon Papers, Box 9.

prevent mass deaths if it had the political will to do so. The signs were not encouraging. Distress was evident throughout the country. Evictions were soaring. Yet it had been decided to close the soup-kitchens, which, though tardily introduced in late March and April, were providing relief to three million by July. The government's finances were jealously husbanded by Charles Wood, the chancellor of the exchequer, and Charles Trevelyan in the treasury. Reflecting and shaping public opinion, *The Times* laid the blame squarely on the inertia of the Irish peasant whose religion was 'Man shall *not* labour by the sweat of his brow'.[33] In mounting alarm the bishops determined on concerted action. Their annual meeting was not due until November, but the situation was too grave to wait until then. They met in Dublin on 18 October and together drew up the most comprehensive memorial they had ever presented to government. In view of the gravity of the situation MacHale and his supporters wanted to appeal directly to the prime minister and then to the queen, but Murray persuaded the bishops to present the memorial first to the lord lieutenant.[34] The remarkable memorial they drew up merits close examination. Raising issues which they never before dared to broach, they challenged basic English assumptions about Irish peasants and criticized government policies.[35]

At the outset the bishops totally rejected the view, held by most English people and recently propounded publicly by *The Times*, that the 'innate indolence' of the people was the cause of their distressed condition and of the Famine.[36] The real causes were penal laws which deprived the masses of the right to property and denied them the fruits of their labour. 'If the labourer is worthy of his hire,' they declared, 'an axiom of natural as well as of revealed religion . . . it would be a violation of those sacred maxims to appropriate the entire crop of the husbandman without compensation for the seed or the labour.' In Ireland, however, the bishops claimed, laws 'sanctioning such unnatural injustice, and therefore injurious to society, not only exist but are extensively enforced with reckless and unrelenting vigour'. While carefully affirming

---

[33] *Times*, 22 Sept. 1847; P. H. Gray, 'British Politics and the Irish Land Question, 1843–1850' (Ph.D. thesis, 1992), fo. 248.

[34] Clarendon to Russell, 23 Oct. 1847, Clarendon Papers, Letterbook 1.

[35] *Nation*, 30 Oct. 1847.

[36] B. Hilton, *The Age of Atonement: The Influence of Evangelicalism on Social and Economic Thought, 1785–1865* (1988), 108–14, 248–50, provides valuable insights into British views of the Famine.

the 'subordinate' rights of property, the bishops insisted that there existed a prior and more fundamental right:

The sacred and indefeasible rights of life are forgotten amidst the incessant reclamations of the subordinate rights of property.... Hallowed as are the rights of property, those of life are still more sacred, and rank as such in every well regulated scale that adjusts the relative possessions of man; and if this scale [of values] had not been frequently reversed we should not have so often witnessed in those heart-rending scenes of the evictions of tenantry, 'the oppressions that are done under the sun, the tears of the innocent having no comforter, and unable to resist violence, being destitute of help from any'.

The government's relief measures, the bishops claimed, were wholly inadequate. The workhouses were overcrowded, fever-ridden, and capriciously managed. The grim choice facing the people was either to starve if they did not enter them or die of contagious disease if they did. '[C]onscious that gratuitous relief has a demoralising tendency, and may be perverted ... into means of proselytism', they called instead for productive employment. As to remedial measures, the bishops were willing to leave them 'to the wisdom of her Majesty's government', but called for a fair arrangement between landlords and tenants based on commutative justice. They also reminded Clarendon that 'large tracts of land capable of cultivation are now lying waste', that the coasts abounded in fish, and that the country was teeming with other mines of wealth. Finally, they appealed to Clarendon on grounds which would most readily influence him—public order:

In such an awful crisis, which threatens such destruction of human life, [your] memorialists, anxious to preserve the souls of their flock from crime and society from the danger of disorganization, beg ... Your Excellency to use your influence with Her Majesty's government, to procure measures of relief commensurate with the magnitude of the calamity.

In this extraordinary memorial the bishops went beyond the strict bounds of 'religion' to criticize the existing social order, condemn government policy, and express principles of social justice. Previously only MacHale had dared to make similar criticisms, and he had been regarded as a trouble-maker. The bishops' call for special government intervention was out of line with current economic thought, and their emphasis on the sacred right to life over and above the subordinate rights of property was unusually vigorous. Although they shared with statesmen of the time the fear that 'mere gratuitous relief' had a demoralizing tendency, they show no trace in their address of a providentialist explanation of the Famine as God's retributive justice. Likewise Trevelyan's claim that the Famine was 'the judgement of God on an indolent and unself-reliant people' was rejected.[37] Instead the bishops had laid the underlying blame squarely on penal laws which deprived the great bulk of the people of the right to property and to the fruits of their labour; in those conditions the failure of the potato produced the catastrophe.

Clarendon made a cautious reply and returned to the notion of 'self-help', which he proposed as the only solution to the distress. He promised, however, that where local effort was inadequate, 'the sacred and paramount duty of government—the preservation of human life—will be performed'. This unsatisfactory reply disappointed the bishops. They now passed another resolution. They thanked the lord lieutenant for his social and enlightened maxims, but if the lord lieutenant proved unable to help the poor, they must go further. 'To avert the destruction of human life, and the disorganisation of society', they would send a delegation of bishops and clergy from various parts of Ireland 'to lay at the foot of the throne the starving and awful condition' of Ireland.[38]

Despite his suave reply, Clarendon was privately severely critical of the tone of the memorial which, he felt, would give a bad example to the priests and would justify their turbulent behaviour. MacHale, he believed, was the principal author. There was, however, a promising development for Clarendon from the meeting. He had looked forward eagerly to the bishops' delegation in anticipation of meeting the formidable MacHale. MacHale had pleasantly surprised him. He found him quiet-spoken and reasonable, and Clarendon came to the conclusion that, although he might be 'vain and turbulent, he was not a bad man'.[39] Clarendon had charmingly 'milorded' the bishops, which he reported pleased them inordinately, and invited them to dinner; although MacHale had refused, Clarendon was convinced that he regretted turning down the offer. Encouraged, Clarendon now resolved to seize the opportunity and wrote directly to MacHale about the general

---

[37] Hilton, *Atonement*, 113.   [38] *Catholic Directory, 1848*, 245–6.
[39] Clarendon to Russell, 26 Oct. 1847, Clarendon Papers, Letterbook 1. Clarendon to Lansdowne, 26 Oct. 1847, ibid.

situation, expressing his concern at rural disturbances and clerical involvement. The archbishop, surprised that for the first time a government had sought his advice, was gratified. In a long and positive reply, MacHale explained the situation in the west. The total failure of the potato, he told Clarendon, had left the people of Tuam helpless. The burden was greater than the unions could carry and the relief was utterly inadequate. Furthermore, evictions were increasing the swell of human misery and 'the struggling people are burdened with the support of these outcasts from their homes'. Only seasonable measures of relief could prevent 'the threatened derangement of society'. The clergy were in a dilemma:

As long as they [the people] endure such destitution without any prospect of the mitigation of their suffering the peace and order of Society will be exposed to imminent danger and though the clergy should be incessant, as they hitherto have been, in their exhortations to patience, it is to be feared that their exhortations will often lose their effect on men enraged now by the impulses of hunger and despair.[40]

This was particularly so when the clergy could not hold forth any hope that help was on the way. 'So far from being enabled to accompany our exhortations [to patience] with those cheering promises of succour which never fail to exercise their influence,' he added, 'we have only to offer them those arguments which are found in the consolation of religion alone.' MacHale appealed to Clarendon in his position of viceroy to use all his powers to save the starving people. 'The very depression of our social condition', he wrote, 'throws into your hand a larger measure of power than usually falls to the lot of the representatives of Her Majesty.' He concluded on what was for Clarendon a hopeful note: 'The communication with which your Excellency has honoured me I duly appreciate and . . . [hope] that I have shewn every disposition to reciprocate your anxiety for the good name of the clergy and the well being of the people.'

In this moderate letter, which contains none of his customary exaggeration and invective, MacHale described the situation as he experienced it and made a strong yet measured plea for immediate and more intensive relief. The case he put reflected the reality in the west of Ireland and in other parts as well, where ever-present distress had reached crisis proportions. His appeal to Clarendon

[40] MacHale to Clarendon, 9 Dec. 1847, ibid. Box 50.

on the grounds of preventing social disruption was a powerful one. Although their priorities were different—the archbishop wanting relief and the viceroy the assurance of law and order—a convergence of interests was possible, and Clarendon was delighted at the reply. 'I have had a shot at the Lion [MacHale] in his den', he told Russell. 'If I could assist MacHale in relieving the people of Tuam . . . and could continue to communicate confidentially with him I should not despair of making him an instrument of good.'[41] Clarendon believed that MacHale was the key to episcopal co-operation for, as Murray said, if MacHale were to behave rightly 'all the rest of the Prelates would follow.'[42] If, having won MacHale, the viceroy could work together with the whole of the hierarchy in a common effort to meet the pressing needs of the country, much might be achieved. Before this promising break-through could be followed up, a bitter public controversy erupted which placed MacHale in the firing line. It ended abruptly the friendly contact between archbishop and viceroy and eclipsed the good effects of Clarendon's careful wooing of the hierarchy.

Within the Irish government, Clarendon had established a good working relationship with Redington and Somerville. His six months in Ireland and, no doubt, the advice of Redington, who owned land in County Galway, one of the areas worst hit, had revealed to him the appalling situation in the country. He pressed urgently for more generous relief, but here he ran up against the determined opposition of Wood and the treasury. As a more permanent measure, Clarendon proposed a landlord and tenant bill, but this encountered opposition within the cabinet from Lansdowne and others. A third measure which he demanded proved more explosive. This was a coercion bill, which he believed that the disordered state of the country required.[43] When MacHale told Clarendon of his fear that the peace and order of society was threatened by men enraged by hunger and despair, he was not exaggerating. As early as the winter of 1846 there had been hunger marches, food riots, and attacks on food convoys. In Youghal, a crowd tried to hold up a ship exporting oats. Agents suspected of

---

[41] Clarendon to Russell, 10 Dec. 1847, ibid. O'Connell called MacHale the 'Lion of the Fold of Judah' or the 'Lion of the West'.

[42] Clarendon to Russell, 21 Dec. 1847, Clarendon Papers, Letterbook 2.

[43] F. A. Dreyer, 'The Russell Administration 1846–1852' (Ph.D. thesis, 1962), fos. 121–42; Gray, 'British Politics', fos. 181–290.

holding up public works were shot at in Clare, where agrarian crime multiplied manyfold over this period. From Ennistymon, in County Clare, Fr. Patrick Fallon expected infractions of the law at any time from peasants who said they 'prefer[red] to be shot by military while taking away from [*sic*] extreme necessity than die the cruel death of starvation'.[44] Egan of Kerry confided to Murray his fear that the people might no longer bear their destitution with patience.[45] This fear of a breakdown in law and order was a constant concern of the clergy 'anxious to preserve the souls of their flock from crime'. An outbreak of violence would signal their own failure to make religious principles the guide of the people's conduct. They feared, furthermore, the disorganization of society with the suffering that agrarian crimes would bring on innocent and guilty alike. The alarming increase in evictions coming on top of hunger and disease could bring about what they most feared. Outside observers entertained similar fears. *Le Correspondant*, which reported regularly on the Irish situation, commented:

England closes its ears to pleas of Ireland: Lord Clarendon ignores the protestations of the Catholic hierarchy. What means will England have left, however, to prevent a radical revolution in land ownership [la révolution radicale de la propriété] in Ireland . . .?[46]

Clarendon, however, was more concerned than may have appeared. Taking to heart the bishops' and MacHale's warning that social disorder might result if further government aid was not forthcoming, Clarendon now determined to impress on the cabinet that Ireland needed help urgently. In separate appeals to Russell and to Lansdowne, whom he knew to be influential with the prime minister, he communicated his alarm:

I hope Russell will not persist in his notion that Irish evils must find Irish remedies only, for it is *impossible* that this country can get through the next eight months without aid in some shape or other from England. Irish ingratitude . . . and the poverty of England may be urged . . . but none of these reasons will be valid against helpless starvation or servile war . . .[47]

[44] Fallon to Labouchere, 5 Oct. 1846, Distress Papers, State Papers Office, Carton 1410.
[45] Egan to Murray, 24 Jan. 1848, Murray Papers, DDA.
[46] *Le Correspondant*, xx. 470, 1847; cf. xvii. 301–2, 25 Jan. 1847.
[47] Clarendon to Lansdowne, 28 Oct. 1847, Clarendon Papers, Letterbook 1.

In the late autumn of 1847, a number of murders and attempted murders of landlords and agents occurred. Was a 'peasants' revolt' or the dreaded servile war, as Clarendon called it, about to break out? These assassinations appeared to confirm the fears of both the anxious bishops and the jittery lord lieutenant. The reaction of Clarendon and English public opinion to this spate of violence was to bring a new turn in the relationship between government and clergy. The resulting crisis was to involve parliament and the Roman *Curia* and to influence Irish clerical reaction to government in 1848—the year of European revolution.

4

Irish Violence and Roman Intrigue, 1847–1848

'It is quite true that landlords in England would not like to be shot like hares and partridges. But neither does any landlord turn out fifty persons at once, and burn their houses over their heads.... The murders are atrocious, so are the ejectments.'

(Russell to Clarendon, 15 Nov. 1847)

While the lord lieutenant and the bishops were grappling as best they could with the problems posed by the Famine, European attention was focusing on Rome. By 1847 Pius IX's position had become the centre of intense diplomacy, a pivotal point in the liberal and revolutionary movements as the events that took place in Italy began to have an impact on other European countries. Into this world of political manœuvres the British government felt obliged to enter, and Irish affairs, too, became involved. The events that took place in Rome and the decisions taken there were to influence government attitudes up to and beyond the Ecclesiastical Titles Act three years later.

In nineteenth-century Europe, the relationship between religious minorities and governments differed according to whether the minority was Jewish, Orthodox, Roman Catholic, or Protestant. Catholics, given the central position of the pope in their Church, were often accused by governments of dividing their allegiance between a foreign power—Rome—and the nation-state. On the other hand, governments were eager to get Rome to put pressure on Catholic minorities, and Rome often obliged. This, in turn, provoked among Catholic minorities hostility towards government manœuvres at Rome and suspicion of curial complicity. This suspicion lay deep in Ireland, where 'religion from Rome, politics from home' summed up the outlook of many nationalists. Already after just a few months in Ireland Clarendon had noted this attitude.

This jealous outlook was not confined to the Catholic laity; the clergy were, if anything, more concerned, for they feared that if Rome sided with the government, the Church might easily fall under the control of the state or the local hostile establishment. Any suspicion of collusion between the Church and the state, they claimed, would alienate the faithful from the Church. This had been their attitude over the veto controversy in the first decades of the century and it had again surfaced in 1844 when unfounded fears of a concordat caused a violent reaction in Ireland.[1] These fears appeared yet again during the winter of 1847.

The earliest indication of a convergence of interests between Rome and the British government may have been an incident in March 1847. On 14 March, Viale Prelà, the nuncio in Vienna, reported to the secretary of state that the British government was not opposed to the restoration of the Catholic hierarchy in England, but wanted to use the occasion to forward its Irish policies, and was suggesting that Rome should indicate its conciliatory spirit by sending a brief to the Irish bishops urging submission to Britain. On 25 March Pius sent the bishops his encyclical letter expressing sympathy for the famine victims and asking the faithful everywhere to come to their aid. In his accompanying letter he urged that both clergy and people foster public concord.[2]

The convergence of Roman and British interests is clearer in a second incident. The events were apparently unconnected with the United Kingdom. The one eventuality that Metternich, the sheet-anchor of European conservatism, confessed he had never allowed for was the election of a liberal pope in the person of Pius IX. Pius' first move was to grant a political amnesty, then a consulta, or parliament, and a civic guard, and, finally, a more liberal secretary of state, as Cardinal Gizzi resigned and the pope's cousin, the popular Cardinal Ferretti, took his place. This peaceful revolution was shattered within a year. In July 1847 Romans were preparing to celebrate the first anniversary of what they had hailed as the dawn of liberalism for all Italy—the amnesty of 1846. Suddenly, police uncovered, or thought they had uncovered, a plot to overthrow the liberal regime. This shock was followed two days

---

[1] On the concordat controversy of 1844, see D. A. Kerr, *Peel, Priests, and Politics* (1982), 193–223.

[2] Pius IX to Irish bishops, 25 Mar. 1847, cited in G. Martina, *Pio IX, 1846–1850* (1974), 463–4.

later by a greater one. On the anniversary of the amnesty Marshal Radetzky sent General Nugent with 860 Hungarian troops across the Po and into Ferrara, where they marched through the streets in full battle attire. Although he was technically within his rights, Radetzky's action outraged Italian patriots, for whom the two events were proof of Austrian machinations. Their fears were heightened by the knowledge that they could no longer count on France, for since the Spanish marriage of Louis Philippe's daughter, France, estranged from England, had moved closer to Austria and was now regarded as conniving at Austria's Italian moves. In the summer of 1847, with the two Catholic powers taking a conservative line, the reforming pope stood isolated. In a Rome tense with rumour his courageous protest to Austria brought a surge of support for him from liberals everywhere, and advice and offers of help poured in—one surprisingly from Mazzini—while in far-away Buenos Aires Garibaldi placed his sword at the pope's disposal.

In England *The Times* published an article on 5 August signed 'Angloromanus' with the stirring words: 'the feeling of the [Roman] people is strong that England, with a great and generous hand, will protect them. In her unselfish policy there is great confidence that Rome will not become another Cracow.' The author of this article was known to be Nicholas Wiseman, vicar-general of the London district, who was in Rome for discussions connected with the re-establishment of the English Catholic hierarchy. Swept along by the general sympathy for the liberal pope, he assured friends on the consulta that, whatever the threats of Austria or France, England would stand by Pio Nono. Apart from his personal loyalty to the pope, Wiseman saw his move as an opportunity for normalizing relations between England and Rome. Pius grasped at the possibility of English support and asked Wiseman to put the matter to the government. Wiseman wrote to Lord Shrewsbury, a leading Catholic peer, to approach Lord John Russell, and hurried back to England himself to press the point. In a long memorandum to Palmerston requesting him to send an agent to Rome, he declared that 'all interested in the contemplated improvements [in Rome] . . . look to England and its Government as the chief, if not the only source, from which internal aid and countenance can be hoped for'. In his covering letter he claimed that 'it is with his [the pope's] full knowledge and sanction that

I make the present communication, a copy of which I forward to Rome'.[3]

He was pushing a door already ajar. Shortly after becoming foreign secretary, Palmerston had recommended the renewal of diplomatic relations with Rome. In April 1847, Russell announced that he was considering doing so and, in the same month, the British ambassador to France, Lord Normanby, had discussed the matter with Luigi Fornari, the nuncio at Paris.[4] When Wiseman came with a request for aid from the pope Russell and Palmerston were well disposed. A positive response would promote the onward march of liberalism and progress, halt Austrian aggression, and substitute the influence of England for that of France in Italy. An important side-benefit might follow in the form of papal support for the government's Irish policy. When Russell acceded to Wiseman's plea and decided to send Lord Minto, his father-in-law, and keeper of the privy seal, to Rome, Clarendon had seized the opportunity and had set down carefully in his memorandum of 1 October what Pius might do to help the situation in Ireland by forcing the clergy to abandon politics. Palmerston agreed and explained to the queen the Irish aspect of Minto's mission:

Lord Minto would endeavour to obtain from the Pope the exertion of his spiritual authority over the Catholic priesthood of Ireland to induce them to abstain from repeal agitation and to urge them not to embarrass but rather to assist Your Majesty's government in the measures which they may plan for the improvement and for the better government of Ireland.[5]

The Irish dimension to the government's mission, then, was twofold: by restoring better relations with the pope, to gain his support for the government's Irish policies and to ban the clergy from involvement in politics. Minto did not arrive in Rome until 3 November and before he arrived two events took place which affected his mission. The first concerned the Queen's Colleges. The majority of bishops kept pressing for a decision and, finally, Pius referred the question back to Propaganda for reconsideration. Propaganda reaffirmed its condemnation and Pius ratified the decision

---

[3] Russell to Palmerston, 14 Sept. 1847, Wiseman to Russell, 13 Sept. 1847, Royal Archives, J1/34, cited in F. Curato, *Gran Bretagna e Italia nei documenti della missione Minto* (1970), i. 54–60.

[4] Martina, *Pio IX*, 164–6.

[5] Palmerston to Queen Victoria, 31 Aug. 1847, Royal Archives, J1/8, cited in Curato, *Gran Bretagna*, i. 44–5.

by a rescript of 9 October. The timing was unfortunate. Coming when it did the rescript, which appeared to set at nought a decision of the queen in parliament and to encourage the anti-government bishops, was viewed by Palmerston and Russell as an unfriendly act at the very time when England was coming to the pope's assistance. Minto was convinced from his discussions with the pope and the secretary of state, Ferretti, that if he had reached Rome earlier the rescript would never have been sent. One of Minto's first tasks would be to persuade the pope to withdraw his condemnation.

The second and more dramatic event that was to influence Minto's mission was directly linked to the distress in Ireland. As the clergy and Clarendon had feared, the Famine, now in its second year, finally led to serious breaches of the peace. Evictions were a major cause of the trouble. They showed a startling increase; the number of families evicted, 3,500 in 1846, almost doubled in 1847, reaching 6,000.[6] The number of murders increased, and in two months of autumn 1847 there were six assassinations.[7] The most sensational murder was that of Major Denis Mahon, of the 9th Lancers. Mahon, like many of the victims, was an improving landlord who, having inherited a badly managed estate around Strokestown, County Roscommon, proposed to buy out the tenants and give them a passage to Canada. Only a minority accepted and, as the rest would 'neither pay nor go', he evicted over 3,000 of them including, it was alleged, 84 widows. On Tuesday 2 November he was shot dead on his way home. The most sensational aspect of the case was Lord Farnham's allegation in the House of Lords that the local priest, Michael McDermott, had declared during Sunday mass that 'Major Mahon is worse than Cromwell and yet he lives'.[8] For the alarmist Clarendon, who had

---

[6] See discussion and table in Donnelly, 'Landlords and Tenants', in Vaughan (ed.), *A New History of Ireland* (1989), v. 332–49; Vaughan, *Landlords and Tenants in Ireland* (1984), 13–26. The figures for 1849 and 1850 are the evictions recorded by the constabulary.

[7] Constabulary returns reported the number of homicides as increasing from 170 in 1846 to 211 in 1847; firing at the person from 159 to 264; highway robbery from 258 to 342; firing at houses from 162 to 257; and robbery with arms almost doubling from 611 to 1,053 over the same period. Less serious agrarian crimes had halved, however, from 1,303 to 620. *Edinburgh Review*, 93 (1851), 220–1.

[8] *Hansard*, xcv. 675–84, 6 Dec. 1847. Henry Maxwell (1799–1868), 7th Baron Farnham. Farnham worked well with the Catholic bishop of Kilmore in providing relief in Cavan during the Famine. Attacks on a number of landlords and agents in his neighbourhood had alarmed him.

shut himself up in the viceregal lodge, these murders were proof that 'servile war against all landlords and English rule' was about to break out. He redoubled his frantic calls for a special powers act. Russell, who always saw the landlords as the villains, and who had come to power through the rejection of Peel's Irish Coercion bill, replied sharply that:

It is quite true that landlords in England would not like to be shot like hares and partridges. But neither does any landlord in England turn out fifty persons at once, and burn their houses over their heads, giving them no provision for the future. The murders are atrocious, so are the ejectments.[9]

English opinion, however, as expressed in both press and parliament, agreed with Clarendon. When Lord Farnham raised the matter in the House of Lords that opinion manifested itself. Stanley demanded to know if it were not true that the priest had denounced Mahon and that he had been assassinated within forty-eight hours. 'The musket of the assassin', he claimed, 'was discharged at the man whom the priest had denounced the previous Sabbath.'[10] Clarendon threatened to resign; Russell gave way. Parliament and press alleged priestly collusion with assassins. Palmerston, too, without awaiting any verification of the charges, instructed Minto to inform the pope that 'Major Mahon, who was shot the other day was denounced by his priest at the altar the Sunday before . . . that denunciation . . . made all the people in the neighbourhood think the deed a holy one'. He added that scarcely anybody now talked of the Mahon murder without a fervent wish that a dozen priests be hanged.[11] On 30 November Minto brought the matter to the pope's attention. Shocked, Pius promised to do all in his power to put an end to such abuses.[12] *The Times* announced the formation of a 'combination of Protestants' whose members swore 'by a crucified Christ, that for the life of every Protestant . . . we will take the life of the Parish Priest where the deed was committed'.[13] The strength of British reaction was not perhaps unnatural for nineteenth-century politicians schooled in the tradition of English

---

[9] Russell to Clarendon, 15 Nov. 1847, Russell Papers PRO 6G.
[10] *Hansard*, xcv. 680–3, 6 Dec. 1847; 1208–11, 16 Dec. 1847.
[11] Palmerston to Minto, 3 Dec. 1847, Curato, *Gran Bretagna*, i. 240–1, 266–80.
[12] Minto to Palmerston, 28 Dec. 1847, Curato, *Gran Bretagna*, i. 240–1, 266–80.
[13] *Times*, 28 Dec. 1847.

no-popery with its distrust of the priest and his role.[14] The fears expressed by Maher and others that if they spoke out against the 'hecatomb' they would be accused of collusion in violence had not been ungrounded.

McDermott indignantly denied the charge, and assured the public 'by the most solemn asseverations a clergyman can utter, that . . . Major Mahon was never denounced, nor even his name mentioned from any Chapel altar . . . on any Sunday before his death'. He went on, however, to assert that the crime was due to 'the infamous . . . cruelties which were wantonly exercised . . . against a tenantry, whose feelings were already wound up to woeful and vengeful exasperation, by the loss of their exiled relatives, as well as by hunger and pestilence'. The charge against him, he said, was a monstrous calumny and he demanded legal process.[15] Instead of the legal process which he demanded, an anonymous letter signed 'an Irish Peer' now appeared in the press, alleging that McDermott could well say that he did not denounce Mahon at the Sunday mass because he did so on Monday, at the mass of All Saints Day, which was a Catholic feast day.[16] This was to lend fuel to the denunciations: it appeared to show that Irish Catholics were not only violent but essentially untruthful. *The Times* denounced McDermott's denial as a further crime and, calling McDermott 'the Tidd or Chitty of Irish Thugee', rejected his challenge for legal process, alleging that there would be mass perjury:

The voice of an approver or two of bad character . . . could not weigh with a jury against the united testimony of a congregation prepared to perjure themselves in platoons to save their spiritual instructor from the gallows.[17]

The claim of the leading paper of the day, which formed as much as it reflected English public opinion, that Irish Catholics were ready to perjure themselves 'in platoons' sharpened the controversy and did not endear press or British public opinion to Irish Catholics. Other papers and reviews took the same line. The

[14] J. H. Newman, *Lectures on the Present Position of Catholics in England . . . 1851* (1851).

[15] McDermott to editor, *Freeman's Journal*, 10 Dec. 1847.

[16] *Times*, 11 Dec. 1847.

[17] Ibid. 'Thug' was a member of a religious organization of robbers and assassins in India, and 'Thugee' was the name given to the system they operated. 'Chitty' was the certificate given by a master to his servant.

Quarterly Review wrote that 'the substantial fact seems beyond all doubt, that the unfortunate gentleman was . . . designated to popular vengeance by the priest with the full influence of his sacerdotal character; and that within a very short space the vengeance was consummated'.[18]

Ministers took the same line. When the Irish peer's letter was published, Palmerston wrote again to Minto that

it seems pretty well established by what Lord Farnham said that the Reverend Mr McDermott not only incited the people to murder Major Mahon, but quibbled and equivocated in attempting to deny what he had done. He says he did not denounce Major Mahon on any Sunday, because he did it on a Monday; and he says he did not name Major Mahon, because he pointed him out by a description which rendered it needless to pronounce his name.[19]

English Catholic gentry, embarrassed by their Irish co-religionists, entered the debate, accepting the charges of connivance at crime and deceit against the priests. In the House of Lords, Lord Beaumont took the same line as Farnham. The Earl of Arundel and Surrey wrote publicly to MacHale to voice his concern at 'denunciations from the altar, followed by the speedy death of the denounced'. MacHale promised that if priests were guilty they would be suspended from the exercise of the priesthood.[20]

At this point another English Catholic lord entered the arena—Lord Shrewsbury. 'Good Lord John', as many Catholics called him, was a generous patron of the English Catholic Church but given to meddling in ecclesiastical matters, from the concerns of the English College in Rome to Irish affairs.[21] Without further proof, Shrewsbury accepted both the allegations of connivance and duplicity levelled against McDermott and, in a letter to the *Morning Chronicle*, demanded that his bishop take action. With Russell's encouragement Shrewsbury used the occasion to vent his pent-up grievances against MacHale—his criticism of the national schools, his support of the repeal rent, his opposition to Fr. Mathew, the

---

[18] *Quarterly Review*, 163 (Dec. 1847), 284–8.

[19] Palmerston to Minto, 18 Dec. 1847, Curato, *Gran Bretagna*, 258.

[20] For the antagonism of many aristocratic English Catholics towards Irish Catholics and their co-operation with the government against them, see V. A. McClelland, *English Roman Catholics and Higher Education* (1973), 120–5.

[21] R. J. Schiefen, *Nicholas Wiseman and the Transformation of English Catholicism* (1984), 56, 166–71. John Talbot, earl of Shrewsbury (1791–1852).

promoter of temperance. He felt keenly the reproaches cast upon 'the religion which I profess in England, through the excesses of some who profess Catholicity in Ireland'. The responsibility for the famine deaths, which MacHale, Slattery, and other clerics blamed on government incompetence, should be imputed to the 'unerring, though inscrutable, designs of God'. This providentialist assumption was common during this period. Shrewsbury, however, went further and, not unlike Trevelyan and many Evangelicals, interpreted the scale of the disaster in terms of divine retribution for Irish sins.[22] The Irish were to blame, he warned, for God's visitation; God was grievously aggravated by their ingratitude, because 'every sufficient expression of gratitude has been withheld both from the Government and the people of England'. The assassinations were part of 'one great conspiracy against property'. The Irish Church stood accused for 'we are all amazed at the silent apathy which seems to reign within the sanctuary'. The English public, he went on, saw the Church:

[as] a conniver at injustice, an accessory to crime, a pestilent sore in the commonwealth; and so long will she be so proclaimed till we are shown some better reason than has yet been given us why Archdeacon Laffan should remain unreprimanded, and why Father McDermott should still be permitted to exercise his ministry.[23]

Although Catholic leaders in Ireland and in Britain reacted indignantly to Shrewsbury's accusation, his remarks about English public opinion were of more significance than they allowed. The English public had difficulty in understanding the Catholic Irish at any time, and had given generously to the famine victims. The assassinations, though few in number, had been highlighted in *The Times* and in other papers and denounced in the strongest language by leading statesmen. The public, already suffering from some relief weariness, resented what they saw as the murderous response to their generous aid.

Was the charge genuine? Some priests were guilty of denunciations from the altar, though bishops, through synodal legislation and

---

[22] For Trevelyan, see B. Hilton, *The Age of Atonement: The Influence of Evangelicalism on Social and Economic Thought, 1785–1865* (1988), 113.

[23] Shrewsbury to MacHale, *Morning Chronicle*, 4 Jan. 1848; B. Ward, *The Sequel to Catholic Emancipation*, ii: *1840–1850* (1915), 130–45. Laffan made a fiery speech at Cashel in November, placing blame for the Famine on the government, *Nation*, 20 Nov. 1847.

individual action, were attempting to stamp out what they regarded as a serious abuse. There had been a sharp disagreement at a meeting of the Strokestown Relief Committee in September, when Mahon accused McDermott of misusing funds. MacDermott may have spoken intemperately, but it is by no means sure that he mentioned Mahon from the altar and no ground existed for Palmerston's claim that his guilt was well established. A score of respectable parishioners solemnly swore that he had never denounced Mahon. Alarmed at the accusations McDermott's bishop, Browne, went to Strokestown to investigate. 'The result of my inquiries', he affirmed, 'has been that he had not on Sunday, Monday, ferial or holy day, not at any time nor in any place directly nor indirectly denounced Major Mahon'.[24] When the trial took place in July 1848, it transpired that the murder had been planned before the Sunday in question. Two men were executed and others transported, but McDermott's name did not figure at the trial.[25]

Farnham had begun the campaign against McDermott. He was a strong Orangeman and was concerned at recent attacks on landlords and agents in south Ulster. Clarendon, however, must carry the ultimate responsibility for pinning blame on the priest. The anonymous letter in *The Times* which strengthened feelings against McDermott may well have been Clarendon's own work. The day before it appeared, Clarendon wrote to Russell:

I send you a newspaper containing a letter from Fr. MacDermott, the parish Priest of Strokestown, utterly denying that he ever mentioned Major Mahon's name. . . . On reading over the letter, however, it struck me as odd that MacDermott should say that Mahon's name was not mentioned on any Sunday before his death and on speaking to Redington about it, he remembered that Mahon was murdered on the Tuesday and that the day before (Monday) was All Saints Day which is a great festival of the Catholic Church, so the denunciation might have taken place then.[26]

The Irish peer's letter to *The Times* bears similarities to Clarendon's letter. 'The reverend priest is quite right', it said, 'as to the word "Sunday". The late Major Mahon was denounced from the altar on the "Monday" previous to his assassination.' The

---

[24] Browne to Shrewsbury, *Tablet*, 3 Jan. 1848.
[25] B. Donlon, 'The Mahon Murder Trials', *County Roscommon Historical and Archaeological Journal*, 1 (1986), 31–2.
[26] Clarendon to Russell, 10 Dec. 1847, Clarendon Papers, Letterbook 2.

anonymous writer added: 'This fact is known in Dublin Castle.' Given the resemblances to Clarendon's letter and Clarendon's propensity to use the press anonymously, it is more than likely he had the letter written. Before *The Times* letter appeared, Clarendon made the astonishing admission to Russell that Redington, who was also a Connacht landlord and had investigated the matter, did not feel sure that the priest had denounced Major Mahon at all![27] Commenting that Farnham's accusations did not constitute evidence that would connect McDermott with Mahon's murder, he told Reeve, *The Times*'s journalist: 'I have in vain tried by every means in my power to get such [evidence] and Ross Mahon, the Major's cousin and agent who had been doing the same at the place, admitted to Redington that the reports were so various and conflicting that he himself had no notion of what McD[ermott] actually did.'[28] Clarendon never publicly admitted Redington's and Ross Mahon's failure to find any convincing evidence. Instead, a short while after those admissions, he replied to Bishop Browne's protestation of McDermott's innocence: 'I will not disguise from your Lordship that the reports (apparently upon good authority) which have reached me, left little doubt upon my mind that Mr McDermott, without directly naming Major Mahon, had excited the people against that unfortunate gentleman.'[29] Clarendon's aim, apparently, was to make use of the crimes and the atmosphere they created to intimidate turbulent clergy and their bishops and to force more coercive powers from a reluctant Russell. A Crime and Outrage bill passed through parliament in less than three weeks and became law on 20 December. As interesting as the objective reality of the charge of priestly connivance at murder is the fact that it was perfectly credible to Palmerston, Clarendon, and to the press and parliament.

Shrewsbury's indictment of McDermott and the bishops shocked moderates as well as conservatives among clergy and laity alike. To Irish Catholics it was astonishing that the leading English

---

[27] Clarendon to Russell, 10 Dec. 1847, ibid. Letterbook 2.

[28] Clarendon to Reeve, 20 Dec. 1847, ibid. c. 534. In this letter Clarendon, while implying that Lord Glengall was the 'Irish Peer', warned against using the letters as texts for articles 'for', he said, ' "the Irish Peer" generally lies and always exaggerates'. Although at first sight this would appear to indicate that the Irish Peer had no connection with Clarendon, Clarendon's action here was similar to his action six months later when Russell wished to prosecute the bishop of Derry.

[29] Clarendon to Browne, 5 Jan. 1848, Clarendon Papers, Letterbook 2.

Catholic peer could accept and publish in the press unsustained accusations. Clergy who were working untiringly for their people, bringing them spiritual support, supplementing government relief, and preaching resignation to the will of God in their efforts to keep them peaceful, were appalled at what they saw as calumnies on their work. MacHale, as was to be expected, defended himself vigorously, but the accusations ended the promising contacts between him and Clarendon. Others, more moderate than him, complained of slander. From Cavan, Philip Foy, curate at Shercock, complained that 'in this diocese [Kilmore], on the express order of our venerated prelate, every clergyman reprobated those scandalous secret societies of Ribbonmen and Molly Maguires simultaneously last October in every chapel before the slanders were even thought of'. He added bitterly, however, that it was 'hard to teach patience to a man who sees his father and mother or wife and children driven from the houses of their ancestors to the bogs and ditches to starvation and death'.[30] Maher, denouncing the sixteen ounces of food doled out to the poor in Carlow poor house, savagely commented:

The Times . . . descries the priest as 'sending his Thug upon a sacred mission, blessing his weapon and absolving him beforehand of the seeming crime'. Introduce the workhouse dietary of Carlow into England, and will *The Times* tell us how many murders, without sacerdotal prompting, it would produce in a season? . . . Talk indeed of a conspiracy against life! Here we have it . . .[31]

From Kinsale, County Cork, Daniel Murphy, vicar forane to the bishop of Cork, summed up the feelings and fears of the Irish clergy:

The unhappy Shrewsbury has done us all great harm and it is quite clear that he is playing the game of the government for our enslavement and that his letter will be submitted if it has not already been done, to the Holy See as a proof of our rebellious propensities and the necessity of government control over the Irish priesthood.[32]

---

[30] *Freeman's Journal*, 4 Jan. 1848. See T. P. Cunningham, 'The Great Famine in County Cavan', *Breifne*, 2 (1965), 434.
[31] Maher to *Dublin Evening News*, 4 Dec. 1847, cited in P. F. Moran (ed.), *The letters of Rev. James Maher . . . on Religious Subjects . . .* (1877), 30–1.
[32] Murphy to Cullen, 1 Jan. 1848, Cullen Papers, ICA.

The Revd James Cooke, professor of moral theology at St John's College, Waterford, and a good friend of Cullen, commented wryly on the crisis. 'I know not what the English mean to do with us', he wrote. 'The papers and parliamentary speeches last year held up the landlords to the Nation's contempt and execration. This last session they have turned on the priests with the most unaccountable fury; now they attack Priests and people together.' What astonished him most was 'Catholic peers joining in this war-whoop and not a hand or word of the government to check it.'[33] Cooke's allegations were justifiable: Russell, like many other Whigs, had indeed branded the landlords as the culprits but now, by its silence, his government was consenting to what Cooke indignantly denounced as a 'war-whoop' against the people as assassins of the landlords and against the priests as their abettors. Cooke would not have been so astonished if he had known that Shrewsbury was in constant contact with Clarendon, and that Russell had encouraged him to send the letter to MacHale.

This shocked reaction extended to some leading Catholics in England. Lucas in the *Tablet* savagely attacked Shrewsbury for lecturing the bishops, ridiculing his 'hyper-archi-episcopal' instructions to the Irish Church. Fathers Pagani and Luigi Gentili, two zealous and influential Rosminian priests, and Bishops Briggs and Ullathorne, became worried at the continuing denunciation of Irish priests and, suspecting government connivance, they convinced themselves of the existence of a plot against the Church. Minto's mission, they suspected, was to persuade the pope, in his hour of need, to agree to a concordat or to exchange diplomats so that the government could gain control over the Church either by paying the clergy or nominating the bishops. A preliminary step would be the public discrediting of the Irish clergy who opposed such arrangements, particularly MacHale. Pagani believed that Shrewsbury and the earl of Arundel and Surrey, another leading Catholic peer, were the prime movers in a plot 'to prostrate the very head of the anti-colleges and anti-government party'—Dr MacHale. Part of the problem lay in the ecclesiastical politics within the Catholic Church in England. English bishops, including Briggs and William Ullathorne, vicar apostolic of the central district of England, as also Gentili and Pagani, feared that Wiseman identified with the Catholic

---

[33] Cooke to Cullen, 22 Jan. 1848, ibid.

aristocracy and the Oxford converts and wanted to establish close links between the government and Rome. They suspected that his ambition was to become the first archbishop of Westminster and that Shrewsbury was pushing his candidature. If he succeeded, the heads of the Catholic Church in England and in Ireland—Wiseman, Crolly, and Murray—would be government supporters and willing to assist it in its measures to control the Church. The letters, they believed, were not Shrewsbury's own but Wiseman's. Pagani now urged that they act immediately to prevent Wiseman's party getting him in as archbishop of Westminster.[34]

To some extent the incident was a phase in the power struggle in the English Catholic Church between bishops and aristocracy. By the mid-nineteenth century, the aristocracy was losing influence to the bishops, and the influx of so many Irish Catholics, who turned for leadership to the clergy, not to the gentry, helped to swing the decision in favour of the bishops. Shrewsbury told Clarendon that among his motives in continuing the controversy with MacHale was 'to vindicate the rights of the laity' and 'to prove that we are not those passive, abject slaves of our Clergy' which too many suppose'.[35]

Some of Pagani's suspicions were justified. Wiseman wanted the restoration of relations between Britain and Rome, regarding it as part of the normalization of the status of the English Catholic Church. He also recognized, however, the importance of proper diplomatic links for furthering government policies in Ireland because, as he told Greville in December, the misfortunes that befell the government's Irish policy in Rome were 'all owing to there being no English ambassador at Rome, and no representative of the moderate Irish Clergy'.[36] As for Shrewsbury's letter, although Wiseman apparently approved of it, it was not written by him. Its author was the Revd Pierce Connelly, Shrewsbury's eccentric chaplain, whom Shrewsbury now sent to Rome to support the candidature of Wiseman and to discredit MacHale. A further twist in the complicated story of Roman intrigues was that when Connelly went to Rome he did indeed try to discredit the Irish clergy, but also, unknown to Shrewsbury, he used every effort,

---

[34] Pagani to Briggs, Jan. 1848, Briggs Papers, 1754A, LDA.

[35] Shrewsbury to Clarendon, 7 Feb. 1848, Clarendon Papers, Box 58.

[36] C. C. F. Greville, *The Greville Memoirs: A Journal of the Reign of Queen Victoria*, ed. H. Reeve (1903), 7 Dec. 1847, v. 470.

including canvassing Minto's help, to block Wiseman's candidature.[37] Pagani and Briggs were right in suspecting government involvement, for Russell had encouraged Shrewsbury to publish his letter attacking MacHale, and Clarendon remained in close contact with him during the controversy. In December 1847, Russell insisted on appointing Dr Renn Dickson Hampden as bishop of Hereford, stating publicly that the appointment would 'strengthen the Protestant character of our Church, so seriously threatened of late by many defections to the Church of Rome.'[38] These remarks from the liberal prime minister, the champion of religious equality, were a sharp reminder that the English state was still a confessional one and they were noted with dismay not just by Tractarians but by the leaders of the Catholic Church in England and Ireland. Briggs, Gentili, and Pagani were struck by the contrast in the government's attitude: at home ministers were attacking, or condoning the attacks, on the Catholic clergy and Russell was proclaiming his strong Reformation principles; in Rome Minto, cabinet minister and father-in-law of Russell, was displaying a most friendly attitude to the pope. Fearing a government plot against the Church, Briggs, with Gentili's encouragement, now decided to warn Pius IX and drew up a solemn memorial for signature by the bishops:

[W]e most . . . solemnly declare to Your Holiness that British Diplomacy has everywhere been exerted to the injury of our Holy Religion. We read in the public Papers that Lord Minto is friendly received . . . by Your Holiness. . . . At this very time, however, . . . the first Minister of the British Government, the Son in Law of Lord Minto is publicly manifesting in England, together with his fellow Minister, his marked opposition to the Catholic Religion and the Catholic Church. Another cause of our serious alarm is the very general hostile and calumnious outcry now made in both houses of our Parliament and throughout Protestant England against the Catholic Priests of Ireland, falsely charging them with being the abettors of the horrible crime of murder whilst as true Pastors they are striving

---

[37] Pierce Connelly, an American Episcopal priest who had converted to Catholicism. D. G. Paz, *Priesthoods and Apostasies of Pierce Connelly: A Study of Victorian Conversion and Anti-Catholicism* (1986); R. Flaxman, *A Woman Styled Bold* (1991).

[38] Russell to certain lay members of the Church of England, 10 Dec. 1847, *Tablet*, 18 Dec. 1847; see also Russell to the bishops of London, Winchester, Lincoln, etc., 8 Dec. 1847, ibid. For a critical evaluation of Russell's motives, see R. Pattison, *The Great Dissent: John Henry Newman and the Liberal Heresy* (1991), 71–5.

to ... console their ... perishing people and like good shepherds are in the midst of pestilence giving their lives for their flocks.[39]

Twenty of the twenty-six Irish bishops and three or four of the eight English vicars apostolic signed it. The bishops' replies to Briggs reveal a deep distrust of the government all the more striking when one takes into account state benevolence towards the Church in recent years.[40] Even bishops who normally supported the moderate line of Murray voiced serious concern. Egan of Kerry feared that a government representative at Rome 'would not contribute to the liberty of our Churches, English or Irish. I am strengthened in the impression by the violent attacks made of late in Parliament on the Irish Priests'. McGettigan of Raphoe declared that he had not the slightest doubt but that 'the interest now working so successfully at Rome will get the Propaganda to issue some document against the Irish priests'. Blake of Dromore, who wanted a stronger memorial, complained that 'in the midst of our utmost effort for alleviating human distress, we are assailed and calumniated in the most atrocious manner'. The more nationalist bishops—Cantwell, O'Higgins, McNally, Slattery, and MacHale— expressed their opposition in stronger terms. McNally, an able pastoral bishop, who, though a firm O'Connellite, was not extreme, saw it as a threat to the liberty of all Catholics in the Empire and feared that the calumnies would be a pretext for demanding control over the Church. John Derry, the newly appointed bishop of Clonfert, was concerned that the restoration of diplomatic relations with Rome would lead to a veto over Church appointments:

the Ministers who propose it ... do so in the hope of being able thereby to obtain a control over the appointment of the Ministers of our Holy Religion; ... the ... almost immediate effect of such secular control and particularly of Protestant British control, will be to alienate the People from the Pastors; ... it will make the Pastors appear to the oppressed people, as stipendiary agents and agents of their oppressors; in a word, ... it will utterly derange all the existing affectionate relations of Priests and People.

Although these replies were sparked off by the spate of denunciations of the clergy, they are a surprising revelation of the depth of the suspicion in which the bishops held the government. The

---

[39] Briggs Papers, 1693, LDA; Dec. 1847.

[40] The replies of 24 Irish and some English and Scottish bishops are in the Briggs Papers, 1718–1756, LDA.

bishops' constant fear had surfaced again: the government was seeking to control the Church and, if it succeeded, the people would lose confidence in it. The strident abuse of the clergy in Britain had thoroughly reinforced their opposition to any such plan. Russell, they believed, had made clear what they suspected all along: they were living in a confessional Protestant state, and the denunciations in press and in parliament had unmasked the strong anti-Catholic feeling which lay just beneath the surface. The government was trying to turn its Roman flank and they feared that the *Curia*, as in the veto controversy, would be won over. When Pius IX, in response to Minto's urgent representations, took action, their worst fears appeared to be realized. On 3 January 1848, at Pius's request, Cardinal Fransoni, the secretary of the Congregation of Propaganda, sent a sharp letter to the archbishops asking for full information on the press reports that the clergy approved of murders.[41] This Roman rebuke, intended as confidential to the four archbishops, was leaked to the press. Slattery blamed Murray for the leak; MacHale informed Rome, and the pope immediately deleted from his own letter to the bishops a paragraph similar to Fransoni's rebuke.[42] If the letter was a victory of sorts for Minto, the fierce reaction it evoked made the victory a Pyrrhic one. The nationalists, priests and laity, went wild with anger. Remonstrances poured in and protest meetings were held. If Propaganda wanted full information more than one bishop was prepared to provide it. Maginn of Derry appealed to Crolly, the Catholic primate, to defend the clergy to the pope, claiming that 'no clergyman has transgressed the bounds of Christian duty, which makes it incumbent on every follower of the Redeemer to stand by the oppressed against their oppressors—for the poor and the needy against those that strip them'. He added that a love of country 'for which our great pope himself is so distinguished' could not be construed as factious.[43] The elderly French, bishop of Kilmacduagh and Kilfenora, told Cullen of the horrific state of his diocese and the plight and dilemma of the priests:

---

[41] Fransoni to Crolly, 3 Jan. 1848, *Catholic Directory, 1849*, 292. Giacomo Fransoni (1775–1856), cardinal prefect of the Congregation of Propaganda Fide (1834–56).

[42] Slattery to MacHale, 15 Feb. 1848, cited in B. O'Reilly, *John MacHale Archbishop of Tuam: His Life, Times and Correspondence* (1890), ii. 115.

[43] Maginn to Crolly, 21 Feb. 1848, Murray Papers, DDA.

the yellings of the poor, on the Roads, in the streets of our Towns, at all our Houses . . . the heart-rending scenes in the Houses of the poor, lying sick of fever, starvation, of inanition and want, are the daily prospects [*sic*] of our Clergy. . . . In one parish alone [Kilmacduagh] there were twenty-one deaths of heads of Families in four days . . . they all died with the utmost resignation to the Will of God blessing the Priest for a very small temporary help. These are the scenes witnessed by our Clergy in the South and West of Ireland!!! and alas if we dare describe these afflictions of our people and our own Agonies at their heartrending sufferings we are stamped by our Enemies of this English Press and the leading Members of Parliament as 'Surplissed [*sic*] Ruffians and Instigators of the Murder of the Landed Gentry and the Exterminators of the People'!!!

'O, how false are these accusations', French exclaimed, 'as God Knows and only Knows.'[44] French, who was timid and scrupulous, avoided the political arena and the moving account he gave is all the more credible. All four archbishops replied to Rome. Murray, in a reasoned statement, denied categorically that any priest either incited to murder or condoned it. He blamed some landlords for cruel treatment of their tenants, but admitted that some priests, moved by genuine sympathy for the poor, condemned these landlords in the press, at public meetings, and, sometimes, in the chapel and from the pulpit. As a result tenants were inflamed against unjust landlords, and an agrarian conspiracy grew up which, under threat to their lives, prevented almost all landlords from getting their rightful rent and other tenants from taking land from which a tenant had been justly evicted.[45] MacHale, knowing that the charges were aimed in the first place against himself, stoutly defended his conduct in the press and to Cullen in Rome. Crolly, spurred on by other Ulster bishops, lent his authoritative voice to the protests sent to Rome against the charges.

The strongest refutation of the charge came from the Munster metropolitan Archbishop Michael Slattery. Slattery, whom Newman described a few years later as 'mild, gentle, tender and broken', was able but introspective and, though little given to the fiery outbursts of MacHale, was deeply suspicious of the government. In a 31-page vindication of the clergy to Cardinal Fransoni, he denied that the chapels were being used for political harangues, and pointed out that McDermott had been vindicated by the testimony of his

---

[44] French to Cullen, 16 Feb. 1848, Cullen Papers, ICA.
[45] Murray to Fransoni, 3 Feb. 1848, draft, Murray Papers, DDA.

bishop and people. After asserting that the Irish Church had suffered, since the Reformation, under more than 'Egyptian bond-
age', and detailing the work of the clergy during the famine, he
traced the source of all the trouble to one cause: the treacherous
English government, being Protestant, wanted to gain control of
the Catholic Church.[46] It was a fierce attack and duly impressed
Fransoni, who immediately replied soothingly, accepting this impassioned defence—an acceptance which Slattery immediately
published. The manner in which Slattery saw the controversy and
the flavour of his vindication is found in his letter to Cullen:

> The Catholic clergy being the only persons to stand forward against the
> oppression of the People, the Landlords availed themselves of the national
> bigotry of England to raise the cry of murder against them to turn away
> public attention from the numberless murders caused by themselves. Hence
> the calumnies sanctioned by the Government to forward their own pur-
> poses of blackening us in the eyes of Europe and even of Rome, thereby
> to destroy the liberty of our Church.[47]

What shocked him was that 'the same anti-Catholic spirit was
not confined to the rabble, but was displayed in both Houses of
Parliament', above all by Stanley and Palmerston. Slattery's explanation did not make allowance for the English exasperation caused
by the belief that the murders were committed by a people on
whom vast sums of money in relief was being spent, nor for
landlords who feared that they were regarded as legitimate targets
for assassination. Nevertheless, there was truth in his contention
that, if the landlords had started the campaign of accusations,
Clarendon, Palmerston, and possibly other ministers were happy
to use it to 'blacken' the clergy abroad and in Rome in furtherance
of their policies. The deep-rooted Protestant suspicion of the
Catholic Church and its clergy had given the campaign a religious
resonance.

On 27 March, nearly two months after Slattery's letter to Fransoni, seventeen of the bishops sent a joint statement to Pius IX.[48]
This letter revealed most clearly the considered reaction of two-
thirds of the bishops towards the campaign against the clergy, and

---

[46] Slattery to Fransoni, 7 Feb. 1848, Slattery Papers, CDA.
[47] Slattery to Cullen, 28 Jan. 1848, Cullen Papers, ICA.
[48] Irish bishops to Pius IX, 27 Mar. 1848, *Acta* (1848), vol. 211, fos. 362–6,
PFA.

its tone was startlingly bitter. It denounced the accusers of the clergy as modern pharisees, a true brood of vipers, with the venom of asps. They whispered lies not merely against innocent priests, whom they accused of profaning the altars by incitation to murder, but against the bishops whom they accused of looking on and tolerating such infamies. This storm of tongues erupting suddenly as from the very gates of hell, burst over the whole of Europe to reach the citadel of the Catholic world, Rome itself. The leaking of Cardinal Fransoni's request for information was specially denounced for it was done, the bishops claimed, in order to intimidate the Catholic clergy. Some of the calumniators, the letter concluded, were false brethren. Many were in Rome itself and English gold was often their motive. Significantly, this uncompromising statement of views was signed not just by the MacHaleite bishops but by Egan, MacNicholas, Walsh of Ossory, and Walshe of Kildare and Leighlin, all moderate in their outlook.

The fierce anger that surfaces in every paragraph of this carefully written letter to the head of their religion some months after the incidents took place, showed the depth of the bishops' resentment. It was the clearest indication yet of the serious damage that the smear of connivance at assassination had done to relations between the bishops and the government. So bitter was the resentment revealed in the bishops' protest that it was difficult to see how trust could be restored between them and the British governing class. The papal rebuke which Minto and Palmerston had elicited had proved counter-productive.

On the other Irish issue—the Queen's Colleges—Minto could also claim initial success, for the pope intimated his regret at having issued the rescript. Newman, when taking leave of him in early December, reported that the pope showed concern, had read all that the papers had said on the matter, and would have discussed it with him had not Newman's lack of Italian prevented it.[49] In Ireland the government was preparing to make another effort to win the Catholics' approval for the colleges scheme. The Whigs had not initiated the measure and Russell disapproved of its basic 'neutral' or 'godless' thrust, but, politically it was impossible to drop it. Clarendon was willing to modify the religious clauses of

---

[49] Newman to Dalgairns, 21 Dec. 1847, cited in C. S. Dessain and V. F. Blehl (eds.), *The Letters and Diaries of John Henry Newman* (1962), xii. 135.

the act to make it acceptable to Catholics. Towards the end of September 1847 his efforts brought him into contact with an unusual cleric, Francis Nicholson.[50]

Nicholson, who was to play an important role in the negotiations over the next year, was a Carmelite friar attached to the friary at Clarendon Street in Dublin.[51] He was, however, a family friend of the More O'Ferralls, with whom he generally lived when in Ireland. For health reasons he travelled to France and Italy. Kindly, and anxious to please and conciliate, he prided himself on his ability to achieve results through his many contacts, though he was less effective than he imagined himself to be. Clarendon described him to Russell as 'a very useful, friendly little man' and Murray always had a kind word for him.[52] To his opponents, however, he appeared as a meddlesome intriguer. The Roman authorities thought sufficiently highly of him to appoint him, in 1847, coadjutor archbishop of Corfu.[53]

Nicholson, a strong supporter of Archbishop Murray in the controversy between him and MacHale on the Bequests Act, approved of Clarendon's policies, particularly in regard to the new colleges, and offered to press for support for them both in Ireland and in Rome. Nicholson's and Murray's plan was to amend the statutes of the colleges in a manner which would give satisfaction to both Rome and to the British Government. After discussions with some of the bishops, Nicholson reported to Clarendon on 19 November that the number who were well disposed towards the colleges had risen to ten and that he hoped shortly 'to steal one of the Episcopal Fold of the "Lion of Judah"'. He now offered to put Clarendon's revised statutes to Rome and Clarendon accepted this willingly, all the more so since Minto needed someone versed in the colleges affair to second his efforts. To help Nicholson in his Roman negotiations Clarendon gave him an official letter, explaining why he had sought his intervention, and enclosed a copy of the proposed revised religious statutes. This letter, the terms of which were drawn

---

[50] Clarendon to Nicholson, 29 Sept. 1847, *Acta* (1848), vol. 211, fo. 393, PFA. Nicholson to Propaganda, 30 Aug. 1848, ibid. fos. 387–92.

[51] Francis Joseph Nicholson (1803–55), Discalced Carmelite friar; ordained (1829); coadjutor archbishop of Corfu (1846); archbishop of Corfu (1852).

[52] Clarendon to Russell, 4 Jan. 1848, Clarendon Papers, Letterbook 2.

[53] According to his own account, this honour was forced on him 'by the utmost stretch of Papal Authority'. Nicholson to Clarendon, 21 Oct. 1847, Clarendon Papers, Box 20.

up by Murray and Nicholson, was to have a colourful history. All might have gone well if Nicholson had gone straight to Rome. He dallied first in Dublin, then in London, and finally in Paris, visiting bishops, ministers, and nuncios. His poor state of health delayed him further, with the result that, although he originally planned to leave for Rome in November, he was still in London at the end of April 1848. Arriving in France, he was delayed further by the Revolution. By then events in Rome had overtaken him.

Lobbying in Rome had been intense. Minto had spent a full three months there, from 4 November to 3 February, and had taken a strong line on the Irish clergy. Not only had Clarendon and Palmerston briefed him, but Shrewsbury had also provided him with material and Minto assured him that he intended to lay both his letter and 'some of Laffan's and McDermott's effusions' before the Pope.[54] Shrewsbury worked also through his chaplain, Connelly, and his son-in-law, Prince Doria. There was, however, a strong counter-lobby. Wiseman, who knew Rome well, alleged that 'Irish ecclesiastical affairs were managed by MacHale through Fransoni, Head of Propaganda, and Father Ventura, who has the Pope's ear'.[55] Although MacHale's political views had merited a sharp rebuke from Fransoni, who warned him some years previously to avoid political controversies, there is some confirmation of this view.[56] Shrewsbury maintained that the pope believed the MacHaleites because of the Liberal Catholics' criticism of England's attitude to the Famine:

he has been so well prepared to believe them upon the conduct of England in respect to the Irish famine, by Montalembert and Padre Ventura. In his late treatise on the Sicilian question, the latter thus expresses himself: 'The Count de Maistre observed that the people even the most remarkable for wisdom in the management of their own affairs, always run into follies when they undertake to manage the affairs of others. No one . . . denies to the English a more than ordinary share of prudence, justice and generosity. But the English Government with regard to Ireland has never been and never will be either wise, just or generous. *While this people of heroes is dying of hunger, the English Parliament has hit upon no other means of consolation or relief than the passing of a Draconian law to*

[54] Minto to Shrewsbury, 20 Jan. 1848, Curato, *Gran Bretagna*, i. 328.
[55] Greville, *Memoirs*, 7 Dec. 1847, v. 470.
[56] Fransoni to MacHale, 26 Feb. 1839, *Lettere e Decreti* (1849), vol. 321, fos. 155–6, PFA.

punish assassins without giving a thought to the desperate misery which has provoked them to crime. The wretched populace demanded bread and it answered them with grape and Canister.'[57]

Ventura did not allude to the large sums that parliament had voted for relief nor to the generosity of the English people; many friends of England, however, shared Ventura's and Montalembert's incomprehension at its Irish policies and were bewildered at the spectacle of the richest country in the world apparently allowing so many of its citizens to die.[58] Ventura's influence with the pope was significant.[59]

At the same time, Cullen, from his vantage-point in the Irish College, organized the defence of the Irish clergy, as well as opposition to the colleges. Cullen was O'Connellite in politics and combined deep-rooted suspicion of the government with total commitment to the model of the Church he knew in Rome. His was the carefully thought-out *votum* or written advice that had persuaded Propaganda to condemn the colleges. On his return to Rome in January 1848, he used all his considerable influence and his mastery of the Roman system to neutralize Minto's success. The result of this lobbying was soon evident, for before long he was able to report to his friends in Ireland that Slattery's letter and his own representations were bearing fruit, and the pope was more favourably disposed than he had dared to hope. Connelly complained to Shrewsbury of their *'great secret influence'*.[60] Cullen received further support early in March when Thomas Grant, rector of the English College in Rome and agent for the English bishops, presented the Briggs memorandum, complete with the signatures of the bishops, to the Pope. Frederick Lucas, who stridently supported Irish Catholics in his journal, the *Tablet*, organized a meeting on 20 March which packed the Freemasons' Hall in London to overflowing. Although the aristocracy and the bishops were absent, it was attended by leading Oxford converts Frederick Oakely and W. G. Ward (who seconded Lucas's proposal), and by Fr. Robert

---

[57] Shrewsbury to Clarendon, 22 Mar. 1848, Clarendon Papers, Box 58.

[58] J. S. Donnelly, 'The Administration of Relief', in Vaughan (ed.), *New History*, v. 328–9.

[59] Costa, 'Da O'Connell a Pio IX', Un Capitolo del Cristianesimo Sociale del P. Gioacchino Ventura (1847)', in L. Morabito (ed.), *Daniel O'Connell: Atti del Convegno di Studi nel 140° Anniversario della Morte* (1990), 93–115.

[60] Shrewsbury to Clarendon, 22 Mar. 1848, Clarendon Papers, Box 58.

Whitty, vicar-general to Dr Wiseman. The meeting drew up a memorial to the pope which, like Briggs's petition, called into question the government's policies towards Catholics and requested that if a nuncio were appointed there be a complete separation of English and Irish ecclesiastical business, so that there be no suspicion 'that Irish affairs pass to Rome through a medium subjected to the influence or guided by the prejudices of either English Protestants or English Catholics'![61]

To drive home their case, Briggs, Ullathorne, and Gentili intended that some bishops should go to Rome in person. MacHale and O'Higgins decided to go and Maginn joined them later.[62] Gentili, with either Briggs or Ullathorne, had hoped to accompany them, but the two Irish bishops set off on their own. Ullathorne went to Rome a few months later on other business, but probably made clear Briggs's and his own position on Irish affairs and on the Diplomatic Relations Act. MacHale and O'Higgins lost no time and arrived in Rome on Palm Sunday, 16 April.

Minto, who had spent February and March in Naples, now returned to Rome when the revolutions broke out, noting that he would have 'the mortification of finding not a trace remaining of all the labours of my outward-bound journey'. Although he stayed less than a week in Rome he found time to warn the pope against MacHale in Ireland and Cullen in Rome, whom he accused of being 'an agency for propagating falsehood' and of sending out a 'continued stream of misrepresentation'. Pius replied that he had seen communications from Dr Cullen of a very temperate character.[63] Minto's influence faded rapidly with his departure. He had patronized Italian liberals, the most prominent among whom was Ciceruacchio. They were now regarded as dangerous.[64]

Unknown to Minto, the two opponents he warned the pope against were about to join forces. A few hours after Minto's leaving Rome by one gate, MacHale, accompanied by O'Higgins, arrived

---

[61] Ward, *Sequel*, 285–301.

[62] William O'Higgins, or Higgins (1793–1853), appointed bishop of Ardagh and Clonmacnoise (1829), an energetic reforming bishop and an ardent nationalist; strong supporter of O'Connell and of MacHale. J. Kelly, 'The Catholic Church in the Diocese of Ardagh, 1650–1870', in R. Gillespie and G. Moran (eds.), *Longford: Essays in County History* (1991), 63–91.

[63] Minto to Russell, 14 Apr. 1848, Curato, *Gran Bretagna*, i. 194–6.

[64] Ciceruacchio's real name was Angelo Brunetti. His son was the assassin of Count Rossi, the pope's prime minister, in November 1848.

by another. Guided by Cullen they immediately set to work to undo Minto's achievements and arranged an audience with Pius for 27 April. At this very time, Pius was passing through a painful crisis. The expulsion of the Jesuits in many Italian states, including the Papal States, showed that the quickening pace of revolution was outstripping him. More particularly, his attention, like that of most Italians, was on the crisis in Lombardy where, after the Milanese had driven out Radetzky, Charles Albert, king of Sardinia, had declared war on the Austrians and sought to rally Italy, and particularly the pope, to his side. Pius had dispatched his best adviser, Corboli Bussi, to Charles Albert's camp on 10 April. Meanwhile, the papal army, swollen by many volunteers, was preparing to attack the Austrians. The pope was on the horns of a dilemma. On the one hand, carried along by the patriotic sentiment of the hour, he felt he should make common cause with other Italian governments against Austria. On the other, warned by the nuncio in Vienna, Viale Prelá, he was anguished at the prospect of a war waged in his name against a Catholic nation, and fearful that it might provoke a schism in Austria and Germany. When MacHale and O'Higgins visited him he had just finalized the Allocutio of 29 April which many have taken to mark the end of his liberal period. British affairs took second place, yet he accorded them a long audience. The bishops were agreeably surprised, as is shown by the account O'Higgins sent the next day to his confidant, McNally, the bishop of Clogher:

He warmly praised the bishops and priests for their zeal, their courage and their perseverance and said he never believed a word of the calumnies heaped upon them. . . . We explained the nature of our agitation in Ireland, and were delighted to perceive that he understood our view of the subject thoroughly and so far from condemning our conduct, looked upon it as proof of our zeal for religion. His Holiness also explained his mind with reference to the infidel colleges, and assured us that his rescript on that important subject shall never be recalled or modified . . . Minto started for England the day before we arrived; and before his departure waited on the Pope and passed a glowing eulogy on the Bishops and Priests of Ireland!!. His charade is at present understood in Rome and he returns a disappointed and humbled diplomatist.[65]

[65] O'Higgins to McNally, 28 Apr. 1848, McNally Papers, DIO (RC) 1/10B/23, CIDA.

This account is hard to reconcile with Minto's account of his success in Rome. In the interval, Pius, upset by the volatility of Italian events, had also become circumspect in his dealings with England. He was acquainted with the debate in the House of Lords on the Diplomatic Relations bill, in the course of which peers had made insensitive remarks about the papacy: both Wellington's amendment to deny him the title of Sovereign Pontiff and Eglinton's amendment forbidding him to choose an ecclesiastic as ambassador to the Court of Saint James were accepted. His confidence in the British government's wholehearted and altruistic support was shaken.[66] The consul in Rome, John Freeborn, had annoyed the *Curia* by his support of Roman revolutionaries.[67] Whatever the reason, the favourable reception he gave the bishops delighted them. Since Pius, although normally welcoming and affable, was not averse to scolding prelates who had not lived up to his expectations, the interview could be seen as an indication that the criticisms of political involvement contained in Fransoni's letter of 3 January had been put aside. It augured well for the success of the bishops' mission. Apart from convincing the pope that the Irish clergy were innocent of the charges brought against them, they had come to block any papal approval of the colleges, and they now set to work to convince Propaganda, the Congregation which would consider the matter.

On 15 April yet another envoy had set out for Rome to make submissions on the same subject. If one section of the bishops sent MacHale and O'Higgins to counteract Minto and Nicholson, the other section now decided to send a further agent to counteract MacHale and O'Higgins. When MacHale and O'Higgins left for Rome on 1 April, Murray became concerned lest they reach the pope before Nicholson, who was still in London. He decided to send his own representative, John Ennis, parish priest of Booterstown, who had successfully represented the moderate bishops on the related question of national education in 1839. On that occasion, the Whig government had given him every support, including money, and now again Russell generously financed his

---

[66] Russell to Clarendon 23 Apr. 1848, Clarendon Papers, Box 43; Murray to Clarendon, 26 Aug., 2, 3 Sept. 1848, Murray Papers, DDA. Nicholson to Murray, 12 Sept. 1848, ibid.

[67] Martina, *Pio IX*, 165–6.

mission.[68] Clarendon provided him with the revised college statutes concerning religion and a copy of his letter to Nicholson. To give the letter more weight, however, Ennis changed the name of the addressee from 'Archbishop Nicholson' to 'Archbishop Murray'. When he arrived in Rome at the beginning of May, Ennis presented both documents to Propaganda together with certain '*osservazioni*'.

The *osservazioni* set forth Murray's case for laying aside the old distrust of the British government and urged instead co-operating with it. While admitting that the state had made proselytism its policy in the past, he argued that three hundred years of experience had proven to every British government the uselessness of such a policy and that it had now abandoned it. The state had abolished the hated Charter and Bible schools, whose purpose was to bring up Catholic children in the Protestant faith, and in their place set up the national system of education. Similarly, army and navy schools, where children had also been brought up Protestant, now had their Catholic chapels and state-paid Catholic chaplains. The legislation over the previous twenty years showed the government's benevolent intentions: Catholic emancipation had been granted, ten Protestant sees had been abolished, and the Maynooth Grant increased. The laws against the regular clergy, embodied in the Emancipation Act, had never been put into effect. As regards the new colleges, apart from the bishops' inability to prevent Catholics from sending their sons there, the faith of the students would be safeguarded for they would be under the surveillance of deans approved by the bishops. Finally, in a general comment, Murray claimed, that 'in no other European nation is the exercise of religious liberty safer or sounder' than in the United Kingdom.[69]

This measured and positive assessment of the relationship between Catholics and the government focused on the issue of education and proselytism, for long a sore point for Catholics. It would remain an issue unless they were convinced that they could trust

---

[68] The support which Melbourne's government gave Ennis in 1839 included introductions to the nuncio in Paris and the French ambassador at Rome who had been instructed by his government to support the mission. On both occasions English Catholics with Roman contacts (Lord Clifford in 1839 and Lord Shrewsbury in 1848) played a role. R. Brent, *Liberal Anglican Politics: Whiggery, Religion, and Reform, 1830–1841* (1987), 226–7. John Ennis (1792–1862) was a nephew of Archbishop Troy, Murray's predecessor in the see of Dublin.

[69] J. Ennis, *Osservazioni* [Observations], a broadsheet in Cullen Papers, DDA.

the government. Murray was appealing for this trust. His claim that Catholics had equality before the law and that the freer constitution of the United Kingdom conferred advantages on religion not available in many European countries was accurate enough. Nevertheless, long after emancipation, the Protestant ascendancy remained firmly in control and Catholics were far from having attained that equality to which the law entitled them; key areas in the judiciary and in higher government office had almost no Catholics. Furthermore, since none of the new colleges was to be Catholic and religion was virtually excluded from them, Catholic higher education would remain in an inferior position to that of the Established Church, which possessed the prestigious Trinity College in Dublin. Whether Peel's and Russell's efforts to redress the balance justified co-operation with government was the point on which the two sides differed.

Whatever the effects Ennis's documents had on the *Curia*, MacHale came into possession of them almost immediately. His counter-measures were masterly. He promptly published the letter and the statutes in the Irish newspapers. Clarendon was doubly embarrassed. Astonished at reading his private letter in the public press, he found himself denounced for underhand dealings. His alleged anti-Catholic activities in Spain twenty years before, when he was 'plain Mr Villiers', were raked up to infuriate Catholic and nationalist opinion. Even Crolly, who had supported him, lost confidence in him.[70] On the other hand, the Orange press raised a howl of protest, accusing him of submitting the statutes to the pope for approval before presenting them to parliament, and Russell had to face some difficult questions in the House of Commons. Murray, too, was wrong-footed, for the altered letter had blown his cover and shown him in league with the lord lieutenant behind the back of his episcopal colleagues. Embarrassed, he explained that Clarendon had never addressed any such letter to him; in turn, this denial discredited Ennis in Rome, where the *Curia* was displeased to find that Ennis had tampered with the documents submitted to them. Finally, Nicholson, who having at last reached Paris found himself marooned there by the revolution, was taken aback to discover, through the public press, that Ennis was acting

[70] Crolly to Murray, 13 Apr. 1848, Murray Papers, DDA.

in his place. This was to damage the mission in Rome, for when Nicholson finally arrived there at the end of July he and Ennis became involved in mutual recriminations. Both felt aggrieved, as Nicholson reported to Hamilton, Murray's archdeacon:

he [Ennis] told me that Mgr. B[arnabò] remarked to him, 'Woe be you, Ennis, Dr N[icholson] has ruined you with the Pope.' . . . The Pope thinks Ennis an impostor who should be sent home. . . . I have not met E[nnis] since nor do I intend to after his language to me when last we met. He has bungled things.[71]

Murray was forced to write to 'my two unharmonizing friends' and to recall Ennis.[72]

Having sown confusion in the enemy camp MacHale, O'Higgins, and Cullen, with the advantage of knowing their opponents' case, drew up for the *Curia* an extensive criticism of the colleges scheme. The main thrust of their argument on education was that when education excluded religion it would, as De Maistre had maintained, poison the whole nation. Furthermore, they claimed that the government could not be trusted. If the government were in good faith in their amendments to the statutes why did they not bring in a new bill guaranteeing the changes? They added a history of government antagonism, past and present, real and imaginary, to the Catholic Church. They cited Russell's Protestant defence of Hampden's appointment who, they told the pope, was an intimate of Archbishop Whately and Blanco White, the one a latitudinarian, the other an apostate. In an impassioned appeal they wrote: 'Wherefore, most Holy Father, *time Anglos et dona ferentes* . . . give little credence to men who never keep their promises.'[73] In general their statement reflected the suspicions manifested in the bishops' replies to Briggs a few months earlier which the accusations of the clergy conniving at assassinations had provoked. On the question of the amendments offered by Clarendon, their wariness was justified for it emerged later that Clarendon and Russell were unable to enact them.

Beside this distrust of the government, distrust for their fellow

---

[71] Nicholson to Hamilton, July 1848, Hamilton Papers, DDA.
[72] Murray to Clarendon, 2 Sept. 1848, Clarendon Papers, Box 50.
[73] *Brevi Rilievi sopra il Sistema d'Insegnamento Misto che si cerca di stabilire in Irlanda nei collegi così detti della Regina* (1848).

bishops was beginning to rankle. On 14 September both MacHale and O'Higgins wrote to Slattery and Maginn respectively, asking them to inform the majority bishops of what was taking place in Rome.[74] The tenor of both letters was the same. O'Higgins complained that 'everything that systematic lying, or British intrigue, as well as the base conduct of false brethren could effect, was called unscrupulously into requisition'. The efforts of Ennis and the change he had made in the address of the letter had pointed to Murray as the chief among the 'ecclesiastical abettors' of Clarendon, whom O'Higgins dismissed contemptuously as 'a heretical viceroy'. If Crolly's volte-face in 1845 on the colleges issue had angered these bishops, Murray's secret intrigues had inflamed them still more. What most exasperated these bishops was what they believed was Murray's presumption in dealing with the government on their behalf without their knowledge or consent. 'Let us hope', wrote O'Higgins, 'that henceforth no man will attempt to treat with Government on a subject affecting our whole body, without first obtaining our explicit consent'.[75] Clarendon's letter as submitted to Propaganda by Ennis was addressed to Murray and read: 'Your Grace had the goodness to promise that you would convey to Rome, for the consideration of the Pope, the amended statutes of the Queen's Colleges.'[76] This implied that Murray, without consulting his fellow bishops or even showing them the new statutes, had promised Clarendon to lay the matter before the Pope. What MacHale and O'Higgins did not know was that the letter had been addressed to Nicholson, who was not a bishop of the Irish Church and was going to Rome on his way to his diocese in Corfu. Ennis's change of addressee was producing unfortunate consequences. The accusation that Murray was acting on their behalf without their consent was one to which bishops like Slattery often returned and they were to raise it at the Synod of Thurles. With feelings now running so high it was difficult to see how harmony among the bishops could be restored.

So discreetly did the MacHaleites distribute their document to the cardinals that their opponents learned of it only days before

[74] MacHale to Slattery, 14 Sept. 1848, Slattery Papers, CDA; O'Higgins to Maginn, 14 Sept. 1848, J. Monahan, *Records relating to the diocese of Ardagh and Clonmacnoise* (1886), 164.

[75] O'Higgins to Maginn, n.d. [end of June 1848], Monahan, *Records*, 165.

[76] *Quarterly Review*, 88 (1850), 257.

the meeting of Propaganda. Propaganda, unhappy at having the same question referred to them for the third time in three years, wrote on 29 June to each individual bishop to ascertain again his opinion. All but two replied.[77] O'Donnell of Galway suspended judgement and pointed out that the statutes had not the sanction of parliament, a point also made by Egan of Kerry who, however, was in favour of the colleges. Blake of Dromore was not opposed, but expressed a hope for more concessions. In all, fifteen bishops declared against the colleges, nine generally in favour, and one suspended judgement.[78] The two who did not reply were Kennedy of Killaloe and Browne of Kilmore, whose opinions, had they come, would have raised the number of supporters to eleven. The lines of argument followed closely on those put forward by Ennis on the one hand and MacHale and O'Higgins on the other: the minority asserting the good faith of the government and the soundness of the guarantees for the faith of the students, the majority challenging that claim. The minority further asserted that university education was necessary and that the Church was unable to provide it. Moreover, they were convinced that the government would erect the colleges one way or the other and that Catholic students would attend them. In addition to the bishops' views Propaganda sought the advice of two consultors. These consultors were the same two who had advised the Congregation in 1846, Corboli Bussi and Cullen, and they now repeated their advice, Corboli Bussi favouring the colleges, Cullen strongly opposing them.[79] Propaganda met in a general Congregation on 25 September and renewed its decision against the colleges. It took the defensive, but pastoral, view that the students' faith might suffer from 'the grievous and intrinsic dangers' of the colleges, and pointed out that most Irish bishops agreed. In a rescript published on 11 October—the

[77] Propaganda to Irish Bishops, 29 June 1848; *Acta* (1848), vol. 211, fo. 366, PFA.

[78] Pietro Ostini, 'Ristretto con sommario sopra la controversia per nuovi Collegi detta della Regina da attuarsi in Irlanda', Sept. 1848, ibid., fos. 348–410. Ostini was the 'ponente', or reporter, to the meeting, whose task it was to set out the problem in a neutral fashion and present the documentation.

[79] For the 1846 meeting, see Kerr, *Peel*, 346–7. Giovanni Corboli Bussi (1813–50), secretary for the Congregation of the Consistory (1845); pro-secretary for State (1846). Leader of the liberal wing in the *Curia* and a strong Italian nationalist, he worked with Rosmini for a customs union in Italy and, in 1848, conducted an important mission to Charles-Albert, king of Sardinia.

third in the same vein—it advised confirming the ban on the colleges, and again urged the founding of a Catholic university. Nicholson was disappointed and blamed Ennis. Corboli Bussi, too, believed that Ennis, in his zeal, had overstated his case.[80] Well satisfied with their work, MacHale and O'Higgins left Rome on 14 November, the eve of the assassination of Count Rossi, Pius IX's minister of the interior, in the last public coach to leave the troubled city. Challenged on the road to Civitavecchia, they blustered their way past nervous revolutionary guards who feared that Pius might flee the city, which indeed he did on 24 November.

These missions to Rome in the year of revolution had mixed success. The initial hopes of Pius IX and of Wiseman that Minto's mission would strengthen the pope's position proved illusory; Metternich never really approved of Radetzsky's move into Ferrara, and an agreement was reached between Austria and the papal government. In any case, the Austrians had been effectively warned off by Palmerston's note of 11 September 1847, and Minto's mission brought no further benefit to the pope. Minto's effort to bolster the pope against France and Austria and yet to restrain revolution in the Italian states failed. It is more likely that, as Cullen claimed, Minto's presence encouraged the radicals by raising their expectations of reform. In the long term Minto's mission marks the awakening of English interest in, and support for, the Risorgimento. MacHale and Cullen proved more than a match for Ennis, Nicholson, and Minto in dealing with the colleges issue. Nicholson had dallied on the way, Ennis had blundered ahead, and Minto, occupied with his role of adviser to the Italian states, did not understand the situation well enough. Propaganda had given the education question a fair consideration and, in the end, took the safer course of following the opinion of the majority of bishops whose anxieties about the faith of the students it perceived as genuine and whose distrust of government it felt it could not ignore. Roman confidence in the government, moreover, had already been shaken by Eglinton's amendment to the Diplomatic Relations bill forbidding the appointment of an ecclesiastic as papal ambassador. This Eglinton clause nullified the purpose of the Act

---

[80] Nicholson to Grey, 9 Oct. 1848, Earl Grey Papers, Department of Palaeography and Reference, University of Durham; Corboli Bussi to Nicholson, Oct. 1848, ibid.

and laid at rest the fear of Pagani, Briggs, and the Irish bishops that the government, with the help of Rome, were on the point of establishing control over the Irish Church.

How well founded was this fear in 1847? In the past, governments had expected and sought such control through 'securities' such as the veto on the appointment of bishops and, as a result, the bishops were suspicious of similar moves, particularly if an approach were made to Rome. Great changes, however, had taken place over the previous fifty years. Although Russell and Clarendon, and indeed Peel during his administration, would have been glad to obtain what influence they could over the Church, by 1848 they did not expect the control over it that would have been regarded as normal in 1799 or 1808. A change had also occurred within the Church over the same period. The papacy's increased prestige and the renewal of the Church in Europe had an impact on the Irish Church. New leaders—Doyle, O'Connell, and MacHale—had given it strong, independent leadership. Although its faithful were for the most part poor, the national schools were now giving them a basic education. Pastorally the Church had made great strides as the increase in religious orders, missionary endeavours, and the reforming synods of recent decades indicated. This renewed Church would have been far less amenable to state control than in 1799 when the bishops, under pressure from Castlereagh and Cornwallis, agreed to accept the veto. The fears of the bishops in 1848 were excessive but, no doubt, they felt that eternal vigilance was the price they had to pay.

The repercussions of the Mahon murder and the wave of violent denunciations it evoked were damaging enough. British public opinion had always been critical of what it perceived as Irish indolence and dependence on government and, as weariness at the continuous demand for relief set in, that criticism manifested itself from the autumn of 1847 in protests against more expenditure on Ireland. Clarendon had earlier lamented the success of Repeal party candidates as alienating British opinion just when Ireland stood in most need. The assassinations and the sharp reaction by press, peers, and parliament deepened that alienation. It would render Russell's conciliatory efforts more difficult in Parliament and within his own cabinet. In turn, as the bishops' replies to Briggs and their letters to Rome in March and July revealed, the resentment at the accusations and the Roman intrigues, left little ground for hope of a reconciliation between them and the government.

Other events in the momentous year of 1848 were to affect relations between Britain and Ireland. A revolutionary fever swept Europe and Ireland had not remained immune.

5

The Church: Authority and Revolution

'First make your peace with God . . . Secondly—arm quietly!'
(Revd James Birmingham, *Nation*, 15 April 1848)

During the first six months of Russell's administration those clerics who took a part in public affairs had been drawn into a controversy in the Repeal Association on the legitimacy of physical force as a means to attain independence. Because of the nature of the issue involved—the legitimacy of force—many clergy, anxious that their people shun violence and remain within the constitutional bounds set by O'Connell, were actively concerned. The dispute in 1846 was for long a theoretical one but, suddenly, in February 1848, the whole debate on the use of physical force shifted dramatically from the arena of fiery rhetoric, so beloved of the cultural and romantic Young Ireland nationalists of the *Nation*, to become a starkly live issue.[1] The acknowledged head of Young Ireland, since the death of Thomas Davis in 1845, was William Smith O'Brien (1803–64), MP for Limerick, and the group included Charles Gavan Duffy (1816–1903), editor of the *Nation*, and John Blake Dillon (1816–66). The catalyst was the revolution of February in France where, with astonishing ease, the government of Louis-Philippe was toppled. The February revolution had an electrifying effect throughout Europe. Metternich had quipped that 'when France catches cold, Europe sneezes' and this was certainly true in 1848. From Berlin to Milan, and from Paris to Budapest, governments were under threat. Metternich, the anchor of conservative Europe for thirty years, fled for his life. In England, the Chartists grew bolder, but it was in Ireland that the French example could prove most dangerous to the government. As Lewis exclaimed in some dread, 'the sparks blown over Europe by the French Revolution find a train of disaffection towards the

[1] D. Gwynn, *Young Ireland and 1848* (1949), 67–97.

English connection ready laid in Ireland'. O'Connell's agitation had sharpened the political consciousness of many Irishmen and the ravages of the Famine had created widespread disorder. The Young Irelanders, and especially John Mitchel, the most revolutionary-minded of them, might seek to exploit the situation.[2] What would be the attitude of the clergy if sparks from Europe set off an explosion?

Support of properly constituted authority had always been part of Church teaching. In Ireland, since the final defeat of the Stuarts, the Church had tried to come to terms with the problem of existing within a Protestant state. Their difficulty was how to meet the oft-repeated challenge of a dual allegiance for, if they professed loyalty to a foreign power in Rome, how could they claim to be loyal to the British state? On the outbreak of war between England and France in 1756, the archbishop of Armagh and other bishops had told their clergy to pray for the king. The first clear use of Church authority to curb organized violence came during the Whiteboy disturbances, when in 1764 Thomas Troy, the bishop of Ossory, told the people that they ought to be amenable to the laws of the nation. When the French Revolution appeared to threaten Ireland, Troy, then archbishop of Dublin, appealed to the people to beware of 'the French disease' and its fatal fruits. Why should they revolt against 'the best of kings' and bring about the religious and social anarchy that had occurred in France?

The first bishop to appear to depart from this line of response was James Warren Doyle, the very able bishop of Kildare and Leighlin.[3] In a letter to Alexander Robertson, MP, published in the *Morning Chronicle* in May 1824, he declared that 'if a rebellion were raging from Carrickfergus to Cape Clear, no sentence of excommunication would ever be fulminated by a Catholic prelate'. There was a shocked reaction. The Catholic primate, Archbishop Patrick Curtis of Armagh, complained to the duke of Wellington, then a cabinet minister, that Doyle had 'clumsily placed the . . . Catholic bishops and clergy . . . in an odious point of view'

---

[2] O'Reilly to Cullen, 22 Mar. 1848, Cullen Papers, ICA. John Mitchel (1815–75) split from the main Young Ireland group to found his own more outspoken paper, the *United Irishman*, in February 1848.

[3] T. G. McGrath, 'Politics, Interdenominational Relations and Education in the Public Ministry of James Doyle, O.S.A., Bishop of Kildare and Leighlin, 1819–1834' (Ph.D. thesis, 1992), fos. 30–41, is the most complete account of the incident.

and promised to suspend him if he did not atone his error.[4] In Maynooth College Louis Delahogue, an *émigré* French theologian, exclaimed in dismay, 'Mon Dieu, il prêche la révolution!' and organized the professors of theology to issue a public statement. This statement, dubbed 'the Sorbonne manifesto' because the prime movers were Delahogue and another *émigré* French theologian, François Anglade, emphasized the care with which they fulfilled their duty of training future Irish priests as loyal citizens:

In discharging this solemn duty we have been guided by the unchangeable principles of the Catholic religion, plainly and forcibly contained in the . . . precepts of St Peter and St Paul. . . . Our commentaries on these texts cannot be better conveyed than in the language of Tertullian. 'Christians are aware who has conferred their power on the Emperors: they know it is God, after whom they are first in rank. . . . We Christians invoke on all the Emperors, the blessings of long life, a prosperous reign, domestic security, a brave army, a devoted senate, and a moral people'.[5]

In reality, Doyle, far from preaching revolution, was merely denouncing government misrule in dramatic terms.[6] There was, however, a difference between Delahogue's and Anglade's outlook and that of Doyle. Theirs was linked with the *ancien régime* theory of the divine right of kings, while Doyle's was essentially the Whig one of contract between prince and subjects. Doyle made the point that the Irish clergy of the post-revolutionary era 'had imbibed the doctrines of Locke and Paley, more deeply than those of Bellarmine or even Bossuet on the divine right of kings'. One of the Maynooth professors to sign the 'manifesto', under pressure from Delahogue, was John MacHale. His views, however, were not very different from Doyle's and he was sharply critical of the Established Church and general misgovernment. The commissioners inquiring into Maynooth in 1826 had rebuked him for criticizing the Established

---

[4] Curtis to Wellington, 2 June 1824, Wellington (ed.), *Dispatches, correspondence and memoranda of Field Marshal Arthur Wellesley Duke of Wellington* (1886), cited in McGrath, 'Doyle', fo. 37.

[5] W. J. Fitzpatrick, *The Life, Times and Correspondence of the Right Rev. Dr. Doyle, bishop of Kildare and Leighlin* (1861), i. 320–8, 341–5. The text of the Sorbonne manifesto is given in J. Healy, *Maynooth College: Its Centenary History* (1895), 361.

[6] The same letter contained his unprecedented proposal for the union of the Anglican and Catholic Churches.

Church, but he defended himself, claiming that he was only 'using the privileges of a British subject'.[7] His views, and those of the other professors at Maynooth, were regarded as significant because it was there that most Irish priests trained. In 1848, the president, Laurence Renehan, described the Young Irelanders as 'speakers of sedition and seducers of the people to the gallows or a bloody grave.'[8] One of the professors in theology, Edmund O'Reilly, told his friend and mentor, Cullen, in March 1848, that Mitchel's writings were 'downright treason'. Another of the theology professors, Patrick Murray, who had denounced the trials of the Young Irelanders as rigged, used the argument of 'prescription' to prove that the government was the legitimate government. Shortly after the rebellion he examined the Church's teaching on rebellion.[9] Obedience to the legitimate civil power in all things lawful and without respect to the religion professed by that power was, he concluded, the 'defined and solemn teaching of the Church'. Nevertheless, he added, it was the common opinion of many theologians that it was lawful to resist by force, and even to depose, a tyrannical ruler, but only on stringent conditions: the tyranny must be unbearable; it must be manifest to men of good sense and not just revolutionaries; the evils following from submission must be greater than those resulting from rebellion; there must be no other method of getting rid of the tyranny; there must be a moral certainty of success; and the revolution must be conducted or approved by the community at large. His friend and colleague, George Crolly, who was also on the staff in 1848, published a textbook of theology thirty years later in which he gave what he believed was the common Catholic position that rebellion was justified only if the tyranny was general and most oppressive and proportionality existed; only the existence of a most serious reason could justify the evil that a rebellion can bring.[10] Murray and Crolly were right; this was

---

[7] *Eighth report of the Commissioners of Irish Education: Roman Catholic College of Maynooth, PP 1826–7*, xiii. 829–31.

[8] Renehan to Kennedy, 4 June 1848, Renehan Papers, MCA.

[9] P. Murray, 'The Right of Resistance to the Supreme Civil Power: Is It in any Case Allowable?', in id. *Essays Chiefly Theological*, (1852), iv. 379–407. Patrick Murray (1811–82), professor of theology; author of works on systematic theology.

[10] G. Crolly, *Disputationes Theologiae de Justitia et Jure ad Normam Juris Municipalis Britannici et Hibernici Conformatae* (1877), iii. 176–8. George Crolly (1810–78), professor of theology; author of works on moral theology; nephew of Archbishop Crolly.

mainstream Catholic theology. The attitude of the Irish Church, then, did not differ from that of the Church in Europe.

The question of loyalty, moreover, had not arisen in an acute form since Emmet's rebellion in 1803, for, serious though the tithe war in the 1830s had been, it had focused on the single issue of the tithes. During the second quarter of the century some success had been achieved in checking rural violence. On the one hand, the government, better informed through the work of royal commissions and parliamentary committees, had improved its policing and its administration of justice. On the other, the clergy's constant denunciation of violence had received powerful support from O'Connell. His constitutional movement may have been the decisive factor, for, given the endemic nature of peasant violence, only the dominating personality of O'Connell and his apparent invincibility could dissuade the more desperate peasants from resorting to their own rough justice. For the clergy, it was of great importance to be able to channel the rebellious feelings of their parishioners away from secret societies into O'Connell's orderly movement. The banners in Conciliation Hall, the movement's headquarters, proudly proclaimed this principle and denounced those who used violence as bringing disgrace on Ireland. The distinction between threats of violence and violence itself was probably not always clear to the millions who followed O'Connell. At the monster meeting in Mallow in 1843, he appeared to touch the limit when he told his audience that the time was coming when 'you may soon have the alternative to live as slaves or die as free men'. O'Connell never went as far again, and later tried to soften the impression he had made. During this period, the clergy gave almost unanimous support to O'Connell, content to believe that he could achieve repeal in the same peaceful way in which he had achieved emancipation.

The impatience of the Young Irelanders with O'Connell's leadership, distrust of his son, John, and opposition to a Whig alliance, led to serious disagreement within the Repeal movement. By the summer of 1846 O'Connell, exasperated at their continual criticism and anxious to work with the Whigs now back in power, determined to use the violent tones of their speeches and writings to force them into line. At the meeting of the Repeal Association on 13 July, O'Connell proposed to the delegates the report on 'Physical Force'. One section stated that all political amelioration

could be sought successfully only by peaceable, legal, and constitutional means, to the utter exclusion of any other.[11] Mitchel
immediately rejected this as an 'unsound and abstract principle'
and the editor of the *Nation*, Charles Gavan Duffy, took the same
line as Mitchel. John Kenyon, parish priest of Templederry in
County Tipperary, the most outspoken of the clerical supporters
of the Young Irelanders, claimed, in a careful statement, that the
question was an open one. 'Though I conceive', he said, 'the moral
force doctrine to be false and visionary, I admit it is a beautiful
vision . . . but I would never resign my right to the opposite doctrine.'[12] When the meeting resumed on 28 July, one of the young-
est of the Young Irelanders, Thomas Francis Meagher, brilliantly
defended their position in his famous 'sword' speech in which he
described the patriot's sword as a sacred weapon blessed by God.[13]
When an irate John O'Connell interrupted and forced the issue of
the peace resolutions, Smith O'Brien, Gavan Duffy, Mitchel,
Meagher, and other Young Irelanders left Conciliation Hall and
later set up the Irish Confederation. Mitchel, in turn, separated
from them and, in February 1848, set up his own more militant
paper, the *United Irishman*. Among those who left there was one
priest, Charles Patrick Meehan, the democratic and eccentric curate at SS Michael and John's church in Dublin. There now began
an abstract debate between Young Ireland and Old Ireland that
preoccupied the Association for the next six months. Almost without exception the clergy rallied to their old hero, O'Connell, and,
after the meeting, those two staunch O'Connellite bishops,
Cantwell, bishop of Meath, and O'Higgins, bishop of Ardagh,
rushed to his support. Cantwell enunciated the conditions for
clerical support and warned that 'to pursue a course of physical
force would prove fatal to the temporal and eternal welfare of the
flocks committed to our pastoral care'.[14] O'Higgins's comment was
more dismissive: 'we have no physical force men in this diocese.
Neither have we, thank God, any schoolboy philosophers, false
and sanguinary Repealers or Voltairian newspapers.'[15] Other

---

[11] *Nation*, 18 July 1846.

[12] *Limerick Reporter*, 30 July 1846. John Kenyon (1812–69).

[13] Thomas Francis Meagher (1823–67), later successful general in the American Civil War. His fiery speech led Thackeray to dub him 'Meagher of the sword'.

[14] *Tablet*, 8 Aug. 1846.

[15] Ibid.

O'Connellite bishops followed suit. The fiery MacHale distanced himself from any suspicion of physical force.[16] McNally of Clogher, Coen of Clonfert, Foran of Waterford, and Blake of Dromore expressed their support for moral force alone, while Slattery told Cullen that the Young Irelanders were 'latitudinarian in religion and revolutionary in politics', and Maginn of Derry ridiculed the Young Irelanders as 'half crazy, strutting with not less pompous folly than distinguished Smollett's Sir Launcelot Greaves, armed capapie with a rusty sword and a gun'.[17] The general feeling of the clergy expressed at meetings throughout the country was summed up by Fr. Michael Meehan, curate in the parish of Kilrush, County Clare, when, denouncing violence, he extolled 'the [national] spirit, weaned by O'Connell from the midnight folly of rebellion—taught by him the secret of moral power'.[18] The Young Irelanders were branded as dangerous. Lucas, in the *Tablet*, commented: 'The heaviest blow that has lighted on our friends of the *Nation* . . . the heaviest scourge that has been laid upon their backs is the double thong wielded by prelatic fingers and knotted with the censures of God's anointed Bishops'.[19] The *Evening Mail*, the organ of the Orange party, commented sarcastically on the support the bishops rushed to give O'Connell: 'the old tactician moves his bishops, and now the Game will end in checkmate.'[20] *The Times* agreed:

Old Ireland has beaten its young rival. The priests have done it. . . . The people follow their pastors; their pastors are guided by their prelates; the hierarchy are devoted to O'Connell. . . . The grand secret of O'Connell's success must be found in the religious accompaniments of his agitation.[21]

The bishops who came out against the doctrine of physical force were O'Connell's most ardent supporters on the bench and their motive was to rally to his defence. They disliked those young men who had dared challenge their hero and who, they suspected with some reason, were opposed to clerical influence in national politics. Kenyon, however, renewed his claim that the legitimacy of physical force was an open question, quoting the Anglican

[16] *Tablet*.
[17] *Pilot*, 9 Aug. 1846; statements from other bishops appeared on 10, 11, 12 Aug.; Slattery to Cullen, 2 Aug. 1846, Cullen Papers, ICA.
[18] *Nation*, 22 July 1846.   [19] *Tablet*, 8 Aug. 1846.
[20] C. G. Duffy, *Young Ireland: A Fragment of Irish History* (1884), ii. 245.
[21] *Times*, 13 Aug. 1846.

theologian, William Paley, in support of the contract theory of government, and the French Catholic theologian, Bailly, on the legitimacy of a just war.[22] In 1848 Kennedy of Killaloe, one of Murray's supporters on the bishops' bench, raised doubts about the condemnation of the legitimacy of physical force, confiding to Renehan that he was 'one of the vast numbers, who felt indignant against the late Mr O'Connell, for his unjustifiable treatment of the Young Ireland party, for the ostensible ground, that they refused to forswear that principle [of resistance]'.[23] Although Kennedy was temperamental and made this comment after O'Connell's death, he and the other bishops were familiar with theological reasoning justifying rebellion in certain circumstances.

An incident in November of 1846 sheds light on the attitude of both the bishops and the Young Irelanders. The 'physical force' men, aggrieved at what they saw as misrepresentation, drew up a memorial in their defence. Four of them, including Frs. Kenyon and Meehan, came to the bishops' annual meeting in Marlborough Street and presented it to Crolly for submission to the bishops. Gavan Duffy, who was probably one of the delegation, related many years later what happened:

After a delay of half-an-hour, during which the deputation constantly expected a summons, Dr Derry, Bishop of Clonfert, brought back the document unopened. He told them that the Archbishop of Dublin, Dr Murray, was of opinion they ought to be heard in their own defence, and other prelates concurred with him; but the Archbishop of Tuam, Dr MacHale, declared that he would retire on the instant if the Young Irelanders were admitted.[24]

This is a tribute to the fairmindedness of Murray, who although poles apart from the politics of the Young Irelanders, was willing to hear their point of view, whereas MacHale was not. Duffy never forgot the insult, and over thirty years later wrote that 'it may be doubted whether the conduct of the Irish Executive [towards the Catholic bishops] was . . . more unjust or unreasonable

[22] *Nation*, 8 Aug. 1846. Louis Bailly (1730–1808), a Jesuit, published *Theologia dogmatica et moralis* (1789), a standard treatise on moral theology used in most French seminaries, and in Maynooth College. It was rigorist and Gallican and was placed on the Index in 1852 'until corrected'.

[23] Kennedy to Renehan, 8 June 1848, Renehan Papers, MCA.

[24] Duffy, *Young Ireland*, ii. 159.

than the refusal of which the Archbishop of Tuam was the mouth-piece.'[25]

The controversy over assassinations made the clergy more receptive of the startling news from France towards the end of February. The success of this February revolution, the moderate behaviour of the new government, and its liberal measures, caught the imagination of nationalists throughout Europe, and appeared to herald a new dawn for freedom. The republican clubs in France proclaimed their intention of aiding downtrodden nations, and foremost among them they numbered Italy, Poland, and Ireland. At the great rally of 15 May when 50,000 demonstrated in Paris, Daniel Stern noted that 'A crowd of onlookers displayed for one another's inspection the Polish eagle, the harp of Ireland and the Italian tricolor.'[26] In Ireland, Charles Gavan Duffy wrote an editorial in the *Nation*, commencing: 'Ireland's opportunity, thank God and France, has come at last! Its challenge rings in our ears like a call to battle'.[27] To the infectious example of France were quickly added those of nationalists in Germany, Italy, and the Habsburg Empire. Not without reason did it appear to be the 'Springtide of the Peoples'.

What was extraordinary about the revolution in France was the part played by the Church. Clergy and people appeared united in a fervent attempt to create a better world. Jesus Christ was invoked as the liberator, the hope of a new society. In Paris, Archbishop Affre promised the new government loyal support; in Bordeaux, Archbishop Donnet declared that the flag of the Republic would always be a flag of protection for religion; in Lyons, Archbishop de Bonald claimed that now the Church would no longer envy conditions in the United States, and Bishop Parisis of Langres proclaimed that henceforth Christianity would claim for its own those sublime words—Liberty, Equality, Fraternity. Not surprisingly George Sand wrote: 'The Gospel is the religion of the people. This is why we have seen the cross carried in triumph in the New Republic; this is why there was no war against the crosses in the churches as in 1830; this is why the trees of liberty were

---

[25] Duffy, ibid.

[26] D. Stern, *Histoire de la Révolution de 1848* (1985), 518. Daniel Stern, pseud. of Marie de Flavigny, comtesse d'Agoult (1805–76), author of works on history and philosophy.

[27] *Nation*, 4 Mar. 1848.

blessed by holy water.'[28] Daniel Stern, too, noted that during two months the clergy of Paris blessed trees of liberty and commented that the people's cause was that of the priest and that Jesus was the first to give the world the republican formula—Liberty, Equality, Fraternity.[29] During the Restoration period, the clergy, particularly at the close of a parish mission, had torn down the tree of liberty and planted a cross in its place, whereas in the July revolution of 1830 the reverse had taken place. Now both cross and tree of liberty were honoured.

In Italy it was a similar story. Archbishop Romilli of Milan had given 'the five glorious days' revolt his enthusiastic approval in his pastoral of 1 April and in other pronouncements. In Rome, clergy sported the tricolor cockade, an action that only two years earlier would have meant imprisonment. Most significant of all was the apparent sanction of the cause of national independence by Pope Pius IX, who by his amnesty in 1846 and still more by his courageous stand against Austria in July 1847, had shown his sympathy with the Italian nationalists. He was hailed by the *Nation* as 'the Baptist of the new faith of freedom'.[30] Then, on 10 February 1848, he concluded a *Motu Proprio* with the words 'O Great God, bless Italy and preserve for her always this most precious of all gifts, the Faith.' 'God bless Italy' were the only words retained, re-echoing throughout nationalist Italy as his speech was interpreted as a blessing on Italian national aspirations. Pius, like most Italians, wanted the Austrians out of Italy. Within the *Curia*, Corboli Bussi equated the revolt against the Austrians, which had erupted in Milan, with the American revolution, and justified it on the grounds of the necessity of vindicating rights which had been for long trodden under foot. The watching world could not know the debate within the *Curia*, but the departure of the papal army for Lombardy and its entry into the war against Austria was reported with ever-growing excitement. The fervour of those days was intoxicating. In his authoritative life of Pius IX, Giacomo Martina

---

[28] George Sand, *La Vraie République*, 11 May 1848, cited in P. Coulon and P. Brasseur, *Libermann 1802–1852: Une pensée et une mystique missionaires* (1988), 42–3.

[29] Stern, *Révolution*, 274.

[30] Years later the editor of the *Nation*, Gavan Duffy, recounted how Pius IX was regarded as 'the appointed head of the nations striving for freedom'. C. G. Duffy, *Four Years of Irish History* (1883), 540.

writes that 'The ferment in the [Italian] seminaries . . . drove many priests and friars to take a rifle in their hand as if in that way they could reconcile the love of their country and the priestly mission.'[31]

In Ireland, the impact of the European revolutions was electric. Mitchel had been alone in preaching rebellion but now, with the exhilarating news from France, Duffy and the other Young Ireland leaders proclaimed that if self-government were denied 'then up with the barricades'.[32] It is in the context of the heady atmosphere of revolution in Europe and reaction in Ireland that the attitude of the Irish clergy in the spring of 1848 is best understood. Smith O'Brien, impressed by the involvement of the priests in the revolution, returned from the delegation to Paris in April fervently hoping that in Ireland they might play a similar part. There was soon evidence that his wish might be fulfilled. As the significance of events in Paris, Milan, Venice, and Berlin sank in, an increasing number of priests, aggrieved by the distress of the people and smarting at the accusation of promoting assassination, caught some of the spirit of their European colleagues. All at once the easy triumph of the revolution on the continent appeared to bring the goal of independence, which had eluded O'Connell, within reach.

Clarendon noted the new mood with alarm. Early in March he reported to Russell that 'a spirit of disaffection throughout the country among the lower orders is universal' and that the priests promoted it.[33] Some confirmation of his fears was not long in coming. Protests multiplied when the government, on 21 March, issued summonses against O'Brien, Mitchel, and Meagher on charges of seditious speeches and writings, and later arrested Mitchel. At a meeting in Limerick on 3 April, Fr. Michael O'Brien promised that the priest would 'brave any danger to wrest their [his countrymen's] souls and bodies from the debasement, destitution, and destruction of foreign rule'.[34] The following day in Waterford, Fr. Nicholas Coughlan declared that the social contract between people and government was broken:

[31] G. Martina, *Pio IX 1846–1850* (1974), 197–8.
[32] D. Gwynn, *Young Ireland and 1848* (1949), 157–70.
[33] Clarendon to Russell, 9 Mar. 1848, Clarendon Papers, Letterbook 2.
[34] *Nation*, 15 Apr. 1848.

England's treatment of us for the past two years would abundantly prove that there is *practically* no government in this kingdom, and, therefore, in conscience, no allegiance is further due. . . . Again in allegiance there is a contract, and . . . should either party fail to supply the due conditions, then it falls to the ground . . . it is pretty clear that *one* of the contracting parties was found wanting. The unworthy deaths of some 800,000 honest men attest it. . . . And, as to this heavy scourge coming from holy Providence, I believe none of it; I rather believe it comes *from beyond the [Irish] channel* . . .[35]

By 8 April the *Nation* claimed that 'The Irish movement . . . has suddenly changed from a procession to a muster', and the principal reason was that 'The Catholic Clergy are coming into it in large detachments. The priests of Limerick, Clare, and Clonmel are ready if peaceful means are not quickly successful, to bless the banners of the people.'[36] The *Limerick Reporter* asserted that 'one of the signs of the times is, the bold position now being taken by so many of the Catholic clergy . . . they will no longer continue peace-preservers for England to the wholesale famine slaughter of their flocks'. The newspaper reported the passionate cry of a Limerick priest that it was 'far better to die as men died in Berlin, Vienna, and Paris than that another million should die the death of Skibbereen'.[37] The clerical example was catching. Within the next few weeks a score of clergy spoke out publicly in like vein. Among the first were some priests from Kerry, where the Famine had been severe. On 9 April the Revd Mathias McMahon, at a meeting at Causeway, spoke of Ireland 'at last preparing in earnest to get rid of the robber rule of England'. A short time later, Fr. Murray of Molahiffe looked forward to 'the liberation of our country'.[38] Owen O'Sullivan, parish priest of Killorglin, took a far stronger view. At a repeal meeting in Killarney attended by seven priests, he complained that the people were dying in millions and declared:

Louis Philippe was a bad man and therefore a determined people armed and hurled him from the pinnacle of greatness. But, bad though he was, no man in France died of famine. Was that the case under the 'base, bloody, and brutal Whigs'? Seek the answer from the millions of our poor countrymen who are rotting in their graves because of the misrule of

---

[35] Ibid. 4 Apr. 1848. [36] Ibid. 8 Apr. 1848.
[37] Ibid. 15 Apr. 1848. [38] Ibid. 22 Apr. 1848.

England . . . if their constitutional appeal [were] treated with ridicule, he for one . . . was prepared to take his stand with the people.[39]

From neighbouring Tipperary James Birmingham of Borrisakane spoke out vehemently. Birmingham, in an open letter to Meagher, protested his loyalty to the queen and friendship towards the English people and Irish Protestants, but denounced the government and advised the people to vow to lessen by one man at least, the enemies of their native land and to die.[40] These bellicose words were surprising from Birmingham who, in 1841, had bravely resisted the tide of O'Connell's movement and refused to have anything to do with the repeal rent, claiming that he was a man of peace and that the people were too destitute to contribute. In nearby Templederry, on 16 April, Kenyon held a mass meeting in support of Mitchel, Meagher, and Smith O'Brien, declaring that 'every man ought to conquer this government that is lying like a load of lead on the heart of his country . . . or die', and twice elicited a promise from an aroused crowd to die for the arrested men.[41] Waterford clerics also came out strongly. On 21 April Fr. Patrick Byrne, curate at Carrick-on-Suir, County Tipperary, invoking the example of the Milanese insurgents, claimed that the priests were determined to stand by and with the people, and would be found amid the fighting, invoking Heaven's blessing upon it.[42] Although most of these fiery statements came from Munster, they were not confined to that province. A few priests in the west joined in. Michael Curley of Castlebar said that only the application of the principles of justice would prevent 'a conflict between a tyrant government and a people driven to desperation.' James Hughes, parish priest of Claremorris, recalling Paley's thesis that the duty of allegiance is neither unlimited nor unconditional, reminded Russell that 'Pius IX conceives that there may be cases in which the extreme argument of arms is the only one that is just— is the only one that is possible'.[43] In Ulster one of the few clerics to speak out publicly was Bishop Maginn of Derry, who informed George Poulett Scrope, the member for Stroud, that:

For myself, as a Christian Bishop, living as I am amidst scenes that must rend the heart of any having the least feeling of humanity, though attached

---

[39] *Nation*, ibid.   [40] Ibid. 15 Apr. 1848.   [41] Ibid. 22 Apr. 1848.
[42] Ibid. 29 Apr. 1848.   [43] Ibid.

to Our Queen . . . I don't hesitate to say to you that there is no means under heaven that I would not cheerfully resort to to redeem my people from their present misery; and sooner than allow it to continue, like the Archbishop of Milan, I would rather grasp the cross and the green flag of Ireland and rescue my country, or perish with its people.[44]

Duffy related later that after the French revolution Maginn had become impatient for action and that 'one day—so one of his priests assured me—mooted the proposal that he and they should go to a gunsmith's in Derry, and openly buy rifles'.[45]

In private others were expressing similar opinions. Father Laurence Forde told Paul Cullen, his old friend and master, that 'People talk of barricades and street fighting that before would shudder at the thought of it. I have no hesitation in saying that in case of outbreak, the Clergy will be with the people to a man.'[46] Forde went on to express his hope for a peaceful settlement of what he called 'the national Question', but felt that if the government did not yield before too long, 'a conflict of doubtful issue is inevitable'. On 14 April Cooke of Waterford told Tobias Kirby, vice-rector of the Irish College, that, while he prayed that the government 'would give us peace and keep us from the horrors of a civil war', he feared that disaffection was becoming 'very general and very desperate'.[47] The revolutionary stance received support from abroad. Lucas, in the *Tablet*, appeared to accept the legitimacy of resistance and was content to leave 'the question of [the] prudence [of rebellion] . . . to coming events'.[48] The *Nation* now printed Bishop Hughes's fiery lecture of 20 March 1847 in New York where he declared:

In a crisis like that which is now passing, the Irish may submit to die rather than violate the rights of property; but in such a calamity . . . the

---

[44] T. D. McGee, *A Life of Rt Rev Edward Maginn, Coadjutor Bishop of Derry, with Selections from his Correspondence* (1857), 101. On Maginn, see also, J. A. Coulter, 'The Political Theory of Dr Edward Maginn, Bishop of Derry, 1846–9', *Irish Ecclesiastical Record*, 5th ser. xcviii (1962), 104–13.

[45] Duffy, *Four Years of Irish History*, 629–30.

[46] Forde to Cullen, 3 Apr. 1848, Cullen Papers, ICA. Laurence Forde (1820–70), studied at Irish College, Rome (1837–45); one of Cullen's theologians at the Synod of Thurles and later his vicar-general.

[47] Cooke to Kirby, 14 Apr. 1848, Kirby Papers, ICA. Tobias Kirby (1804–95), vice-rector of the Irish College, Rome (1836–50); rector (1850–91); titular archbishop of Ephesus (1885).

[48] *Nation*, 15 Apr. 1848.

Scotch will not submit; the English will not submit; the French will not submit; and depend on it—the Americans will not submit. Let us be careful, then, not to blaspheme Providence by calling this God's famine.[49]

Although this powerful indictment of the government's conduct of famine relief was not intended to incite rebellion, its publication a year on fuelled anti-government anger. These clerical outbursts in April are as surprising as they are significant. A flamboyant style of oratory and a patriotic rhetoric was common at this time, but these speeches went beyond that rhetoric in their intensity and directness and alarmed not merely the lord lieutenant but bishops and fellow priests. Although the priests whose belligerent speeches were recorded constituted no more than a score out of a total of three thousand parish clergy, others were sympathetic with such views. Michael Doheny, one of the Confederate leaders, in his account of the rebellion written shortly after he had escaped to America, claimed that he knew of 'several priests who were fully prepared to take their share in an armed conflict; in fact, the vast majority of those I met at the time'.[50]

The question arises as to why these priests took such a strong line against the government. Although resentment at the accusations made by press and parliament that they were the abettors of assassination was a factor, bitterness at the famine deaths constituted the main element in their complaints. The themes that surfaced again and again in their grievances were 'the millions rotting in their graves', 'Skibbereen', 'wholesale famine slaughter' for which they placed the blame, not on Providence, but on misrule. Whether or not this blame was justified has been the subject of impassioned debate from the Famine to the present day.[51] A further and most

[49] J. Hughes, *A Lecture on the Antecedent Causes of the Irish Famine in 1847 delivered . . . by the Right Rev. John Hughes, D.D., Bishop of New York at the Broadway Tabernacle, March 20th 1847* (1847).

[50] M. Doheny, *The Felon's Track, or History of the Attempted Outbreak in Ireland, embracing the Leading Events in the Irish Struggle from the year 1843 to the close of 1848* (1849), p. xxviii.

[51] J. S. Donnelly, 'The Great Famine: Its Interpreters, Old and New', *History Ireland*, i, no. 3 (1993), 27–33. As early as 1861 John Mitchel, in *The Last Conquest of Ireland (Perhaps)*, accused the government of slaying a million and half of men, women, and children. This stark charge has generally been rejected. More often, remoteness and an unfeeling *laissez-faire* attitude has been attributed to the government, in particular to Trevelyan; Woodham-Smith, *Great Hunger*, 58–61, 139–49, 375–6; J. Hart, 'Sir Charles Trevelyan at the Treasury', *English Historical Review*, 75 (1960), 99; Donnelly, 'Administration of Relief', 296–8; J. M.

emotive complaint arose with the increase in evictions. In 1846 between 3,500 and 3,600 families were evicted. In 1847 the numbers almost doubled to 6,026. In 1848 it rose sharply again to 9,657. If observers could see the Famine as the work of inscrutable providence, it was far more difficult to see the same hand in the work of the landlord's eviction posse levelling cabins. So heartrending were some eviction scenes that Poulett Scrope raised the matter in Parliament, and his revelations and the corroborating evidence produced by Peel provoked shocked reactions.[52] A scandalized Russell wrote to Clarendon that 'the murders of poor cottier tenants are too horrible to bear and if we put down assassins we ought to put down this Lynch law of the Landlords'. When he raised the matter with his cabinet colleagues, however, he failed to get any effective response. Hobhouse relates the cabinet's reaction:

Lord John drew the attention of the Cabinet to the horrible instances of ejectment instanced the evening before in the House of Commons by Poulett Scrope. Clanricarde said he was afraid there was no cure for the evil. If the tenant is not ejected by a certain day he claims the right to stay another year, and if he cannot be persuaded to go by day light, nothing is left but to force him out by night, and so he is forced out in a winter night and dies of cold and starvation by the road side. There was a general shudder amongst us all but I did not hear a remedy suggested.[53]

Hernon, 'A Victorian Cromwell: Sir Charles Trevelyan, the Famine and the Age of Improvement', *Eire-Ireland*, 22/3 (1987), 15–29; Hilton, *The Age of Atonement* (1988), 109–13, 162. Austin Bourke exonerates Trevelyan, the civil servant, and blames Russell, the prime minister; 'Apologia for a Dead Civil Servant', in *Visitation*, 170–7. During the Famine, Archdeacon O'Sullivan, who was greatly involved in organizing relief, visited Trevelyan and showed no distrust of him or of his policies. Because of its central administrative position the Dublin government's views are, however, of weight. Bessborough called Trevelyan 'the guide of Charles Wood' and asked Monteagle's help to 'open his [Wood's] eyes' to the real situation in Ireland; Bessborough to Monteagle, 30 Sept. 1846, Monteagle Papers. Clarendon denounced Trevelyan as Wood's evil genius and complained that they 'sat coolly watching and applauding what they call "the operation of natural causes"'; Clarendon to Lewis, 29 Dec. 1848, Clarendon Papers, c. 532/1. After disputes with Trevelyan, Edward Twistleton, chief commissioner of the poor laws, resigned, claiming that the indifference of parliament was leading to a policy of extermination; Clarendon to Russell, 10, 12 Mar. 1849, ibid., Letterbook 4. Trevelyan was not alone in his severe attitude. In his important study, *Atonement*, Boyd Hilton draws attention to the contemporary religious outlook that viewed the Famine as a providential visitation. Peter Gray's 'British Politics and the Irish Land Question, 1843–1850' (Ph.D. thesis, 1992), is an impressive study of the question.

[52] *Hansard*, xcvii. 1007–9, 24 Mar. 1848.
[53] Diary of Lord Broughton, 25 Mar. 1848, Add. MSS 43752, vol. 9, fos. 2–3.

Some time later Clarendon was shocked by the figures for Kilrush in County Clare. 'It appears', he told Sir George Grey, 'that 4,000 persons have been evicted and 900 houses levelled since November last! The misery has been beyond description but the law has not been violated!' Hoping to avoid bad publicity, he asked Grey to suppress the facts for 'the case is too shocking for publication if it can be avoided'.[54] The suppression of such facts could not hide them from the clergy, who witnessed the evictions and saw their flocks perish. Distressed though Russell was by the evictions, he took no effective action. With such afflicting grievances it is not surprising that many in Ireland found the revolutionary example from Europe tempting. Clarendon noted that disaffection was 'shared and promoted by the Young Priests everywhere and by the old ones in many districts and it is showing itself strongly since the events in France and the People believe that a Revolution made by themselves without trouble, leads to a Government that feeds the whole nation'.[55] The Repeal Association was no longer an adequate outlet for these pent-up grievances. John O'Connell's Repeal bill in April 1848 was rejected. When Russell declared that as long as he had breath he would oppose the repeal of the Union, Clarendon warned him that 'Some bishops and many priests wrote to John O'Connell saying that your speech had put an end to peaceful agitation and they must now look to the national Convention.'[56] Prominent nationalist priests, hitherto pillars of O'Connell's non-violent movement, abandoned it. At a repeal meeting, during which John O'Connell urged moderation, Fr. John Miley echoed the wish for a peaceful solution, and went on to state ominously:

if the same ordeal is in store for us that has been reserved for neighbouring countries, and that a baptism of blood be necessary for the liberties of Ireland, so far as the Catholic clergy are concerned, I am of opinion that their position and their duties will be in no respect different here from those of the Catholic clergy in the newly-emancipated states of the Continent.[57]

This statement from a priest who had been the faithful companion of O'Connell in his last journey across Europe and was

---

[54] Clarendon to Grey, 13 July 1848, Clarendon Papers, Letterbook 3.
[55] Clarendon to Russell, 9 Mar. 1848, ibid. Letterbook 2.
[56] *Hansard*, xcviii, 478, 18 Apr. 1848; Clarendon to Russell, 27 Apr. 1848, Clarendon Papers, Letterbook 2.
[57] *Nation*, 22 Apr. 1848.

identified with constitutional methods indicated a significant shift in attitude.[58] An alarmed John O'Connell appealed for support to Slattery lest the people turn to leaders ready to act 'upon heated and wild impulses', but the archbishop told him that it was useless to expect a united effort from clergy amidst the diversity of feeling.[59] It was clear to Slattery that the great Repeal movement was dying and that, even if he had wished, he could not pump life into it. As Clarendon observed, it was losing out to Mitchel and the Young Irelanders' Confederation. The situation as it had developed left some clergy open to the stimulus of the exciting events in France and Italy, where Catholicism and revolution appeared to go hand in hand. Most of those priests were of the younger generation and came from the same geographical area—a broad belt stretching across the south and west of Ireland, from Kilkenny and Waterford, through Tipperary and Limerick, across to Kerry, and up to Clare and Galway. The northern half of the country saw fewer protests: Connacht had never been to the fore in O'Connell's Repeal movement, and Ulster's strong Protestant population may have forced the clergy, with the exception of Maginn, to be more circumspect in their protests. In Dublin, where the clubs were better organized, there was less need for their leadership and, in any case, Murray kept as tight a rein on them as he could.

The month of May saw no decrease in the political fever. Smith O'Brien and Meagher had been arrested on charges of sedition but the jury disagreed, and their release was hailed as a triumph by the Confederates. In Dublin, the trial provoked scenes of wild excitement, and at the many protest meetings throughout the country the priests were prominent. In Waterford city a soirée was given in honour of the leaders of the Confederation at which a number of priests spoke.[60] Nicholas Coghlan, chaplain to the asylum, reminded his hearers that 'Pius IX, the greatest reformer the world ever produced, tells men, by his heroic acts, that liberty is worth fighting for'. Patrick Kent, curate in Ballybricken parish, referred to the thousands of coffinless dead, the victims of starvation, and told his audience that, 'in the whispered words of the great bishop of Derry, tyranny is not government, and that allegiance is due

---

[58] John Miley (1785–1861), rector of Irish College, Paris (1849).
[59] O'Connell to Slattery, 31 May 1848, Slattery Papers, CDA; Slattery to O'Connell, 1, 16 June 1848, ibid.
[60] *Nation*, 13 May 1848.

only to protection'. In Limerick Fr. Michael O'Brien, after coun-
selling patience, proclaimed that 'if Irishmen have no protection
on this earth but their own right arms, then I will be prepared to
cry with Mr Meagher, "Up with the barricades, and invoke the
God of battles" '.[61] Father James Hampston of Kenmare advised
the people to get arms and pikes for there was no law against it.[62]
Father Byrne, from Carrick-on-Suir, sought justification in St
Bernard and Innocent III, claiming that 'to feed the starving Irish—
to rescue them from a roadside death—to free them from a
yoke . . . as galling as that of the Saracen' was as religious a cause
as the Crusades.[63]

If some bishops allowed their clergy free rein to express their
support for the Confederation, others made every effort to bridle
them. Murray, despite his years, was foremost. Propaganda's letter
of 3 January gave him to understand that at last Rome was ready
to discourage political clerics. In February he brought pressure to
bear on Maynooth's president:

Observations have lately reached me . . . expressing surprise and regret,
that the President of the Royal College of Maynooth was not among
those who, on a recent occasion, thought it right to testify their respect
for Her Majesty, by appearing at the Levee of Her Representative. . . . It
was said, that when it was remarked to you, that your absence . . . had
been unfavourably noticed, you replied, that you would not, if you attended the Levee, be able to govern the College. This, if it had a shadow
of truth in it, would be a sad tale for Maynooth.[64]

This questioning of his loyalty and the implied reflection on the
spirit prevailing in his college startled Renehan, who denied the
statement attributed to him, giving as his reason for his absence
the fact that neither he nor his predecessor, 'so distinguished for
intense veneration to even the most Tory Government', had ever
attended the levee. With a touch of malice, Renehan added that:

should your Grace and the Trustees advise me to the contrary and author-
ize me, notwithstanding the resolution passed by the last summer Board,
to join what some may consider a manifestation not of loyalty or respect

---

[61] *Nation*, 3 June 1848.
[62] Report of Edward Ledger, sub-inspector of police, to Inspector General,
Clarendon Papers, Box 24/2. James Hampston was a priest who had been suspended by his bishop.
[63] *Nation*, 13 July 1848.
[64] Murray to Renehan, 18 Feb. 1848, Renehan Papers, MCA.

only, but to some extent also of politics, I shall feel a pride and pleasure in following whatever course your Lordships may recommend as most becoming the President of a ... purely ecclesiastical college, and most expressive of loyalty to the Queen and to the Irish Viceroy.[65]

Renehan had neatly countered Murray's move, for he knew well that Murray would not dare raise the question of attendance at the Castle with the trustees, who included MacHale and Slattery, both of whom regarded Murray as a government bishop. Moreover Renehan was in constant communication with Slattery, who was his bishop. Checked in Maynooth, Murray next turned his attention to his own clergy. He called a meeting of the Dublin priests, and warned them that he would insist on the pope's mandate on clerical politics being obeyed. 'No dissentient voice and only one *murmur* ... raised against it'.[66] When Peter Cooper, a curate in Murray's own parish, attacked the government for its 'machinations for her [the Church's] enslavement', Murray brought him before his council, accused him of exciting the people, and forbade him from appearing in the pulpit again. Cooper's answer was that if the pulpit were closed to him the press was open, and to the press he was resolved to go; at the same time he wrote for support to Slattery. The cautious Slattery did not come out openly in his favour but complained to Cullen of Murray's tactics.[67]

With the upsurge of support for revolutionary ideas in the aftermath of the continental rebellions, Murray became more alarmed. To Cullen he explained his concern at the threatening situation:

What I always dreaded has occurred. A section of the Repealers are arming themselves openly, and proclaiming their intention of availing themselves of the first favourable moment to come into hostile collision with the Authorities of the State, except the Repeal of the Union be at once granted. Government is making corresponding preparations to meet the threat; and God grant, that our Island which has lately opened its bosom so frequently to give an untimely grave to its perishing children, may not soon, through the rashness of its fiery Patriots, have to endure a still more grievous calamity in the horrors of Civil War. Our angry politics and particularly the sums of money sent by Priests from the most distressed districts of the country to Conciliation Hall have done much to

---

[65] Renehan to Murray, 19 Feb. 1848, ibid.
[66] Clarendon to Shrewsbury, 24 Feb. 1848, Clarendon Papers, Box 43.
[67] Slattery to Cullen, 21 Mar. 1848, Cullen Papers, ICA.

impede the current of charity which was coming from England to our relief.[68]

Murray was hoping to win over or to neutralize the influential and well-placed rector of the Irish College, whom he knew was supporting MacHale and his party. In his concern over the drying-up of aid from England he was expressing the deep-felt irritation of English people, who could not understand why the Irish response to their generous alms was a threat of violence and rebellion. In Dublin, however, he was removed from the distress and desperation of the west and south. Murray now determined to take the unusual step of appealing publicly to his faithful and, in a moving letter to the press, recalled his experience during the rebellion of 1798:

Fifty years ago I witnessed the miseries which a convulsion—such a scene like this might give birth to—inflicted on the political, social and moral condition of this unhappy country. Can anyone be surprised that a thrill of horror should rush through my soul at the thought of the recurrence of such a calamity? May God in his mercy avert it![69]

Murray did not believe a rebellion justified, but theoretical arguments concerned him less than the real horrors of civil war. In this he had been consistent in his stance since emancipation in 1829. In 1831 he had prohibited clerics from engaging in politics and refused publicly to be counted as a Repealer.[70] When the Clontarf meeting was proclaimed in 1843, he had complained to his confidant and helper, Archdeacon Hamilton, that he 'trembled to think on the effects of a struggle . . . but for the prudence of our poor people . . . the shores of Clontarf would be again steeped in torrents of blood' and expressed his astonishment at 'those ministers of the religion of peace who had lent the influence of their sacred character to prepare the way for such a catastrophe'. Now, he feared, that catastrophe was at hand.[71]

Bishop Kennedy of Killaloe was also active. His first encounter was with Anthony Nolan, the parish priest of Monsea. Nolan, a priest of 60 years of age, had taken a strong line against secret societies and faction fighting, but had denounced offenders from

[68] Murray to Cullen, 8 Apr. 1848, copy, Murray Papers, DDA.
[69] *Tablet*, 12 Apr. 1848.   [70] Ibid.
[71] Murray to Hamilton, 13 Oct. 1843, Hamilton Papers, P1/35/0, DDA. The reference is to the battle of Clontarf in 1014.

the altar, an abuse that bishops attempted to eradicate. On 6 January 1848, returning after illness to his chapel in Puckane, County Tipperary, Nolan found twenty-one ejectment processes nailed to the chapel door. Enraged, he denounced, during mass, the police constable responsible, expressing his surprise that the women and children did not hunt him into his barracks. Clarendon complained to Kennedy and the bishop suspended Nolan for three months.[72] Emboldened by his success in bringing Nolan to heel, Kennedy now required Birmingham to withdraw his support from the Young Irelanders and, after an unedifying public exchange of letters, Birmingham agreed. Kennedy next turned his attention to Kenyon. Kenyon was the most prominent whole-hearted priest supporter of the Young Irelanders. He had supported Mitchel in his revolutionary statements, and when, after Mitchel's transportation to Bermuda in 1848, the now reunited Young Ireland party decided to elect a new executive council, Kenyon with Meagher headed the poll, receiving more votes than Smith O'Brien, Duffy, Dillon, or Doheny. Bishop Kennedy first warned him to break his connection with Mitchel's republican paper, the *United Irishman*. Although Kenyon appeared to accept, a few weeks later he made his violent speech at Templederry, and Kennedy threatened to suspend him unless he withdrew forthwith from active involvement with all Young Ireland activities. Kennedy's harshness made him unpopular with his clergy and some of them complained to Rome. Propaganda asked Slattery, Kennedy's metropolitan, to investigate, but the archbishop, who had also been approached by Kenyon, explained that it was not his custom to interfere in neighbouring dioceses, merely advising Propaganda to counsel peace to the bishop. Privately, as he revealed to Cullen, he was highly critical of Kennedy's actions. The Congregation cautioned Kennedy on his over-frequent use of suspension.[73] Aware of his unpopularity, Kennedy wrote to Renehan at Maynooth, defending his condemnation of the rebellious priests. Since Kenyon had offered redress, Renehan cautiously suggested that it was up to Kennedy 'to decide whether it may not be better for religion, for the credit of the priesthood, for the peace of the Church, and still more for

---

[72] I. Murphy, *The Diocese of Killaloe 1800–1850* (1992), 187–90.
[73] Cullen to Slattery, 4 July 1848, Fransoni to Slattery, 8 July 1848, Slattery to Fransoni, 4 Aug. 1848, Slattery Papers, CDA. Murphy, *Killaloe*, 377–8.

the public peace of the country to accept such reparation'. Kennedy, although wary of Kenyon's evasive language, decided to reinstate him. In less than a week Kenyon declared publicly that he had not retired from political strife, and believed 'that no honest Irishman, who is master of his own actions, ought to retire from it till his country is delivered from . . . her subjection to a cruel and greedy government of foreigners'. Whether this was a further quibble on words or not, the correspondence between them was to prove important some months later.

Kennedy now sought Renehan's opinion on the political debate of the day. What, he asked, was his opinion 'as to the duty of obedience to our Rulers in the present circumstances of our unfortunate country?'[74] Renehan answered with considerable circumspection. The constitution of these realms, he admitted, supposed that in certain cases resistance to the civil authorities was lawful and even a duty. The present case turned on the question of the validity or invalidity of the Act of Union. Whatever the theoretical rights of the argument for resistance, however, it was highly dangerous 'when publicly propounded to inflammable mobs who cannot understand the nice distinctions of the orator . . .'. The bishop was right in censuring their actions, not as errors, but 'as foolish, imprudent, unpriestly and scandalous incentives to or, at least, occasions of crime'. Their rhetoric, he concluded, could lead to a rebellion and seduce the people to the 'gallows or a bloody grave'.[75] Kennedy, who had been advised by another theologian of the legitimacy of resistance given certain conditions, agreed that 'to the abstract principle, no British Government could object, England herself having successfully acted on it on more than one occasion'. What he objected to was priests urging the immediate, and therefore violent, rejection of British rule.[76] Civil war would be the result, he concluded, and few were willing to face that 'except that unhappy class who are so steeped in misery, as to be easily persuaded that no change could be for the worse for themselves'. In demanding that Kenyon and Birmingham withdraw from Young Ireland, Kennedy was able to take his stand on the two recent directives from Rome, both of which discouraged clerical involvement in politics.

[74] Kennedy to Renehan, 2 June 1848, Renehan Papers, MCA.
[75] Renehan to Kennedy, 4 June 1848, Renehan Papers, MCA.
[76] Kennedy to Renehan, 8 June 1848, Renehan Papers, MCA.

This short debate on the morality of physical force is interesting in both what it omits and what it asserts. Fifty years before, Archbishop Troy had condemned the United Irishmen on the ground that they were a secret society, and that the change they wanted to bring about in Irish society was to be on the model of infidel revolutionary France. The charge of being a secret society could not be levelled against the Young Irelanders, nor did the revolutions of the spring of 1848 appear as anti-religious as that of 1789. O'Connell's agitation against the Union had left its mark, for Renehan saw it as the fundamental question on which the argument turned. If the Union were illegal, as O'Connell had maintained, then both he and Kennedy would find force theoretically justifiable. Kennedy's attitude, like Renehan's, was not dissimilar to the Whig view of rebellion. Both were less concerned, however, with the abstract theory than with the possible practical effect—civil war. Neither of them believed that rebellion had a chance of succeeding, and were anxious to steer people away from it. They were also emphatic in condemning the involvement of clergy in fomenting unrest; it was unworthy of their calling and contrary to recent papal exhortations.

Events moved fast. On 27 May, after trial before a packed jury, Mitchel was convicted of treason and immediately put aboard a ship for Bermuda. This action by a determined government incensed all varieties of nationalists. It also led to widespread sympathy from the Chartists in England and a closer understanding between them and the Irish Confederates and Repealers. A spate of protest demonstrations followed in both countries. Irish nationalists of all hues attempted to form a common front, and on 12 June the Repeal Association and the Irish Confederation agreed to unite as the Irish League. In bringing about this united effort, the clergy were to the fore. Miley, with the lawyer Colman O'Loghlen, drew up the principles of the League and up to two hundred priests wrote to the *Nation* to support it.[77] A few insisted on the O'Connellite principle of moral force alone; others were more ambivalent, but demanded a more vigorous approach to the government on Irish grievances. Many added their execration of the treatment of 'the brave and the patriotic John Mitchel', who only

---

[77] Sir Colman O'Loghlen (1819–77), later judge-advocate-general in Gladstone's ministry (1868).

a few months earlier had merited clerical condemnation for advocating violence. At least four bishops also lent their support to the new League, denouncing the mismanagement of famine relief and warning of the consequences if concessions were delayed. Thus Cantwell of Meath and his clergy declared that 'The priest will preach obligation in vain while the political economists of the government criminally sacrifice the lives of the people.' Foran of Waterford and his clergy claimed that all Irish people wanted was 'that which every other people in Europe are now possessing or recovering—the means of living on their native soil, and the power of legislating for their own benefit'. Maginn was more outspoken and, in a fearful description of the havoc wrought by the Famine, denounced the government as solely concerned with the maintenance of law and order and indifferent to the ruin and death of the people:

our merchants bankrupt, our farmers . . . beggars, the bravest of our country rotting in heaps on the shores of the stranger and the remainder . . . gaunt spectres flitting over . . . the loveliest land on earth . . . at every elbow a spy or informer . . . tens of thousands of military or police ingloriously watching the convulsions and writhings of the starving victims of misrule, lest, in their agony, the slightest symptom of disaffection should pass unnoticed or unpunished.[78]

Despite the clamour of the nationalist priests, it would be a mistake to believe that all the clergy were as committed to the new League as they had been to O'Connell's Repeal movement. If two hundred priests expressed their support, that did not mean that they wanted revolution, and more moderate voices were raised. Murray was attempting to rein in his clergy and used the retreat he organized in June for his priests at Maynooth College to bring home to them the gravity of the situation. On 28 June, when the bishops were in the college, he took a major initiative. He and like-minded bishops met, and republished the decrees of the episcopal meeting of 1834.[79] These decrees, based on Murray's own decrees of 1831, had requested all priests 'to avoid . . . any allusion at their Altars to political subjects, and carefully to refrain from connecting themselves with political clubs'. Murray's move caused a furore among the other bishops, who complained that they had not been consulted even though some of them were

[78] *Nation*, 24 June 1848.   [79] Ibid. 8 July 1848.

present in the college. MacHale and O'Higgins were in Rome, but Slattery, Cantwell, Derry, and Browne of Elphin publicly dissociated themselves from it, Browne pointing out that no such resolution was proposed to the bishops' meeting, much less adopted.[80] Father Byrne of Carrick-on-Suir contrasted the actions of Murray and Crolly with that of an earlier archbishop of Dublin: 'the great Lawrence O'Toole encouraged . . . King Roderick and other Irish princes to unite for the total expulsion of the English marauders. . . . Would to heaven his successors in Armagh and Dublin had imitated his example.'[81] Sharper criticism came from the able pen of a Dublin priest, Thaddeus O'Malley, who questioned both the competence of Murray and his associates and the binding value of the resolution. He asked 'whether it is in the competence of a few of the prelacy to impart a new life . . . to a resolve which emanated from the entire body under circumstances very different from the present, and which, from never having been acted upon by your lordships, may fairly be deemed to have become obsolete'. It was difficult to refute O'Malley on this point since the 1834 resolutions had been broken almost as soon as they had been issued, Murray being one of the few bishops who tried to enforce them. O'Malley further challenged the bishops with the example of the Catholic Church elsewhere:

The great and striking moral phenomenon of our day is the almost simultaneous resurrection throughout all Europe of oppressed nationalities. . . . The Catholic Church in other lands has given to the holy cause of national freedom its heroes or its martyrs, each confronting danger differently in different circumstances—the Lombard bishop braving death as a soldier because the battle was to be won—the Frank braving death as a pacificator, because the battle was won. With such examples, with the still higher example of our noble Chief Pontiff, who has preserved the Catholic religion in Italy by making himself the head apostle of Italian freedom, is it for you, my Lords, to shrink from a struggle the most righteous of all?[82]

O'Malley was a highly talented and independent-minded, if controversial, figure. Some of his fellow clergy had suspected him of connivance with the government which had appointed him rector of the university of Malta, despite ecclesiastical disapproval. His intervention showed that a battle was taking place for the minds

---

[80] Ibid. 15 July 1848.   [81] Ibid. 13 July 1848.   [82] Ibid. 15 July 1848.

and hearts of the clergy. It was the hour of 'oppressed nationalities' throughout Europe and the question O'Malley raised was whether the Irish clergy should stand aloof when the cardinal archbishops of Milan and Paris and, above all, the pope, had supported their own countrymen's strivings for freedom.

Murray had again been challenged, this time in his attempt to present his stand as the official attitude of the hierarchy, but he battled on. The involvement of the clergy in the Young Irelanders' Confederate clubs, which had spread throughout the capital and the country, became his main concern in July. Father Meehan was the first president of one of the Dublin clubs. Murray now formally requested his parish priests to inform him if any of their priests were involved in the Irish clubs. There were forty-seven parishes, but only seven replies have survived, and none of them reported involvement in the clubs or the procuring of arms. Two vicars forane—John Grant of Wicklow and Alexander Roache of Bray—revealed, however, that some of their priests refused to stop their people forming clubs and others had 'eccentric' views on politics.[83]

It was developments on the continent, however, that again made most impact on the attitude of the clergy. The euphoria of the spring had given place to dissension. Conscious of his role as father of all Catholics, and dismayed at the rumblings of a possible schism, Pius IX, in his Allocutio of 29 April, declared himself unwilling to wage war against Austria. He appealed to the Austrian emperor to withdraw from Lombardy and Venetia, 'confident that the German nation itself, being honestly proud of its own nationality, will not engage its honour in an attempt to shed the blood of this Italian nation'. This appeal, which shows some confusion in Pius' own attitude, did not prevent the disillusion of Italian nationalists, who believed that he was abandoning their national aspiration of Italy for the Italians. His popularity declined overnight, and the new prime minister, Terenzio Mamiami, sharply defined the pope's function as to pray, bless, and pardon. The papal soldiers, defeated at Cornuda and Vicenza, returned to

<hr>

[83] Michael Dungan to Murray, 24 July 1848, Murray Papers, DDA; John Grant to Murray, 2, 5 July 1848, ibid.; Alexander Roache to Murray, 5 July 1848, ibid.; Eugene Clarke to Murray, 29 July 1848, ibid.; John Gowan to Murray, 29 July 1848, ibid. It is probable that Murray did not write to the nine parishes in the city of Dublin.

Rome and blamed Pius. By the end of June the situation in Rome was getting out of hand.

Events in France were adroitly used by Clarendon to influence public opinion. Secretly, he had begun to subsidize the *World*, a shady journal run by William Birch, who had been imprisoned for libel.[84] After the April elections in France Clarendon's private secretary, Corry Connellan, who acted for him, impressed on Birch the importance of using the news against the Young Irelanders:

> The French news ought to turn to account . . . the defeat of Ledru Rollin and the vigorous proceedings of the Provisional Government in making arrests. I presume that tomorrow's mail will bring us an account of the capture of Blanqui and Cabet, the great Communist leader. The *morale* of that might be applied to Mitchel and Co.

When the workers' revolution broke out, the archbishop of Paris, Denys-Auguste Affre, was shot at the barricades on 25 June while attempting to mediate.[85] Monsignor Parisis tried to explain to the National Assembly that the shooting was not the fault of the rioters, but he was shouted down with cries of 'assez, assez' by furious conservatives, and the press portrayed it as murder by the revolutionaries.[86] The death of Affre, who had organized aid for victims of the Irish Famine and had been supportive of the February revolution, was a shock to many in Ireland, and John O'Connell wrote to the Paris clergy to express his sympathies.[87] To Clarendon the shooting was a godsend; gleefully he wrote to the duke of Bedford that 'the priests have taken alarm at the death of the Archbishop of Paris who, poor man, never did a better thing in his life than getting himself murdered'.[88] The clergy, he told the home secretary, Sir George Grey, have 'a deadly fear of the clubs induced by the recent events at Paris and the salutary murder of the Archbishop'.[89] Clarendon played on this fear with considerable adroitness. He maintained regular contact with Delane, editor of *The Times*.[90] In Ireland he succeeded in persuading or

---

[84] K. B. Nowlan, *The Politics of Repeal: A Study in the Relations between Great Britain and Ireland, 1841–50* (1965), 195.

[85] R. Limouzin and J. Leflon, *Mgr Denys-Auguste Affre, archevêque de Paris, 1793–1848* (1971), 339–61.

[86] Ibid. 350. *Le Correspondant*, 25 June, 2 July 1848.

[87] Limouzin and Leflon, *Affre*, 359–60.

[88] Clarendon to Bedford, 8 July 1848, Clarendon Papers, c. 80.

[89] Clarendon to G. Grey, 8 July 1848, ibid., Letterbook 2.

[90] Clarendon to Reeve, 21 Aug. 1848, ibid., c. 534.

paying editors and journalists to do the same. He was successful in influencing the *Dublin Evening Post*, a leading liberal paper and an O'Connellite organ, which now supported the government's policy. One of Clarendon's ablest collaborators was Dr William Cooke Taylor, a biographer and historian, whom Russell agreed to pay £500 a year.[91] 'What is more use than anything', he told Grey, 'is Dr Cooke Taylor's articles in the *Dublin Evening Post* connecting the Clubs with infidelity and *proving* that every Irish priest must expect the fate of the Archbishop of Paris. . . . The clergy are getting really frightened not for the State but for themselves . . .'.[92] In a self-congratulatory tone he confided to Lansdowne:

I caused the tide of sacerdotal influence to turn against the Clubs. At first it was inclined towards them but during the last five weeks Cooke Taylor and I have kept up such an uninterrupted fire of anti infidel articles founded upon the experience of all French revolutions, that their Reverences have struck their flags and have since been coming over in flocks.[93]

The editor of the *Nation*, Gavan Duffy, complained bitterly of this successful war of propaganda, and O'Malley attempted to counter Clarendon's effective press campaign by underlining the difference between Ireland and France. He appealed to the bishops not to lend any countenance to the hireling organs of the government, denouncing the members of these clubs as Jacobins, Socialists, and Communists.[94] Later, Patrick Murray, a Maynooth theologian who had been hostile to the Young Irelanders, complained of the skilful presentation of events in France to turn people against the Confederation and of the misinformation propagated by the *Post*:

Three times a week these foul and fetid jaws were opened to vomit forth such abominable slanders as modest men could sometimes hardly read without a blush and timid men without a shudder . . . if a convent were sacked in one place and its inmates violated; if a church were desecrated in another place . . . if anywhere some blasphemy uttered or some theory of organised plunder advanced—if there occurred an anti-social commotion

---

[91] Clarendon to Russell, 16 Apr. 1848, ibid. Letterbook 2. William Cooke Taylor (1800–49) had written on history and translated Beaumont's *L'Irlande sociale, politique et religieuse*. Cooke Taylor had earlier been a paid writer for the Anti-Corn Law League and wrote a highly effective piece of propaganda: *Notes of a Tour in the Manufacturing Districts* (1842).
[92] Clarendon to G. Grey, 5 July 1848, Clarendon Papers, Letterbook 3.
[93] Clarendon to Lansdowne, 16 July 1848, ibid.   [94] *Nation*, 15 July 1848

among the canaille of the faubourgs . . . straightaway the Young Irelanders were blamed.[95]

Undoubtedly, Clarendon's press campaign and events on the continent produced an effect. By early July many clergy had become wary of the rhetoric from the clubs, which were in some disarray.[96] Clarendon's satisfaction changed to alarm when he learned that the laity were not tamely following their priests, as he hastened to tell George Grey:

The priests . . . are now like Frankenstein. They recoil at the monster of their own creation. They are daily becoming more powerless before that monster and they must go with the stream or perish. They are perfectly aware of the danger of the clubs, that they lead to civil war and anarchy, and above all to infidelity and the loss of their influence (which is their existence) . . . and they have consequently . . . denounced them. It has been useless. The people are rushing in their thousands to the clubs.[97]

Although there was some truth in this claim, it was exaggerated. Since the beginning of the year Clarendon had been predicting a rebellion and, on St Patrick's Day, placed the armed forces, the Trinity College students, and the Bank of Ireland officials on full alert. His constant forebodings annoyed and amused the cabinet, and Russell opened his every communication with trepidation. The gossip in the London clubs had it that his 'womanish alarms' would cause him to be replaced by Hardinge. Still, as July wore on, the signs in Dublin, including reports from secret agents, were disquieting and Clarendon decided to act. He first took the precaution of packing his children off to the safety of England.[98] His immediate target was the newspapers. He had already suppressed Mitchel's paper, the *United Irishman*, and now he suppressed the *Irish Tribune* and the *Irish Felon*, organs of the more revolutionary party, and arrested leaders including Meagher and Duffy, the proprietor of the *Nation* whose offices were raided. On 21 July he proclaimed the city and county of Dublin under the 1847 Coercion Act. A bill suspending habeas corpus was rushed through parliament and became law on 25 July. The moves were successful,

---

[95] Duffy, *Four Years of Irish History*, 745.
[96] R. Davis, *The Young Ireland Movement* (1987), 156–68.
[97] Clarendon to George Grey, 19 July 1848, Clarendon Papers, Letterbook 2.
[98] Clarendon to Bedford, 26 July 1848, ibid., c. 80.

and the remaining Young Ireland leaders scattered towards the south where Smith O'Brien had already gone to prepare for a rising. It was there, far away from the influences of the Castle, that the decisive confrontation between government and Young Ireland would be fought out. There, too, the influence of the priests was to be of great moment. Would they side with the Confederates? Clarendon's great fear was that events had now moved beyond their control. Willy-nilly, they might be sucked into the vortex:

They might give a great impulse to the movement by joining it, they can do little or nothing to check it and if things were to continue in their present state for another week there is hardly a priest throughout the whole south of Ireland who would not feel his life as well as his means of existence depended upon his joining the Rebellion. This is a hard fate for men many of whom are well disposed, but it is the result of the voluntary system . . . and of the agitation which they themselves have done.[99]

At the end of July the rebel leaders decided to take the field, choosing the counties of Kilkenny, Tipperary, Limerick, and Waterford as the most promising ground to raise the standard of rebellion. The first effort was at Carrick-on-Suir. To their disappointment the clergy, some of whom, like Byrne and Nolan, had written in fiery language of a holy rebellion, gave no support and some openly denounced the whole idea. Popular reaction appeared to bear out some of Clarendon's fears, for the police reported that 'When the priest implored his flock not to join the Club nor to go to Doheny's meeting, a man rose in the chapel, abused him furiously and called him an enemy of his country and the congregation applauded and went to the meeting.'[100] Smith O'Brien then led his force to Mullinahone in County Tipperary. Here, too, they encountered clerical opposition. The account Doheny gives is astounding. 'O'Brien addressed the people. . . . The two clergymen, Rev Mr Corcoran and Rev Mr Cahill, appeared by his side, and openly resisted his advice. They warned the rebels of the terrible consequences . . . unless they speedily abandoned their folly and returned home. At their clergy's advice more than half of the three

---

[99] Clarendon to Russell, 25 July 1848, ibid., Letterbook 2.
[100] Michael Doheny (1805–63), barrister, prominent Young Irelander, and later co-founder of the Fenians; author of *The Felon's Track* (1849).

thousand rebel army melted away.'[101] How a real revolutionary could allow this to happen is difficult to understand.

Much depended now on whether other parts of the south would rise. Anxiously, the rebel leaders awaited the arrival of Kenyon to their aid or news of his diversionary move in west Tipperary on the Limerick border. When no news came they finally contacted him in his parish house in Templederry, imploring him to begin a diversionary tactic at once. To their amazement, he told them that he could not think of acting on that suggestion; it was not becoming of a priest, he told them, to begin a bootless struggle! Smith O'Brien now marched towards Ballingarry, a few miles from Mullinahone, and a skirmish with the constabulary took place. The police barricaded themselves in Widow McCormack's farmhouse, shot dead two of the peasants, and wounded several more. Just then two local curates, Philip Fitzgerald and Patrick Meagher, rode up. Fitzgerald recounted what transpired:

Mr O'Brien asked what I would advise them to do, and said he would act as I would recommend. . . . I was never more perplexed. I saw that if they returned to the house, the police would very probably be all killed . . . and as a consequence, that martial law would be proclaimed throughout the district and the atrocities of '98 again renewed.[102]

Having negotiated in vain with the police inspector, Fitzgerald advised Smith O'Brien to postpone hostilities to another time. Shortly afterwards, on the arrival of police reinforcements, the rebels dispersed. This was the pathetic end of the Young Ireland 'rebellion', which Mitchel described as 'a poor extemporised abortion of a rising'.[103] In a minor incident in west Limerick, the people of Abbeyfeale took the warrant for the arrest of Richard O'Gorman, one of the Young Ireland leaders, from the policeman and 'would have killed him but for the intervention of the priest'.[104] Not a single priest took part in the rebellion except Fr. Edmund Prendergast, parish priest of Ballingarry, who was senile and who cheerfully marched off at the head of the rebel army and returned to fraternize as happily with the soldiers a few days later. The only

---

[101] Doheny, *Felon's Track*, 170.

[102] P. Fitzgerald, *Personal Recollections of the Insurrection at Ballingary in July 1848* (1861), 28–9.

[103] J. Mitchel, *Jail Journal* (1854; repr. 1921), 72; entry for 24 Oct. 1848.

[104] Clarendon to Russell, 6 Aug. 1848, Clarendon Papers, Letterbook 3.

real help the Young Irelanders got from the clergy was after the
rebellion. Maginn provided clerical attire to smuggle Thomas
D'Arcy McGee out of the country. Father Patrick Meehan, who
had publicly strongly opposed the Young Ireland doctrine of
physical force, sheltered O'Gorman, and rowed him out to a waiting
ship that took him to America.[105] Archdeacon O'Sullivan related
how Doheny escaped:

my worthy curates had no small share in getting him out of the country.
The Tuosist curate [Michael O'Leary] gave him a suit of clothes which he
did not put on until he arrived in Bristol to which place he got from Cork
in the garb of a peasant taking cattle over. In Bristol he became priest
with Father O'Leary's clothes on him and a breviary under his arm and
thus escaped to America, first I believe to France.[106]

In Tipperary the parish priest of Clonoulty, John Mackey, and
his curate, Michael O'Carroll, took pity on Meagher and his companions, who were suffering from exposure, and brought them
food. Meagher at first refused to shelter in the priests' house, but
at the insistence of Miss Mackey, the parish priest's sister, finally
agreed. The priests persuaded them that they had no chance of
escaping and went to Dublin to plead with Redington and Clarendon on their behalf.

The bishops and clergy presented a petition to the lord lieutenant asking for clemency for the rebels generally. An irate Clarendon,
believing that the clergy were only seeking to restore their lost
popularity with their people, insisted that it should be turned
down out of hand. While there was truth in his claim, Clarendon
did not reckon with the ambivalence towards rebellion among
even moderate nationalists who, while opposed to violence, could
still feel some sympathy for the defeated rebels. Even the very
loyal Archdeacon O'Sullivan apparently accepted without difficulty the involvement of his two curates in smuggling Doheny to
America. Father Fitzgerald, who had played a key role in containing the rebellion by his advice to Smith O'Brien at Ballingarry,
was opposed to the Young Irelanders because their doctrines led
to civil war 'and as a minister of religion . . . I felt bound to dis-
countenance them'. Yet shortly after the rebellion, he roundly

---

[105] Murphy, *Killaloe*, 205–7.
[106] O'Sullivan, diary, 26 Aug. 1851; see also Doheny, *Felon's Track*, 253, 277–
81.

condemned what he saw as the total failure of the government to prevent the famine deaths. An ingrained conviction that the government, because of its failure to redress Irish grievances, bore some responsibility for the outbreak lurked in the recesses of many Irish minds.

The fiery statements of some clerics in the months before the rebellion, together with the action of the Clonoulty priests, provided grounds for some Orangemen and sections of the press to claim large-scale clerical participation. In particular, they declared that Maginn, Kenyon, Birmingham, Mackey, and three other priests had been involved and were being shielded by Catholic officials.[107] To Russell's annoyance, the *Times* took up the story.[108] Clarendon was unhappy and asked that the Attorney General contradict it officially in Parliament.[109] There was little substance to the report, but the accusation against Maginn is complicated, and it is difficult to establish firm conclusions. Duffy related later that Dr Gray, the editor and proprietor of the *Freeman's Journal*, came to him when he was in prison in Newgate and told him that the bishop had authorized him to assure him that if the rebellion were postponed until the harvest was stored, 'he would join it himself with twenty officers in black uniforms. . . . The same overture was made by the same intermediary to O'Brien.'[110] When Clarendon went through Smith O'Brien's papers, he claimed that he found correspondence 'proving that Dr Maginn . . . was as cognizant of all that was going on and as much implicated as any of them'.[111] Startled, Russell wanted to force Maginn out of the country, but Clarendon pleaded that it would be far better to hold the matter over his head as a hidden threat. 'I would much rather have it conveyed to him that his proceedings were known and make fear of exposure the security for his future good behaviour'.[112] When the charge was leaked to the *Derry Sentinel* a few months later, Maginn denied it outright and wrote directly to Redington challenging its authors:

[107] Memorandum of Orange Lodge to Clarendon, 19 Oct. 1848, Clarendon Papers, Box 7, 71/2.
[108] Russell to Clarendon, 1 Nov. 1848, ibid., Box 43.
[109] Clarendon to Russell, 2 Oct. 1848, ibid., Letterbook 2.
[110] Duffy, *Four Years of Irish History*, 629–30.
[111] Clarendon to Russell, 6 Aug. 1848, Clarendon Papers, Letterbook 3.
[112] Russell to Clarendon, 8 Aug. 1848, ibid., Box 43; Clarendon to Russell, 10 Aug. 1848, ibid., Letterbook 3.

it was . . . untrue that any letters of mine abetting treason, could be found in Mr O'Brien's portfolio, for I wrote none. . . . If there have been . . . such letters why . . . are they not produced? . . . I now fling defiance at the monster [of calumny] and dare it to prove any word or deed of mine adverse to the lawful sovereign . . . or to produce from Smith O'Brien's portfolio, or any other, any letter of mine exciting to . . . rebellion . . .[113]

Redington replied that:

having no knowledge and not believing that any letter . . . bearing your signature and inciting Mr O'Brien to rebel . . . [was] found in the port-folio . . . I cannot but come to the conclusion that your correspondent has been misinformed in stating that some person high in authority in the Castle, had made a communication that such was the fact. This I think entirely disposes of the matter, as far as the matter has induced your Lordship, not unnaturally, to make vindication of your character . . .[114]

The Smith O'Brien papers contain no corroboration of the al-legations, and Smith O'Brien's memorandum of his interview with Maginn that same week records: 'I returned to Dublin and . . . attended the second meeting of the [new] League, having first had an interview with . . . Dr Maginn . . . who promised the adhesion to it of himself and his clergy upon the condition that its proceed-ings should be kept within the bounds of constitutional opera-tion.'[115] The *Derry Sentinel*'s claim that its source was some person high in authority in the Castle is similar to the claim of the 'Irish Peer' whose 'Letter' on the Mahon affair played a part in raising the tension. It may well have originated with Clarendon who, as we have seen, was not above using the press to make anonymous insinuations. His reluctance to accede to Russell's wish to expose Maginn publicly, and his suggestion that he merely make Maginn aware that the government knew of his treasonable acts, indicate that the evidence was not as clear-cut as he had pretended. Clarendon had probably exaggerated the significance of the in-criminating documents and leaked this to the *Sentinel*. On the other hand, a certain ambivalence is apparent in Maginn's attitude, and he both spoke and wrote in so fiery a manner as to provide ground for the belief that he approved of the course the Young Irelanders adopted.

---

[113] Maginn to Redington, n.d. [Sept.] 1848, McGee, *Maginn*, 168–9.
[114] Redington to Maginn, 3 Oct. 1848, cited in McGee, *Maginn*, 168–9.
[115] Gwynn, *Young Ireland*, 221.

Clarendon, expressing the wish that '48 would be for Ireland what the '45 had been for Scotland, presumably hoped that it would be the last rebellion. He determined that the best course to adopt was to ridicule it. Although they enforced the law, neither he nor Russell were vindictive in their treatment of the rebels. The '48 has gone down in history as a pathetic, ludicrous affair where, fortunately, casualties were few. Certainly, despite the high motives and character of its leaders and the honourable conduct of the insurgents, it is difficult to dignify it with the title of rebellion. The credit or blame for reducing it to 'a cabbage-garden rebellion' has been variously assigned to the rebels' ineptitude, the peasants' passivity, or the government's decisiveness. The role of the clergy was also important, and a variety of sources attest their influence in containing it. Clarendon was explicit on the point. Within a few days of the Ballingarry incident, he announced triumphantly that 'The rebellion is over . . . the priests are still rebuking the flock for their folly.' They played, he believed, a decisive role. 'The conduct of the Clergy as a body has been really admirable. In the disaffected districts they performed their duty at great personal risk and with the utmost certainty of losing their influence.'[116] Redington praised the priests at Ballingarry and Mullinahone and told Maginn categorically how gratified he was that 'the clergy of our Church have shown their determination to support the cause of order and peace'.[117] Stipendiary magistrates and detectives reported a bitterness among the people against the priests 'for not going with them and siding with their enemies'.[118]

Rebels also blamed the priests.[119] Doheny's account recorded that some Irish–Americans asserted 'that the entire failure was attributable to the Catholic priests, and that in opposing the liberation of Ireland they acted in accordance with some recognised radical principle of the Church'. Doheny denied both claims, but criticized 'the acts and language of those among them, who interposed and unhappily exercised baneful influence on the abortive attempt of their unfortunate country'.[120] He disclosed how the priests in Mullinahone and in Ballingarry advised against continuing in arms

[116] Clarendon to Russell, 3 Aug. 1848, Clarendon Papers, Letterbook 3.
[117] Redington to Maginn, 3 Oct. 1848, cited in McGee, *Maginn*, 168–9.
[118] Clarendon to G. Grey, 6 Aug. 1848, Clarendon Papers, Letterbook 2.
[119] Duffy, *Four Years of Irish History*, 690.
[120] Doheny, *Felon's Track*, pp. xxviii–xxix.

and also recorded that Fr. Patrick Laffan, curate in Fethard, had 'read the names of the proscribed traitors for whose persons a reward was offered'.[121] Other rebel leaders told a similar story. Lewis related the account given by Smith O'Brien and Meagher shortly after their arrest. When Smith O'Brien blamed the town dwellers, Meagher added that they had been deserted by the priests, who at the beginning encouraged them to rise, and when they found that the force against them was large, exhorted their flocks to be quiet 'who, when they were told, fell down like spaniels!'.[122] John O'Mahony, another of the leaders, was highly critical of the priests in south Tipperary, at least, whom he accused of originating the movement towards rebellion, telling the people to make pikes, to form clubs and promising to lead them on the day of action.[123] The bitterness of failed revolutionaries is evident in those criticisms, but they were not without substance. Smith O'Brien himself, in a speech he prepared but never delivered, gave his own explanation:

Much has been said by Party writers about the disloyalty of the Catholic Clergy, but it is my sincere belief that it was through the instrumentality of the superior order of the Catholic Clergy that the insurrection was suppressed. For my own part I feel convinced that we were defeated, not by the military preparations of Lord Hardinge or of General MacDonald, not by the system of espionage organised by Lord Clarendon but by the influences brought into action by the Catholic Clergy. Whatever merit therefore is connected with the repression of our effort is due chiefly, if not solely, to the Catholic Hierarchy.[124]

This statement, which is part of his frank account of the rebellion, was written after months of reflection, at a time when he expected to be condemned to death. As the studied opinion of the leader of the rebellion it merits serious consideration. The role he attributed to the hierarchy was borne out by the facts. Murray made sure the Dublin clergy gave it no support. Crolly and Slattery were strongly opposed to the rebellion. MacHale's absence in Rome saved him from an embarrassing position, but it is almost certain that he

[121] Ibid. 184.

[122] Lewis to Clarendon, 4 Nov. 1848, Clarendon Papers, c. 530.

[123] John O'Mahony, *Personal Narrative of my Connection with the Attempted Rising of 1848*, cited in J. Newsinger, 'Revolution and Catholicism in Ireland, 1848–1923', *European Studies Review*, 9 (1979), 465–6.

[124] Cited in Gwynn, *Young Ireland*, 234.

would have taken the same line as Slattery. Kennedy forced Kenyon, the most committed of the priests, to refuse to act. Walsh of Ossory, Ryan of Limerick, Egan of Kerry, and Delany of Cork also discouraged rebellious agitation.[125]

It was not merely government officials and rebels who believed that the priests' intervention had been decisive. In clerical circles, too, the priests' role in persuading the people not to rise in rebellion was acknowledged. Murray stated it categorically at the time and later, in an official report to the Cardinal Prefect of Propaganda, he informed him that the priests had acted with outstanding zeal and at the risk of their lives to prevent bloodshed and to restore order.[126] From Maynooth College, the bursar, Thomas Farrelly, told R. M. Bromley, the government auditor of accounts:

The 'would be leaders' have woefully miscalculated their strength in that quarter . . . I believe they imagined the whole population with the Catholic clergy at their head would have risen as one man to join them, whereas the Priests have everywhere opposed their progress and effectually prevented the people from joining in their Quixotic enterprise.[127]

Farrelly was anxious to present the priests in a good light, but the revolutionary language of some priests provided some grounds for the rebels' illusions. His account of the priests' attitude during the rebellion was probably correct, because Maynooth College, with over five hundred priests and students, kept itself well informed about clerical life and opinion throughout the country. As Farrelly expected, his letter found its way quickly into the lord lieutenant's office. The combined evidence, then, from government, rebel, and clerical sources indicates that the clergy, particularly the bishops, played an important role in confining the rebellion to a tiny proportion of the people. On the other hand, it is difficult to imagine that the rebellion would have succeeded even if the priests had not taken a stand against it. Militarily it was a fiasco—poorly planned and premature. It had no leader of military talent and arms and provisions were in short supply. Psychologically, too, the people were not ready. Smith O'Brien, many years later,

---

[125] Clarendon to Russell, 17 Mar. 1848, Clarendon Papers, Letterbook 2; *Tablet*, 15 Apr. 1848.
[126] Murray to Cardinal of Propaganda, 22 Dec. 1849, *Acta* (1851), vol. 213, fos. 171–5, PFA.
[127] T. Farrelly to R. M. Bromley, 10 Aug. 1848, Russell Papers, PRO 30/22/7C, fos. 331–2.

said quite simply 'that the people preferred to die of starvation at home, or to flee as voluntary exiles to other lands, rather than to fight for their lives and liberties'.[128]

This comment betrays a certain over-simplification, for the inefficient leadership of O'Brien played a major part in the ignominious collapse of the rebellion. The government's decisive action, the sudden suspension of habeas corpus, the police raids in Dublin which left the Confederation disorganized, and the superior forces of the crown, made it extremely unlikely that the rebellion would have succeeded even if the clergy had not worked against it. What clerical opposition ensured was that the conflict was minimized: had it not been for their action, more peasants would have stayed with Smith O'Brien at Mullinahone and others from Counties Tipperary, Kilkenny, Carlow, Limerick, and Kerry might have swelled his ranks. Clerical intervention prevented a massacre and made the rebellion a relatively bloodless one. This, in turn, removed the justification for the type of severe repression that followed other revolts. This was the only rebellion between 1798 and 1921 which did not see many deaths of policemen, soldiers, and innocent people, or the execution of some of the rebels.

The clergy's motives in opposing the rebellion varied. Although some, in the spring of 1848, appear to have accepted that force might be necessary, they constituted, with the doubtful support of Bishop Maginn, a small proportion of the 2,000 priests in Ireland. When the actual rebellion came, even they changed their minds. They saw that pike-carrying peasants without food or guns, with no officers but journalists and poets, could never topple the might of English rule. The indecisive behaviour of the leaders as they marched from one town to another added to the conviction that the venture was hopeless. Doheny recorded that 'a very respectable gentleman, a witness of [the] proceedings [in Carrick-on-Suir]', defended the conduct of those who discouraged the rebellion, 'on the ground that the preparations seemed . . . to preclude the possibility of success; and that it was the sacred duty of every man capable of appreciating the position and resources of the people, the difficulties of the enterprise and the consequence of failure, not alone to Carrick but the entire island, at all hazards to prevent a useless wreck and slaughter.'[129] Father Fitzgerald, who rode up to

---

[128] Duffy, *Four Years*, 690.   [129] Doheny, *Felon's Track*, 164.

Smith O'Brien at Ballingarry on the fateful day of the rebellion, gave his own explanation some years later:

On the one hand, a numerous army, well-appointed and disciplined and supplied with all the munitions of war, on the other, an undisciplined and unarmed peasantry, without leaders of any knowledge or experience and destitute of everything that could render success certain or even probable. This weighed also heavily with me . . . for that there should be carnage at all, was much to be lamented, but that it should be entirely on one side, and especially on the side of a poor and oppressed population, with whom all my sympathies were enlisted, and with whom I in every way identified, was an idea from which I recoiled instinctively.[130]

The journalist A. M. Sullivan, who later on was closely associated with Gavan Duffy in the *Nation*, depicted their reaction to the disarray and muddle of the Confederates. 'The clergy rushed into the midst of the rebels demanding "Where are your arms?" they said; and there were no arms. "Where is your commissariate?"— the multitude were absolutely without food; "Where are your artillery, your cavalry? Where are your . . . officers?" . . . The gathering thousands melted slowly away . . .'.[131]

This graphic picture was close to the reality. Without food, leadership, or arms, the insurrection was hopeless.[132] The sufferings during the rebellion of 1798 were not forgotten. In Mullinahone, Cahill and Corcoran warned the people of the terrible consequences that would befall them. Renehan denounced the Young Irelanders as 'seducers of the people to the gallows or a bloody grave'. This attitude has often been seen as ambivalent; it can, however, be argued that it was by far the most realistic. Like Fitzgerald's, the sympathies of the priests were with their parishioners, and many of them shared their aspirations, but they saw clearly the utter hopelessness of this ill-prepared rebellion and

---

[130] Fitzgerald, *Recollections*, 34.

[131] A. M. Sullivan, *New Ireland: Political Sketches and Personal Reminiscences of Thirty Years of Irish Public Life* (1877), 91. Alexander Martin Sullivan (1830–84), joined the staff of the *Nation* in 1855 and became editor and proprietor in 1858.

[132] John Blake Dillon, one of the principal leaders, related that some '30 rust-eaten fowling pieces and some few auxiliary weapons of the most despicable description' was all they had. Most of the army melted away because they had 'no idea where breakfast was to be had, except under their own roofs'. B. O'Cathaoir, *John Blake Dillon, Young Irelander* (1990), 106, 83.

took the courageous step of opposing the rebel leaders to their faces in order to save their people.

It could be argued that the apparently revolutionary section of the clergy did not really support revolutionary methods, but hoped that England would yield repeal to pressure and threats, as the governments on the continent had yielded to external agitation. As such their activity could be seen as no more than O'Connellite moral force pushed to the limit. This is certainly true for many, but it does not completely explain the fervour during the months following the revolution in France. Never before had priests used such revolutionary language, the unequivocal meaning of some of their public statements indicating a willingness to bless a revolt if it had a chance of success. They weighed up the proportionality of good and evil, and the famine deaths appeared to provide sufficient justification. The attitude of the Irish clergy can be better understood in the context of the conduct of the French and Italian clergy in the spring of 1848 and, like the Young Irelanders generally, they were carried away by the ease with which established regimes collapsed throughout Europe. Why they turned aside at the last moment had much to do with the deteriorating situation in Italy and France, culminating in the death of Archbishop Affre; after June, most French Catholics had turned against the revolution and, in Ireland, Clarendon drove home the lesson. The ineptitude of the Confederates as leaders of a revolution, fear for the lives of their faithful and for their own, and perhaps, as Clarendon suggested on one occasion, for their property, combined to make them withdraw from an obviously futile and dangerous venture and to persuade their people of the folly of the rebellion. For most of them the rebellion, short-lived and confined to a tiny area, never reached them and the army, whose green or tricolour flags they might have been prepared to bless, never materialized. In County Tipperary, where the rebels took the field, at least two priests, who had voiced fiery sentiments, were faced with the dilemma. In Carrick-on-Suir, where the Confederates contemplated beginning the rebellion, Fr. Patrick Byrne was criticized by Duffy for not giving it support. Certainly a few days later Byrne implored the Confederates to delay the rebellion, but the decision not to begin there was the result of earnest pleading by the clubs.

Kenyon's attitude is more puzzling. Given his fiery speeches and his position on the council of the Confederation, he was expected to come out early in the rebellion once the rebels took the field. Kenyon's refusal to help the rebellion contrasts not only with his prior involvement with the leaders of the movement, but even with an entry he made in his parish register a few days before when, on 27 July, he wrote: 'This evening I have heard of a rebellion in south Tipperary under William Smith O'Brien—may God speed it.' Amazingly, Kenyon retained the friendship of many of the leaders, such as Mitchel, to the end. When, in 1861, the Fenians brought home the body of Terence Bellew McManus, another prominent Young Irelander, for a national burial that was to be an emotive statement of the ideals of advanced nationalism, Kenyon was chosen to preach. Many years later Thomas Clarke Luby, one of the Fenian leaders, explained Kenyon's inaction during the 1848 rebellion on the grounds that his bishop had lifted his suspension on condition that he did not 'take the initiative' in the rebellion. Why he never informed his fellow conspirators that he would be unable to act is difficult to understand. Kenyon appears to have been torn between his nationalist feelings and his desire to continue functioning as a priest. He certainly expected to be arrested and perhaps executed, and had made his will, which he sent to his bishop. With some justification, Kennedy claimed to have saved him from jail or exile.

The revolutionary movement of 1848 has generally been written off as a farcical shambles. Although Gavan Duffy glorified it as the year of the Young Irelanders, many historians, like contemporary public opinion in Britain, have dismissed it as a ludicrous skirmish in the Widow McCormack's garden. Some reassessment is necessary for in Ireland, as throughout Europe, 1848 had been an astounding year, full of contrasts and contradictions, not least for the Church. The year began with fierce denunciations of their collaboration in assassination. Embittered by these attacks and by the famine deaths and evictions, they welcomed the intoxicating news from Paris, Rome, and Milan. Some of them hoped that similar changes could come about in Ireland with the same ease as in France. Judging the evil of rebellion to be outweighed by the evil of famine deaths, a number appeared ready to throw in their lot with the Confederates. How many is difficult to assess, but twenty or so were reported in the press as using language which could be construed as showing willingness to join in a revolt. It is possible that their strong statements were no more than rhetoric or the intemperate reaction of the hard-pressed pastors of a starving people. Even if others held the same view, they constituted a small proportion of the total number of priests. The tight discipline imposed by bishops limited their scope and the discouraging sequence of events in France and Italy, which Clarendon exploited effectively as counter-revolutionary propaganda, made them draw back. The hopelessness of an ill-prepared insurrection finally made them decide either to stand aloof or to prevent their people from taking part in it. It was a chastening moment for the clergy. It remained to be seen what use a triumphant government would make of their discomfiture.

In his assessment of people and their behaviour Clarendon waxed hot and waxed cold. A few weeks after requesting Russell to give the priests special mention in parliament for their courageous stand against the rebels at great risk to themselves, he became annoyed with them when they pleaded on behalf of the rebels.[133] He again sent alarming reports to the cabinet, foretelling a new and more dangerous rebellion in which this time the clergy would take the lead. At the same time, since the people now turned on them as traitors this would be 'an excellent opportunity', he suggested, 'for rendering the Priests more independent of the People'. This suggestion fitted in exactly with what Russell had in mind.

For almost twenty years Russell had been maturing a plan to achieve the integration of the Catholic Church into the United Kingdom as a central part of his whole Irish policy. The main plank of this scheme was to be the endowment of the Catholic Church in the shape of state salaries for the clergy and other benefits. When a similar scheme had been mooted earlier, the bishops had opposed it vociferously. Now, however, after suppressing the rebellion, the government was in a strong position. The destitute people were unable to support their priests. The clergy were feeling the shock effects of famine, emigration, rebellion, and a reinvigorated Protestant mission. The time seemed ripe. If, as Clarendon believed, a rift had developed between priests and people over the priests' role in the rebellion, the autumn of 1848 might well prove the moment to bring forward a comprehensive plan that would win over an impoverished and alienated clergy to the side of the government, and make them the main

---

[133] Clarendon to Russell, 13 Aug. 1848, Clarendon Papers, Letterbook 3.

supporters of government policies in controlling a restless people. Were it to prove successful, a major step, they believed, towards the assimilation of Irish Catholics, their incorporation into the constitution and the permanent conciliation of Ireland would have been accomplished.

6

Endowment or Independence?
Russell's 'Great Settlement' Foiled,
1848–1849

'the one Grand Question . . . the payment of the Roman Catholic Clergy'.

(Russell to Clarendon)

For a Church that sees its task as a mission to a large population, the provision of clergy is a priority; the Irish Catholic Church, with its highly developed sacramental system, needed a numerous clergy to administer its rites and preach the Christian gospel. Yet in the early years of the nineteenth century it was failing in this requirement for, despite strenuous efforts to provide more clergy, the ratio of priests to people in 1845, though showing great variations from diocese to diocese, stood at 1 : 3,000, a figure that compared unfavourably with the proportion within the Established Church (1 : 408) or the French Church (1 : 847).[1] Candidates for the priesthood were ample: the resources to educate them and to support them in the ministry were scarce. Peel's generous Maynooth Grant of 1845 went some of the way towards solving the first problem, but almost immediately the Famine dramatically complicated the second.

The income of parish priests varied considerably from diocese to diocese and from parish to parish. It possibly averaged £150 a year in the 1840s.[2] The curates, however, were far worse off. They

---

[1] S. J. Connolly, *Priests and People in Pre-Famine Ireland, 1780–1845* (1982), 32–6; D. A. Kerr, *Peel, Priests, and Politics* (1982), 7, 51–2. The first reliable figures are for 1834, when the ratio of priests to faithful was 1 : 2,985. The number of priests increased by over 200 over the next decade, but the population also increased.

[2] Kerr, *Peel*, 34–7; D. Keenan, *The Catholic Church in Nineteenth-Century Ireland: A Sociological Study* (1983), 227–31; J. O'Shea, *Priests, Politics and Society in Post-Famine Ireland: A Study of County Tipperary 1850–1891* (1983), 20–3, 314–16.

constituted 58 per cent of the parish clergy and normally were not promoted to a parish until their late forties. In some parishes they received a third or less of the parish income; in other parishes the parish priests provided their keep and a salary, which ranged from £30 to as little as £10. At the onset of the Famine, the widespread starvation and fever called for more priests to minister to the sick, and especially to bring them the last rites which Catholics passionately wanted and claimed as their due. The increase in illness and mortality among the clergy made these demands more difficult to meet. As the Famine continued and emigration increased the situation changed. The deepening poverty of the people and, as deaths and emigration took their toll, the decreasing population, meant that parishes were poorer and could afford fewer priests. The situation in the diocese of Elphin illustrates the dilemma this created for bishops. In 1845 the diocese was seriously understaffed with a total of 92 priests for a population of 310,000 or a ratio of 1 : 3,848. Yet in 1847, the bishop, George Browne, was forced to block ordinations and told Renehan, the Maynooth president, of 'the improbability . . . of there being vacancies for a series of years to provide for one third of those young men whose studies are now nearly completed and who must necessarily remain without ordination until vacancies occur'.[3] By 1850 bishops from all four provinces were forced to hold up ordinations. Edward Walsh of Ossory told Renehan that 'having four priests and two deacons, one of whom is two and the other one year at home after having read four years theology at our seminary, without any immediate prospect of providing a mission for any of them, I must reluctantly withhold faculty to promote . . . to priesthood any of the young students in Maynooth College'.[4] McNally of Clogher, while acknowledging that he was 'greatly in want of priests', believed he could not provide a living for them.[5] His neighbour, James Browne of Kilmore, told Renehan that in Cavan 'the population is diminished to such an extent that one curate is deemed sufficient in some parishes in which hitherto two had hard labour, whilst in some others the parish priest would consider himself equal to the duty without a curate at all'.[6] The bishop of Killaloe reported a

[3] Browne to Renehan, 30 Apr. 1847, Renehan Papers, MCA.
[4] Walsh to Renehan, 15 May 1849, ibid.
[5] McNally to Renehan, 28 Dec. 1849, ibid.
[6] Browne to Renehan, 9 Apr. 1850, ibid.

similar situation.[7] From Clonfert, Bishop Derry put the dilemma of many bishops to Renehan:

I am entirely at a loss what to do with these young men now in college. It would be mischievous to have more priests ordained than can be supported. It is also a great disappointment to *them* to be refused ordination after their long and laborious and probably expensive preparation.[8]

David Walsh, who was bishop of the prosperous diocese of Cloyne in north and east Cork and of the poorer diocese of Ross in west Cork, reported that 'so great . . . is the depression . . . and so strong in consequence are my apprehensions that the insufficient supply of Priests I have at present will not find the means of support for the coming half year, that I am extremely unwilling to embarrass myself with a great number . . . than the exigencies of the Diocese indispensably require'.[9] The anguish of a bishop for his priests comes through in French's account of the problem in his dioceses of Kilfenora and Kilmacduagh:

As melancholy Starvation, heartless Extermination, and unexampled Emigration of our people to the shores of the United States of America, have rendered this poor diocese (in common with the West of Ireland) a wilderness, I am in apprehension it would be imprudent at present to call to Holy Orders such of my subjects [as] have not finished their full course . . .[10]

Renehan, who understood the plight of the unfortunate students, pleaded the case of one John Nestor who had completed his course. French replied that he did not know how he could provide for him when ordained, and asked Renehan to bend the rules of the college and let him stay on another year, for the times might mend. If not, French could think of only one solution—'let him propose for the foreign mission or for America, as *I can't give him bread*'.[11] The situation was slow in improving. In 1851 Walsh of Ossory was still forced to report to Renehan that he was unable

[7] J. Newman, *Maynooth and Victorian Ireland* (1983), 106.
[8] Derry to Renehan, 2 June 1851, Renehan Papers, MCA.
[9] Walsh to Slattery, 25 May 1848, Slattery Papers, CDA.
[10] French to Renehan, 8 May 1850, Renehan Papers, MCA.
[11] French to Renehan, 14 May 1850, ibid. P. Hamell's index shows that Nestor had been ordained deacon in 1849, but there is no record of his ordination to the priesthood. P. J. Hamell, *Maynooth Students and Ordinations Index, 1795–1895* (1982), 131.

to provide for the young priests coming from Maynooth.[12] In November 1853 it was Slattery's turn to complain to Renehan that he had too many students for whom he could not provide. What is remarkable is that the problem was not confined to the poorer western districts but hit dioceses like Cloyne and Cashel in Munster, Clogher and Kilmore in Ulster, and even Ossory in the more prosperous province of Leinster. For students who had been preparing for the ministry for several years the situation was distressing; they could not go back to the lay state, particularly if they had reached sub-diaconate. The social pressure was great and the refusal of ordination occasioned shame and often economic hardship to their families who had financed their studies and hoped for some recompense. It created difficulties, too, in Maynooth when students whom Renehan and the staff considered fit for ordination were kept back.

Not merely were the bishops forced to refuse ordination but mounting pressure came on them to reduce the number of priests serving in the dioceses. 'I am tortured by the applications of Parish Priests to remove curates in consequence of the depopulation of their Parishes', Browne of Elphin exclaimed.[13] Browne of Kilmore told Shrewsbury that he had several well-qualified priests just come from Maynooth, but was obliged to quarter them out amongst their relatives instead of employing them in their ministry. 'And this', he explained, 'not because there was not the most crying need for their services, but because neither he [the bishop] nor his people had the means of supporting them!'[14] The situation was worse in Kilmacduagh. 'My poor Parish Priests', the bishop complained, 'are obliged to dismiss their curates, owing to the scanty means of subsistence for themselves!' For many young priests the only solution was the one that their fellow countrymen were adopting in their hundreds of thousands—to take the ship to America. By 1849 many were leaving the country. French complained that 'three of my poor Curates have called for their "Exeats" and want to [go] to America'.[15] In Kilmore, too, the number of

---

[12] Walsh to Renehan, 25 May 1851, Renehan Papers, MCA.

[13] George Browne to Renehan, 4 May 1850, ibid.

[14] Shrewsbury to Clarendon, 9 June 1848, Clarendon Papers, Box 58; James Browne to Renehan, 8 Sept. 1847, 9 Apr. 1850, 27 May 1851. Renehan Papers, MCA.

[15] French to Renehan, 8, 14 May 1850, ibid. An exeat is the official permission given by the bishop to one of his priests to leave the service of the diocese.

priests seeking exeats increased substantially. The diocese of Down and Connor, which included the rapidly growing city of Belfast where the Catholic population more than doubled between 1834 and 1861, was extremely short of priests and was one of the few dioceses willing to accept priests from other dioceses. The bishop, Cornelius Denvir, warned those intending to come that the emoluments 'are very limited'.[16]

Apart from the plight of those younger clerics and curates for whom their bishops could not provide, priests suffered both through an increase in work and a reduction in income. Sick-calls multiplied and, increasingly, the priests were called out to attend the dying. As early as April 1846 Bishop Egan described the situation in his diocese of Kerry and the pressure on the clergy:

the priests are absolutely exhausted having to attend so many sick calls and in many instances are obliged to walk, their horses being unable to carry them through want of sufficient feeding and the priest not getting as much as would purchase oats for his horse.[17]

Archdeacon O'Sullivan, the parish priest of Kenmare, related how he was followed everywhere by hungry people and often prayed that he could go far away from it all. In the diocese of Cork matters were no better. The vicar capitular, Thomas Barry, reported that the diocese needed many more young priests 'in consequence of the mortality of Priests . . . and the great necessity of having a sufficient number to attend to the great multitude of the dying'.[18] From Derry, Maginn reported the increased labours of the mission and the need for more priests.[19] Slattery told Renehan that 'The priests here are harassed to Death by duty and the distress of the people'. No wonder Bishop McNally warned the president of Maynooth that the young men coming out of the seminary did not realize the frightful difficulties facing them, or that a pious bishop like French prayed that 'the almighty God, in his mercy, spare both clergy and people!' The Famine spared neither and by 1848 many priests were in dire need. At the beginning of the Famine, some priests had small farms and were cushioned from its

---

[16] Denvir to Renehan, 19 June 1849, Renehan Papers, MCA. Between the years 1834 and 1862, the Catholic population of Belfast increased from 19,712 to 41,406. W. E. Vaughan and A. J. Fitzpatrick, *Irish Historical Statistics: Population 1821–1971* (1978), 52.

[17] Egan to Renehan, 22 Apr. 1846, Renehan Papers, MCA.

[18] Barry to Renehan, 21 May 1847, ibid.

[19] Maginn to Renehan, 10 Mar. 1847, ibid.

effects by their savings and the support of more prosperous farmers. As the Famine progressed, however, what surplus they had was used up providing relief and making up for the shortfall in their income. Strzelecki, who had spent much of 1847 and 1848 in the distressed areas and who was well received by the priests, told Clarendon in 1848 that the 'clergy are reduced to extreme want—even of common necessities' and a year later he reported that many of them were in a state of beggary and without decent clothes. He repeated this claim in his evidence to the select committee on Irish Poor Laws, adding that 'In some instances, where priests were confined with fever, I found in their cabins nothing available beyond stirabout . . . there was no tea, no sugar, no provisions whatever; in some of their huts, the wind blew, the snow came in, and the rain dripped.' Other witnesses before the same committee, who also had been involved in poor relief, confirmed his reports.[20] The following June Redington reported that 'the priests have suffered severely, some of them are almost starving'.[21] Murray, who distributed an enormous amount of relief directly to priests and was the recipient of their letters of appeal and of thanks, knew of priests who were starving and others who were unable to leave their cabins or perform their duties for want of shoes.[22] Some precise information on the drop in clerical income is available. Bishop McGettigan of Raphoe told Redington that his own income had dropped from £500 to £200. The income in Thurles parish dropped from £225 in 1844 to £177 in 1847.[23] O'Sullivan kept a careful account of the income of his parish of Kenmare, which shows that from £348 in 1842 it plummeted to £116 in 1848.[24]

[20] Strzelecki to Clarendon, 26 Aug. 1848, Clarendon Papers, Box 58; Clarendon to Russell, 27 Aug. 1849, ibid., Letterbook 4; *Report and Minutes of Evidence of the Select Committee, Lords, on Irish Poor Laws 1849*, xvi. 979–80, 4 May 1849; Joseph Bewley, secretary of Society of Friends, ibid. xvi. 98, 25 May 1848; Phillip Reade, ibid. xvi. 238, 25 Mar. 1848.
[21] Clarendon to Russell, 9 June 1849, Clarendon Papers, Letterbook 3.
[22] Clarendon to Russell, 4, 16 Oct. 1848, ibid.
[23] O'Shea, *Priests, Politics and Society*, 314. This income was shared among the priests of the parish. Some other sources of income also existed.
[24] O'Sullivan, diary, under entry for 10 Jan. 1849. This did not include the salary of £60 paid to him as chaplain to the workhouse. Normally the total amount would be divided with his two curates. He had this to say on parish income in 1843: 'The revenues of the Parish now may form a subject of curiosity hereafter. The first year [1839] it provided £250, the second £270, the third £340. . . . A great deal to be said for the services rendered but the poor people certainly are willing to contribute to our support as far as their means will allow them.' Diary, 11 Oct. 1843.

The decrease varied from parish to parish, but in general a sharp fall occurred. Hard hit though many parish priests were, the curates were hit still harder. Many parish priests in the poorer parishes could no longer afford the paltry sum of £10 or £20 which constituted the curate's salary.[25] It was not surprising that the question of providing salaries for the clergy should now surface as a major topic of political discussion.

A provision for the Catholic clergy formed a major part of the important project—mooted by many thoughtful observers—of endowing the Catholic Church. It had a long history. By the end of the eighteenth century, statesmen sought to secure some control over the Church which, it was by then evident, had retained the allegiance of the majority of the people. They believed that while the privileged position of the Established Church should be maintained, the Catholic Church, by a type of concurrent endowment, could be rendered less dependent on the people, more accountable, and more liable to support the state, if it could be integrated into the constitution. Payment of the clergy, some control over the training of the students, and a royal veto over the appointment of the bishops were the main elements in this scheme. The question came up for consideration for the first time in 1782, with the relaxations of the penal laws. In 1799, during negotiations on the Union, the government had gone so far as to establish a list of the Catholic clergy with a view to paying them salaries. In the aftermath of the 1798 rebellion, the bishops were under pressure to accommodate the government and unwilling to be regarded by the laity as blocking their hopes for full emancipation through a refusal to co-operate with government proposals. They agreed to accept payment of the clergy and a royal veto on the appointment of bishops, though on well-defined conditions.[26] In the face of George III's opposition Pitt failed to procure emancipation, but Henry Addington, who succeeded him in 1801, although opposed to emancipation, favoured paying the clergy. Castlereagh, who as chief secretary had been involved in the negotiations with the bishops, rejoined the government on the understanding that such a scheme would be put into effect, but related later that the bishops

---

[25] O'Shea, *Priests, Politics and Society*, 22–3, 313; Kerr, *Peel*, 32–7.
[26] P. O'Donoghue, 'The Catholic Church and Ireland in an age of Revolution and Rebellion, 1782–1803' (Ph.D. thesis, 1975); Kerr, *Peel*, 64–5.

refused the offer while the claims of the laity for emancipation were not satisfied.[27]

The controversy over the veto was part of the same attempt to control the Church, although the emphasis had shifted to the manner of appointing bishops. The bishops took a stand against the veto at their meeting in 1808 and both clergy and laity united in refusing Roman pressure to accept the measure.[28] The question of payment of the clergy again emerged when Sir Francis Burdett, the reforming member for Westminster, brought forward a bill for emancipation. To facilitate its passage through parliament, he included two 'securities' or 'wings', one of which was the payment of the clergy. O'Connell accepted this proposal, claiming that it had the approval of the leading bishops of the day, Murray and Doyle. Doyle indignantly told O'Connell that he would rather resign his see than accept a salary, 'for if my hand were stained with Government money, it should never grasp a crozier or a mitre ever after be fitted to my brow'.[29] The matter of the 'wings' was not put to the test, for the House of Lords rejected Burdett's bill and, when emancipation did come four years later, Peel felt it unwise to press for any securities.

In 1833 Russell, in his first sketch of his Irish policy, had concluded that a provision for the priests was a priority. Shortly afterwards George Lewis, who asserted that the two great remaining Irish grievances were the economic and the ecclesiastical, made the same point. In a comprehensive study of the matter, Lewis made a reasoned case for the endowment of the Catholic Church, which, he warned, should be done for the common good and with no intention of interfering with the Church's independence.[30] Other influential writers like Charles Greville and Nassau W. Senior

---

[27] B. MacDermot, *The Irish Catholic Petition of 1805* (1993), 174–6.

[28] C. D. Leighton, 'Gallicanism and the Veto Controversy: Church, State and Catholic Community in Early Nineteenth-century Ireland', in R. V. Comerford, M. Cullen, J. R. Hill, and C. Lennon (eds.), *Religion, Conflict and Coexistence in Ireland: Essays Presented to Monsignor Patrick J. Corish* (1990), 135–58.

[29] W. J. Fitzpatrick, *The Life, Times and Correspondence of the Right Rev. Dr. Doyle, Bishop of Kildare and Leighlin* (1861), i. 451; T. G. McGrath, 'Politics, Interdenominational Relations and Education in the Public Ministry of James Doyle, O.S.A., Bishop of Kildare and Leighlin, 1819–1834' (Ph.D. thesis, 1992), fos. 63–93.

[30] G. C. Lewis, *On Local Disturbances in Ireland and the Irish Church Question* (1836), 341–429.

advocated the same cause.[31] In 1837, when Russell was home secretary, he raised the issue, but the bishops took alarm and passed a resolution at their annual meeting expressing their 'unalterable determination to resist, by every means in our power, a measure so fraught with mischief to the independence and purity of the Catholic religion in Ireland'.[32] O'Higgins, who was in Rome earlier in the year, had told Pope Gregory XVI that every bishop in Ireland would 'beg his bread throughout any diocese rather than ever receive a pension', words which the pope warmly approved.[33] O'Higgins was given to exaggeration, but the influential Kinsella, bishop of Ossory, who had travelled to London in 1835 to oppose payment of the clergy, explained his opposition to Tocqueville: 'if we received money from the State, they [the people] would regard us as officials of the State, and when we advised them to respect Law and Order they would say "That is what they are paid for"'.[34] Russell nevertheless asked Mulgrave, the lord lieutenant, to sound out Archbishop Murray. Murray, while conceding that Catholics would be more prepared to receive the offer from the government then in office than from any other, added: 'I think it would require a little more time thoroughly to extend to questions concerning their religion that utter confidence which for the first time they [Catholics] feel in everything affecting their temporal concerns.' Mulgrave concluded that, excellent though the idea was, it was not advisable '*at this moment*' and Russell decided to defer it.[35] The problem of correct timing was a critical one and was to surface again. In 1843, at the height of the repeal agitation, Whig leaders—Russell, Macaulay, and Lord Jeffrey—discussed provision for the priests. Nassau Senior put it forward as his 'cheval de bataille', in his important article on Ireland.[36]

[31] N. W. Senior, *On National Property and on the Prospects of the Present Administration and of their Successors* (1835); C. Greville, *Past and Present Policy of England towards Ireland* (1845).

[32] Meetings of the Irish Bishops, 10–13 Jan. 1837, DDA.

[33] Nicholson to Hamilton, 1 Feb. 1837, Hamilton Papers, P1/38/11, DDA.

[34] A. de Tocqueville, *Journeys to England and Ireland*, ed. J. P. Mayer (1958), 147.

[35] Mulgrave to Russell, 11, 23, 27 Dec. 1837, Russell Papers, PRO, 30/22/2F, fos. 218, 237–8, 240–7.

[36] Senior to Napier, 14 Nov. 1843, cited in S. L. Levy, *Nassau W. Senior 1790–1864: Critical Essayist, Classical Economist, and Adviser of Governments* (1970), 136.

Russell, however, disliked Senior's patronizing attitude to Irish Catholics and made it clear that unless the feelings, pride, and ambition of the Irish people were satisfied, offers to pay the clergy would be regarded as a bribe.[37]

In 1846, when announcing the programme of the new government, Russell regarded endowment as the major plank in his long-term reforms. In view of the opposition to the measure, he promised, however, that he would not touch it 'until opinion changes'.[38] A year later, during the elections, he told Clarendon that he had 'no thoughts of paying the priests as you will see by my City speech'.[39] Peel, however, during the same election campaign in his address to the Tamworth electorate, made a strong case for paying the priests and pointed out how favourably Britain treated the Catholic Church in Malta and Canada.[40] In July 1848 Peel told Sheil that direct endowment of the clergy should come.[41] Although for Russell this was an assurance of Peel's support, it was also a reminder that Peel was overtaking him on Irish policies, both factors to spur him to action. Now, in 1848, Russell believed the time had come to press forward with the great design he had so long nurtured. In March, faced with a deteriorating situation in the country, the Irish government, Redington, Somerville, and Clarendon, made a measured case for delaying no longer in implementing the scheme:

When every Crown . . . in Europe is tottering we cannot govern Ireland . . . without some extensive measures of conciliation . . . so long as the priests are dependent for their daily bread upon the evil passions of their flock and so long as every Catholic is offended by the dilapidated state of his Church and the wretched hovels in which the priest is condemned to live, you may rely on it that things cannot materially improve.[42]

An enthusiastic Redington drew up a memorandum which Russell laid, slightly altered, before the government. The increasing danger of an outbreak of violence in Ireland, he reminded his colleagues,

---

[37] Russell to Napier, 1 Dec. 1843, cited in Levy, *Senior*, 137–8.

[38] Russell, *Hansard*, lxxxvii. 1179, 16 July 1846.

[39] Russell to Clarendon, 22 July 1847, Clarendon Papers, Box 43.

[40] *Nation*, 24 July 1847.

[41] W. T. McCullagh, *Memoirs of Richard Lalor Sheil* (1855), ii. 387–9.

[42] Clarendon to Russell, 23 Mar. 1848, Clarendon Papers, Letterbook 2. Sir William Meredyth Somerville (1802–73), 1st Baron Athlumney; MP Drogheda (1837–52); chief secretary for Ireland (1847–52).

made it necessary for them to give urgent attention to measures to meet the crisis. He would agree to Clarendon's repeated request for a suspension of habeas corpus, but it must be balanced by concessions, the two most important of which would be a bill to control ejectments and payment of the priests. A sum of £400,000 a year was to be levied by a land tax in Ireland and paid over to the Roman Catholic members of the Bequests Commission, to be spent by them 'either in the purchase of glebe-houses and glebe lands, or in the payment of the Parish Priests of Ireland'.[43] As usual the prime minister was ahead of his colleagues, who advised caution. Grey suggested that they postpone the measure until the following year 'to arrange in concert with the Catholic Hierarchy and the Pope the details' and, as Wood, Lansdowne, Palmerston, and Clanricarde took a somewhat similar line, the matter was postponed.[44] Yet it was very much in the air. Peel told Sheil that the timing was right for the priests were in dire poverty;[45] Bentinck was also well disposed.[46] On the night he rushed the suspension of habeas corpus through the Commons, Russell dined with Sheil, Greville, and Ward in Richmond, where all agreed that the payment of the priests must be attempted soon.[47] Charles Buller, Liberal member for Liskeard, produced a plan for Ireland incorporating payment as a central point. Even as Smith O'Brien's rebellion broke out Greville was firmly convinced that the government should take up the endowment scheme and 'in spite of all the opposition which pride, prejudice and bigotry will throw in its way, it must be forced through'. The collapse of the rebellion furnished Greville with added reasons for pressing ahead with the plan.

The most satisfactory part of the business is the good conduct of the Catholic clergy, who appear to have very generally used their influence on the people to deter them from their rebellious course. It is to be hoped

---

[43] Russell, memorandum to cabinet, 30 Mar. 1848, Russell Papers, PRO 30/22/7B.

[44] Grey on Russell's memorandum 30 Mar.; Wood, n.d.; Palmerston, 31 Mar.; Clanricarde, Apr. 1848, Russell Papers, PRO 30/22/7B.

[45] McCullagh, Sheil, ii. 387–9.

[46] Greville to Clarendon, 3 May 1848, Clarendon Papers, c. 521; Somerville to Clarendon, 1 June 1848, ibid., Box 27; Redington to Clarendon, 12 June 1848, ibid., Box 24/2.

[47] C. C. F. Greville, *The Greville Memoirs: A Journal of the Reign of Queen Victoria*, ed. H. Reeve (1903), 24 July 1848, vi. 214.

that the recollection of their behaviour on this trying occasion will have a considerable effect in paving the way for the payment of the Irish clergy, when this vital question comes on, as very soon it must.[48]

A new factor, Russell noted, had emerged with the radicalization of the revolution in Europe. 'The priests and we are in the same boat to row against the current of infidelity and communism setting in with Mitchel and Duffy.'[49] Endowment of the Catholic Church constituted the corner-stone of Russell's Irish policy. Without it, as he told Clarendon, the policy was 'lame and imperfect'.[50] When Clarendon made difficulties, he repeated that 'it is the measure [to] which I have always looked forward as the finishing stroke to a national policy towards Ireland—it fills up Mr Pitt's outline of 1800 which in 1849 is yet incomplete'. Whig politicians favoured endowment in order to exercise some control over a clergy whose influence, though real enough, they often exaggerated or misunderstood. Many of them believed like Clarendon that the priests would not abandon 'agitation upon which *they depend for their daily bread*'.[51] Others insisted that the priests were of the same origin and shared the same prejudices as the people and, since the priests depended on the populace for their living, the only way to separate them was to salary them. This was the constant theme of Nassau Senior as well as of many Tories. Russell substantially shared this view, but there was a more positive side to his policy. Justice for Ireland was a real motive with him, even if that justice consisted in what a good Foxite Whig thought was best for Ireland rather than what the Irish wanted. Despite his dislike of Catholicism, Russell had no difficulty in accepting it as the religion preferred by the vast majority of Irish. 'It is no question of the supremacy of the Pope. . . . It is a question of the happiness of a people long vexed by religious injustice and political oppression.'[52] The Established Church, he was convinced, had proved a tragic failure: 'The Irish Protestant Church had been, from its beginning in the reign of Elizabeth, foreign to the soil, ill-planted and ill-nurtured, a scare-crow rather than a tree, a fountain

---

[48] Greville, ibid. 5 Sept. 1848, vi. 227; 31 July, vi. 216.
[49] Russell to Clarendon, 8 Aug. 1848, Clarendon Papers, Box 43.
[50] Russell to Clarendon, 28 Feb. 1849, Clarendon Papers, Box 26; J. Prest, *Lord John Russell* (1972), 292.
[51] Clarendon to Russell, 6 Aug. 1848, Clarendon Papers, Letterbook 3.
[52] J. Russell, *Recollections and Suggestions, 1813–73* (1875), 297.

of bitterness and animosity rather than a fertilizing stream'.[53] The duty of the state, he affirmed, 'is not to choose . . . that doctrine which the Legislature . . . may consider to be founded in truth, but to endeavour to secure the means by which they can inculcate religion and morality among the great body of the people'.[54] Russell, too, hoped that his scheme would produce a better, more educated type of priest. Encouraging Clarendon to try to persuade Archbishop Crolly to join the Privy Council early in 1848, he explained his policy: 'My object has always been to raise the Roman Catholic clergy. Anything that can be devised that will give them rank, power and responsibility I should be glad to see.'[55] Peel's grant to Maynooth College had intended a similar effect and as such it was welcomed by Russell. In his *Recollections* he contrasted unfavourably the life of an Irish priest whose miserable living conditions prevented him from engaging in intellectual pursuits with that of a French priest, who was able to devote his leisure time to study.

Now in autumn 1848 Russell prepared to put his plan into action. The timing, at last, was right. The moderates among the bishops had been vindicated by the rebellion fiasco and the pope, according to Redington, would accept. The priests were impoverished for their dues had dried up. They had lost credit with the people, Clarendon believed, by first encouraging rebellion and then flinching from it. Although the government no doubt exaggerated the extent of the support the clergy gave to rebellion and the people's consequent disillusionment, the radicalization of the 1848 revolutions had frightened Catholic clergy in Ireland as it had throughout Europe. As Russell cheerfully told Redington, 'the Pulpit's laws, the Pulpit's Patrons give, / And those who live to please, must please to live'.[56] To the disgruntled Clarendon, critical alike of government weakness and clerical politics, Russell defended his more lenient outlook—Ireland, he reminded Clarendon, was 'solemnly promised by the Act of Union *equality of privileges*'. It was better, he added, that they try to keep the majority of priests with them than antagonize them.

[53] Russell, *Recollections*, 286–7; J. P. Parry, *Democracy and Religion: Gladstone and the Liberal Party, 1867–1875* (1989), 32–6.
[54] Prest, *Russell*, 80.
[55] Russell to Clarendon, 11 Feb. 1848, Clarendon Papers, Box 43.
[56] Prest, *Russell*, 290.

An incident had already occurred which, in the sensitive atmosphere surrounding the relations between the government and the Church, may have influenced the outcome. In August, in the unlikely setting of a debate on public works, Lord Ellenborough and Lord Monteagle suggested that provision be made for the endowment of the Catholic Church. Stanley intervened in the discussion to declare that 'he was not satisfied with the doctrine . . . that the Roman Catholic clergy, in being placed in a position of perfect independence of their flocks, should at the same time not be connected with the State. It would be a matter of policy, or, he would say plainly, of police with him'.[57] This was a poisoning of the wells because, as an irate Clarendon complained, by 'declaring that the priests must become agents of the Government, for it amounted to that, he [Stanley] will compel them to renounce and refuse that which if becomingly offered, they would gladly accept'. Stanley had deliberately touched on the most sensitive issue in an insensitive fashion: the last thing the clergy would accept was to become government gendarmes. The bishops who opposed endowment were alerted.

Notwithstanding this incident Russell, eager to get his plan off the ground, now travelled to Ireland to discuss the whole Irish policy with the Irish government and particularly Clarendon, and with Redington, the principal contact with Murray. At the viceregal lodge he discussed at length the twin policies they intended to pursue—provision for the Catholic clergy and land reform. Redington suggested the provision of glebes and the upkeep of churches, but Russell felt it was not enough and decided that a generous provision for salaries be financed by a land tax. The pope would be consulted beforehand, but no concordat or formal agreement would be sought.[58] The decision not to insist on conditions pleased Redington:

no fairer opportunity . . . can offer for doing so [endowing the Church] in so far as the condition of Ireland was concerned . . . they [the Irish Catholics] and the Pope should be assured that 'the object is not to weaken in any way the spiritual influence of the Roman Catholic Clergy but to secure temporal peace'. You have wisely determined not to negotiate the arrangement of any thing connected with the Catholic Church by means

---

[57] *Hansard*, c. 1134, 4 Aug. 1848.
[58] Russell to Redington, 6 Sept. 1848, Russell Papers, PRO 30/22/7D.

of a Concordat, as I am well aware any overture on that point would not be favourably received by the Court of Rome, especially as such a measure would be unpalatable to the Roman Catholic body in Ireland.

An offer without strings attached was so important for Redington, aware of Catholic suspicions as regards government moves at Rome, that he spelled out the conditions:

especial care being taken to let it clearly be seen, that it is not the wish or object of the British Government to place the Roman Catholic Church in Ireland in servitude to the temporal power. This will be best shewn by their not seeking for a Concordat or requiring any conditions such as in former times were suggested—a veto on the appointment of the Bishops or the like.[59]

Redington remembered the divisive veto controversy, the furore that the scare of a concordat had aroused in 1845, and the backlash the Minto mission had unleashed. If the settlement contained the slightest suggestion of impinging on the Church's influence, the clergy and Rome would reject it out of hand. Well satisfied with his trip, Russell left Ireland on 9 September, and in October asked Clarendon to come over and put the plan to the cabinet 'as part of our general scheme'.[60] There were two main difficulties to be overcome: the fear of the Irish bishops and the fury of the anti-Catholics. Redington sounded out Murray. Murray was not optimistic and predicted that the bishops would renew their rejection at the forthcoming annual meeting, although 'secretly the Majority of the Clergy would not join in that feeling—especially the curates.'[61] As it turned out the bishops, who had advanced their meeting from November to October because of the state of the country, were primarily concerned with the Famine but, alerted by Stanley's remarks, they pre-empted the government move on salaries. Underlining their solidarity with their people, they declared that 'having shared in the prosperity of their flocks, the clergy of Ireland are willing to share in their privations, and are determined to resist a measure calculated to create vast discontent—to sever the people from their pastors, and ultimately to endanger Catholicity in this country'.[62]

---

[59] Redington to Russell, 7 Sept. 1848, ibid.
[60] Russell to Clarendon, 6 Oct. 1848, Clarendon Papers, Box 43.
[61] Redington to Clarendon, 4 Oct. 1848, ibid., Box 24/7.
[62] *Catholic Directory, 1849*, 312–13.

This was the strongest rejection yet of endowment and it was woven into the emotive question of famine suffering. Whether or not, as Murray appeared to doubt, the bishops' sentiments were shared by the starving curates, the reason given undoubtedly goes to the heart of the matter: any measure that appeared to sever the people from their pastors alarmed the bishops and was to be firmly rejected. Although Murray believed it was a foolish decision, he was unable to resist it. Since MacHale, the leader of the anti-government party, and his ally O'Higgins were absent in Rome, the resolution was a clear indication that most bishops took a different line from Murray on this issue.[63]

Russell nevertheless determined to stick to his plan. 'Circumstances', he told Clarendon, 'are in other respects so favourable for a great settlement that I should not be deterred if all the bishops concurred in a *nolle prosequi*.' He called a special cabinet meeting on 24 October to which he summoned Clarendon and proposed to entrust an annual sum of £340,000 to the Catholic hierarchy for the endowment of the Catholic clergy.[64] There was general agreement except for Wood. Grey, who endorsed the scheme but wanted it as part of a larger plan to prevent further agitation, believed that the government should carry the scheme but would be turned out of office. At this comment Russell stoutly declared that he would rather fail by trying to carry it than not try at all. 'It was the duty of Government', he maintained. At last Russell was courageously preparing to implement a programme which, for over twenty years, he had considered to be the key to the Irish problem.

A preliminary obstacle was papal approval, but when Palmerston's brother, Sir William Temple, envoy to Naples, approached Pius IX he raised no objection but left it to the Irish bishops. Russell now appointed a cabinet committee to work out the details. This was a tactical mistake for, given the composition of the cabinet, it would have been better if Russell had formulated his own scheme since no other minister was as interested in its success as he was. Difficulties arose immediately. Wood opposed giving any more money for Irish purposes. With Sir George Grey he argued that neither parliament nor country would be disposed to

[63] Clarendon to Russell, 16 Oct. 1848, Clarendon Papers, Letterbook 3.
[64] Broughton, diary, 24 Oct. 1848, Add. MSS 43753, fos. 46–8; Grey, Journal, 24 Oct. 1848, c. 3/14, UD.

advance money in any shape for Irish purposes.[65] As Palmerston had remarked: 'that we ought to pay the Catholic Priests is manifest; how we can accomplish it is quite another thing'.[66]

Wood had listed what he believed were the three main difficulties: the impossibility of raising such a large sum, the extreme unpopularity of the scheme in England, and the probability that the bishops would reject it. As regards the first, Russell decided on a separate tax on Ireland. This would avoid an English or Scottish outcry of 'Rome on the rates', but Redington feared that the Presbyterians of the north would baulk at paying a tax to subsidize the Roman clergy.[67] The second difficulty was not unconnected and constituted the most immediate one for Russell's weak government, with its precarious parliamentary majority. In addition to voluntarists who opposed state endowment of religion, the 1847 election had returned many members sensitive to Protestant views and already in August they had begun to organize.[68] The anti-Catholic National Club set up a subcommittee 'to consider of the best mode of arousing the sense of the Country to the dangers which will result from the endowment of Romanism by the State'.[69] Peel confessed that he was dispirited by this no-popery feeling, but felt it could be overcome. By November, however, Greville noted that 'Protestant bigotry and anti-Catholic rancour continue to flourish with undiminished intensity'.[70] Clarendon was taken aback at the strength of Protestant opposition he encountered when he came to England. Stanley, noting the strength of this Protestant feeling, was anxious that the scheme be abandoned and brought pressure to bear on Russell through his brother, the duke of Bedford, who wrote that 'the question is surrounded by difficulties. Hardinge says that unless you are pretty sure of carrying it, it would be a pity to raise a storm, and to expose your friends to its pelting. Stanley . . . says that the opposition would come chiefly from your own supporters.'[71] Russell knew that it was Stanley who was trying, with some success, to persuade Hardinge that the

[65] Greville, *Memoirs*, 11, 15 Nov. 1848, vi. 243–4.
[66] Palmerston to Clarendon, 11 Oct. 1848, Clarendon Papers, c. 524.
[67] Greville, *Memoirs*, 15 Nov. 1844, vi. 244.
[68] G. I. T. Machin, *Politics and the Churches in Great Britain 1832–1868* (1977), 183–92.
[69] J. Wolffe, *The Protestant Crusade in Great Britain, 1829–1860* (1991), 236.
[70] Greville, *Memoirs*, 7 Nov. 1848, vi. 124–5.
[71] Russell to Clarendon, 4 Nov. 1848, Clarendon Papers, Box 43.

scheme was impracticable. The dilemma, as Clarendon had explained to Lewis, who, like Greville, kept up his advocacy of the scheme, was that 'if we get no previous assurance of support from the Catholics, and those who desire the measure are lying low to see which way the wind may blow, the Government may get into a useless scrape'.[72]

Clarendon was right for, given the strength of the opposition in England, the attitude of the Catholics—the third major difficulty Wood pinpointed—would be decisive. The timing for an approach to the bishops was unfortunate, for the opponents had forestalled the government and brought the bishops' meeting to issue a statement. It would now be difficult for the bishops to go back on their decision. Despite Russell's light-hearted dismissal of the bishops' statement, Redington advised allowing the longest interval possible to elapse between the declaration of the bishops and making a new approach to them. In Dublin the nationalist press, alarmed by Stanley's remarks, came out in support of the bishops' statement.[73] Redington, however, who regarded the measure as one of fundamental importance, advised persevering despite all opposition.

I am satisfied from long consideration that a great opportunity has presented itself for dealing with the whole Irish Question, and probably laying the sane foundation for peace and prosperity in this most troublesome portion of Her Majesty's dominions. The bigotry of England and Scotland and the proclaimed indifference (to say the least) of the Irish prelates of the Roman Catholic Church may well make the Cabinet pause and hesitate but I think the proper course will be to determine upon what is right to be done for this country and persevere with those measures, heedless of the opposition of the MacHaleites.

Redington believed the measure could go far towards a permanent solution of the Irish problem, and he now invited two of Murray's most influential supporters, Fr. Ennis and Dean Meyler, to dinner to sound them out further on the matter. When he told them that the proposal to endow the Church was one without any strings attached, they expressed their opinion that, had the bishops known this, they would not have opposed it.[74] This was encouraging so, at the cabinet's request, Redington again consulted

---

[72] Clarendon to Lewis, 2 Nov. 1848, ibid., c. 532/1.
[73] *Freeman's Journal*, 14 Oct. 1848.
[74] Redington to Clarendon, 31 Oct. 1848, Clarendon Papers, Box 24/2.

Murray in what was to be a decisive meeting. He chose a bad day. Murray was in low spirits because the new Roman rescript renewing the condemnation of the colleges had just come. When Redington put his case for clerical salaries and made it clear that they would be given without conditions, Murray replied that he had assumed that all along and that the distinction of endowment *with* securities or *without*, had never arisen in the bishops' discussions. He revealed that even Crolly, who normally supported him, was opposed on the grounds that endowment 'might relax the energies of the priesthood' and the highly respected Kinsella, who had recently died, had been strongly opposed to state provision on principle. Since the bishops had frequently and so recently declared against the measure they could not change their mind at present. The recent rebellion, too, posed a problem, he added, for 'the priests had lost much influence with the people by not supporting them in rebellion and if they became stipendiaries of the state they would lose the remainder'. On a practical level, Murray pointed out that the amount the government was prepared to offer the priests would not compensate for what some of the clergy in the south received in fees for baptisms, marriages, and funerals. When Redington said that there would be no prohibition on their continuing to receive those fees, Murray replied that 'if the Clergy get the Stipend, the parishioners will soon reduce the fees'. Murray was categorical in his pessimistic appraisal of the success of the scheme, Redington remarking that 'he adhered to this opinion throughout'. Redington's enthusiasm could not withstand Murray's pessimism: 'I think this opinion of Dr Murray almost conclusive against stirring in the matter. It is true that he has the weight of years upon him and that he dreads the idea of another question being mooted upon which differences will arise'. Reluctantly Redington concluded that the scheme must be abandoned, for 'the fact is that the clergy will not be soothed and I believe that the maintenance of Churches and all must be given up'.[75] When Clarendon read Redington's letters to the cabinet the pressure mounted against Russell's plan. By the third meeting of the committee on 11 November, Grey noted in his diary that 'we have pretty well ascertained that we must give up the endowment of the priests'. Writing to Clarendon, who was still in London for the

[75] Redington to Clarendon, 5 Nov. 1848, ibid.

cabinet discussions, Somerville resignedly remarked that 'After what has passed on your side of the water, and here between Redington and Dr Murray, I look upon the Endowment question as abandoned for the present.'[76]

Russell had made endowment central to his plan for Ireland and to abandon it meant abandoning his great settlement. He explained his dilemma to Monteagle:

recommendations have come from all quarters, especially (though indirectly) from Archbishop Murray not to stir the question . . . at present. Two reasons are given. 1. That the priests are in bad odour from their blowing cold on the insurrection—and would suffer more if pay followed upon loyalty; 2. That the young Maynooth curates, since Peel's settlement, are likely to be favourable to endowment, but are not yet strong or numerous enough to have weight.[77]

Both reasons need examining. Although in certain areas priests were in bad odour because of their opposition to the rebellion, it is unlikely that this unpopularity was widespread. If the clergy had accepted a government stipend it is possible that their attitude to the rebellion would have been used against them. The other reason Russell gives is more surprising. When, twenty years later, Gladstone was drawing up his plan to achieve that equality between the Churches that Russell had attempted, the president of Maynooth argued for concurrent endowment. Yet the Maynooth priests did not support it.

Russell, however, had also to take Protestant opposition into account: 'the repugnance of Episcopal, Presbyterian, Baptist, Independent and Roman Catholic', he told Monteagle, '[was] such as to defeat any measure for the present'.[78] Together with the lack of enthusiasm on the part of his cabinet colleagues, this opposition finally proved too much for Russell. On 5 December he admitted to the cabinet that the scheme would have to be abandoned. It was a major disappointment for him. Unfortunately, too, having staked all his hopes on this measure, he had nothing to substitute for it and this meant that he went before parliament in 1849 with no important measures for Ireland. Still, he hoped that the project had been postponed rather than abandoned. The dream had for so

---

[76] Somerville to Clarendon, 10 Nov. 1848, ibid.
[77] Russell to Monteagle, 18 Nov. 1848, Monteagle Papers, NLI.
[78] Russell to Monteagle, [12 Nov. 1848], ibid.

long formed a large part of his thinking that he determined to return to it again with new vigour the following year.

The views of the clergy on this important question were difficult to ascertain. Clarendon maintained:

if the vote of the clergy could be taken by ballot the question would be carried by an immense majority though they will not dare express themselves favourably to it in the dioceses of opposing bishops. They [the bishops], according to Dr Murray, can get on pretty well and can afford to wait for better times without doing the unpopular act of accepting payment, and they care little about the Curates, many of whom are starving.[79]

How accurately Murray gauged the situation of the priests is not easy to ascertain, for little written evidence is available. Some of the scanty surviving correspondence of the clergy are letters to Cullen and Kirby, rector and vice-rector respectively of the Irish College in Rome. Relations, ex-alumni, and friends of Cullen— Cooper in Dublin, Maher in Carlow-Graigue—took the same fiercely independent stance as Cullen himself. Nevertheless, some supporting evidence can be found from other clerics for Murray's view. The most interesting and fullest expression of opinion is that of Archdeacon O'Sullivan. He noted in 1844 'that the poor people certainly are willing to contribute to our support as far as their means will allow them'. In May 1847, reflecting on what was for him the tragedy of proselytism in Kenmare, he noted that the people were not instructed. The reason for that was the shortage of priests:

The number of priests to attend to them is too small, the parishes too extensive; with a population of over 10,000 and an area of near 60,000 statute acres, how could myself and my curates come at all the calls, and attend to the instruction of the people . . . What can one of my curates do this day who has a [sick] call thirteen miles from here more than go and return?[80]

The pastoral needs were not being met and the reason was simply that 'We have not priests enough, and if they are multiplied what is to support them?' This brought him to consider the question of a government salary, and his firm conclusion was that

---

[79] Clarendon to Russell, 4 Oct. 1848, Clarendon Papers, Letterbook 3.
[80] O'Sullivan, diary, 23 May 1847, KrDA.

without it 'we cannot much longer get on'. The bishops were removed from the grim reality of the situation in which the priests found themselves:

The Bishops, no doubt, are unanimously opposed to it. They lose no opportunity in recording their determination of resisting it, but this is because they have not the trouble of wringing it out of the miserable creatures from whom we are obliged to extract it. It is because they do not come into collision with the hard fisted as we needs must, for example sake often, as much as for any other reason, if we wish to get anything. It is because they get clean and clear in one lump sum from their vicars who must undergo the odium of its collection. From the number of remittances I have made the Bishop for the last years I was vicar general in Dingle, I calculated his income must be about £1300 a year, and no wonder he should not seek nor wish for a change.[81]

O'Sullivan examined the argument that accepting a stipend would give the government a say in the appointment of bishops, and here he was as firm as its most vehement episcopal opponents: 'Perish the day that we would give the Crown any control in the election or ratification of our Bishops.' It was a false argument, he was convinced, for the government would not look for control. A major advantage which he hoped would result from clerical salaries was that it would keep priests from engaging in popular politics, in which he felt they were too involved. O'Sullivan told Lansdowne that he believed that 'all the priests of this diocese [Kerry], as far as I can ascertain, are favourable to it'. When O'Sullivan dined with the metropolitan chapter in Dublin, however, he found a different opinion prevalent. 'They were unanimous against it,' he noted 'because, as I told them, they got their offerings from rich respectable people and had not to wring it from the poor creatures we have to deal with.'[82]

Although the clergy in Dublin were poorer than O'Sullivan allowed, his assessment of the situation in Kerry is credible for, in company with the bishop, he visited all the parishes more than once and knew the priests and how they lived. He himself was reasonably well off. The entries in the privacy of his diary are the serious comments of a well-informed priest. Other priests shared O'Sullivan's view. The Reverend James Browne of Ballintubber told Count Strzelecki what he thought was the general opinion:

[81] Ibid.   [82] Ibid. 29 Nov. 1847.

There are reports that a State provision is about being made for the clergy. I apprehend the Measure will not be countenanced by the Prelates, but the Clergy are reduced to extreme want, even of common necessities. And unless some provision be made for them, their position is degrading in the extreme.

In his covering letter to Clarendon, Strzelecki remarked that this was an opinion he had heard expressed 'on many occasions by many other Clergymen'.[83] The Reverend John Forrest of Newmarket, who was opposed to endowment, admitted to Kirby that 'the great bulk of the priests would grasp at it as a boon. Some of them are badly off but the great body are well enough'. He concluded that 'If the bishops allow any latitude to the priests in the affair of a pension the affair will be settled.'[84] Patrick Murray of Maynooth, who argued strongly against endowment, claimed that from his personal knowledge and from testimonies above all suspicion there was 'a considerable number of the Irish clergy, who entertain opinions not unfavourable to a state endowment', which included 'men as able, as learned, as zealous . . . as any of those with whom they differ'.[85]

The opinions of O'Sullivan, Browne, Forrest, and Murray tally with those of Archbishop Murray and indicate that priests, in some areas at least, would have welcomed salaries. Several of those who opposed the idea were the better-off priests. Others, however, like Cullen, Maher, Forrest, and Cooper opposed it on the same ideological grounds as the bishops: freedom for the Church from all state control. For many of those, too, a national feeling would have played a role in their opposition.

It is more difficult to ascertain the views of the laity. Most of the Repealers and Young Irelanders would have abhorred state payment as betokening the enslavement of that most important national institution, the Church, to the state. As late as 1844 O'Connell, amid roars of approval from the crowds, reminded them of the veto controversy 'when the people cried out "we will have no Soggart Sassanagh"'.[86] Archbishop Kelly of Tuam was

---

[83] Strzelecki to Clarendon, 26 Aug. 1848, Clarendon Papers, Box 58.
[84] O'Sullivan, diary, 10 July, 29 Nov. 1847, KrDA; Forrest to Kirby, Kirby Papers, ICA.
[85] P. Murray, 'State Endowment of the Catholic Church in Ireland', in id. (ed.), *The Irish Annual Miscellany* (1850), i. 72–3.
[86] *Tablet*, 7 Dec. 1844. 'Soggart Sassanagh' means Saxon priest.

probably right when he claimed in 1825 that 'However much the people may have complained, I think they would prefer, notwithstanding, to support their own clergy, to seeing them paid by the State.'[87] After years of famine, however, some would have welcomed the easing of the burden of supporting the clergy. Whatever their feelings, neither laity nor priests were consulted.

Catholic opposition to Russell's plan for salaries came from the bishops, priests like Cooper in Dublin, and theologians like Patrick Murray. Since payment was against neither the teaching of the Church nor its practice in continental Europe, even in countries where the ruler was not Catholic, the roots of this opposition and the particular circumstances that aroused such hostility need examining. Apart from the long history of hostility between the British government and the Irish Catholic Church, part of the difficulty in 1848 must be sought in recent insensitiveness of both parties to one another's susceptibilities. Many Irish Catholics felt that if Ireland were truly part of the United Kingdom more would have been done to prevent the mass famine deaths and growing number of evictions. The clergy were becoming increasingly worried about proselytism. On the other hand, the English press and parliament believed, when landlords were shot and rebellion broke out, that Irish Catholics were biting the hand that fed them. Denunciations of the clergy as abetting assassination and Minto's negotiations in Rome made the clergy believe that the government wanted to control them and made them suspicious of its apparent favours. Stanley's remark bracketing endowment with policing deepened that suspicion and, having put their opposition on record at their meeting shortly afterwards, it would have been difficult for the bishops, as Murray pointed out, to reverse it so quickly. If he raised the issue, another bruising conflict would be the result. The bishops' letters to Briggs less than a year earlier gave an insight into their feeling; three-quarters of them expressed mistrust of government intentions, even the moderate Delaney of Cork, maintaining that it was working 'for the purpose of impairing their [hierarchy's] influence and obtaining for themselves [the government] a right of interference'.[88] Clarendon was scarcely exaggerating a year later when he complained to Henry Tufnell, the

---

[87] *Reports from the Select Committee appointed to inquire into the State of Ireland ... PP 1825*, viii. 260.

[88] William Delaney to Briggs, 24 Dec. 1847, Briggs Papers, 1709 LDA.

chief whip, that 'nothing can make the Irish clergy believe that the British Government is not always plotting for the destruction of the Roman Catholic religion'.[89]

At the root of their opposition was this suspicion, understandable enough in view of the long history of bad relations. Trust was essential for any conciliation scheme, especially for the proposed endowment of the clergy, which of its nature would bring priests and bishops into closer contact with the government and, as they feared, make them dependent on it. It was too much to expect that Irish Catholic bishops would place their Church in such a position of dependence on the British state, which was still a strongly Protestant one and fundamentally hostile to their faith. For the bishops, in particular, who perceived themselves as guardians of the faith, the priority was to avoid popular alienation from the Church. Financial considerations took second place. A number of them, such as Kinsella, O'Higgins, and MacHale, would have held views similar to those of the French Liberal Catholics whose leader, Abbé Félicité de Lamennais, had, in 1830, denounced 'the scrap of bread thrown to the [French] clergy . . . [as] the title-deed of her subjection' and cited the Irish refusal to accept state payment as the example the French should follow. This concern for the Church's freedom was the main difficulty, and was the one advanced by Patrick Murray in his comprehensive article, where, citing the example of the French Church, he wrote: 'The danger which I dread in the state endowment of the priesthood, is . . . from a narrowing of the Church's liberty, an intermeddling in her own proper affairs.'[90] Furthermore, even those who might have been willing to accept salaries were reluctant to incur the odium of taking an unpopular move and Clarendon acutely observed that 'the Bishops will be afraid of the People and the Priests will be afraid of the Bishops'.[91] A few years earlier a well-placed, if unsympathetic, observer, Maria Edgeworth, had criticized Sydney Smith's advocacy of salaries for the clergy as too facile a solution, commenting that it did not take into account 'that the clergy love power as other men do—as well as money—and that their love of

---

[89] Clarendon to Tufnell, 28 Apr. 1850, Clarendon Papers, Box 70.

[90] Murray, 'State Endowment', 76–7. Lamennais's article appeared in his journal, *l'Avenir*, 18 Oct. 1830, cited in L. Le Guillou and N. Roger-Taillade (eds.), *Journal Intime Inédit* (1990), ii. 111.

[91] Clarendon to Russell, 4 Nov. 1849, Clarendon Papers, Letterbook 5.

power over their flocks cannot easily be bought off'.[92] The clergy would have described this power as influence for the spiritual welfare of the people. In any case Peel's concessions, the Bequests Act, and in particular the generous Maynooth Grant, on the very eve of the Famine, had eased the critical financial burden for the bishops, if not for the priests, in the nick of time.

In the autumn of 1849 Russell again opened up the question of Catholic endowment. Peel had assured Russell that, in England, the endowment had become far less unpopular than it had been and, thus encouraged, Russell cheerfully expressed his determination 'to make it even popular'. The fact that the question was not raised at the annual bishops' meeting was also a hopeful sign that their open antagonism had diminished; McGettigan of Raphoe told Redington that if it had been raised they would not have ventured to record their annual protest against it as the distress and privations of the clergy were so dreadful that they would thankfully accept a provision. McGettigan added that 'some curates do not scrape together £25 a year'. Still, despite the undoubted distress among many of them, he doubted whether the clergy could be brought openly to declare their desire for endowment. While Redington was willing to co-operate fully, Clarendon was more difficult to persuade. Greville may have been right in asserting that Clarendon was opposed to the scheme for, certainly in 1849, he poured cold water on it. He told Lewis that parliament was not ready for 'large measures'.[93] When Monteagle told him of a meeting he had had with the Limerick clergy, whose bishop, John Ryan, favoured endowment, Clarendon was alarmed and expressed the fervent hope that the clergy would not abandon their previous unwillingness to accept payment 'for *their* unwillingness is a better reason than our inability to do that which in the present hourly-increasing bigotry of England and Scotland must be unpopular'.[94] To Russell he pointed to the renewed sectarian bitterness as a new difficulty. When Russell brushed aside this objection, Clarendon again raised the objection to taxes. Only magic, he remarked sceptically, could make the plan popular with 'Irish Proprietors and

---

[92] Maria Edgeworth to Richard Butler, 3 Apr. 1845, cited in M. Hurst, *Maria Edgeworth and the Public Scene: Intellect, Fine Feeling and Landlordism in the Age of Reform* (1969), 144.

[93] Clarendon to Lewis, 10 Oct. 1849, Clarendon Papers, c. 532/1.

[94] Clarendon to Monteagle, 26 Oct. 1849, Monteagle Papers, NLI.

English and Scotch bigots'. He had believed in the scheme, he said, 'until the question was on the *tapis* last year and I had the opportunity in England of ascertaining for myself how bitter and uncompromising the feelings of Dissenters were upon the subject and how alarmed and angry the representatives of all large constituencies were at the supposed intention of the government'. 'If that same state of things exists', he said, and if Russell proposed endowment, 'you will go out of office *re infecta*'.[95] Alarmed by Clarendon's prediction that the measure would fail, Russell decided to consult Tufnell, who told him that the proposal would upset the government and that the measure would indeed fail. On hearing this Russell, without even putting it to the cabinet, tamely decided that 'we must put it off for another year'. In contrast to the previous year, the reason for postponing it in 1849 had less to do with opposition from the bishops than opposition from Protestants. It was the anticipated opposition from that source that Clarendon used to pour cold water on Russell's enthusiasm. Twenty-five years later Russell was still recommending concurrent endowment instead of disestablishment of the Anglican Church and the payment of the priests as a panacea for Irish ills, but never again would he have the opportunity to put his favourite scheme to the test.[96]

The Church's view of state endowment had changed from acceptance in 1799 to rejection fifty years later. As on the related question of a veto, a shift in attitude is noticeable in the post-Napoleonic period. By the 1830s rejection of clerical salaries had become the common attitude among bishops. Government outlook had also changed. During the eighteenth century and up to Catholic emancipation, endowment was regarded not merely as liberating the clergy from dependence on an unruly peasantry, but also as a necessary control over a body whose loyalty was often questioned. Russell's plan of 'concurrent' endowment of the Catholic Church, however, was more positive in its thrust. It was principally intended to conciliate Catholics by upgrading their religion and its ministers. It was aimed also at producing a better-educated and more gentleman-like priest, similar to the French *curé* if not the

---

[95] Clarendon to Russell, 20 Nov. 1849, Clarendon Papers, Letterbook 5.
[96] S. Walpole, *The Life of Lord John Russell* (1889), ii. 433; Russell, *Recollections*, 243.

Anglican vicar. Lewis had argued cogently for endowment without any strings attached and this is what Russell proposed. He
rejected a settlement that would be seen by Catholics as no more
than a bribe.

The decision not to press ahead with this scheme in 1848 and
1849 marks an important turning-point in Russell's Irish policy
and in his political life. The corner-stone of his Irish policy was
the endowment of the Irish Church; without it he had simply no
grand plan for Ireland. The opposition to it was formidable yet
it is surprising that he gave up so easily on his favourite solution.
Peel faced as difficult a problem when, having already alienated
his supporters by his change of opinion in 1829 on Catholic
emancipation, he introduced a type of Catholic endowment in the
increased and permanent Maynooth Grant of 1845. Gladstone,
too, faced as great a struggle in 1869 when he abolished all en-
dowments. One major difference was that Peel and Gladstone
could count on Catholic support on those issues whereas Russell
could not. This does not completely explain Russell's failure. Either
Russell had not thought the matter through and made contingency
plans for possible difficulties, or he lacked the courage to persevere in the face of all obstacles. Probably both are true. When the
time of decision came, he quailed before the double threat of
Protestant opposition and Catholic reluctance. Yet he knew the
extent of the opposition from both sides beforehand and had dismissed the one and disregarded the other. Many years later, referring to Gladstone's ability in carrying Disestablishment, he made
an interesting admission:

My political character is very much the reverse of that which Sydney
Smith . . . attributed to me. . . . My disposition has always been favourable to compromise and moderation. . . . I felt, however, that boldness,
which, according to Lord Bacon, is the first quality of a statesman, was
required as the primary quality for dealing with the Irish Church . . .[97]

It is not unlikely that this statement is a tacit admission of his
timidity in tackling decisively the issue closest to his heart. Greville
believed that firmness was necessary, and that was what Russell
lacked. He was a sick man during much of 1848 and lack of support from his colleagues, including Clarendon, forced him to shrink

[97] Russell, *Recollections*, 285.

from the difficulties. In June 1848, Greville confided to Clarendon that:

> Whether it be by their fault or their misfortune, it is evident that this Government has been continually falling in public estimation . . . John Russell himself appears a great failure. He has been unlucky in his own and his wife's health . . . his wife torments him to death.[98]

Given the strength of the opposition it might have been wiser for Russell to accept Redington's plan of a provision for glebes and places of worship which was acceptable to the bishops and would conceivably have caused less opposition among Protestants, to whom it could have been proposed as a logical extension of the Maynooth Grant. In the weak position in which he found himself, it was understandable that Russell shrank, in Bedford's words, from raising a storm and exposing his government and party to its pelting. Yet, since he had made the measure the centrepiece of his Irish policy, its postponement and virtual abandonment left him with few cards to play.

The other great measure for Ireland was the Encumbered Estates Act. Other studies have examined the economic and social aspects which were central to this Act. The significant improvement Russell hoped it would bring formed an integral part of his wide-ranging, indeed sweeping, reform plan for Ireland. Realizing how revolutionary it was, he spelt out carefully the probable consequences:

> This is a serious change. The new proprietors will not be separated from the clergy and the people by religion and habits; but they will not be united to the Government by the feeling that the English connexion is their only security. We ought not therefore to adopt this change, without looking forward to the ultimate consequences—the Roman Catholic Church united with the State and the displacement of 'one stratum in the social hierarchy' of Ireland—viz. the Protestant gentry.[99]

This was a quite radical approach and surfacing here again was Russell's general plan which involved the establishment of a Catholic parson and a Catholic squire working in harmony with the state. The Encumbered Estates Act of 1848, however, proved

---

[98] Greville to Clarendon, 23 June 1848, Clarendon Papers, c. 521.
[99] Russell to Clarendon, 13 Dec. 1847, ibid., Irish deposit, Box 43; Prest, *Russell*, 275.

abortive and had to be amended, along lines suggested by Peel, in a new Act in 1849.[100] Though it was an important piece of legislation, and a number of Catholic merchants acquired land through it, Russell's expectations from it were not fulfilled. Furthermore, since his scheme to endow the clergy never got off the ground, by 1849 his great plan for Ireland had stalled.

In 1843 Russell had been able to claim that Peel and good government in Ireland were a contradiction and could fairly contrast the tranquillity the Whigs' government had brought in the 1830s with Tory rule, which had resulted in a situation where 'Ireland was occupied, not governed'. By 1849, after the catastrophic Famine, the Young Ireland rebellion, the renewed Coercion Acts, the botched Encumbered Estates Act, and the collapse of the plan for Catholic endowment, his claim to understand and govern Ireland better was open to question. As John Prest points out, Russell had always thought himself superior to Peel on Ireland, and when this was no longer so the upheaval in the political firmament told upon his temper.[101] His failure damaged his own party's belief in him as the expert on Ireland. There still remained the possibility that in 1850, in an improving economic climate, he could relaunch his plans. In the course of that year, however, important changes took place in Ireland, within the Catholic Church, and in his own relations with Catholics which rendered a resumption of his plan for Catholic endowment or any other major reform more difficult.

---

[100] J. S. Donnelly, 'Landlords and Tenants', in Vaughan (ed.), *New History*, v. 346–9; J. C. Brady, 'Legal developments, 1801–79', ibid. 456–7.
[101] Prest, *Russell*, 292–302.

7

Conflicts and Resolutions: Protestant Missioners, Archbishop Cullen, and the Synod of Thurles, 1849–1850

'"There are no riches, nor treasures, nor honours, nor worldly wealth", Saint Augustine wisely declared, "greater than the Catholic Faith".'

(Synod of Thurles, September 1850)

Over most of Europe revolution had ground to a halt by the end of 1848. On 21 November a new government under Schwarzenberg came to power in Austria, Franz Josef became emperor a fortnight later, and almost simultaneously Louis Napoléon was elected president in France. In Rome, however, the revolution was only beginning. On 15 November, as Russell's cabinet committee was attempting to work out its plan for the Irish clergy, Count Pellegrino Rossi, a key figure in the papal government, was assassinated. The pope fled to Gaeta and his attitude towards Liberalism underwent a complete change.

In Ireland the situation in 1849 was as bleak as ever. The Young Ireland rebellion had further alienated many in England. Officially the Famine was over, and Trevelyan had said that no more funds were available for relief. The Society of Friends wound up its outstanding operations in June 1849, pointing out that the problem was 'far beyond the reach of private exertion'. Yet in fact 1849 and 1850 were years of terrible distress in many areas. Cholera had broken out again and the blight reappeared in May. People were exhausted by three years of famine, and even those with some reserves found them now exhausted. In May, alarmed by the distress, a new relief committee was set up in Dublin: the Royal Exchange or General Relief Committee with Fr. Spratt as its energetic secretary. What the government would do was the question uppermost in most Irish people's minds. Russell's plan of paying

the priests would at least have relieved the Catholic poor of a
heavy burden, enabled the clergy to help their parishioners, and
injected much-needed money into the system. It would also have
been an indication of the government's intentions to proceed with
far-reaching measures for the improvement of Ireland. Having
dropped it, however, Russell did not replace it with any other
relief measure. In growing desperation, Clarendon complained again
and again to Bedford of the seriousness of the situation in Ireland
and Russell's weakness in cabinet:

It grieves me beyond expression to see Lord John is not master in his own
Cabinet and that on more than one occasion he should be compelled to
write to me, that having no real support, he was obliged to yield or to
break up the Cabinet.... Lord John himself has written to me saying
that we now see the fatal effects of meeting Parliament without any
plan.... I have ... expressed my fears that the doctrines of Trevelyan,
whose mouthpiece C. Wood is, would prevail.... C. Wood, backed by
Grey, and relying upon arguments (or rather Trevelyanisms) that are no
more applicable to Ireland than to Loo Choo, affirmed that the right
thing to do was to do nothing—they have prevailed and you see what a
fix we are in.[1]

Clarendon was right. From the home office, Lewis confirmed
that both sides of the House of Commons saw the absence of a
plan as a capital error and a proof of Russell's inefficiency.[2] Greville,
acknowledging that the people in Ireland were dying of hunger
and no one knew what to do, commented: 'All call on the Government for a plan and a remedy, but the Government have no
plan and no remedy; there is nothing but disagreement among
them; and while they are discussing and disputing, the masses
are dying.'[3] The absence of a plan was disastrous both for Ireland
and for the government's credibility. Clarendon's conviction that
Trevelyan was to blame was corroborated by Lansdowne, who told
Greville that Trevelyan was the real author of Wood's scheme to
refuse giving or lending money and to let misery and distress run
their course. A more widespread resistance to Irish relief schemes
existed, however, for when Wood proposed a grant of £50,000
Greville reported that 'the English members and constituencies

---

[1] Clarendon to Bedford, 16 Feb. 1849, Clarendon Papers, Box 80.
[2] Lewis to Clarendon, 14 Feb. 1849, Clarendon Papers, c. 530.
[3] C. C. F. Greville, *The Greville Memoirs: A Journal of the Reign of Queen
Victoria*, ed. H. Reeve (1903), 9 Feb. 1849, vi. 274.

have become savage and hard-hearted towards the Irish and one after another of all parties jumped up and opposed the grant.'[4] Russell gave his own assessment of the situation to Clarendon:

the great difficulty of this year respecting Ireland is one which does not spring from Trevelyan or C. Wood but lies deep in the breast of the British people. It is this. We have granted, lent, subscribed, worked, visited, clothed the Irish,—millions of money, years of debates etc etc—the only return is calumny and rebellion. Let us not grant, lend, clothe etc etc anymore, and see what that will do. Such is the result to which MacHale, J. O'Connell, and Smith O'Brien have brought us. Now without borrowing and lending we could have no great plan for Ireland and, much as I wished it, I have to see that it is impracticable.[5]

Faced with such obstacles, only a strong-willed prime minister could press through any costly new policies for Ireland in 1849. Russell, unable to get his way in cabinet, made ineffectual threats to resign if he were continually thwarted.[6] Nothing was done. Irish affairs, after topping the political agenda for a brief moment, slipped into the background. Clarendon, under pressure from many quarters, began to despair. 'I am sadly out of spirits', he confided to Monteagle, 'if I ever allowed myself to despair about *anything* I would be inclined to do so now about Ireland.' He felt, he complained, like an animal tied and baited with the woes, the complaints, and remonstrances of one man after another and his only hope was that the future would not be so diabolically bad as the present seemed to indicate.[7] As it became clear that the government lacked the energy, the resources, or the political will to deal with the problem many, faced with continuing distress, began to lose hope. Thousands, even among the less distressed, abandoning the struggle, forsook their farms and fled the land. Mass emigration began to Britain, Canada, and America. Evictions had increased to reach a frightening total of 13,384 families for the year.[8] Tenants began to organize resistance and, in October 1849,

---

[4] C. C. F. Greville, ibid.

[5] Russell to Clarendon, 24 Feb. 1849, Clarendon Papers, Box 26.

[6] Russell to Clarendon, 17 Jan. 1849, ibid.

[7] Clarendon to Monteagle, 20 Feb. 1849, Monteagle Papers, NLI.

[8] This number constituted 19.46% of all net evictions recorded by constabulary, 1849–80; T. W. Moody, F. X. Martin, and F. J. Byrne (eds.), *A New History of Ireland: A Chronology of Irish History to 1976* (1982), 325. For an assessment of eviction figures see W. E. Vaughan, *Landlords and Tenants in Ireland 1848–1904* (1984), 13–26.

two Catholic curates in Callan, County Kilkenny, Thomas O'Shea and Matthew O'Keefe, launched the first successful Tenant Protection Society. Before long, numerous priests and nine bishops had publicly declared their support for the Tenant League that emerged from this movement and a union was forged with Ulster tenants.[9] Priests and Presbyterian ministers sat on the same platform advocating tenant rights. Given the worsening religious antagonism in the country, it was uncertain how long this League of North and South, of Orange and Green, as enthusiastic nationalists called it, would last.

With Wood and his supporters in cabinet and at the Treasury intent on giving Ireland as little as possible from the imperial exchequer, the government brought in the Rate-in-Aid bill, which levied a rate for relief on the already hard-hit Irish Poor Law unions. This was quite a change, for the burden of relief was shifted from the United Kingdom to Ireland. A new furore was the immediate result. Lansdowne and the Irish proprietors were incensed. The measure contradicted, as Clarendon admitted, the very notion of a United Kingdom and Russell's own assurance that, in the time of its need, the poorer part of the kingdom could look for support to the richer part which would prove, he had said, that the two islands formed but one undivided realm. It enraged the Ulster Protestants, who did not want to be taxed for the support of Connacht and Munster.[10] They became 'demented with rage', Clarendon alleged, and 'quite as ready for rebellion as the Clubs and Confederates were last year'.[11] Angry at 'this selfish and rebellious spirit' in Ulster, he concluded that even the best of Irishmen were but *'plated savages'*.[12]

In Ulster, hostility between members of the Orange Order and Ribbon Society, an agrarian and nationalist movement, erupted in 1849.[13] Clarendon reported attacks on a Catholic St Patrick's Day procession near Downpatrick during which a policeman and a

---

[9] In Tipperary, the ratio of priests to laymen on the League's organizing committee was 31 : 22; J. O'Shea, *Priests, Politics and Society in Post-Famine Ireland, A Study of County Tipperary 1850–1891* (1983), 60.

[10] J. Grant, 'The Great Famine and the Poor Law in Ulster: The Rate-in-Aid Issue of 1849', *Irish Historical Studies*, 27 (1970), 634–52.

[11] Clarendon to Bedford, 9 Mar. 1849, Clarendon Papers, Box 80.

[12] Clarendon to Bedford, 29 Mar. 1849, ibid.

[13] For sectarianism in Ulster, see D. Hempton and M. Hill, *Evangelical Protestantism in Ulster Society, 1740–1890* (1992), 47–102.

woman were killed.[14] Worse was to follow. The bloodiest encounter between Catholics and Orangemen in Ulster since the foundation of the Orange Order in 1795 took place on 12 July. The Orangemen returning from a celebration in the grounds of Lord Roden, grand master of the Orange Society of Ireland, passed through a Catholic district at Dolly's Brae, near Castlewellan in County Down. Ribbonmen blocked their way. In the ensuing battle many Catholics were killed and the homes of Catholics sacked and burned.[15] The inquest was unable to discover those responsible for the killings. Clarendon was outraged and ordered an inquiry. On 13 September, at Castlewellan Petty Sessions, Roden, although indirectly implicated, presided, and he and his fellow magistrates refused to take informations against Orangemen involved. At the session on 9 October they again refused. This was too much for Clarendon, and he dismissed Roden and two of his colleagues from the magistracy. Clarendon, hoping for support from *The Times*, or 'to bespeak the attention of that *tout puissant* journal', explained to Reeve that 'when I received Berwick's report and the evidence and found how much the loss of life . . . and the brutal outrages committed . . . were attributable to the indiscretion and party spirit of the Magistrates I could come to no other conclusion than that they ought to be removed from the Bench'.[16] Their removal provoked an indignant outcry from the Orangemen, who accused Clarendon of persecuting Roden and other loyal Orangemen. 'The North is in a state of Rabies', Clarendon told the home secretary, 'because Roden's dismissal is a token that Law and Order and Roman Catholics are not to be trampled on with impunity.'[17] Apart from accusing him of subservience to the pope in the matter of the colleges, Orangemen charged Clarendon with double-dealing in 1848 by willingly accepting the arming of the Ulster Protestants while pretending to the Catholics that he would never countenance it. The influential *Quarterly Review* asserted that

---

[14] Clarendon to George Grey, 18, 19 Mar. and 7, 14 July 1849, Clarendon Papers, Letterbook 6. A. Macaulay, *Patrick Dorian, Bishop of Down and Connor, 1865–1885* (1987), 75.

[15] Estimates of the number of Catholics killed vary. J. Lee, *The Modernisation of Irish Society, 1848–1918* (1973), 50, gives the figure of 20; Macaulay, *Dorian*, 75, mentions 3; whereas D. J. Hickey and J. E. Doherty, *A Dictionary of Irish History since 1800* (1980), 134, put the number at 30.

[16] Clarendon to Reeve, Clarendon Papers, c. 534.

[17] Clarendon to Grey, 19 Oct. 1849, ibid., Letterbook 4.

'arms were supplied, and supplied to Orangemen', and published details alleging that Major Turner, Master of the Horse, had given the Dublin Orangemen £600 for the purchase of arms and that this move was secretly authorized by Clarendon.[18] Isaac Butt (1813–79), a barrister, and founder and editor of the *Dublin University Magazine*, made similar charges, alleging that Corry Connellan, Clarendon's secretary, was covertly, on behalf of Clarendon, encouraging the Orangemen, and that as a result of his negotiations with Steward Blacker, a leading Orangeman, the Orangemen had acquired five hundred stand of arms.[19] It appears that Captain Kennedy, an army engineer, had advanced £500 or £600 to arm the loyalists. Clarendon knew of this arms deal, but claimed that it was not government money and denied that he ever handed out musket or cartridge.[20] Did the viceroy engage in secret negotiation? Given the tense circumstances in the months leading up to the rebellion, it is probable that he closed his eyes to Kennedy's activity or even secretly encouraged it. All he admitted was of greeting with 'fair words' those who promised support. As he told Russell at the time, the Orangemen 'must not be encouraged and yet they ought not to be too much snubbed, for many of these people mean well to the institutions of the Country though hostility to the Catholics is doubtless their moving principle'.[21] Russell had indeed advised Clarendon '*in extremis*, not to rebuff offers of help from Orange associations, and to envisage arming the Protestants'.[22] Yet, even when Wellington advised it, Clarendon resisted the temptation to call out the yeomanry, telling Russell, who was prepared to agree to that step, that 'the time may come . . . but that time *has not yet arrived*'.[23] Whether or not his 'fair words' were misinterpreted by some loyalists, he was now paying dearly for them.

[18] [J. W. Croker], 'Lord Clarendon and the Orange Institution', *Quarterly Review*, 86 (Dec. 1849), 228–94; id., 'Lord-Lieutenant Clarendon', ibid. 480–91. John Wilson Croker (1780–1857), conservative politician and writer.

[19] [I. Butt], 'Ireland under Lord Clarendon', *Dublin University Magazine*, 39 (1853), 377–83. Isaac Butt (1813–79), professor of political economy at Trinity College (1836–40) was a Tory; later founder of the Home Rule movement. James Corry Connellan (*c*.1807–85), called to Irish bar (1836); private secretary to Bessborough (1846) and then to Clarendon (1847).

[20] Clarendon to Delane, 2 Dec. 1849, cited in A. I. Dasent, *John Thadeus Delane, Editor of 'The Times', His Life and Correspondence* (1908), i. 96–100.

[21] Clarendon to Russell, 15 Mar. 1848, Clarendon Papers, Letterbook 2.

[22] Russell to Clarendon, 19 Mar., 3 Apr., 17 July 1848, ibid., Irish Box 43.

[23] Clarendon to Russell, 28 July 1848, ibid., Letterbook 3.

From October 1849 to the end of February, Clarendon was harassed by Orangemen in Ireland and Roden's influential friends among the Tory party in England. Stanley raised the matter in the House of Lords. Clarendon was forced to cross to Westminster, where he made a spirited defence of his reasons for dismissing Roden.[24] Clarendon was pleased, and in a list of his achievements which he drew up for the *Edinburgh Review* he included 'Dolly's Brae and its consequences among which will be the extinction of Orangeism!'[25] At his behest the government brought in a Party Processions Act, making it a criminal offence to parade with firearms or carry banners or sing songs 'which may be calculated . . . to provoke animosity between different classes of Her Majesty's subjects'.

Yet Clarendon was able to please neither side, for Ulster Catholics were disappointed that their appeal to the lord lieutenant to dismiss all the magistrates who refused to take informations in the Dolly's Brae affair had been rejected.[26] These angry controversies and public disclosures nettled Clarendon, showing him more clearly the rough realities that faced any chief governor in Ireland. Disappointed at the meagre results of his policies, disgruntled by Russell's soft approach, annoyed with Catholics and Orangemen alike, he had become increasingly disillusioned with his role in Ireland and with Russell's government. Under attack on many fronts, he expressed his frustration to Bedford:

Every day I am obliged to contradict some fresh calumny and falsehood and this together with the prospect of next winter, agrarian murders beginning again, and ruin staring every body in the face make my office almost unendurable. I have nothing like rest of mind and that would wear out a cast iron man.[27]

The autumn, however, marked a personal success for Clarendon. For some time both he and Russell had wanted Queen Victoria to visit Ireland. Clarendon hoped that her visit would give a much-needed boost to the Irish economy, and both he and the prime minister believed that it would be a symbol and celebration of the

[24] *Hansard*, cvii. 603, 1004, 1129; *Nation*, 16, 23 Feb. 1850. Edward Stanley (1790–1869), Lord Derby (succ. 1851), chief secretary for Ireland (1830–3); prime minister (1852).
[25] Clarendon to Lewis, 28 Apr. 1850, Clarendon Papers, c. 532/2.
[26] Macaulay, *Dorian*, 75–6.
[27] Clarendon to Bedford, 17 Oct. 1849, Clarendon Papers, Box 80.

unity of all subjects in the United Kingdom. It was finally agreed that she should come on 3 August. Would the Catholic clergy welcome her appropriately? The three archbishops—the archdiocese of Armagh had been vacant since Crolly's death in April—had sharply different reactions to the news of the visit. MacHale demanded that the bishops meet her in Dublin and explain to her the real state of the country.[28] Slattery proposed that an address, detailing the sufferings from the Famine and other Irish afflictions, be presented to her.[29] Murray, who normally drafted the hierarchy's addresses, circulated a draft address of warm welcome.[30] MacHale, accusing it of passing over the state of the poor in silence, angrily rejected it:

I could not affix my signature to any form of address deficient in the expression of those evangelical duties to our flocks, suffering from famine and cruelty, on which Christian bishops should not be silent. . . . I regret I find no allusion whatever to the sufferings of the people, or the causes under the control of legislative enactment by which their sufferings are still aggravated.[31]

MacHale drew up a draft text which drew attention to the mass mortality that 'has in several parts of Ireland, diminished your Majesty's subjects by a fourth, and in some by a half', the 'cruel evictions' and suffering from famine. Slattery insisted that the bishops would not sign a milk-and-water or merely complimentary address.[32] Murray now inserted a reference in his text to 'the many woes of our suffering poor', but his change did not go to the heart of his two colleagues' objections. MacHale complained that 'it leaves the original address still liable to the same objections of being entirely silent on the hideous cruelty inflicted, for want of legislative government protection, on our flocks whom we see daily through the operations of those very cruelties perishing unpitied before our eyes'.[33] Slattery refused Murray's invitation to the queen's levee to kiss hands and complained of the queen's indifference to the Famine. Murray replied that she had sent a

[28] MacHale to Slattery, 7 July 1849, Slattery Papers, CDA.
[29] Murray to Slattery, 25 July 1849, ibid.
[30] Ibid. *Catholic Directory 1850*, 134–5, gives the text of the address.
[31] MacHale to Murray, 30 July 1849, cited in B. O'Reilly, *John MacHale, Archbishop of Tuam: His Life, Times and Correspondence*, 2 vols. (1890), ii. 189.
[32] Slattery to Murray, 23 July 1849, ibid. ii. 188.
[33] MacHale to Murray, 1 Aug. 1849, ibid. ii. 196.

circular appeal for Ireland to all her churches.[34] Tempers were frayed, but to Murray's and Clarendon's relief the timid Slattery decided not to go ahead with a rival address. The bishops, he decided, should remain silent. The people would be surprised at their expression of a loyalty and happiness which they did not share. Murray saw the objections as mere trouble-making and, forwarding to Clarendon MacHale's reply, he made the pained comment: 'Your Excellency will perceive by the accompanying letter what I have to endure from some of my Brethren.' 'I would be sorry', he told Slattery, 'that her [the queen's] attachment [to Ireland] should be turned by a cold reception into dislike.'[35] In the end Murray persuaded twelve bishops to sign his address.

The incident was not insignificant, for it illustrated again the difference in outlook between the archbishops. Murray trusted in the government's good will, valued its efforts at famine relief, and believed that more could be achieved by working with it than by opposing it. Yet, despite his correspondence with clergy in the stricken areas, he was removed from the scenes of starvation and eviction that MacHale witnessed daily. Moreover, Slattery and MacHale were expressing an anger against the government that was shared by many: other prominent clergy criticized the visit. Appalled at the costly preparations amid such suffering, Miley told Spratt that the celebrations in Dublin were 'like illuminating a graveyard—like fireworks in Glasnevin, or like shutting out, with a gorgeous curtain, one half of a long ward of an hospital, crowded with all kinds of disease and suffering'.[36] Some of the press, nationalist and conservative, and members of the Irish aristocracy were hostile. The *Evening Mail* demanded that the funds be spent 'not on illuminations but on Her Majesty's starving subjects'. Lord Monteagle refused to attend the pageant in Dublin Castle, and Lord Fitzwilliam took the same line.[37] 'A great *lie* is going to be acted there', he claimed, 'I would not have her [the queen] go *now* unless she went to Killarney workhouse, . . . Galway, Connemara and Castlebar. *That* would have been my tour for her.'[38] The mood

---

[34] Murray to Slattery, 1 Aug. 1849, Slattery Papers, 1849/54, CDA.

[35] Murray to Slattery, 21 July 1849, ibid. 1849/49.

[36] *Nation*, 19 Jan. 1850. Glasnevin is the main cemetery in Dublin.

[37] For views and reservations as regards the visit, see C. Woodham-Smith, *The Great Hunger: Ireland, 1845–9* (1962), 384–406.

[38] Fitzwilliam to Monteagle, 2 Aug. 1849, Monteagle Papers, NLI, cited in Woodham-Smith, *Great Hunger*, 387.

of the clergy and others had changed since autumn 1846. Then bishops and clergy had been slow to speak out collectively against the mass deaths. Now they were in bad temper, and many felt that a protest should be made at the highest level. Despite such mixed feelings at her visit, the queen, who was accompanied by Prince Albert and their four children, was well received and the visit marked a gratifying, if passing, success for Clarendon. Yet the squabble over her reception was more important than at first appeared: it revealed a growing tendency to blame the government for an inadequate response to the Famine and an anger at attempts to conceal the extent of the catastrophe.

In the decade after 1849, age-old religious animosities, already evident in nineteenth-century Ireland, began to rise alarmingly. The reason was proselytism. Most great religions, convinced that they are entrusted with a divine message of salvation, feel morally bound to propagate that message by making converts or proselytes. Yet, because of the sharply contrasting ways in which it is perceived, proselytism has always been a highly sensitive issue. What one religious group regards as praiseworthy missionary activity the opposing group perceives as immoral poaching, often, indeed, as little short of demonic. More than religious experience and conviction are involved, essential though these are, for closely, often inextricably, intertwined with the spiritual dimension of conversion are its social and political aspects. Socially, converts are drawn into a rival culture and often face ostracism or persecution for abandoning their community and its values. If conversions are sufficiently numerous they can tilt the balance of influence and power in the community and the consequent shift can upset the whole religious, and even political, equilibrium of a country. The proselytizing group, if it becomes politically dominant, might hail conversion as facilitating the assimilation of the converts to its own political values, a consequence which the rival group may greet with corresponding alarm.[39]

Of critical importance in conversions is the means adopted. It is not unusual for a dominant group to use preferential treatment to entice people to conform to their religion; indeed, the very fact of conforming to the religion of the dominant group almost auto-

---

[39] D. A. Kerr, 'Religion, State and Ethnic Identity', in id. (ed.), *Religion, State and Ethnic Groups* (1992), 10–12.

matically brings with it advancement and increased opportunities—educational, social, political, and financial—to the convert. Yet material advantages might attract converts for the wrong reason and, if money, food, clothing, or land are used to win converts, this may be interpreted as bribery. If the community is a tightly knit one the potential tension is enormous. All these elements came together in nineteenth-century Ireland and, particularly, in the closing years of the Famine.[40]

Since the Reformation, the ever-present antagonism between Catholics and Protestants had flared up with renewed violence at different points in Irish history and the period after the Napoleonic wars was one of those points. The Catholic Church was undergoing a revival in Europe, and in Ireland Doyle, O'Connell, MacHale, and Catholic leaders generally adopted more confident and independent attitudes than had been common earlier. At much the same time, the Established Church was undergoing a renewed missionary thrust as the Evangelical movement made its influence felt. Evangelicals, embarked on extensive missionary campaigns abroad, determined also to bring the light of the gospel to the Irish Catholics on their very doorstep. They were determined to achieve what the Reformation had failed to do and to win Ireland over to the reformed religion through this 'Second' or 'New' Reformation. Although this missionary thrust had been building up in the early decades of the century, the beginning of this new phase of activity, or 'Protestant Crusade' as it has been called, is conveniently dated from the episcopal charge of William Magee, Anglican archbishop of Dublin, in 1822.[41] A religious war of words and missionary endeavour broke out between Catholics and Protestants. Enthusiastic Evangelicals preached and distributed tracts and bibles at fairs and in villages, organized lessons and schools, and engaged in controversies with the priests. The early efforts were concentrated in Dublin and in County Cavan where, with the enthusiastic support

---

[40] It was not surprising that proselytism could be a source of great dissension and that in some countries governments felt it necessary to lay down elaborate rules governing conversions. In Austria intending converts were obliged to report to the priest of their original persuasion, who could interview them twice but had then to issue a certificate for the political authorities. A supervisory body might be asked to verify the age, physical and mental fitness, and free will of the convert.

[41] D. Bowen, *The Protestant Crusade in Ireland, 1800–1870* (1978); J. Liechty, 'Irish Evangelicalism, Trinity College Dublin, and the Mission of the Church of Ireland at the End of the Eighteenth Century' (Ph.D. thesis, 1987).

of the local landlord, Lord Farnham, they achieved some initial success. In the 1840s successful evangelizing took place in west Kerry and in the west of Ireland, particularly Achill, where the Revd Edward Nangle set up a Protestant colony.[42]

During the Famine, proselytizing efforts redoubled, for many Evangelicals saw that catastrophe as a providential opportunity. For the missioners, the main motivation was to rescue the people from the darkness of popery and priestcraft and to bring them to the pure light of the gospel. In turn, this would make the people peaceful and more open to political integration. The missioners singled out the priests as forming a barrier between the people and the word of God. When the Catholic clergy reacted strongly, Evangelicals attributed their opposition to deceit and obscurantism and to resentment caused by loss of income and power. To attribute their anger to these reasons alone would be to miss the principal motivation of the priests and misunderstand the whole controversy. For the priests the spiritual welfare of their people was a sacred trust and they believed that they, as pastors, were answerable for the eternal salvation of the faithful. Convinced that the loss of the Catholic faith was the greatest of all evils, and that such apostasy would endanger eternal salvation, bishops and priests were aghast at the prospect of their people abandoning the faith. The struggle between the two parties was essentially a struggle for souls. The economic dimension also existed, but was far from being a main motivation on either side.

A lethal ingredient in this missionary activity was the means it adopted or was perceived to adopt. During the Second Reformation in Cavan, it was alleged that Farnham had given material benefits—shoes, clothing, or an acre or two of land—to the converts. Catholics accused some Evangelical missioners of making wholesale use of food, clothing, and money during the Famine to persuade starving Catholics to attend Protestant services and send their children to Protestant schools. Before long the tag of 'souperism' was being applied to the efforts of the proselytizers, and the converts were taunted as having 'taken the soup'.

The increased activity of Protestant missioners was quickly noted. In Counties Cork, Limerick, Kerry, Mayo, Sligo, and Dublin

---

[42] Bowen, *Protestant Crusade*, 109. Edward Nangle (1799–1883), secretary of the Sunday School Society of Ireland, editor of the *Achill Missionary Herald*.

bishops, priests, and laity began to complain of aggressive proselytism and in some cases of souperism.[43] For the local priests this
activity, coming on top of the misery of the Famine, was a bitter
trial and one many of them felt powerless to deal with. Michael
Gallagher, parish priest of Achill, told Synnott that 'poverty . . . has
compelled . . . the greater number of the population to send their
children to Nangle's proselytising, villainous schools. . . . They are
dying of hunger and rather than die, they have submitted to his
impious tenets.'[44] For Michael Hart, parish priest of Ballycastle,
County Mayo, in the Killala diocese, the Presbyterian ministers
from Belfast were the enemy. They had bought land, he complained, and set up a colony, and many attended their Sunday
service 'for the sake of meal and money; but, thank God, as yet
no perverts'. Hart complained that the Presbyterians received
rations from relief associations which enabled them to entice people
to attend on Sunday. He hoped to banish them 'as soon as the
Lumpers makes [*sic*] their appearance'.[45] Other priests were less
sanguine. William Flannelly, parish priest of Ballinakill, Clifden,
County Mayo, told Murray that 'it cannot be wondered if a starving
people be perverted in shoals, especially as they [the proselytizers]
go from cabin to cabin, and when they find the inmates naked and
starved to death, they proffer food, money and raiment, on the
express condition of becoming members of their conventicle.'[46]
Some local landlords, according to the priests, helped the proselytism. From Kiltullagh near Castlerea, County Mayo, Patrick
McLoughlin complained that the local incumbent, R. Blundell,
used his influence over the principal landlords or their agents, 'in
removing poor Catholics from their holdings. . . . It is well understood that if they go to Church, that they will not be disturbed.'[47]
Sometimes the quality of the converts was called into question.
Peter Fitzmaurice, parish priest of Omery and Ballindoon, County
Mayo, vicar forane in the Tuam diocese, commented wryly: 'Thirteen bible readers under a bankrupt landlord are . . . changing bad

---

[43] On souperism, see T. O'Neill, 'Sidelights on Souperism', *Irish Ecclesiastical
Record*, 5th ser., 71 (1949), 50–64; D. Bowen, *Souperism: Myth or Reality? A
Study of Catholics and Protestants during the Great Famine* (1970); R. E. Foster,
Modern Ireland, 1600–1972 (1988), 329.
[44] Gallagher to Synnott, 5 Jan. 1848, Murray Papers, DDA.
[45] Hart to Synnott, 19 June 1848, ibid. Lumpers were potatoes of inferior quality.
[46] Flannelly to Murray, 6 Apr. 1848, ibid.
[47] McLoughlin to Synnott, 15 Apr. 1848, ibid.

Catholics into good Hypocrites.'[48] Understandably, many of the converts were among the poorest Catholics for it was they who most needed help; a standard criticism the Catholics made of the mission was that it directed itself especially towards the most vulnerable: the very poor and the children. From the Presentation convent in Galway, Sr. Mary O'Donel appealed for help to keep the convent school open to counteract the work of the missioners:

At no period did our National School stand in need of help . . . more than now when Heaven and Earth as the Preachers say, are working to carry out the great work of 'Reformation'. *Money* is to be no obstacle, no sum will be refused to bring over the poor. . . . 'Fly from Babylon' is, I believe, the watch word. The priests are called impostors but we [the nuns] are pitied and my darkness is *awful*. I could not give you an idea of their *raving* but the money is plentiful with them and the people are many degrees worse off than in 1846. We are struggling to keep on our break-fast as the only meal they [the school-children] have and to clothe the destitute orphans . . .[49]

As a Catholic view of the situation, Sr. O'Donel's description is an interesting account of the preaching and outlook of the missioners. The bishops were worried. At their annual meeting in 1847, the whole bench of bishops had protested against proselytism to the lord lieutenant. When he omitted to mention it in his reply, they complained of his silence 'as to the unchristian abuse of public and private charities evinced by the wicked attempts at proselytism and demoralization to which they were in some parts of the country perverted.'[50] Clarendon's reply is not recorded. Rome was also worried. As early as November 1847, Fransoni wrote in person to Slattery, complaining about the proselytism in Cork and Kerry, and requesting him to investigate and take the necessary steps to prevent it.[51] A year later he wrote again, urging the bishops to oppose the work of the proselytizing societies and to succour the poor, and Monsignor Alessandro Barnabò, secretary of Propaganda, informed Slattery directly of the pope's concern at the corruption of the poor by the proselytizing societies.[52] If anything

[48] Fitzmaurice to Synnott, June 1848, ibid.
[49] O'Donel to Synnott, 9 Mar. 1849, ibid.
[50] Minutes of the Irish Bishops, 26 Oct. 1847, DDA.
[51] Fransoni to Slattery, 27 Nov. 1847, Slattery Papers, CDA.
[52] Fransoni to Slattery, 4 Oct. 1848, ibid.; Barnabò to Slattery, 24 Sept. 1848, ibid.

was needed to galvanize the bishops into action it was a reprimand from the pope that they, the shepherds of the flock, were
neglecting their primary duty of safeguarding the faith of the people.
They had already protested more than once to the government
about souperism and now some bishops, like Derry of Clonfert,
issued pastoral letters strongly condemning the proselytizers.

In 1849 the issue took on a new importance. In that year Alexander Dallas founded the Society for Irish Church Missions to
Roman Catholics with headquarters in London and branches
throughout the United Kingdom.[53] By 1854 it had 125 different
mission stations in 24 different parts of the country.[54] It generated
great fervour and, in England particularly, large sums of money
were donated to finance its work. Meetings at which returned
missioners recounted their adventures and successes in Connacht
were enthusiastically attended and generously supported. From
then on the Evangelical mission to Irish Catholics was better
organized. A systematic effort was mounted in the west and south-
west of the country, but Dublin was especially targeted. No effort
was spared to use what was regarded as the providential occasion
of the Famine to win the native Irish for Protestantism. Schools,
workhouses, magdalens all became the arena of a bitter struggle
for the souls of the poor. Before long even the famine relief
committees, which had seen priest and parson work together, were
being accused of sectarianism. In Dublin the older General Relief
Committee was reactivated and clashed with Spratt's Royal Exchange Committee. When Miley tried to raise money in London
for Spratt's committee he was told 'that our Committee was altogether a Popish and priestly concern, and that in labouring for
us they would be helping to support that which was the curse of
the country'. 'One is set for aiding the Pope and putting down the
Godless Colleges', wrote Lord Cloncurry humorously, 'the other
for aiding the landlords and not the tenants.'[55] In Belfast the

---

[53] Alexander Dallas (1791–1869), rector of Wonston, Hampshire, founded the
Society on 29 Mar. 1849 with headquarters at Exeter Hall.

[54] A. Dallas, *The Story of the Irish Church Missions, continued to 1869* (1875),
133, cited in J. L. Prunty, 'The Geography of Poverty, Dublin 1850–1900: The Social
Mission of the Church, with Particular Reference to Margaret Aylward and Co-
workers' (Ph.D. thesis 1992), fo. 126. This important thesis breaks much new ground
on the work of the Church Missions and on the Catholic counter-movement.

[55] *Cloncurry and his Times*, 546–7, cited in P. O'Dwyer, 'John Francis Spratt,
O. Carm., 1796–1871' (Ph.D., 1968), fo. 142.

relations between Protestants and Catholics had deteriorated; the 1848 rebellion, Dolly's Brae, and the competition between Protestant and Catholic immigrants were the main causes. Protestant proselytism was met by Catholic reaction and the fierce religious antagonism sparked off, in 1857, the worst riots in Belfast's history to date.[56]

By 1851, the Evangelical campaign throughout the country was triumphantly announcing that 35,000 Catholics had converted. Edward Stopford, Archdeacon of Meath, believed that 5,000 had conformed in Tuam and that forty parishes showed an increase in the number of Protestants.[57] Almost as important as the achievements of the missionaries was the manner in which their successes were trumpeted forth in the bitter religious polemical literature of the day. Early in January 1852, Robert Bickersteth, rector of Saint Giles in the Fields in London and secretary of the Mission, in a lecture to the Young Men's Christian Association, was able to claim:

Within four years of the commencement of the work, an impression has been made which has far exceeded the most sanguine expectations of the founders of the Association, aroused the attention of the empire, and wrung from the Romish hierarchy the unwilling admission that their power in Ireland is fast approaching destruction.[58]

Some claims were accurate, others exaggerated, Catholics alleging that they were made to impress benefactors in England to keep the funds flowing. The campaign nevertheless generated fervent hopes and corresponding anxieties. Coming on top of the mass deaths and the great exodus to the New World, enthusiastic Evangelicals claimed—and Catholic clergy feared—that the numerical superiority of Catholics in Ireland was at last being challenged. Would Ireland soon cease to be Catholic? Catholic anger was unbounded. When a hundred preachers were sent to Ireland by the 'Protestant Alliance' they were warned that, if they preached,

---

[56] A. C. Hepburn, 'The Catholic Community of Belfast, 1850–1940', in M. Engman (ed.), *Ethnic Identity in Urban Europe* (1992), 44; Macaulay, *Dorian*, 74–84.

[57] T. P. O'Neill, 'Sidelights on Souperism', 60–3.

[58] R. Bickersteth, *Ireland, A Lecture to the Y.M.C.A., on 6 Jan. 1852* (1852), cited in D. N. Hempton, 'Bickersteth, Bishop of Ripon: The Episcopate of a Mid-Victorian Evangelical', in G. Parsons, *Religion in Victorian Britain, iv: Interpretations* (1988), 49.

the churches would be torn down over their heads.[59] Even the moderate and broad-minded Archdeacon John O'Sullivan fiercely denounced what he called 'cursed souperism'.

Now I am no agitator ... [Yet] if Souperism were to invade my parish in the morning, before evening would Father John become the greatest agitator in the Country. He would be a Tenant Right man, a Defence Association man, a Repealer, Anything, Everything, to stir up and excite the people. Prayers and Rosaries and Missions and Forty Hours ... are the only weapons Dr Cullen depends on. ... Rome knows very little and Dr Cullen seems to know less of what a Priest on a country mission must recur to in order to meet Soupers.[60]

O'Sullivan condoned the rough handling that the missioners received and admitted that his preaching provoked his parishioners to break the doors and windows of the Protestant church and beat the parson 'within an inch of his life'.[61] His violent reaction is an indication of the passions that proselytism of their 'flocks' could excite in the clergy. He roundly condemned his bishop, Egan of Kerry, for dealing too gently with Catholics who had returned to the Catholic faith. Egan was not the only bishop to be criticized for being too weak in opposing proselytism. Denvir in Belfast and Murray in Dublin also came in for similar criticism. A few years later, the bishops of the province of Cashel were still smarting from rebukes from Rome, which some attributed to Cullen's denunciations. In Dublin, the struggle between Catholics and the Protestant missionaries quickly became as acrimonious as in Connacht or Kerry. Hospitals, orphanages, poor-houses, and schools, all became centres of struggle between the two religions, with each accusing the other of using those institutions to proselytize those most vulnerable. Spratt, who had worked closely with Protestants before and during the Famine, became involved in controversy about the running of hospitals.[62] Ellen Smylie set up schools and homes to care for waifs and strays, many of whom were Catholic,

[59] O'Neill, 'Sidelights on Souperism', 60.

[60] O'Sullivan, diary, 13 Apr. 1854, 767–9.

[61] 'That they [the church door and windows] were broke and the Parson beat within an inch of his life is a fact', he wrote in his diary, 'but not by me. He came three successive Sundays while I was at the National Synod of Thurles to preach to the people as they came out from Mass, and he paid for it the Sunday after I came home, but tho' my language no doubt excited and stirred up the people I took good care not to commit myself.' Diary, 10 Mar. 1854.

[62] O'Dwyer, 'Spratt', fos. 153–66.

and was accused of bringing up the children of poor Catholics in the Protestant faith. In those homes, picturesquely called 'Birds' Nests', the Church Mission Society paid for the schooling, and private charity for the maintenance, of the children. Here as elsewhere, however, it was not easy in practice to distinguish disinterested charity from sectarian proselytism. Margaret Aylward and some companions founded St Brigid's orphanage in north Dublin to counter the Protestant mission.[63] Later she and her companions were to become the Sisters of the Holy Faith. Cullen, at first reluctant to become involved, gave them his support. The threat of proselytism united all shades of Catholic opinion and stirred up the strongest passions. In a country with such strong religious feelings and a history of religious wars any mingling of relief with proselytizing was highly dangerous.

One particularly unsavoury case came before the Kenmare Quarter Session where the Bible-reader stripped a boy called Jones of the clothes he had received because he ceased to frequent the Bible school. The magistrate, in finding for the boy, remarked that, though he might not like the religion of the majority, such conduct would prove the curse of the country.[64] This was the fear among many Anglicans. The primate, Lord John George Beresford, was cold towards the Protestant mission activity.[65] The Anglican archbishop of Dublin, Richard Whately, while defending the Protestant clergy against charges of souperism, was concerned at attempts 'to induce persons to carry on a system of covert proselytism by holding out relief to bodily wants and sufferings as a kind of bribe for conversion'.[66] Clarendon, despite his strong dislike of Catholicism, was concerned. When Russell's brother, the duke of Bedford, told him that the Irish Mission Society had formed a branch in Bedford, he warned him of the dangers involved:

A Protestant movement is going on in the Diocese of Tuam and I hope some of the conversions may be sincere and lasting but one cannot feel sure when food and clothing are generally brought in aid of the Scriptures. If a Branch of the Irish London Society is established at Bedford I suppose you can hardly avoid subscribing to it. As Lord Lieutenant I

---

[63] Prunty, 'The Geography of Poverty', fos. 187–311.
[64] *Nation*, 19 Jan. 1850; *Tablet*, 19 Jan. 1850.
[65] Bowen, *Protestant Crusade*, 273–90.
[66] R. Whately, *The Right use of National Afflictions, being a Charge Delivered ... on 19 and 22 Sept. 1848* (1848), 4–5.

should not venture to do so as its objects are proselytising and *if* it effects some good, it is at the cost of much bad blood.[67]

Bad blood was certainly created. A Quaker, Alfred Webb, wrote after the Famine:

a network of well-intentioned Protestant associations spread over the poorer parts of the country, which in return for soup and other help endeavoured to gather the people into their churches and schools, really believing that masses of our people wished to abandon Catholicism. . . . The movement left seeds of bitterness that have not yet died out, and Protestants, not altogether excluding Friends, sacrificed much of the influence for good they would have had if they had been satisfied to leave the belief of the people alone.[68]

There is much truth in this assertion. The bitter reaction to the Protestant missions was among the worst legacies of the Famine. Converting to another religion occurred for many different and often complex reasons, the most important of which was personal conviction. Catholics, both clergy and laity, however, were convinced that many missioners had held out hope of food and material relief to win over the famine-stricken poor and that the hope of relief was a deciding factor in the conversions. The tag of souperism lived on in Irish folk memory, casting a shadow over the impressive relief work of the Church of Ireland and the Protestant clergy, many of whom died of famine-related disease. Claim and counter-claim poisoned relations, deepened the religious division, and influenced attitudes for decades to come.

The concern for the faith of their people was the reason for the continuing Catholic mistrust of the education provided by the state. Since the eighteenth century Church leaders had feared that education would be used for proselytizing purposes. In 1820 the Catholics withdrew from the Kildare Place Society, the government-supported education board, when the society began to subsidize the schools of Protestant missionary societies.[69] In 1838, a number of bishops denounced the national schools, claiming that the religious

---

[67] Clarendon to Bedford, 4 Aug. 1851, Clarendon Papers, Box 80.
[68] Cited in Foster, *Modern Ireland*, 329.
[69] The Kildare Place Society, or Society for the Promotion of the Education of the Poor in Ireland, was established 1811 and, from 1815 to 1831, received a substantial government grant. At first it was accepted by the Catholics, but in 1820 Daniel O'Connell, the duke of Leinster, and Lord Cloncurry retired from the board.

textbooks used were of a proselytizing tendency.[70] In 1845 the bishops expressed their fear of the new academic or Queen's Colleges because they deemed them dangerous to the faith and morals of the Catholic pupils.[71] In 1846, in a *votum* drawn up for the use of Propaganda, Cullen advanced a well-argued case against the colleges as constituting a danger to the students' faith, and it was this advice that the Congregation followed.[72] Fate was soon to involve Cullen even further in the issues of colleges and proselytism, for Rome's condemnation of the colleges did not bring an end to the controversy.

Disappointed though he was with the renewed Roman condemnation of the colleges despite his strenuous efforts to avert it, Clarendon felt he had no other course but to press ahead with the plans for them. In December 1848 he announced that they would open their gates the following autumn and that they would eventually form a new Queen's University. The government's plan was attractive. No fewer than twenty professorships and four administrative posts in each college were announced, for which immediate applications were invited. At the same time, it promised scholarships for the students. For many middle-class Catholics the colleges had certain enticements: inexpensive university education for their sons without the need of travelling to Dublin or abroad and a number of educational posts. Applications for the professorships poured in, many of them from Catholics.[73] As the applicants normally asked for a recommendation from their bishops this raised fresh problems. The bishops in Cork, Galway, and Belfast, where

---

[70] I. Murphy, 'Primary Education', in P. J. Corish (ed.), *A History of Irish Catholicism*, vol. v, fasc. 6, 1–52; E. Larkin, 'The Quarrel among the Catholic Hierarchy', 121–44; D. A. Kerr, *Peel, Priests, and Politics* (1982), 58–64.

[71] *Tablet*, 21 May 1845.

[72] For Cullen, see P. Mac Suibhne, *Paul Cullen and his Contemporaries, With their Letters*, 5 vols. (1961–77); E. R. Norman, *The Catholic Church and Ireland in the Age of Rebellion, 1859–1873* (1965); Lee, *Modernisation*, 42–51; P. Corish, 'Cardinal Cullen and Archbishop MacHale', *Irish Ecclesiastical Record*, 5th ser. xci (1959), 393–408; id., 'Cardinal Cullen and the National Association of Ireland', *Reportorium Novum*, iii (1962), 13–16; id., 'The Radical Face of Paul Cardinal Cullen', in P. J. Corish (ed.), *Radicals, Rebels and Establishments* (1984), 171–84; E. Larkin, *The Making of the Roman Catholic Church in Ireland, 1850–1860* (1980); id., *The Consolidation of the Roman Catholic Church in Ireland, 1860–1870* (1987); E. D. Steele, 'Cardinal Cullen and Irish Nationality', *Irish Historical Studies*, 19 (1975), 239–60; D. Bowen, *Paul Cardinal Cullen and the Shaping of Modern Irish Catholicism* (1983).

[73] Clarendon says between two and three thousand! Clarendon to Russell, 10 June 1849, Clarendon Papers, Letterbook 6.

the colleges were established, viewed the applications with sympathy, for academic posts did not often come the way of educated Catholics. The government was optimistic. Redington reported that, despite the rescript, the bishops of Cork and Belfast would not stop Catholics attending, but that Bishop O'Donnell of Galway, whom he described as 'a worthy old man', might 'under the dictation of MacHale, take some strong step' such as persuading Dr William Kirwan, parish priest of Oughterard, the newly appointed president of the Galway college, to step down.[74]

The question of appointments would be crucial if those for whom the colleges were destined were to be satisfied. Apart from Kirwan in Galway, another Catholic, Sir Robert Kane, was appointed president of the Cork college and Dr Henry Cooke, the leader of orthodox Presbyterians, president of the Belfast college. As for the appointment of professors, the Presbyterians were well satisfied, Cooke claiming that the appointments in Belfast had been made 'with a view to satisfying the Presbyterian people', and the Presbyterian General Assembly at a special meeting on 2 and 3 October passed a resolution expressing its confidence in 'the qualifications and character of the persons appointed'.[75] From the point of view of Catholics, however, the matter was less satisfactory. In their first reaction to the bill the bishops had asked that a fair proportion of the professors be Catholics, and singled out six sensitive areas where Catholics could not attend 'without exposing their faith or morals to imminent danger, unless a . . . Catholic professor will be appointed for each of these chairs'. Furthermore, Clarendon had promised Murray that 'in the Council, Professorships, and other posts, of each College, the Catholic religion will be fully and appropriately represented'.[76] When the appointments were made public it emerged that very few of the professors—some seven of the sixty—were Catholic, and in none of the areas where the bishops asked specifically for Catholic professors was a Catholic appointed.[77] Although it is unlikely that Clarendon

[74] Redington to Clarendon, 25 Oct. 1848, ibid., Box 24/2.

[75] *Northern Whig*, 4 Oct. 1849, cited in T. W. Moody and J. C. Beckett, *Queen's, Belfast, 1845–1949: The History of a University* (1959), i. 78–9.

[76] Clarendon to Murray, 19 Mar. 1848, cited in *Royal Commission on University Education in Ireland, Second Report, PP* 1902, xxii. 189.

[77] W. K. O'Sullivan, *University Education in Ireland: A Letter to Sir John Dalberg Acton, Bart., M.P.* (1860), 17. F. McGrath, *Newman's University: Idea and Reality* (1951), 70; the *Freeman's Journal* gave the proportion of Catholics as one-fifth, Moody and Beckett, *Queen's*, i. 65.

intended to go back on his commitment or totally to reject the bishops' request, it is difficult not to see in the final appointments a disregard for their position. He had first referred the selection of professors to the council of presidents and vice-presidents of the colleges which contained only two Catholics out of six. Clarendon, however, took a close interest in the appointments and probably took the final decision.[78] The strongly Protestant *Evening Mail*, which in the wake of the Maynooth Grant had been hostile to Peel's scheme in 1845, now rejoiced at the appointment of what it saw as enlightened professors. Since the colleges, however, were designed primarily for Catholics, the appointment of so few Catholic professors confirmed opponents' distrust of government policy.[79]

Those opponents, taken aback by the government's move on the colleges, were quick to criticize it. The decision to set up another university, instead of granting the degrees from the old and well-established Dublin University, was seized upon in order to ridicule the 'gingerbread degrees' of the new arrival.[80] A speech by Raymond de Vericour, newly appointed professor of English literature at the Cork college, added fuel to the fire when he was interpreted as praising Rabelais and Montaigne and attacking medievalism. The professor apologized but was reprimanded.[81] Feelings were running high. The redoubtable MacHale, determined not to let the government keep the initiative, called a synod of his province of Tuam for 23 January where it was resolved to proceed with the setting up of a Catholic university.[82] Since MacHale had proved unable to provide sufficient Catholic primary schools in his diocese to replace the national schools which he refused to allow, his action on the university was no more than a gesture of defiance, but it was a signal to his colleagues. Other bishops were equally alarmed and reported the matter to Cullen in Rome. Slattery suggested a committee to look into the matter, meetings were held, and the question was to come up for discussion at the bishops' meeting in November. In a letter to Renehan, Slattery bared his indignation at Clarendon's supporters among the bishops. Up to

[78] Clarendon to Monteagle, 2 May 1850, Monteagle Papers, NLI.

[79] Despite the bishops' opposition to the colleges, one third of the students in the years 1849–51 were Catholic. *Report of Her Majesty's Commission appointed to inquire into the Progress and Condition of the Queen's Colleges at Belfast, Cork and Galway, PP 1857–8*, xxi. 364.

[80] *Freeman's Journal*, 6 Dec. 1848.

[81] *Report into Queen's Colleges, 1857–8*, xxi. 7–8.

[82] *Acts of Tuam Synod*, 23–6 Jan. 1849, Murray Papers, DDA.

this, he claimed, on matters ecclesiastical the rule had been 'Roma locuta est, causa finita est'—once Rome has spoken the matter is decided; now people were treating papal rescripts on the colleges as so much waste paper:

> Now, however, the system of Canonical Law which . . . derives its inter-pretation of Papal Rescripts . . . from the teaching of the Vice Regal Patron of Borrow's Bible in Spain is put forward in the castle organ by his venal scribes with Conway [editor of the *Dublin Evening Post*] to blackguard and bludgeon every one no matter how sacred his character that dares to speak or think or act against the Government Scheme of Academical Education.[83]

With the archbishops of Tuam and Cashel firmly opposed to the scheme, and Murray of Dublin in favour, the attitude of the archbishop of Armagh was of crucial importance. Crolly had been the first to break ranks and come out in favour of the colleges in 1845, maintaining this position as head of the pro-colleges party thereafter. In November, however, Maginn reported that the archbishop had now decided against the colleges.[84] This report is sur-prising, although Crolly had expressed disillusion with Clarendon when the nationalist press revealed the lord lieutenant's support for George Borrow's work in Spain as agent of the British and Foreign Bible Society. Crolly may have changed his mind then or he may have seen acceptance of the rescript as obedience to the Holy See. It was not to matter, for Crolly suddenly fell ill of cholera and died within the day on 6 April 1849.

Crolly's death left open the key see of Armagh, whose bishop was primate of all Ireland and thus titular head of the Church. Given the division of the bishops and clergy on the question of sup-port for government policies, particularly as regards the colleges, the appointment of a successor aroused more than usual interest and some apprehension. Whigs like Richard Bellew, a Catholic landowner and Whig MP for County Louth, and Clarendon, who regarded Crolly as well disposed, saw his death as a disaster and feared an intransigent successor. The MacHaleites wanted some-one less amenable to government views. Local and regional interests

[83] Slattery to Renehan, Renehan Papers, 6/3/36, MCA. When Clarendon was ambassador in Spain he had given some support to George Borrow, agent for the British and Foreign Bible Society.
[84] Maginn to Slattery, 27 Nov. Slattery Papers, CDA; Cantwell to Slattery, 29 Nov. 1848, ibid.

were also important. Since the middle ages the diocese had been divided into two quite distinct parts often distrustful of one another, an Ulster section, composed mainly of County Armagh, and a Leinster section, composed mainly of County Louth. Armagh had remained more traditionally Irish in customs, language, and outlook. Louth, on the other hand, had been exposed to Anglo-Norman influences from early on. The Catholic archbishop resided in Drogheda, the chief town of County Louth, at the extreme south-eastern tip of the diocese, but Crolly, conscious of the city of Armagh's prestige as, traditionally, the seat of St Patrick, had begun to take up residence there.

In 1829 Propaganda had accepted, with certain modifications, a plan put forward by the Irish hierarchy for the selection of bishops. The procedure thenceforth was that, when a vacancy occurred, the parish priests met and proposed a *terna* or three names in order of merit: *dignus*, or worthy, *dignior*, or more worthy, and *dignissimus*, or most worthy. The bishops of the province then met, discussed the *terna*, and sent their recommendation, with their comments, to Rome. They were expected to recommend one of the three, though they were free to change the order. The final choice was left to the pope, who normally chose one of the *terna*. This was the procedure followed in choosing a successor to Crolly.

Undoubtedly there was canvassing and intrigue. Pressure mounted on the parish priests whose task it was to vote for the *terna*.[85] When they met on 22 May, twenty-six of them (mainly Armagh priests) voted for Joseph Dixon, professor of scripture at Maynooth College, twelve (mainly Louth priests) voted for Michael Kiernan, parish priest of Dundalk, County Louth, and twelve (mainly Louth priests) for John O'Hanlon, prefect of the Dunboyne foundation for senior students at Maynooth College. When the seven bishops of the Armagh province met they were divided between Dixon and O'Hanlon. Denvir, McGettigan, and Browne of Kilmore recommended Dixon. Cantwell, Higgins and McNally, all MacHaleites, equally strongly recommended O'Hanlon. The seventh bishop, Blake of Dromore, finally agreed to vote for O'Hanlon.[86] Both

---

[85] A. Macaulay, 'Dr Cullen's Appointment to Armagh, 1849', *Seanchas Ard Mhacha* (1980–1), 3–36.

[86] There were eight bishops in the province of Armagh in addition to the archbishop of Armagh. The bishop of Derry had been mentally ill for some years; his coadjutor, Edward Maginn, who had effectively ruled the diocese since 1845 had died in January 1849, and a successor, Francis Kelly, was not appointed until 3 August 1849.

parties canvassed for their candidate. Rome hesitated. The three archbishops were consulted. Murray considered Dixon the most suitable. Of O'Hanlon he merely remarked that when he consulted his Maynooth colleagues some years earlier on his suitability for his home diocese, they felt they could not recommend him.[87] Slattery and MacHale were in favour of O'Hanlon. Fransoni, perplexed by the division of opinion on the three candidates, wrote to Slattery in July.[88] Slattery recommended Paul Cullen as an alternative.[89] A few days later, whether independently or not, MacHale gave his advice. After recommending O'Hanlon he added that 'in as much as I only find one of the three candidates designated whom I judge worthy, I should most earnestly recommend, in case the Rev. Dr O'Hanlon is not chosen, the Very Rev. Paul Cullen . . .'.[90] Rome accepted the advice of the two bishops with alacrity. The *Curia* knew and respected Cullen and had often consulted him on the Church in English-speaking countries. Propaganda then recommended him and Pius IX appointed him. Cullen apparently resisted the appointment, but in December it was announced that he was to be the new primate and, on 24 February 1850, he was consecrated archbishop of Armagh in the church of Santa Agata dei Gothi in Rome.

Reaction to Cullen's appointment varied. Among the Irish clergy it was generally favourable, as he was known to be both able and pious and some, especially those who had known him in Rome, looked to him to heal the division in the Irish Church. In the months before his return to Ireland he received congratulations and advice from more moderate clerics who hoped he would not side with either MacHale's or Murray's party. Murray congratulated him, commenting to Propaganda that he was most suitable. Even James Hamilton, the Scottish convert priest, while fearing that he had been nominated by the anti-English party, thought well of him, commenting to Minto that 'through what I know of his character, I am in hopes that he will prove less troublesome than

[87] O'Hanlon's colleagues in Maynooth, including the president, Renehan, were strongly of opinion that he was in no way suitable for episcopal office. O'Reilly to Cullen, 22 May, 30 Apr. 1849, Cullen Papers, ICA.
[88] Fransoni to Slattery, 30 July 1849, Slattery Papers, 1849/53, CDA.
[89] Slattery to Fransoni, 28 Aug. 1849, ibid.
[90] MacHale to Propaganda, 1 Sept. 1849, *Scritture originali riferite nelle congregazioni generali dell'Anno 1849*, vol. 975, fos. 563^r–564^v, PFA. Macaulay, 'Cullen', 29–31.

might have been feared'.[91] Shrewsbury, Bellew, and the Irish Whigs were unhappy, as was Clarendon, for whom the appointment appeared a further threat to his hopes of maintaining a balance between Protestants and Catholics. 'The Pope . . .', he told Russell to whom, one suspects, he was delighted to have bad news to announce, 'is about to play us a shameful trick by appointing Dr Cullen Primate in disregard of all the rules by which such appointments are regulated.' 'Dr Cullen is . . . notorious', he claimed, '. . . as the agent of MacHale and the most malignant enemy of the English and the English government in Ireland.'[92] He called him 'the devil incarnate' sent to punish the government for the Eglinton amendment to the Diplomatic Relations bill. Later Clarendon claimed that 'Cullen had a mission to put them [the colleges] down for he and his Master [Pius IX] . . . fear the consequences of education and of looking in the light of reason on winking Virgins and Esatic [*sic*] Nuns and they make no secret of the necessity of teaching history not according to fact and acknowledged truths but according to the dogmas of the Catholic faith.'[93] Clarendon's reaction was that of a nineteenth-century Liberal who perceived the Roman Church as opposed to the advance of civilization.

Clarendon's claim that, in the appointment of Cullen, the pope had disregarded all the rules, a claim that Russell later advanced in parliament to justify the Ecclesiastical Titles bill, needs correcting. Although the pope rarely overrode the choice of the local Church, it was always understood that the final decision lay with him. Papal appointment of Cullen reflected Roman perplexity at the sharp division between the supporters of Dixon and O'Hanlon; when, subsequently, two of the three archbishops consulted suggested Cullen, Rome was pleased to be able to place in Armagh a man whom they knew and trusted. The consultations Propaganda made as to the suitability of O'Hanlon and Dixon show that, had the Armagh bishops made a clear choice of any one candidate, the question of appointing Cullen would not have arisen. It was not

---

[91] Hamilton to Minto, 30 Dec. 1850, Russell Papers, PRO 30/22/9A. Cullen, however, called Hamilton a 'meddler' and 'a poor little, contemptible, "pious fool", like Lord S[hrewsbury] who . . . was going about with Lord Minto, introducing him to the people here', Cullen to MacHale, 28 Jan. 1848, cited in O'Reilly, *MacHale*, ii. 112.

[92] Clarendon to Russell, 5 Jan. 1850, Clarendon Papers, Letterbook 5.

[93] Clarendon to Reeve, 20 Oct. 1852, ibid., c. 534. Twenty years later Clarendon still referred to Cullen as 'that viper'.

part of a tit-for-tat policy on the part of the pope. Nor was it a deliberate attempt to ultramontanize the Irish Church, though the knowledge that Cullen held views acceptable in Rome would have weighed in his favour. On the other hand, whereas Cullen was not the devil incarnate, nor the tool of MacHale, as Clarendon claimed, he was totally distrustful of the government and unwilling to co-operate with Clarendon as Crolly, Murray, and their predecessors in Armagh and Dublin had been.

Cullen was to bring changes to the Irish scene. Born in 1803 of well-to-do farmer stock, he was educated for the priesthood at Carlow under Bishop Doyle, and then in Rome, his father alleg-edly refusing a free place for him at Maynooth, because he would not have his son take the oath of allegiance or accept the king's money.[94] His academic career in Rome was distinguished, and after his ordination in 1829 he was appointed professor of Greek and oriental languages in the College of Propaganda, with respons-ibility for the Polyglot press. In 1832 he was appointed rector of the newly re-established Irish College in Rome. The Irish bishops used him as their Roman agent, which increased his influence and gave him an insight into the working of the Church in Ireland and in Rome. Energetic, zealous, and single-minded in his devotion to his Church, he had become highly respected and influential in Roman ecclesiastical circles. Charles Russell, later president of Maynooth and a reliable witness, reported in 1843 that 'everyone to whom I speak tells me that he [Pope Gregory XVI] will not refuse Dr Cullen anything he asks'.[95] Archbishop Nicholson, who took a different line from him on a number of issues, referred sarcastically to him as 'the Pope of Ireland'.[96] The next pope, Pius IX, also thought well of him. During the period of the Roman Republic, Cullen had stayed on as head of the Irish College, took over the management of the important College of Propaganda, and successfully prevented the Mazzinian government from abolish-ing it. It was while the pope was still at Gaeta that he appointed Cullen, then in his forty-seventh year, archbishop of Armagh. Cullen had trained and worked in Rome from 1820 to 1850 during a period when the Catholic Church, and the Roman See in particular, had experienced a remarkable revival. Zealous Catholics turned to the papacy which, in the person of Pius VII, had emerged from the revolutionary period with enhanced prestige. First Joseph de Maistre, with his seminal work *Du Pape*, then Liberal Catholics in their combat against Gallicanism in France, sought to ally pope and people. Religious orders devoted to Rome were restored or founded as a confident Church engaged in new efforts to re-evangelize the old world and send missionaries to the new. Roman liturgy and Roman devotions were introduced and progressive Catholics everywhere were turning to Rome as the centre of unity and authority and as the mainstay of the Church's independence against state encroachment. This was the exciting reforming Church that Cullen experienced in his youth and early manhood in Rome and with which he identified.

Cullen became archbishop at a moment when a small, but ultimately quite significant, change was taking place in one of the informal yet vital structures of the Irish Church. The annual meeting of the bishops was the nearest thing to a synod that the Church possessed. From the late eighteenth century, and particularly since the early nineteenth century, when it became an annual event, the meeting became the most important means the bishops possessed to develop and formulate common policies. It had proved quite successful in promoting a united approach to the problems facing their Church. From 1838, however, the meetings had become the scene of disagreements between the bishops on the questions of national education, the Bequests Act and the Queen's Colleges. Since the meetings' resolutions were reported in the newspapers, these divisions became public knowledge. Weary of the continuing wrangling, the bishops decided at their meeting in 1849 that in future the meetings should follow synodal procedure and that a proper national synod should be held on the Tuesday after the summer meeting of the Maynooth Trustees.[97] Their decision was to bring a greater change than they realized and its immediate effect was that, on 6 April 1850, Pius IX appointed Cullen apostolic delegate with the task of presiding over the synod.

---

[97] Bishops' meeting, 7 Nov. 1848. Contrary to what was stated later, the decision to hold a national synod did not originate with Cullen.

The synod gave Cullen a heaven-sent opportunity to press his views on the bishops. What authority an apostolic delegate possessed no one quite knew, and Clarendon was told that Cullen would arrive 'armed with Powers such as were never before given to an Irish Bishop, so I expect a large crop of trouble from him'.[98] Egged on by MacHale, Slattery, and Cooper, Cullen immediately brought powerful pressure to bear on Delany of Cork and O'Donnell of Galway, the bishops in two of the cities where the colleges were located, sending them copies of the recent documents from Propaganda which warned against the colleges.[99] Within three weeks of his arrival in Armagh, Cullen had formally convened the synod for 15 August, but his ill health forced him to postpone it and it finally opened on 22 August in Thurles, County Tipperary, the seat of Slattery, the archbishop of Cashel. It was to last a full three weeks.[100] The four archbishops and twenty bishops were present. Egan of Kerry, MacNicholas of Achonry and French of Kilmacduagh and Kilfenora were unable to attend and were represented by proxies. All twenty-seven had the right to vote. The bishops were each accompanied by a theologian, and Cullen claimed as legate the right to two theologians. The provincial superiors of the religious orders —Jesuits, Dominicans, Franciscans, Augustinians, Carmelites, Discalced Carmelites, Vincentians, and the abbot of Mount Melleray, Bruno Fitzpatrick, were also present. The provincials had no vote, but it was decided that Fitzpatrick, as a mitred abbot, should have a vote, bringing the number voting to twenty-eight. This decision which, according to Cullen, was taken 'by the unanimous decision of all the bishops' was to prove significant.[101]

One of the first acts of the synod was to write a letter of support

---

[98] Clarendon to Russell, 20 Apr. 1850, Clarendon Papers, Box 70.

[99] Delany to Cullen, 22 May, 2 June 1850; Cullen to Delany, 30 May 1850; MacHale to Slattery, 1 June 1850; MacHale to Cullen, 11 June 1850; O'Donnell to Cullen, 8, 11 June 1850; Cooper to Cullen, 1850, Cullen Papers, Section 39/1, File I, DDA.

[100] J. Ahern, 'The Plenary Synod of Thurles', *Irish Ecclesiastical Record*, 75 (1951), 385–403; 78 (1952), 1–20; Larkin, *Making of the Church*, 27–57; D. Keenan, *The Catholic Church in Nineteenth-Century Ireland: A Sociological Study* (1983), 200–12; J. Whyte, 'Political Problems: 1850–1860', in P. Corish (ed.), *A History of Irish Catholicism*, vol. v, parts 2 and 3 (1967), 7–12; P. C. Barry, 'The Legislation of the Synod of Thurles, 1850', *Irish Theological Quarterly*, 26 (1959), 131–66.

[101] Abbot Bruno, when signing the decrees, added 'e privilegio admissus', *Decreta Synodi Plenariae Episcoporum Hiberniae Apud Thurles Habitae Anno* MDCCCL (1851), 62.

to the exiled conservative archbishop of Turin, Luigi Fransoni. Apart from being a gesture of solidarity, this was intended by Cullen as a signal that the Irish Church was ranging itself against the liberalism of the modern state. It was Fransoni's strong views on clerical exemption that had brought on him the wrath of the Sardinian government. In the first week the synod dealt with religious reform. In this it was continuing the work of recent local synods as the Irish Church attempted to conform to the model of a counter-reformation Church. The administration of the sacraments was to be brought in line with Roman custom. Priests were exhorted to live piously, to dress clerically, and to read the Bible, the lives of the saints, and a complete theological course. The duties of bishops, parish priests, and curates were carefully set out.

The synod devoted no fewer than eleven articles to faith, citing the words of St Augustine that there was no greater treasure in this world than the Catholic faith, and the Council of Trent's description of it as the foundation of all justification. While thanking God that Ireland never produced a heresy, the synod warned that every effort must be made to guard the precious treasure of the faith. Proselytizers were singled out as the arch-enemies of the Church and were denounced as degraded men (*perditos homines*), who sought by money, gifts, and all kinds of corruption to turn the starving, afflicted poor from their faith.[102] Proselytism, the synod warned, harmed not just the people's faith but also their morals, for either they abandoned their faith or hypocritically pretended to be converted. To counter the efforts of the proselytizers the synod exhorted the clergy to preach the pre-eminence of the faith and the dangers of apostasy, and to invite Vincentian Fathers and Jesuits to give missions in the parishes. The synod's emphasis on faith is remarkable. It is in the context of 'safeguarding the faith' that the articles on education, which constituted the core of the synod's legislation, are best understood.

As regards the national schools the synod maintained the *status quo*, while warning against changes in the ownership of the schools which the government had hoped to introduce. The most contentious issue, however, was not the national system but the colleges, and the effort to produce a common policy on this thorny issue constituted the very reason for the synod. Cullen tried to pre-empt

[102] Ibid. 13.

dissidence by appealing to the authority of the pope. The bishops' task, he stated when the question came up, was merely to accept the Roman rescripts since they had no competence to change what the pope had ratified. He cited Pius IX's letter to the Italian bishops of 8 December 1849 to illustrate papal views on education:

it is incumbent on you ... to be vigilant in all these things, which regard ... the education of ... youth. For ... the modern enemies of Religion and human society, with a most diabolical spirit direct all their activities to this point that they may pervert the minds ... of youth. Wherefore ... there is no attempt from which they shrink, that ... they may altogether withdraw ... every institution destined for education, from the authority of the Church and the vigilance of Her holy pastors.[103]

Cullen was quickly disillusioned. The bishops launched into a full discussion. McGettigan, bishop of Raphoe, the senior bishop in Cullen's own province of Armagh, immediately distanced himself from the rescripts declaring that they did not concern him. To Cullen's argument of the danger to youth inherent in the colleges, Browne of Kilmore replied that every college had certain dangers, while O'Donnell of Galway claimed that those in charge of the new colleges were honourable men on whom they could rely. Another bishop, possibly to embarrass Slattery who had been educated in Trinity College, asked why that university had not incurred the same condemnation. Other bishops pointed out that the colleges would provide the Catholic community with the opportunity of higher education which the bishops could not provide. The most serious difficulty raised was when one bishop expressed the fear that the condemnation of the colleges might lead to a schism. Murray suggested that Rome did not understand the situation in Ireland, and proposed that the bishops should now adopt the same attitude as they did in 1816 when they successfully challenged the letter of Cardinal Litta recommending the veto.[104] Since the bishops' stand over the veto was quite exceptional, to recommend the same procedure again was to adopt an unusually strong line.

Cullen, on whom fell the main burden of replying to these objections, was taken aback at the strength of the opposition, but, well prepared, he argued his case forcibly. The trial of strength came on two motions put forward by Cullen which forbade clerics,

---

[103] Thurles 1850, file III; notes (in Cullen's handwriting), DDA.
[104] Thurles 1850, file IV; notes (in Cullen's handwriting), DDA.

on the pain of suspension *ipso facto*, from accepting office in the colleges. The supporters of the colleges, maintaining that the rescripts were binding only on those to whom they were addressed, contested those propositions. As the twenty-four bishops voted, it became clear that they were evenly divided, Murray's supporters proving more numerous and more united than suspected. All depended on the proxies. Two of the three proxies voted for the propositions as did the abbot of Melleray. Cullen's proposition then passed by a majority of fifteen to thirteen. Nevertheless, the margin was slender. On 2 September a dramatic development took place. Bishop Egan's procurator, John McEnnery, who had voted with the minority, made a solemn declaration before the synod that, after serious reflection, he could not reconcile his vote with obedience to the Holy See; he then retracted it and voted for the condemnation of the colleges.[105] According to Archdeacon O'Sullivan, who was at the synod, McEnnery had yielded to undue pressure by Cullen and his supporters.[106] Although O'Sullivan was hostile to Cullen and wrote his account three and a half years after the event, his account is probably an accurate one. After McEnnery's change of mind, Murray's supporters were more clearly in a minority. The fifth proposition declaring that parents should reject and avoid the colleges because of serious (*gravia*) and intrinsic dangers to the faith and morals of Catholic students, was carried by sixteen votes to twelve.

What was remarkable was the vigour with which the minority fought their case, even after Cullen's solemn warning that, by opposing the rescripts and Barnabò's letter to him, they were opposing Rome. The size of the minority was also remarkable. When the colleges question first came up in 1845, the minority bishops numbered only eight. Now the number had risen to thirteen. Seven bishops had died in the interval. In the dioceses of Ossory and Ferns, Walsh and Murphy, reversing their predecessors' stance, had decided to support the colleges. In Armagh, on the other hand, Cullen had taken a different line from Crolly and opposed them. More surprising, perhaps, was the change of heart by four bishops—Blake of Dromore, Egan of Kerry, Haly of Kildare and

---

[105] Thurles 1850, file IV; diary, DDA. Peter Cooper, one of the most fervent opponents of the colleges, had been appointed one of the secretaries to the synod and appears to have written the diary.
[106] Diary, 13 Feb. 1854, KrDA.

Leighlin, and O'Donnell of Galway. All had voted against the colleges in 1845, but now they supported them. This change is all the more remarkable in view of the repeated condemnation of the colleges by Rome and the powerful pressure the new primate and apostolic delegate applied to dissuade anyone from voting against what he represented to be the express wish of Rome. Why they changed their position is not clear but the real, if not completely successful, attempts of Clarendon to improve the college statutes and Murray's persuasive example undoubtedly played a part. All three suffragan bishops of the Dublin province sided with Murray.

Despite this unexpectedly stubborn opposition, the minority bishops were no match for Cullen who had obtained the condemnation he wanted. He was also successful in promoting his favourite scheme of a Catholic university. With great skill he had the proposition accepted unanimously and even persuaded Murray, who believed the venture impractical, to go on the committee of eight bishops charged with promoting it. A further triumph, indeed his master stroke, was his composition, in the name of the synod, of an address purporting to explain the main thrust of the bishops' deliberations, their corporate views and decisions. It was normal for the bishops to present an address or memorial to the lord lieutenant at the end of their annual meeting. Cullen, however, directed this address to the Catholic clergy and laity and, in its final form he presented it to the bishops on 9 September, at the end of the synod's sessions. It was then published in the name of the synod. The address, a wide-ranging and ably written document, went beyond issues discussed at the synod to take a stand on problems facing the country.[107] It first, however, addressed the issue of the colleges and, by the solemn manner in which it invoked papal authority, it attempted to dispose definitively of the problem:

After a most searching ... examination of the statements and facts that were urged on either side, availing himself of every resource of counsel ... demanding and receiving from every member of the Irish Episcopacy his individual opinion, making it the object of his long and anxious deliberation, and pouring forth his soul to Him who promised to abide with his Church even to the consummation of time, the successor of Peter pronounces his final decision on the subject.

[107] *Catholic Directory 1851*, 184–200.

There is pious exaggeration here. While it is certain that Pius IX, who took the Church's role in education very seriously, viewed the issue of the Irish colleges as important, and had consulted each of the bishops, he was in the middle of a revolution and facing more pressing problems. The address then concluded:

all controversy is now at an end—the judge has spoken. THE QUESTION IS DECIDED. Recognising, with reverential awe, in that decision the voice of Him who hath said, 'He who hears you, hears me' ... this Synod has received not only with profound respect but unanimous acclamation, the decisions which were asked for in the name of the Irish Church.

The Irish bishops always received papal briefs with great respect, but Cullen was overstating, if not misstating, their reaction. The address, then, returned to an issue that united all the bishops— that of proselytism. While bitterly condemning the proselytizers, the address emphasized that 'none have been more loud and indignant in reprobating a system ... offering a mess of pottage for the glorious inheritance it seeks to purchase, than the respectable and enlightened portion of our Protestant brethren'.

A more unusual feature of the address was the attention it paid to the social issue of the day—the distress in the country. The bishops' appeal to the government in 1847 had been repeated at their 1848 meeting, but the synod's address went much further.[108] It first called on well-off Catholics to help the suffering poor. It then firmly asserted the bishops' right and duty, enjoined on them at their episcopal ordination, to defend the poor. Since, it said, the canons of every council from Chalcedon to Trent express 'concern for the Poor' the bishops would be guilty of 'criminal neglect if they suffer the Poor to be oppressed without raising their voice in their defence and vindication'. In making this strong defence of their right to speak, Cullen and the bishops had in mind the vigorous complaints, in December 1847 and early 1848, that clerical intervention was promoting rural violence. Having first cleared the ground, they spoke out categorically, protesting in powerful and indignant terms against the eviction of the poor:

We behold our poor not only crushed and overwhelmed by the awful visitation of Heaven, but frequently the victims of the most ruthless oppression that ever disgraced the annals of humanity. Though they have

---

[108] *Catholic Directory 1849*, 312–13.

been made to the image of the living God, and are purchased by the blood of Calvary, though the special favourites and representatives of Jesus Christ, we see them treated with a cruelty that would cause the heart to ache if inflicted on the beasts of the field. . . . The desolating track of the exterminator is to be traced in too many parts of the country—in those levelled cottages and roofless abodes where so many virtuous and industrious families have been torn by brute force, without distinction of age or sex, sickness or health, and flung upon the highway to perish in the extremity of want.

Solemnly warning the oppressors, in other words evicting land-lords, that the arm of the Lord was not shortened, it concluded in the apocalyptic words of St James that 'the hire of the labourers, who have reaped down your fields, which by fraud has been kept back by you, crieth, and the cry of them has entered into the ears of the Lord of Sabaoth' (James 5: 4).

The address owed most to Cullen and affords an insight into his outlook and priorities. Yet, assented to by the hierarchy, it showed the Irish Church in a most assertive light. Neither Doyle nor MacHale had spoken so strongly, and the bishops' memorial to Clarendon in 1848 was tame compared to the address. In their defence of the poor the bishops treated them with dignity and respect, and showed indignation and compassion at their suffering. Their angry criticism of evicting landlords was unprecedented in its severity. With evictions reaching a record figure of 104,000 in 1850, their demand for strong action was justified.[109]

The final decree of the synod touched on an internal but sensitive issue. Entitled 'On Avoiding Dissensions among Ecclesiastics', it decreed that no bishop should take on himself the responsibility of approving or putting into effect any government law which related to Catholic education, ecclesiastical goods, or the rights of the Church, before all the bishops had examined and approved that law. Where difference of opinion arose or where the question was of major importance and could not be settled by the bishops, the matter should be referred to the Holy See. This decree was a censure of Murray. Yet, although he had supported the national school system, the Charitable Bequests law, and the Queen's Colleges and continuously co-operated with the government, he scarcely deserved this reprimand, for he was generally unwilling to

---

[109] Donnelly, 'Landlords and Tenants', in Vaughan (ed.), *A New History of Ireland* (1989), v. 337–43. Vaughan, *Landlords and Tenants*, 15–17.

give the government more than his personal opinion and advice and did not claim to act for the whole bench of bishops. The section of the decree concerning reference to the Holy See contained nothing new, but it further strengthened ultramontane tendencies in the Irish Church.

The Dublin government's reaction to the synod was at first dismissive. While keeping himself informed of its proceedings, Clarendon ridiculed it. 'A medieval farce called a national synod has been enacting at Thurles', he told Russell, adding that the moderate bishops would force the 'rampant ones' to refer all contested matters to Rome. This he believed would be a point gained, for 'Dr Wiseman may persuade the Pope that he has been misled by MacHale and Cullen'.[110] In an effort to upstage any decision of the synod on a Catholic university the *Dublin Evening Post*, a paper that supported the government plan, announced that the royal sanction had been given to the statutes constituting the colleges a university.[111] When it became known that the bishops were split down the middle on the colleges, the government was pleased. Redington commented 'that taking away the vote of the Abbot of Mount Melleray, the first resolution and the third were only carried by one vote and this, it may not be unfairly considered, was the vote of the Primate recently sent from Rome to govern a see in Ireland to which he had not been elected by the suffrages of the clergy'.[112] This complacent attitude changed with the publication, in the name of all the bishops, of the synodical address. Clarendon was furious. In a reply to George Grey, who had accepted his first evaluation of the synod, he complained 'that the mummers at Thurles have not been as harmless as you suppose' for they were setting the poor against the rich. To Russell he complained angrily that the address, 'for intolerant Bigotry . . . is worthy of the Middle Ages, of Louis Blanc for its socialist doctrines and of the Devil for its misquotation of Scripture'. It was high time to enquire whether 'we shall permit a set of men under the mask of religion and in the name of a foreign power to preach a crusade against civilisation and to stir up different classes against each other'. While urging Russell to inform the pope of the government's displeasure, he blamed the Eglinton clause in the Diplomatic Relations Act, alleging

110 Clarendon to Russell, 31 Aug. 1850, Clarendon Papers, Box 6.
111 *Dublin Evening Post*, 27 Aug. 1850.
112 Redington to Clarendon [Aug. 1850], Clarendon Papers, Box 25.

that it was partly 'to avenge himself for this . . . that the Pope sent Dr Cullen as Primate in violation of all the rules that govern the election of bishops'. Clarendon's account provoked Greville to anger at the synod. His 'dander was up against the Thurlites', and he promised to lash the 'Fanatics' in the leader columns of the *Times*; both he and George Grey grasped at the possibility of a 'schism'.[113] Clarendon held out little hope of lay defiance of the synod's decrees, 'for not only is obedience a fundamental doctrine of the Church of Rome but fidelity to the Pope is part of an Irishman's political creed'.[114] All depended on the pope, he believed, for if he gave it 'the go by' the address would be inoperative.

The mention of a schism arose from the sharp public controversy that had broken out among Irish Catholics occasioned by the pronouncement on the colleges in the synodical address. If Cullen believed that, when the synod ended on 10 September, the colleges issue had been finally decided, as the address claimed, a further shock was in store for him. Although outmanœuvred, the minority bishops showed no sign of yielding. The following day, before they left Thurles, Murray and his supporters among the bishops drew up an appeal to Pius IX pointing out the damage the synod's decisions would do.[115] An anonymous 'memorandum' appeared in the *Dublin Evening Post* claiming that many bishops 'were averse to any publication from the Synod regarding the Queen's Colleges except the Rescripts, until certain points . . . should have been submitted to the final judgment of his Holiness'. It further revealed that on some points 'the opinions of the Bishops are so nearly balanced as to admit of a majority of one only'. As regards the synodical address, it stated that it contained statements of which many bishops disapproved.[116] The memorandum was but the first shot. The condemnation of the colleges in the address had dismayed the lay Catholics who supported them and John R. Corballis, a Dublin solicitor and commissioner on the Board of National Education, wrote a public letter to Murray on 30 September asking whether Catholic parents were now forbidden

---

[113] Grey to Clarendon, 27 Sept. 1850, ibid., c. 522; Greville to Clarendon, 17 Sept. 1850, ibid., Box 14; Greville to Clarendon, 28 Sept. 1850, ibid., c. 522.

[114] Clarendon to Grey, 5 Oct. 1850, ibid., Letterbook 6.

[115] Murray and twelve bishops to Pius IX, 11 Sept. 1851, *Acta* (1851), vol. 213 fos. 163–238, PFA.

[116] *Dublin Evening Post*, 21 Sept. 1850.

to send their sons to the colleges, pointing out that for over fifty years they had been permitted to send their children to Trinity College. Murray replied that a petition signed by thirteen bishops had been sent to the pope asking him to refuse his sanction 'to certain proposals on points yet undecided relative to the subject of Academical Education.'[117] It is likely that both the Memorandum and Corballis's letter had the sanction of Murray and were aimed at countering the synodical address and delaying or blocking the condemnation of the colleges. They were partially successful. The strongest supporters of the colleges had been the Young Irelanders. On the publication of the synodical address, Charles Gavan Duffy, the only leading Young Irelander left on the scene, unwilling to contribute to further dissension among Catholics, had accepted the decision against the colleges. This changed when he saw the memorandum and the reply to Corballis and he now expressed his hope that Murray's appeal to Rome would succeed.[118]

The anti-college party was infuriated at the turn of events. MacHale, Slattery, Cantwell, Murphy of Cloyne, and Kelly of Derry complained to Kirby, Cullen's successor as rector of the Irish College, who duly forwarded their grievances to the Congregation.[119] Writing to Propaganda, Cullen placed the blame squarely on Murray:

The real question to be decided is whether one ought or ought not to obey the decisions of the Holy See; whether the Pope ought to rule the Church in Ireland through the majority of the bishops, or whether, on the other hand, the English government ought to rule it by means of the archbishop of Dublin.[120]

This was an overstatement, for it was not true that Murray or his twelve supporters were prepared to allow the government to dictate to the Church. Yet the fact that Redington was able to relay to Clarendon much of the day-to-day debate of the synod and the votes on the colleges indicated that Murray's party was in constant contact with government officials. This lent substance

[117] *Nation*, 5 Oct. 1850; *Dublin Evening Post*, 2 Oct. 1850.
[118] *Nation*, 5, 12, 19 Oct. 1850.
[119] Cullen to Kirby, 2 Oct. 1850; MacHale to Kirby, 26 Nov. 1850; Cantwell to Kirby, 6 Oct. 1850; Murphy to Kirby, 4 Oct. 1850; Kelly to Kirby, 14 Nov. 1850; Kirby Papers, ICA.
[120] Cullen to Propaganda, 8 Oct. 1850, *Acta* (1851), vol. 213, fo. 207, cited in Whyte, 'Political Problems', 10.

to the suspicion of some bishops that the ageing archbishop had fallen under government influence and roused jealousy among others who were denied this access to government. Yet, although his opponents attributed Murray's refusal to accept defeat to either Whig influence or personal obstinacy, he had a good case. The arguments in favour and against availing themselves of the colleges were finely balanced, and the bishops so evenly divided, that he believed it possible to persuade Rome to reverse its decision as it had done on the national education system. This was the view of Archdeacon O'Sullivan, who assured Corry Connellan that 'the Pope will never over-rule the opinion of so large and respectable a minority'.[121] Although the question of the faith of the students was involved, the issue was not one of doctrine but a practical judgement as to whether or not the colleges would prove dangerous to the Catholic youth of Ireland. The history of over a decade of dissension, however, between Murray and MacHale cast its shadow over the debate. Murray had a further cause of dispute with the MacHaleites, for he considered they had slandered him at Rome by one of their publications.[122] Apart from the different assessment each side made of the issues, there existed a marked difference in attitude. Edmund O'Reilly, professor of theology at Maynooth, summing up the difference of approach between the Murray and MacHale parties, justly remarked that 'there are two scopuli to be avoided—passiveness and turbulence. There may be perhaps too much of the former on the one side, too much of the latter on the other side.'[123] Cullen had taken over MacHale's opposition, tempering his turbulence, and had deliberately broadened the agenda of the synod of Thurles to include many other practical matters concerning faith and discipline, turning it into a platform from which to launch his campaign as the reformer of the Irish Church.

While this open controversy about the colleges was rocking the Irish Church, a no less remarkable dialogue had gone on between Russell and Clarendon on the same subject. For some time neither of them had been happy with the colleges scheme on grounds not far removed from those of the bishops. Sir James Graham, Peel's

---

[121] Connellan to Clarendon [Sept. 1850], Clarendon Papers, Box 9.

[122] Murray to Secretary of Propaganda, 9 Mar. 1850; Cullen to Secretary of Propaganda, 27 Feb. 1851; *Acta* (1851), vol. 213, fos. 163–238, PFA.

[123] O'Reilly to Cullen, 11 Dec. 1844, Cullen Papers, ICA.

home secretary from 1841 to 1846, had been the architect of the Colleges bill, and now Clarendon poured scorn on 'Graham's experiment', pronouncing it unsuitable to Ireland.[124] 'The Colleges', he had told George Grey, 'were well meant but I think they are a mistake i.e. not adapted to the present wants of the country.' It was hard to justify the policy of forcing a neutral or, as many would say, a godless education on a country where all groups, Protestant, Catholic, and Dissenter, wanted denominational education. Nevertheless, the government was caught in a dilemma, as Clarendon admitted:

> Once established, however, we have a political as well as an educational interest in their success. After all the factious uproar that has been raised against them and all the intrigues that have been carried on at Rome, it is important to show that neither Pope nor Prelate can prevent that which the British Government has determined shall be.[125]

This dogmatic political stand was not the best ground on which to introduce a major reform of Irish education. Clarendon, however, made every effort to persuade the government to make the colleges less unacceptable to the Catholics. '[W]e are bound', he told Russell, 'to do what we can to render them places of good moral and religious instruction. Above all it is our duty to remove the godless stigma cast upon them by MacHale and Inglis.'[126] Central to his plan of removing the 'godless tag' were halls of residence where the students would be supervised and given religious instruction. The idea had a history. To meet in some way the bishops' criticism, Graham, in July 1845, had introduced an amendment allowing the Board of Works to lend money for the construction of the halls of residence which would be supervised by the Churches. During the parliamentary debate Russell had demanded that the halls be made part of the university and that the religious instruction given in them be endowed equally with the rest of the university courses. Peel's government refused. Clarendon now wanted to return to Russell's suggestion. If the halls were recognized as part of the university scheme and deans of residence in charge of them paid by the state, this would amount to the endowment of some religious education in the colleges,

[124] Clarendon to Monteagle, 2 May 1850, Monteagle Papers, NLI.
[125] Clarendon to George Grey, 15 Jan. 1849, Clarendon Papers, Letterbook 3.
[126] Clarendon to Russell, 23 May 1849, ibid., Box 26.

remove the slur of 'godless' colleges, and give the bishops control over the religious education of their students. Such a concession might well tilt the balance among the bishops and would enable Murray to reopen the case in Rome. The cabinet, however, recommended that the deans' remuneration should come from fees. Clarendon replied to the argument that paying the deans was paying for the propagation of error by pointing out that it could no more be objected to than the payment of Catholic chaplains in jails, workhouses, and the army.[127] The cabinet refused to go further.[128] Clarendon replied sharply that 'to make such a fallacious provision would be looked upon as equivalent to a determination that there should be no religious instruction'. Launching into an attack on the principle involved he demanded to know 'upon what ground can we say that a Professor of Latin or Agriculture shall have £250 a year secured to him by the State but that the teacher of religion and the superintendent of morals shall depend on what he can scrape together?'. Clarendon felt so deeply on the matter that he threatened to abandon the colleges policy altogether:

I have so strong a feeling about the impropriety of any educational establishment being without the certain means of religious instruction and about the impolicy after all that has passed, of such an establishment being instituted by the government and that essential element of education being left to chance, that I doubt at present whether I can bring myself to interfere any further with the Colleges. Parliament may object and bigotry and economy combined may refuse to grant the small sum necessary but we don't know that till it is tried.[129]

Russell was moved by Clarendon's outburst to consult Graham, who had introduced the bill in 1845. The cautious Graham told him, however, that it would not be possible to support any charge for religious instruction in the colleges; the act intended private boarding houses only, presided over by persons in whom the parents could have confidence; he and Peel could hardly go further without being accused of breach of faith. Russell concluded that the difficulties confronting any change would be insurmountable and gloomily explained the political reality to Clarendon:

[127] Clarendon to Russell, 23 May 1849, ibid., Letterbook 4.
[128] Russell to Clarendon, 3 June 1849, ibid., Box 26.
[129] Clarendon to Russell, 6 June 1849, ibid., Letterbook 4.

new grants for Deans of Residence will be objected to (1) By Graham and the Peelites—(2) By Inglis and those who oppose the teaching of error—(3) By the rigid Economists who will not like spending the money. Let me add to this that the Cabinet are heavily if not quite all against it, and I have said enough to shew that we cannot expect any successful move.[130]

Clarendon rejoined that Graham had made a mistake and that it was time to remedy it.

It is quite true as Graham says that the measure as introduced by him makes no provision of the kind and that in fact the contrary principle was professed but what was the consequence? Why that Inglis and MacHale joined in the outcry against the Godless system of education and even those most friendly to the institution felt that a great mistake had been committed and must if possible be repaired.[131]

Clarendon denounced the selfishness of the cabinet's attitude: 'The Cabinet feeling is, I am sure, to let the Catholics scramble on or go to the dogs as the case may be, provided there is no trouble in Parliament.' He had, he confessed, 'a very strong feeling upon the subject, not only because I believe that the determination not to secure religious instruction will be fatal at once to these Colleges, but I think it exceedingly wrong on the part of a Government to leave to chance a question of such extreme importance.'[132] Clarendon's arguments were similar enough to those of Cullen and other bishops who opposed the colleges. A perplexed Russell now decided to consult Peel. Peel advised him that if the government asked parliament for anything for the deans of residence it might raise a storm. Peel also explained his own difficulty in 1845 when he brought in the bill, confessing that 'after Maynooth . . . he did not know how to estimate the strength of the Protestant feeling'.[133] This remarkable admission explains the botched nature of the consultations in 1845 when the Colleges bill was introduced. On that occasion the then lord lieutenant, Lord Heytesbury, had not adequately consulted the bishops before the bill was introduced into parliament. When the bishops' reservations became known, Peel was in a dilemma. Only three weeks before, a majority of his party had voted against him on the Maynooth Grant,

---

[130] Russell to Clarendon, 22 June 1849, ibid., Box 26.
[131] Clarendon to Russell, 24 June 1849, ibid., Letterbook 4.
[132] Ibid.
[133] Russell to Clarendon, 29 June 1849, ibid., Box 26.

taunting him with betraying the Protestant interest. If Peel had changed the Colleges bill already before parliament in response to the bishops' criticisms, the Tories would have accused him of again betraying the country and bowing to the wishes of the Roman clergy.[134] Indeed, in reply to Russell's criticisms during the debate in 1845, Peel betrayed his fear that Inglis, Spooner, and the no-popery section of his party might accuse him of covertly endowing the Catholic Church.[135] Heytesbury, too, when Graham questioned him on his consultation of the bishops, had replied that 'we must not lead the Catholics to imagine that they have a right to be consulted in all such matters'.[136] The furore about the Maynooth Grant had had a paralysing effect on Peel's government and was responsible for an initial flaw in the Colleges bill that was never completely rectified.

Russell had never liked the system. During the parliamentary debate in 1845 he had argued that the bishops should be recognized 'as a part of your [government] plan' and should have been properly consulted. He felt that the bishops' memorial of May 1845 showed that they mistrusted the measure and that they feared 'that the faith and morals of the middle orders ... would be endangered'.[137] Russell's doubts remained when he came to power and it is probably significant that nothing was done regarding the colleges until Clarendon took up the matter in the autumn of 1847. By then the 1847 election, with its anti-Maynooth overtones, had returned a more Protestant parliament, and so narrowed Russell's room for manœuvre. Now, in the aftermath of the synod, he voiced his grave misgivings about the scheme and told Clarendon that Trinity College for the Established Church, Cork for the Roman Catholics and Belfast for Presbyterians would have been a far better scheme and would have worked well.[138] Clarendon protested that Russell's ideas would mean abandoning the principle of mixed education and would perpetuate sectarian animosities.[139] Russell replied that the plan was a bad one from the beginning, for the Catholic Church 'was sure to be startled by the

---

[134] See Kerr, *Peel*, 290–351.
[135] *Hansard*, lxxx. 1283–4, 2 June 1845.
[136] Heytesbury to Graham, 13 May 1845, Graham Papers.
[137] *Hansard*, lxxx. 1239–40, 1247–8, 2 June 1845.
[138] Russell to Clarendon, 1 Oct. 1850, Clarendon Papers, Box 26.
[139] Clarendon to Russell, 4 Oct. 1850, ibid., Letterbook 6. By mixed education was meant education of Catholics and Protestants together.

entire exclusion of religious instruction'. Even Clarendon's improvements, which had cost the lord lieutenant so dear, were not safe for, as Russell warned him, 'there is no Parliamentary security for the permanence of your regulation'.[140] When Clarendon remarked that to drop mixed education would put Ireland back fifty years, Russell made a measured case for separate education:

it would only put Ireland in the condition of England and Scotland which are not so far behind Ireland as Irishmen may suppose. Nay, Trinity College Dublin is in my plan, and I believe Belfast will be. Thus you have two of the great religious sections into which the British Islands are divided, with their own universities and the Roman Catholics alone made the subject of a Graham experiment.[141]

The exchange of views indicated a better understanding of Irish realities on the part of Russell than his lord lieutenant possessed. Like Liberals generally, Russell believed that the state should intervene in education, but, on grounds that were pragmatic as well as theoretical, he opposed the exclusion of religion from education. His views may be gleaned from his reply, as home secretary, to the debate in 1838 on national education in England. The education provided, he said firmly, should be religious; merely secular education should be rejected, for it 'would fail to implant in the minds of the children that religious and moral culture which was necessary'.[142] While he was referring here to English primary education, he apparently held similar views as regards Irish college education. In view of his wish to place the Catholic Church on an equal basis with the Established Church, he was anxious that the new system, which was intended primarily for Catholics, should not relegate religion to an inferior position.[143] In a country which had deeply held religious views, all three religions wanted an education that would be religious as well as scientific. Anglicans, in general, were opposed to neutral education, and both Presbyterians and Catholics sought, with growing success, to make the national system *de facto* denominational. Even Murray and his

---

[140] Russell to Clarendon, 1 Oct. 1850, Clarendon Papers, Box 26.
[141] Russell to Clarendon, 7 Oct. 1850, ibid., Box 26.
[142] *Hansard*, xliii. 731–2, 14 June 1838.
[143] For a full evaluation of Russell's educational views and policies, see R. Brent, *Liberal Anglican Politics: Whiggery, Religion and Reform, 1830–1841* (1987), chs. 5 and 6; P. Mandler, *Aristocratic Government in the Age of Reform: Whigs and Liberals 1830–1852* (1990), 182–93.

supporters accepted mixed education only on condition that safe-guards were present. Had they known that the prime minister believed that the guarantees contained in Clarendon's revised regulations were not safe, they would have withdrawn their support.

By 1850, however, despite these strong misgivings, it was too late to abandon the scheme, imperfect though it was. Clarendon, determined not to let an act of the queen in parliament be blocked by the 'mummers of Thurles', prepared to fight, encouraged by the fact that the margin by which the anti-colleges bishops had won was slight. He decided on tactics to win over Rome. Richard Lalor Sheil, a Catholic and old friend of O'Connell, was to be sent to Florence to act as the government's special agent in Rome. Clarendon would provide him with his detailed criticism of the synodical address, listing all the government had done for the Catholics. Nicholas Wiseman, the foremost English bishop, who was setting out for Rome on affairs concerning the Roman Catholic Church in England, would be asked to help. With Clarendon's encouragement, too, Lord Shrewsbury was already using his influence in Rome and that of his son-in-law, Prince Doria, to the same purpose. If Murray and so many bishops now wrote to assure Rome that the colleges posed no threat to the faith, the combined effort of so many influential Catholics gave good reason to hope that the pope might delay, or even cancel, the Thurles condemnation. There was some contradiction between Clarendon's outburst against the bishops for interfering in national affairs and his own willingness to appeal to the pope, but he was determined that the scheme should go ahead with as much approval as possible, and the chances of success, he believed, were good.

Before Roman negotiations got under way, and while the paper war between supporters and opponents of the colleges was still raging, a new development occurred in England that was to have profound repercussions on the situation in Ireland up to the end of Russell's administration.

8

Cardinal's Hat or Archbishop's Gauntlet? The 'Papal Aggression': The Ecclesiastical Titles Act and Ireland

'Under our feet we'll stamp thy Cardinal's hat
In spite of Pope or dignities of Church.'
(Lord Chancellor on Cardinal Wiseman, 9 Nov. 1850)

'Dr Cullen has thrown down the glove.'
(*Times*, 22 Aug. 1851)

'We cannot leave his glove on the ground.'
(Russell to Clarendon, 2 Oct. 1851)

The year and a half from the calling of the synod of Thurles to the resignation of the government in February 1852 witnessed an unexpected but bitter and prolonged dispute between the Whig government and the Catholic Church. During this period the Whigs' religious policies appeared to become less liberal while the Catholic Church in Britain and Ireland moved towards Ultramontanism. The remarkable events of those eighteen months had profound consequences in Ireland, for the government and the Church, and for their relations with one another.

The public dispute between the Irish bishops on the colleges, which had continued after the closure of the synod, saw appeals and counter-appeals to Rome. It was suddenly overshadowed by events which had little to do with Ireland and her affairs—'the papal aggression'.

The history of the papal aggression has been the subject of numerous studies.[1] Most of these concentrate on the British aspects

---

[1] O. Chadwick, *The Victorian Church* (1966), i. 271–309; E. R. Norman, *Anti-Catholicism in Victorian England* (1968), 52–79; W. Ralls, 'The Papal Aggression of 1850: A Study in Victorian Anti-Catholicism', *Church History*, 43 (1974), 242–56.

of the question, but the Irish dimension merits special treatment here because of its impact on the relations between government and Church.[2] The origin of the controversy concerned the restructuring of the Catholic Church in England, which by the middle of the nineteenth century had problems both of organization and orientation. The steady flow of converts of social and intellectual standing, many of them clergy, from the Oxford movement brought about tensions between older, more conservative, Catholics who clung to their established ways, and the new converts, supported by Nicholas Wiseman, vicar apostolic of the London district. What changed the Catholic Church in England, however, from a tiny minority estimated at 80,000 in 1767 to the three-quarters of a million recorded in 1851 was the mass influx of Irish Catholics.[3] This influx had started well before the Famine, but had become a veritable flood during and after those terrible years. Apart from attempting to assimilate the Oxford converts, the Church in England had to cope with this enormous number of Irish Catholics who now formed the majority of the faithful. Difference of race, language, political outlook, social habits, and even of religious practice rendered the task difficult and posed problems for relations between the two groups of co-religionists. 'Freedom and religious mood drew Catholics to splendour, even to ostentation, to display the majesty and mystery of Catholic faith, to build cathedrals prominent in the city square. Irish labourers tied them to back streets and slums, to tin sheds and converted halls.'[4] Tensions were inevitable. On the one hand, during the Famine, bishops like Briggs, converts like Lucas, and wealthy English Catholics had contributed generously towards relief in Ireland and towards the education of the Irish poor in England; on the other, there had long been misunderstandings between sections of Irish and English Catholics. Despite the fact that by 1850 the great majority of Catholics in Britain were Irish-born, or of Irish parentage, very few Irish clergy were in positions of influence, a fact that, with cultural change, different habits of religious practice, and the insufficiency of Catholic chapels, contributed to the leakage

---

[2] G. I. T. Machin, *Politics and the Churches in Great Britain, 1832–1868* (1977), 209–28, and E. Larkin, *The Making of the Roman Catholic Church in Ireland, 1850–1860* (1980), 58–95, pay attention to the Irish dimension.

[3] J. Bossy, *The English Catholic Community, 1570–1850* (1975), 297.

[4] Chadwick, *Victorian Church*, i. 271–2.

of Irish Catholics from the Church. On political issues distrust existed between the English Catholic aristocracy and Irish Catholics. Different stands on the veto question and attitudes towards Daniel O'Connell had not endeared Irish Catholics to the English Catholic gentry, who saw themselves as the representatives of the Catholic community in the United Kingdom and lectured Irish Catholics, including bishops, on their conduct.[5] Some, like Shrewsbury, lived or wintered in Rome and assisted the government in its efforts to influence the pope against what they perceived as Irish extremism.[6] This activity did not pass unnoticed or unresented by Irish political and Church leaders. In England the presence of so many Irish Catholics had contributed to reducing the leadership role of the Catholic aristocracy; the Irish workers' immediate loyalty was not to the gentry but to the local priest and the bishop.

Unlike the Irish Church, which had preserved a Catholic hierarchy from the Reformation, the English Catholic Church was governed by vicars apostolic who had powers similar to bishops. The majority of the English clergy petitioned Rome for a properly constituted hierarchy. Anxious to avoid Protestant protests in England, Rome had taken the advice of English Catholic leaders. This was to wait until a Whig government was in power, to act when parliament was not in session, and to avoid taking the names of any existing sees. Yet the timing proved unfortunate. Recent years had seen hundreds of thousands of Irish Catholics flooding into English cities, competing for jobs and causing resentment among the native English by their different lifestyle. Furthermore, the Church of England was in disarray. In 1845 John Henry Newman, the leader of the Oxford movement, had joined the Church of Rome, and a steady stream of some of the Church of England's finest men had preceded or followed him. Then, in 1847, Russell appointed Renn Dickson Hampden, regius professor of divinity at Oxford, as bishop of Hereford. Many churchmen believed that Hampden had Evangelical Protestant views on the Trinity, and thirteen bishops protested publicly against his appointment. Russell refused to listen. Suspecting that all Hampden's opponents held

---

[5] R. Swift and S. Gilley, *The Irish in the Victorian City* (1985); id., *The Irish in Britain, 1815–1939* (1989); R. Gray, *Cardinal Manning: A Biography* (1985), 143–7.

[6] One of Shrewsbury's daughters married Prince Borghese, and another Prince Doria. Lord and Lady Shrewsbury normally spent the winter months in Rome.

Newman's Catholic views, Russell determined to defend the Protestantism of his Church. His insensitive actions dismayed many loyal Churchmen. The so-called Gorham case had caused further dissension. Dr Phillpotts, the bishop of Exeter, had refused to institute the Revd George Gorham to a living in his diocese, claiming that his views on baptism were unorthodox. When the Privy Council upheld Gorham's appeal, many believed that it had decided that a denial of baptismal regeneration was not a bar to a living in the Church of England. Bewildered churchmen resented what they saw as the state's reassertion of Erastianism; a few, like Henry Wilberforce and Lord Feilding, now followed Newman's example and converted to Catholicism. Others resented what they saw as Romanizing trends among Tractarians and some high churchmen. Wiseman had unwisely entered the Gorham controversy and some Protestants suspected, with some reason, that the over-sanguine vicar apostolic had dreams of leading the Church of England into the papal fold. It is possible that he conveyed some of his hopes to the Roman *Curia*.

It was in this charged atmosphere that the papal brief of 29 September 1850 created, or restored, the English Catholic hierarchy and, on 7 October, Wiseman issued a pastoral letter 'Out of the Flaminian Gate'. Wiser heads like Newman and Bishop Ullathorne wanted the Catholic hierarchy restored quietly, but the brief, and Wiseman's letter, made it a public issue. Included among the seats of the new dioceses was Westminster which, although not the name of an Anglican see, was a name that 'rang loud with the history of England'.[7] Wiseman's pastoral letter was couched in flamboyant and exuberant tones. 'We govern and continue to govern', he wrote, 'the counties of Middlesex, Hertford, and Essex as ordinary thereof, and those of Surrey, Sussex, Kent, Berkshire, and Hampshire, with the islands annexed, as administrator with ordinary jurisdiction.' A triumphalist note sounded in such statements as 'your beloved country has received a place among the fair Churches, which, normally constituted, form the splendid aggregate of the Catholic communion; Catholic England has been restored to its orbit in the ecclesiastical firmament, from which its light had long vanished'.[8] Wiseman wrote with the enthusiasm of

[7] Chadwick, *Victorian Church*, i. 290.
[8] Wiseman, *From the Flaminian Gate*, cited in B. Ward, *The Sequel to Catholic Emancipation*, ii: *1830–50* (1915), 305–8.

a man who saw his choicest dream being realized and who cherished even greater hopes for the future of the English Catholic Church.[9] Although his words intended no more than to delimit the areas where he would exercise spiritual jurisdiction over Catholics, the claim of a Catholic prelate to govern and administer English counties was irritating in the extreme to Anglicans, clear though it should have been in the mid-nineteenth century that Rome had no territorial claims on England. Queen Victoria was reported as exclaiming 'am I queen of England or not?'[10] A further difficulty was to emerge. Pius IX and Wiseman believed that the government knew of the intention to restore the hierarchy and had raised no objection. Although they had grounds since Minto's visit for believing this to have been the case, a misunderstanding had arisen and the government could equally claim that it had never been informed. Both the pope's action and the manner in which Wiseman had announced it offended Protestant feelings.

When the brief reached the British press toward mid-October, *The Times* reacted strongly against its exalted curial language. It blew the issue out of proportion, describing the papal brief, or 'bull' as it came to be known, as a clumsy joke and 'one of the grossest acts of folly and impertinence which the court of Rome has ventured to commit since the crown and people of England threw off its yoke'.[11] A few days later *The Times* drew attention to the dispute between the archbishop of Turin and the Piedmontese state, asking 'are not the same "authorities" at this moment defying the government and laws of Sardinia and waging open war there with the Crown?'[12] Two days later it published and commented sharply on Wiseman's pastoral. *The Times*, whose influence was never greater, was partly responsible for stirring up the controversy. It labelled the papal action as 'papal aggression' and the name stuck. *Punch*, too, played a significant role, and over the following months no issue was complete without several cartoons and witty, and often unpleasant, articles on papal bulls and scheming cardinals. The Catholic Dicky Doyle, its leading cartoonist, resigned in protest.[13] *The Times* had caught the mood, the sales of *Punch* soared, and the popular press followed suit. Clergy,

[9] S. Gilley, *Newman and his Age* (1990), 264.
[10] Ward, *Sequel to Emancipation*, ii. 287.   [11] *Times*, 22 Oct. 1850.
[12] Ibid. 27 Oct. 1850.   [13] Richard Doyle (1824–83).

laity, and Protestant societies throughout the land now denounced pope and cardinal. On Guy Fawkes' day their effigies were burnt on bonfires all over Britain. *Punch* depicted Pius IX in the cellars of the Palace of Westminster, as 'THE GUY FAWKES OF 1850, PREPARING TO BLOW UP ALL ENGLAND'. Many Dissenters, concerned about Catholic civil rights, declined to join in the outcry, and the influential newspaper the *Nonconformist* commented that 'to associate great religious truths with street mummery and a waste of gunpowder, speaks but little for the boasted enlightenment of the age'.[14] Bishop Ullathorne tried to explain the papal action as intended simply to regularize the position of the Catholic hierarchy, but to little avail. Newman defended it too vigorously in a widely reported sermon and that increased the anger. Some of the Catholic gentry were strongly critical of Rome's action, and one or two left the Church in disgust.

At first the furore was confined to Britain. Among Irish Catholics and Irish Protestants it aroused no more than close interest and some surprise. One clergyman of the Established Church, remarking that in Ireland 'we are used to these titulars, and do not find their existence an insupportable evil', pointed out the excellent relations between the Anglican and Catholic archbishops in Armagh and in Dublin and that Cullen had just paid a visit to the Anglican primate who, moreover, used to drive his predecessor, Crolly, to meetings.[15] The calm in Ireland was shattered in early November. Dr Maltby, the bishop of Durham and an old friend of Russell, wrote to him to ask what he or the government thought of 'the late aggression of the Pope upon our Protestantism' which he believed was 'insolent and insidious'.[16] In an open letter, Russell replied from Downing Street on 4 November. He agreed that the 'aggression' was indeed 'insolent and insidious', castigated the pope for his 'pretension of supremacy over the realm of England', and promised that 'the present state of the law shall be carefully examined, and the propriety of adopting any proceedings with

[14] Cited in S. H. Major, 'The *Nonconformist* and the Roman Catholic Church', *Recusant History*, 19 (1988–9), 190.

[15] An Irish Beneficed Clergyman to *Morning Chronicle*, 15 Nov. 1850, cited in *The Roman Catholic Question: A Copious Series of Important Documents, of Permanent Historical Interest, on the Re-establishment of the Catholic Hierarchy in England, 1851*, ser. 15 (1851), 13.

[16] Durham to Russell, 30 Oct. 1850, Russell Papers, PRO 30/22/8F, fos. 118–19.

reference to the recent assumption of power, deliberately considered'. He singled out the Tractarians, however, as a greater threat, for these 'unworthy sons of the Church of England' constituted a danger 'within the walls'. He concluded with a peroration which entered the sensitive realm of popular theology:

I will not bate a jot of heart or hope, so long as the glorious principles and the immortal martyrs of the Reformation shall be held in reverence by the great mass of a nation which looks with contempt on the mummeries of superstition, and with scorn at the laborious endeavours which are now making to confine the intellect and enslave the soul.[17]

Seldom has a statement by a prime minister evoked such an enthusiastic response. The press applauded him. Protestant bodies throughout the realm acclaimed him. The archbishop of Canterbury, bishops, and deans showered congratulations on him.[18] Russell had emerged as the champion of Protestantism against insidious Romanism. Even though his cabinet colleagues had not seen the letter before it was sent, some welcomed it. Wood, the chancellor of the exchequer, reported that 'Lord John is very proud of his letter which has been wonderfully well received in the city'.[19] The home secretary, Sir George Grey, was also pleased with it.

In view of the striking contrast between the sentiments expressed in the so-called 'Durham letter' and Russell's long-standing dedication to religious freedom, his motives in writing it have been the subject of much debate.[20] Yet with such a public outcry against popery and accusations that royal supremacy and the Established Church were being attacked, a response was a political necessity. After three weeks of discreet silence, the direct, personal appeal of his friend, the bishop of Durham, finally spurred Russell into action. Political calculations were, no doubt, present. Since his popularity and that of his government was waning, there was the hope that this popular issue might restore it, and he may have desired to emulate the success of Palmerston who gained popular and parlia-

[17] J. Prest, *Lord John Russell* (1972), 429–30.
[18] Canterbury to Russell, 9 Nov. 1850, Russell Papers, PRO 30/22/8F, fos. 190–1.
[19] Wood to Clarendon, 8 Nov. 1850, Clarendon Papers, Box 32.
[20] For Russell's motives see Chadwick, *Victorian Church*, i. 297–9; Norman, *Anti-Catholicism*, 57–61; Prest, *Russell*, 319–26; Machin, *Politics*, 210–28; Ralls, 'Papal Aggression', 242–56; D. G. Paz, 'Another Look at Lord John Russell and the Papal Aggression, 1850', *The Historian*, 45 (1982–3), 47–64.

mentary applause by his patriotic stand on the Don Pacifico issue. Here, now, was an issue that matched the feelings of his heart and would win the applause of his countrymen. Some months later Stanley gave his son, Edward Stanley, his own explanation of Russell's action:

Johnny had heard that I meant to publish a strong Protestant manifesto (which I never thought of doing); he remembered how he had tripped up Peel by his Edinburgh letter in favour of entire corn law repeal: and he thought I was going to trip him up in the same way. As it turns out, he has only upset his own government. It is quite a case of retributive justice.[21]

Russell's fear of being out-manœuvred is plausible enough— if he did not act Stanley, or even Disraeli, might take the lead in a more violent no-popery campaign and make himself the champion of the Protestant cause with the support of a Protestant parliament. The fundamental motive for his action, however, should be sought in Russell's religious feelings and his dislike of Catholicism, whether of the Roman or Oxford variety. If either dislike predominated it was hostility to Tractarianism. 'I prefer', he told Brougham on 9 October, 'the Roman Catholic foe to the Tractarian spy.'[22] Puseyism, he was convinced, was weakening the Established Church from within and pushing it Romeward. He regarded Puseyism as popery in disguise or, in the words of Sheil, 'Popery with a bar sinister'.[23] To add to Russell's annoyance, W. J. E. Bennett, one of the signatories of the resolutions against the Gorham judgment and curate-in-charge of St Paul's, Knightsbridge, where the Russells regularly worshipped, engaged in the very 'ritualism' Russell abhorred. Annoyed and concerned at the Romanizing tendencies in the Church, Russell had been anxiously discussing with Clarendon how best to combat them. Clarendon, somewhat waspishly, had encouraged Russell's resentment against Tractarians and Catholics generally. On 28 September Clarendon wrote:

If no voice is raised against the bad example and pernicious influence of such men as the Bishop of London [Charles James Blomfield] and of

---

[21] Stanley's journal, 1 Mar. 1851, cited in J. Vincent (ed.), *Disraeli and the Conservative Party: Journals and Memoirs of Edward Henry, Lord Stanley, 1849–1869* (1978), 51–2.

[22] Russell to Brougham, 9 Oct. 1850, Brougham Papers, cited in Prest, *Russell*, 321.

[23] J. Russell, *Recollections and Suggestions, 1813–73* (1875), 129.

Archdeacons Manning and Wilberforce, mischief will creep on and the clergy will be gradually undermined. The sooner, therefore, the broad line is drawn between real and pseudo Protestants the better. . . . I only wish the . . . fidgety curates who go to seek . . . freedom at Rome would first come to Ireland to . . . observe the slavish submission effected by its [Catholicism's] perpetual interference.[24]

Russell, in reply, encouraged Clarendon's brother Montagu to get up a 'declaration' attesting 'the adherence of the subscribers to the general doctrine of the Reformation, their satisfaction at that great event . . . and their dread of any change which might bring back the Church of England into the bosom of the Church of Rome'. This declaration, he added, should 'avow openly the obedience of its subscribers to all acts of Parliament or Canons which establish the Queen's supremacy in all cases spiritual and temporal without any reservation'.[25] He also suggested a committee of twenty-five clergymen in London for maintaining the principles of the Reformation, but Clarendon told him that Montagu did not think twenty-five trustworthy men could be found.[26] Clarendon encouraged, even incited, Russell. When the no-popery agitation began in mid-October, Clarendon, rejecting Greville's criticism of the clamour, welcomed it. He told Reeve that it was necessary 'to proclaim *à haute voix* that we will not consent to the imposition of the yoke of Rome' and warmly congratulated him on his articles in *The Times* for 'piquing the Roman Catholics of England about their allegiance and implying that they are unfit for liberal institutions if they submit to them [Roman claims]'.[27] Before Russell made any public pronouncement, Clarendon told him that this 'outburst of pure protestantism' would do more than any declaration 'to put down Puseyism and prevent Jesuits, Passionists and

[24] Clarendon to Russell, 28 Sept. 1850, Clarendon Papers, Letterbook 6. Henry Manning (1808–92), archdeacon of Chichester (1840); joined Catholic Church (1851); cardinal archbishop of Westminster. Robert Wilberforce (1802–57), son of the philanthropist; archdeacon of East Riding (1841); joined Catholic Church (1854).

[25] Russell to Clarendon, 30 Sept. 1850, ibid., Box 26. Henry Montagu Villiers (1813–61), younger brother of Clarendon, canon of St Paul's Cathedral (1847–56), later bishop of Carlisle and then of Durham. He was an extremely low churchman.

[26] Russell to Clarendon, 13 Oct. 1850, Clarendon Papers, Box 26.

[27] Clarendon to Reeve, 23 Oct. 1850, cited in H. E. Maxwell, *The Life and Letters of George William Frederick, Fourth Earl of Clarendon* (1913), i. 315; Clarendon to Reeve, 25 Oct. 1850, Clarendon Papers, c. 534.

other Mountebanks from parading the streets'.[28] The timing of Clarendon's letter is significant, for Russell received it at about the same time as he wrote his reply to the bishop of Durham. When Russell's letter appeared, a contented Clarendon wrote to Lewis: 'It will, I hope, damage the real authors of the Thing, those never to be half enough cursed Tractarians.'[29] Although Clarendon felt that it would be wrong to punish 'the reasonable Catholics' and could not see how the pope had contravened the law, the general anti-Catholic tone of his letters stoked Russell's annoyance with both Tractarians and Catholics.[30] 'Mummery', 'slavish submission', 'yoke of Rome', terms which Clarendon constantly used to describe the Catholics' faith, were the terminology of the Durham letter, though they may have been the stock-in-trade of other Whigs.

Although Clarendon's influence was considerable, Russell's own religious feelings were the main incentive for writing the letter. Romanizing trends within the Church of England angered him and in the letter, after denouncing papal interference, he turned to castigate 'those unworthy sons of the Church of England' whom he alleged 'were leading their flocks "step by step to the very verge of the precipice" '. Three weeks later Russell based his justification on the necessity to oppose Tractarians:

The danger I have feared all along has been that the young Tractarian clergy by the weakness and connivance of the Bishops would get possession of the Churches and establish a religion of the higher classes, from which the middle and lower would separate. I think I have done much to save England from this danger and the people will do the rest.

Russell distrusted the bishops and the clergy with their elaborate theologizing and felt he had more in common with the ordinary, straightforward Protestantism of the people. Resentment at Catholic ingratitude in not appreciating his efforts on their behalf surfaced in the letter.[31] Only two months before, Wiseman had assured him that he would be remaining in Rome, but he was now returning in the full panoply of a Roman cardinal to install himself in Westminster; frustration at the Irish situation may also have

---

[28] Clarendon to Russell, 3 Nov. 1850, Clarendon Papers, Letterbook 6.
[29] Clarendon to Lewis, 8 Nov. 1850, ibid., c. 523/2.
[30] Clarendon to Russell, 3 Nov. 1850, ibid., Letterbook 6.
[31] Prest, *Russell*, 320. In the second paragraph of the Durham letter Russell briefly recounted his work for Catholics.

played some part in Russell's response. Greville, who knew him, sharply criticized him for blurting out 'his petulance and imprudence'.[32] Disraeli acutely commented to Stanley that he was simply 'indulging in his hereditary foible—to wit, having a shy at the Papists'.[33] Apart from this political and religious motivation, Russell's own impulsive temperament influenced his reaction. Only a few days earlier he had spoken of first consulting the pope and had explicitly ruled out hasty measures, yet in the end he acted without weighing the consequences.[34]

He was soon to see those consequences, for if Protestant opinion rejoiced at the Durham letter, Catholic opinion was aghast. Wiseman angrily denounced the government for deception. It had, he alleged, concealed the fact that, although it knew of the intended move, it had raised no objection. Clergy and laity, English and Irish, pro-government as well as anti-government bishops, read with amazement the prime minister's letter in which he described their rites, by which they would understand in the first place the mass and sacraments, as 'superstitious mummeries'. The Durham letter, coming from one who had consistently championed religious freedom, caused surprise to the point of disbelief. Edward Stanley recounted an unconfirmed report that when Clarendon first had the letter read to him, he expressed admiration at the cleverness of the forgery, nor until proof arrived, would he admit it to be genuine.[35] This may have been a ploy on Clarendon's part when he realized how sharp the Irish Catholic reaction was, for when the letter first appeared he had told Lewis that 'Lord John's is a good letter and will please the Protestants and was certainly demanded by the . . . feeling of the country'.[36] One reaction is recorded. From Rome Shrewsbury, recounting to Clarendon his many lengthy and, he believed, successful efforts to convince the *Curia* of the government's good faith on the colleges issue, added a hasty postscript to his letter: 'Surely L[ord] John's letter in *The Times* of Nov. 6 is a spurious document! I cannot

---

[32] Greville to Clarendon, 20 Nov. 1850, Clarendon Papers, c. 522.

[33] Derby Papers, Box 145/1, cited in R. Blake, *Disraeli* (1969), 300.

[34] Paz, 'Another Look', 64, believes Russell's response was thoughtless and unpremeditated.

[35] Stanley's journal, 12 Feb. 1851, cited in Vincent, *Disraeli and the Conservative Party*, 39–40.

[36] Clarendon to Lewis, 8 Nov. 1850, Clarendon Papers, c. 523/2.

believe it to be otherwise. From the long-tried and consistent advocate of *civil and Religious Liberty* it is impossible!'[37] Shrewsbury's incredulous reaction was that of many contemporaries: why did Russell break with the tradition of a lifetime, use language insulting to Catholics, and promote no-popery?

Russell's action had serious consequences, for he had repeated the common mistake in England's dealings with Ireland of seeing the situation from an English point of view, rather than that of the whole United Kingdom; he thus failed to foresee the effects of his letter on Ireland. The Lord Chancellor added fuel to the fire in his speech at the Guildhall on 9 November, when he cited Shakespeare's Henry VI:

> Under our feet we'll stamp thy Cardinal's hat
> In spite of Pope or dignities of Church.[38]

Such inflammatory language coming from prominent members of the establishment was bound to annoy Irish Catholics. An alarmed Clarendon reported to Lansdowne that Russell's 'mummeries of superstition' caused an outbreak of 'rabies' in Ireland:

At one fell swoop it appears to have alienated the entire Roman Catholic community of Ireland . . . if the brewers of Southwark . . . were to smash the Cardinal's head as well as his hat I think my Lord Chancellor might be indicted as an accessory before the fact. All these [*sic*] English fuel makes the Irish fires blaze brightly.[39]

Many Catholics had supported the Whigs through thick and thin—More O'Ferrall, Redington, Sheil, Bellew, and others. Although they regarded as unfortunate the manner in which the establishment of the hierarchy in England had been managed by both pope and cardinal, they now felt let down by Russell's slur on their religion. Even Redington, the under-secretary and chief channel of communication with the bishops, doubted if he could continue in office. Russell was unrepentant, for when Clarendon, suddenly aware of the impact of the letter on Redington and other Catholic Whigs, pointed out that some of its terms would offend

---

[37] Shrewsbury to Clarendon, 15 Nov. 1850, ibid., Box 58.
[38] *Tablet*, 16 Nov. 1850. The allusion is to Gloucester's challenge to the bishop of Winchester in Shakespeare's *1 Henry VI*, I. iii. 50.
[39] Clarendon to Lansdowne, 14 Nov. 1850, Clarendon Papers, Letterbook 6.

Catholics, his protest was brushed aside.[40] An unmollified Russell replied sharply:

For thirty years the Whigs sacrificed power to maintain their opinion that the Roman Catholics ought to be admitted to power. The cause was gained, and the Pope applies himself to thwart the English government in every way he can imagine—to insult our Queen—to supplant our religion. And then I am not to defend our religion attacked from without and within. . . . I cannot give up our arms of defence as Protestants to please their [the Catholics'] susceptibility. Let them therefore support Stanley and d'Israeli if they will . . . I cannot bow the flag of England before that of the Pope.[41]

Russell's strong Protestantism, his resentment of ingratitude, and his intemperateness all come to light in this letter. Clarendon had to face the reality of the Irish scene, and he now relayed to Russell the balanced comments of Redington, whom he described as 'the most honourable and loyal person possible':

I think Lord John would have utterly failed in his duty if he had not repelled this aggression . . . but when Lord John, who we, through life, have considered our best friend and the beau ideal of all that is mild and tolerant, declares, though the blow was aimed at the Tractarians, that the forms of our religion are mummeries of Superstition, he not only wounds us in what we hold most dear but places every Roman Catholic who serves him . . . in a painful position by exposing him to the taunts of those disaffected brawlers and turbulent priests . . .

Clarendon went on to defend Redington. It was not fair for Lord John, he insisted, to suggest that men like Redington wished 'the flag of England should bow to that of Rome' or to dismiss their real grievance by suggesting that they go and serve Stanley and Disraeli. Even Archbishop Murray, Clarendon reminded Russell, had felt obliged to convene his clergy for the purpose of congratulating Wiseman, adding: 'For a man like Dr Murray this is a significant act.'[42] Somewhat abashed, Russell expressed his regret for using the offending word 'mummeries', and went on in a letter, which he wanted shown to Redington, to rationalize his use of it:

---

[40] Clarendon to Russell, 10 Nov. 1850, ibid.
[41] Russell to Clarendon, 13 Nov. 1850, ibid., Box 26.
[42] Clarendon to Russell, 15 Nov. 1850, ibid., Letterbook 6.

they [the Catholics] have no right to find fault, if following my diocesan, I use a word as applicable to members of my own church, nearly equivalent to his own word 'histrionic'. And it might very well happen that these practices might be superstitious in our Church, which are not so in the Roman Catholic.

While this explanation went against the common understanding of the letter it also appeared to contradict what Russell had written three days before. Explaining his refusal to write to the duke of Norfolk to say he had been misunderstood, he had told Clarendon that 'the terms used are applied to the Tractarians but I cannot deny that Roman Catholics are open to similar terms of reproach'.[43] To suggest at first that the Pope was trying to supplant his religion and then to change his defence to casuistry on the word 'mummery' showed that Russell had not thought the matter through. Palmerston had recommended similar casuistry to Sheil:

I told Sheil that he should say to the Italians that insolent means unusual and is synonymous with Insolito and that the fair meaning and application of Mummery is that such is the real Nature of Forms and Ceremonies of the Catholic Belief when introduced into the Protestant Ritual where they have no Meaning and no Foundation of Belief and Significance, as they have in their natural Places in the Ritual of the Church to which they belong.[44]

Palmerston was not consistent. A few days earlier he had applauded the no-popery agitation and remarked: 'It is lucky, however, for the English Catholics that there are Catholics in Ireland or Else—!' What this vague menace was is not clear. His subtle explanation of 'mummery' and 'insolent' would scarcely have deceived the *Curia* and it is unlikely that Sheil made use of it. In Ireland, although Redington professed to accept Russell's explanation, it is doubtful how far he and other Catholics were convinced by it. The explanation, taken at its face value, strengthens the argument that the Durham letter was aimed more at Tractarians than at Roman Catholics.

Other cabinet members appear to have been divided in their opinion on the Durham letter. Since they had not been shown it before it was sent they felt less responsible, yet most appeared to

---

[43] Russell to Clarendon, 13 Nov. 1850, ibid., Box 26.
[44] Palmerston to Clarendon, 13 Nov. 1850, ibid., c. 524.

have approved of its sentiments. Wood and George Grey praised it until Clarendon and Sheil told them of the reaction in Ireland. Although Lord Grey and Labouchere apparently had misgivings, the only strong criticism came from Morpeth, now earl of Carlisle, the commissioner for woods and forests. Disgusted with Russell's action, he referred to him in the privacy of his diary, as 'our No Popery Premier'.[45] Outside the cabinet Lewis, realizing the offensive nature of Russell's language, feared that 'the mummeries' would ring long in Lord John's ears. With some foresight he commented that the Irish members would remember the 'mummeries' when the government was hard pressed in the next session. The most outright protest came from Greville. Apart from scathing comment in his diary, he complained bitterly to Clarendon, and, finally, when he could no longer stand what he called 'the torrent of nonsense, violence and folly which the newspapers day after day poured forth', he wrote a long letter to *The Times* on 9 December. To Clarendon, he complained that 'it is really intolerable that he [Russell] should take his pen in his hands and blurt out his petulance and imprudence without consulting anybody, or allowing any one of those who must be committed by it, to see his production'.[46]

Unwittingly, Russell gave a powerful impetus to Ultramontanism. As Clarendon remarked, 'the religious war now raging in England is . . . greatly in favour of the Ultramontanes here for it compels the Roman Catholics to sink all minor differences'.[47] Cullen, Slattery, and MacHale remained suspicious of government intentions, particularly after the 'assassinations' controversy and the intrigues at Rome in 1848. Now their suspicions appeared justified. Cullen, immediately seizing the advantage, wrote to Propaganda three days after the letter was published, enclosing documents to prove his case against mixed education, including the Durham letter. 'The third document', he wrote, 'is a letter written by our prime minister, Lord John Russell "to make known his views on the Catholic religion". He is our most decided enemy. It falls to him, principally, to nominate the professors in the Queen's

[45] Diary, 6, 7, 8, 9, 11 Nov. 1850, cited in D. D. Olien, *Morpeth: A Victorian Public Career* (1983), 372.
[46] Lewis to Clarendon, 12 Nov. 1850, Clarendon Papers, c. 530; Greville to Clarendon, 20 Nov. 1850, ibid., c. 52.
[47] Clarendon to Russell, 19 Nov. 1850, ibid., Letterbook 6.

Colleges.'[48] Cullen drove the point home in an important address to his clergy. Turning to the key issue of the appointments of staff in the colleges, he cleverly used Russell's own description of the Catholic faith and rites to convince his audience that the colleges constituted a snare:

Can we expect that any system which confines the intellect and enslaves the soul, will be fairly and honestly protected and encouraged? Will the mummeries of superstition be promoted? When the appointment of a professor is to be made, if perchance a Catholic is to be selected, will one be chosen who is zealous for our mummeries, that is, who is devotedly attached to the doctrines of our Church? Is it not to be feared that every selection of professors will be made with the object of freeing us from the dreadful state of ignorance in which we, in common with nearly two hundred million of our brethren, constituting the most civilised and enlightened portion of the human race, are placed, in order to make way for the lights and liberty of the reformation amongst us?

He turned then to destroy the position of Murray and his supporters. Russell had been honest in avowing his hostility to Catholicism, he claimed, and so 'our indignation should be reserved for those who think it wise to put the education of Catholic youth in the hands of men who draw so frightful a picture of our doctrine, and who entertain so sincere, so inveterate a hatred of everything Catholic'. His case was a persuasive one: how could a government which so despised the Catholic faith be trusted to appoint staff who would promote that faith? As he insinuated, too, there was an echo of the European clash between Liberalism and Catholicism. His able address undoubtedly influenced waverers among bishops, clergy, and laity. In January 1851, Cullen spoke again but in less polemic tones at the Lord Mayor's dinner in Drogheda, where he promised solidarity with the English Catholics and made a dignified appeal for religious and civil liberty.[49]

If Cullen exulted in the Durham letter as unmasking the Whigs, Murray now saw the ground cut from under him. Dismayed at the attack on his Church and in an attempt to retain the initiative, he convened his clergy and came out on the side of the English

---

[48] Cullen to Secretary of Propaganda, 9 Nov. 1850, *Acta* (1851), vol. 213, fos. 241–2, PFA.

[49] E. Larkin, *The Making of the Roman Catholic Church in Ireland, 1850–1860* (1987), 88.

Catholics, the first Irish bishop to do so. At this meeting of 18 November he attempted to pour oil on the troubled waters:

this change of discipline affects . . . no class of Christians but the members of our own Church. . . . We can readily make allowances for the inconsiderate expressions of unkindness towards us which the advocates of intolerance were enabled to evoke from many a humane, and generous, and upright heart, while the real state of the case was studiously kept out of view; but the delusion cannot continue; the good sense of England will check that spirit of intolerance, so hostile to Religious Freedom and to Social Improvement.[50]

The measured tones of this statement and the readiness to make allowances for reactions in the heat of the moment were typical of Murray and are reminiscent of an appeal he made to the Englishman's sense of fair play during an earlier 'no-popery' scare in 1835.[51] Compared with Wiseman's own defence Murray's plea was mildness itself. Wiseman wrote thanking Murray and renouncing all further faith in politicians.[52] In the past Irish clergy had suspected Wiseman of collaborating with the government. They had had good reason. Clarendon had asked Russell to persuade Wiseman to use his influence in Rome on behalf of the government's Irish policies and, before going to Rome, Wiseman had visited Russell.[53] The visit had excited alarm in Ireland, and from Saint John's College, Waterford, James Cooke warned Kirby that 'Dr W. had an audience with Lord J. Russell!!! before his departure. Was this to get instructions or to take compliments to the Holy Father or Cardinal Fransoni?' The alarm was probably justified, for Wiseman had undertaken to write to Russell 'respecting the feeling of the Holy See on the subject of a minister from England to be sent on a special mission'.[54] The mission was, most likely, to gain support from the Holy See for the government's Irish policies including the colleges. Cardinal Antonelli, the secretary of state, confirmed to Shrewsbury that Wiseman had spoken out against the condemnation of the colleges.[55] The Durham letter,

---

[50] W. Meagher, *Notices on the Life and Character of His Grace, Most Reverend Daniel Murray* . . . (1853), 75–6.
[51] D. A. Kerr, *Peel, Priests, and Politics* (1982), 21.
[52] Wiseman to Murray, 13, 20 Feb. 1851, Murray Papers, DDA.
[53] Clarendon to Russell, 31 Aug. 1850, Clarendon Papers, Letterbook 6.
[54] Wiseman to Russell, 3 Nov. 1850, Russell Papers, PRO 30/22/8F.
[55] Shrewsbury to Clarendon, 2 Nov. 1850, Clarendon Papers, Box 58.

and Wiseman's subsequent 'appeal', in which he bitterly attacked Russell, put an end to any possibility of using Wiseman as a counterbalance to Irish lobbying in Rome. Wiseman asked Sheil to tell Clarendon that 'the Irish Education Question would all have been settled satisfactorily . . . but that [Russell's] letter had rendered it impossible'. Wiseman also told Lady Greville that 'he had seen the Pope before he left Rome and was authorised by him to propose to our Government a sort of compromise with regard to the Irish Colleges which he thought would have been satisfactory'. Now, however, bargaining on the colleges had became more difficult. Wiseman sent Sir George Bowyer, a Catholic convert, to Greville, to explore what could be done to calm the 'aggression' crisis. Greville, anxious to restore harmony, suggested that the best line Wiseman could follow would be to urge the pope not to pronounce against the colleges: Bowyer replied that Wiseman would gladly see this course taken, but that 'Lord John's letter had now made it impossible'. The letter, Bowyer added, would be regarded not only a gross insult, but as a declaration of hostility against the Roman Catholic religion; the pope 'would refuse to place any confidence in the intentions of the British Government when the head of it put forth such a Manifesto'. Although he did his best to combat this view, Greville believed that what Bowyer said was true.[56] So deep was the rift between the Catholic primate and Russell that thenceforth 'Cardinal Wolsey Wiseman', as Clarendon disparagingly called him, did not conduct official business between the English hierarchy and the government; other bishops undertook that role.[57] Cullen, while giving full support to Wiseman and the English Catholics, wrote to Kirby that it was 'hard to compliment the English—as they may turn the tables on us some fine day, and join the government against us'. In a transparent reference to the role of some English Catholics during the 'assassination' controversy, he added, 'if we had caused an uproar as that excited in England [by Wiseman], what would the language of English Catholics be towards us?'[58] Newman, too, for whom

[56] C. C. F. Greville, *The Greville Memoirs: A Journal of the Reign of Queen Victoria*, ed. H. Reeve (1903), 10 Nov. 1850, vi. 374–7; Greville to Clarendon, 14 Nov. 1850, Clarendon Papers, c. 522.
[57] Clarendon to Lewis, 22 Jan. 1850, Clarendon Papers, c. 532/2; J. D. Holmes, *More Roman than Rome: English Catholicism in the Nineteenth Century* (1978), 81.   [58] Larkin, *Making of the Church*, 89.

Liberalism was anathema, was pleased that 'we are rid of them [the Whigs] for ever'.[59]

The difficulty in Ireland was that Russell's decision to legislate against ecclesiastical titles took no account of accepted practice in Ireland nor indeed of his own expressed attitude. In July 1845 he had stated in the House of Commons that 'he believed they might repeal those disallowing clauses which prevented a Roman Catholic bishop assuming a title held by a bishop of the Established Church', adding that 'he could not conceive any good ground for the continuance of this restriction'.[60] The Irish bishops' titles had already been recognized officially. Peel's Charitable Bequests Act of 1844 spoke of bequests 'in trust for any archbishop or bishop . . . of the Church of Rome officiating in any district, or having pastoral superintendence of any congregation of persons professing the Roman Catholic religion'. In the gazetting of the Act, on 17 December 1844, the bishops were given their full ecclesiastical titles (without, however, mention of territorial title) and precedence over the peers.[61] A private Act, the Dublin Cemeteries Act of 1846, referred to 'his Grace Daniel Murray, and his successors exercising the same Spiritual Jurisdiction as he now exercises in the Diocese of Dublin as an Archbishop'.[62]

Clarendon had complicated matters further. When he came to Ireland, his concern to make contact with the bishops had brought him meetings with Archbishop Nicholson, who volunteered to support, at Rome, the government case on the colleges. Nicholson had just been appointed Catholic coadjutor archbishop of Corfu and at his request Clarendon decided that it would be better if all Roman Catholic bishops be addressed no longer as 'Right Reverend Sir' but as 'My Lord' and 'Your Grace', though without recognizing their territorial titles. For him and for Russell this was pure common-sense and no more than the logical conclusion of the Bequests Act. Clarendon pressed Lord Grey to adopt the same style for colonial bishops. Grey raised difficulties. The Catholic bishops' salaries, he claimed, made them unsuited to such a dignity, and he cited the case of the bishop of Newfoundland, who had only £75 a year. Russell, however, was in favour and Grey

[59] Gilley, *Newman*, 264–5.
[60] *Hansard*, lxxii. 290, 9 July 1845.
[61] Kerr, *Peel*, 125, 190.   [62] *Quarterly Review*, 88 (1851), 256.

reluctantly agreed and sent out a circular accordingly.[63] Clarendon believed he had scored a success at little cost. He had gratified his new ally, Nicholson, and, at the first meeting with the Irish bishops, he was convinced he had charmed them by his gracious acknowledgement of their status. Affecting much amusement that Irish Catholic bishops could be pleased by such 'puerilities as empty titles', Clarendon reported to Russell that at his meeting with them 'their pleasure at being "my Lorded" . . . was quite curious'.[64] When the queen visited Ireland in 1849, the official entrée list to Dublin Castle, published in the *Dublin Gazette*, named the Roman Catholic archbishops of Armagh and Dublin before the duke of Leinster and immediately after the Anglican archbishops of Armagh and Dublin. Apart from some mutterings on the part of Orangemen, little attention was paid to these matters until the papal aggression crisis. Disraeli, on the very morrow of the appearance of the Durham letter, made effective use of them in a tart attack on the government:

when the present Lord Lieutenant arrived . . . he gathered together the Romish Bishops of Ireland, [and] addressed them as nobles. . . . On the visit of her Majesty . . . the same prelates were presented to the Queen as if they were nobles, and precedence was given to them over the nobility and dignitaries of the national Church; it was only the other day . . . that the Government offered the Office of Visitor to the Queen's Colleges to Dr Cullen, the Pope's delegate, and *pseudo* Archbishop of Armagh and to Dr M'Hale, the *pseudo* Archbishop of Tuam. What wonder, then, that his Holiness should deem himself at liberty to apportion England into dioceses, to be ruled over by his bishops! And instead of supposing that he has taken a step 'insolent and insidious' should he not have assumed that he was acting in strict conformity with the wishes of her Majesty's Government?

How could they blame the pope? 'The whole question has been surrendered and decided in favour of the Pope, by the present Government, and the Minister who recognised the *pseudo* Archbishop of Tuam as a peer and a prelate, cannot object to the

---

[63] Clarendon to Russell, 13 Oct. 1847, Clarendon Papers, Letterbook 1; Clarendon to Grey, Earl Grey Papers, 29 Oct. 1847, 81/2; Russell to Clarendon, 30 Oct. 1847, Clarendon Papers, Box 43; Grey to Governors of Colonies, 20 Nov. 1847, *Quarterly Review*, 88 (1851), 253.

[64] Clarendon to Russell, 30 Oct. 1847, Clarendon Papers, Letterbook 1.

appointment of a *pseudo* Archbishop of Westminster.'[65] He placed the blame squarely on the Whigs' own policy, with its insistence 'that there shall be no distinction between England and Ireland'. Disraeli had logic on his side. Clarendon's Orange enemies, still smarting from Roden's dismissal from the magistracy over the Dolly's Brae affair, took up the question of government inconsistency. In January 1851, in a 21–page article in the *Dublin University Magazine*, they denounced him as unworthy to be lord lieutenant. As proof of his trucking with popery, they republished Clarendon's letter to Nicholson in which he addressed the bishops as 'My Lord' and 'Your Grace'.[66] Throughout January 1851 the Orangemen kept up a running fire and Clarendon had to explain again and again the mistake over the Nicholson letter and the entrée list.[67] Clarendon engaged in a long and difficult correspondence with Nicholson concerning the leaked letter to the pope. Nicholson, however, disclaimed responsibility and blamed Ennis, Murray's envoy. It was Clarendon who financed and briefed Ennis and gave him a copy of the letter, and it was Ennis who changed the addressee and unwittingly allowed a copy of it to fall into MacHale's hands.

In the controversy over the aggression, all sides waited with expectancy to see what measures Russell would announce when parliament met. He had committed himself to legislate, and both public and parliamentary pressure would scarcely allow him to do otherwise. Looking around the house on the opening of parliament, and noting that the peers were assembled in great numbers, Morpeth, now Lord Carlisle, considered 'the poor Pope to be an unequal match with the throne of Britain thus begirded'.[68] The first sign that the session ahead could be stormy came from the veteran Radical, Roebuck. When the Queen's Speech announced legislation against the assumption of ecclesiastical titles, he denounced Russell's betrayal of liberal principles and read out the list, issued

---

[65] Disraeli to the lord lieutenant of Buckinghamshire, 8 Nov. 1850, cited in *The Roman Catholic Question*.

[66] 'Lord Clarendon's Policy in Ireland', *Dublin University Magazine*, 37 (1851), 136–58. The author was probably the editor, John Francis Waller.

[67] Clarendon to Lansdowne, 26 Jan. 1851, Clarendon Papers, Letterbook 6; Clarendon to G. Grey, 28 Jan., 1, 2 Feb. 1851, ibid.; Clarendon to Bedford, 3 Feb. 1851, ibid., Box 80.

[68] Morpeth's diary, 4 Feb. 1851, cited in Prest, *Russell*, 326.

by the Lord Chamberlain, of the entrée to Dublin Castle.[69] When Russell introduced the bill a few days later he broadened the basis of the argument from a criticism of Wiseman and Pius IX to a denunciation of papal authoritarianism past and present. Denouncing the pope's 'unusual' appointment of Cullen to Armagh, he condemned as presumptuous his signing of the synodical address as 'Paul, Archbishop of Armagh'. The government would have prosecuted him for this insolence, he declared, had not the law officers advised against it. The synod of Thurles came in for bitter castigation:

I point this out to the House as a most important circumstance that on the question of education, that on questions of the occupancy of land, the Synod, which consisted entirely of Roman Catholic ecclesiastics, . . . thought it proper to hold forth to the Irish people and tell them what should be their duty and conduct on those two subjects . . . no language was omitted which could excite the feelings of the peasant class against those who were owners of the land.[70]

When this speech, which contains the official reason that Russell advanced for his decision to bring in legislation forbidding the assumption of ecclesiastical titles, is compared with his reaction in the preceding October and November a significant change of emphasis is evident. The most interesting feature is the omission of all reference to the Tractarians. In the Durham letter the 'danger' which he had singled out as alarming him much more than any aggression of a foreign sovereign was 'the danger within the gates from "unworthy sons" of the Church of England herself'. Now, however, there was no mention whatever of those unworthy sons. This omission can be explained in terms of the measure Russell was introducing which concerned Catholics and not Tractarians.

Of equal interest and more difficult to explain are the new elements Russell introduced, in particular the Irish dimension. The main target of his attack had switched to Cullen and Thurles. Some accounts appear to have accepted that Irish difficulties were uppermost in his mind but, although his view may have changed as the months passed, in November Russell did not mention them as being in the forefront of the grievances the country had sustained.

---

[69] *Hansard*, cxiv. 77, 4 Feb. 1849; letter from Lord Chamberlain's Office, 7 Aug. 1849, in *Dublin Gazette*, Aug. 1849.
[70] *Hansard*, cxiv. 189–90, 7 Feb. 1851.

He appears to have read the proceedings of the synod on 16 November.[71] It was Pius IX's and Wiseman's 'aggression' and Protestant reaction to it, in particular the bishop of Durham's letter, which spurred Russell, already deeply annoyed at Tractarianism, to write. There was no mention then of Cullen or the Irish bishops. Indeed, he had good reason to be heartened by the support for the colleges of fully half of the bishops at Thurles, and he privately shared the dissatisfaction of the other bishops aggrieved at having foisted on the Catholic community what he derisively called 'Graham's experiment'. Furthermore, writing to Clarendon only two days before penning the Durham letter, Russell was still promoting the idea of endowing the Irish priesthood, though he would except the bishops since 'the appointment of Bishops is and shall remain independent of the State . . . I do not think it would be right'.[72] This attitude does not at all correspond to the idea of a man infuriated with the synod of Thurles and anxious to take the first opportunity to vent his rage against the Irish bishops. Neither Russell's reply to the bishop of London on 30 October nor the letter to the bishop of Durham on 4 November mention Cullen, the synod, or the colleges. When urged to use the 'aggression' as a bargaining counter with the pope on the colleges, Russell replied, as late as 9 December, that he did not see how the government could deal directly with 'the Pope's denunciations of the colleges and in fact he has not lately denounced them'. Irish affairs were not uppermost in Russell's mind. He went on to make an interesting restatement of his position:

There is a good letter in the *Times* . . . which I conclude is Charles Greville's. But he, as well as Wiseman and Roebuck, leaves out the important point viz. that the Pope for the first time since the Reformation claimed jurisdiction over the Queen, the Archbishop of Canterbury, and all Protestants in England. A missionary Establishment is clearly directed to its own communion: a fixed Roman Catholic Establishment by the decrees of the Council of Trent extends to all baptized persons.[73]

Although he mentions his feeling of ingratitude that his work for Catholics has not been sufficiently acknowledged, taken together with the rest of his correspondence during November and

[71] Russell to Clarendon, 16 Nov. 1850, Clarendon Papers, Box 26.
[72] Russell to Clarendon, 2 Nov. 1850, Russell Papers, PRO 30/22/8F.
[73] Russell to Clarendon, 9 Dec. 1850, Clarendon Papers, Box 26.

December, this letter corroborates the view that the religious motives of his action were annoyance at Pius IX and Wiseman, compounded by his apprehension that the Tractarians and other high churchmen, who had opposed him on the Hampden issue, were damaging the Protestantism of the Church. Politically, he was resolved not to allow Stanley to steal his 'Protestant' clothes, in the way that Peel had stolen his 'Irish' ones, and he hoped, in the process, to restore his diminishing popularity. Cullen's appointment to Armagh did not provoke the letter, nor did the synod's rejection of the colleges. Neither did the synod's denunciation of evictions for, although the manner in which the synod condemned them annoyed Clarendon, the question was not a priority for Russell when he wrote the Letter. He had been as critical of evicting landlords as the bishops were in their memorial.[74]

Disraeli, rightly detecting in Russell's speech a change of direction, was the first to tax him with it. 'I find', he taunted, 'the noble Lord seeking as the basis of his Bill, not the visit of Dr Wiseman to England, but the synod of Thurles.' Disraeli, however, failed to highlight the omission of all mention of the Tractarians. Why Russell changed direction is not easy to understand. Perhaps he feared that the bill would be ill received by the ultra-Protestants and filled up its 'leanness' by the 'fatness' of his speech. In a tactical manoeuvre he was trying to broaden the basis of his measure, as he explained to Clarendon.[75] His speech was 'too big for our bill', Morpeth noted. It has been argued that, since the anti-Catholics had directed for long their attention to Rome and Ireland, it was impossible for them to change their target to Tractarianism.[76] Russell always shared in the popular anti-Catholicism which lumped together Rome and Irish Catholicism. The papal aggression and the synod of Thurles were but symptoms of the same Roman conspiracy. For whatever reason, Russell, both by his speech and by the tenor of the bill, brought the Irish dimension to the foreground. It was to remain there.

In Ireland, in the weeks before parliament met, the clamour against the Durham letter had become muted, as all sides waited

---

[74] Russell to Clarendon, 15 Nov. 1847, Russell Papers, PRO 6G.

[75] Morpeth's diary, 7 Feb. 1851, cited in Prest, *Russell*, 326; Russell to Clarendon, 8 Feb. 1851, Clarendon Papers, Box 44.

[76] J. Wolffe, *The Protestant Crusade in Great Britain, 1829–1860* (1991), 244–5.

expectantly to see what form the proposed legislation would take. Clarendon told Monteagle that 'this country occupies my attention exclusively and I keep roaring out "whatever you do remember Ireland" '. The Catholics, he added, although in a state of sullen discontent, were quieter than he expected but *'they are waiting'*.[77] Russell's introductory speech and the details which Romilly, the attorney-general, gave of the contents of the bill, brought the reaction Clarendon dreaded. The speech was stronger, the bill more restrictive than Catholics had anticipated. Romilly, who made the ill-fated prediction 'that the House would find that the . . . Catholics would not resist it [the bill]', sought to close any loophole and prevent any evasion. The *Nation* commented:

The Whig bill . . . is not, as we supposed a mere *placebo* for English Protestants. Quite the contrary. It proves to be a . . . well-considered attack upon the Catholic Church in Ireland. Cardinal Wiseman was the target of the 'No-Popery' mob, but Lord John Russell's fire is directed point blank against Archbishop Cullen and his colleagues. The bill is essentially an Irish one. Whatever it proposed to take away from England, she has not enjoyed above a month or two; but it threatens to snatch from Ireland rights long conceded, . . . and even recognized by law.[78]

The *Nation*'s comment was accurate enough. Cullen, not Wiseman, was the target. The bill was no formality. The first clause forbade the assumption of ecclesiastical titles and the fourth compelled bishops and deans to give evidence on oath in prosecutions under the Act not directed against themselves. It was the second and third clauses, however, that dismayed the Irish bishops. The second clause provided that every deed or writing by a Catholic bishop be void if the name of the see appeared in the document. The third declared forfeit to the crown any property devised for a bishop or dean by the title of his see or deanery and this was extended to chaplains and all the bishop's subordinates. Murray was taken aback by the tenor of the legislation. Clause two would render essential business, such as the ordination of priests, extremely difficult for it was in virtue of his title to his see that a bishop ordained priests for his diocese. Clause three would despoil the Church of donations and bequests. Murray complained to Graham, describing how difficult it was for an episcopal Church such as the

---

[77] Clarendon to Monteagle, 14 Dec. 1850, Monteagle Papers, NLI.
[78] *Nation*, 22 Feb. 1851.

Catholic Church to function under the clauses of the bill; Graham read Murray's letter in parliament. To his clergy of Dublin he addressed a pastoral letter which, for a man of his forebearance and moderation, was extraordinary in the bitter disappointment it conveys:

Beloved brethren, The hand of persecution is about to be once more extended over us, and a new element of civil discord cast amongst us. . . . In the bitterness of my heart, therefore, I call on you and your flocks to send up to the Lord of mercy your fervent supplication that He . . . may inspire our rulers with that wisdom that sitteth by His throne, that they may execute justice with an upright heart, not for the benefit of a faction, but for the peace and happiness, and social welfare of the entire people. . . . We know our flocks, and they know us. . . . We are their Bishops; they know us to be so, and yet a law is proposed forbidding us under penalties which we could not pay, and the non-payment of which would doom us to a prison, to acknowledge, even to our own flocks, that we are what they know us to be, the pastors whom the head of our Church, acting according to its known discipline, has placed over them.

Murray pointed out that the poor, already reeling under the effects of famine and pestilence, would also be the victims of the new law. If alms for them were confided expressly to the bishop—and Murray received donations for the poor and famine-stricken from all over the world addressed to him as archbishop of Dublin—they could be confiscated and 'employed by Protestant hands to corrupt the faith'. He ended with a bitter complaint against the government's hypocrisy and ingratitude. 'And this, too,' he wrote, 'is for us called religious freedom; and this is the return which the Catholic clergy are to receive for their efforts in the hour of trial for the preservation of public order.'[79]

If Catholic ingratitude had stung Russell, Russell's ingratitude had stung Murray, for no one had worked harder to keep the country loyal and to prevent a serious rebellion. As he was the prelate most respected by all sides in parliament for his moderation, his pastoral caused a stir. *The Times*, so instrumental in stirring up the controversy, was now moved to reflect on the gravity of the crisis and expressed its fears of a Catholic backlash:

The movement among the Roman Catholic body has received additional impetus by the publication of the pastoral of Archbishop Murray, and

[79] *Nation*, 22 Feb. 1851.

there is little doubt that such of the laity as may have held back, from disinclination to coalesce with the professional agitators, will feel coerced . . . to take part in the common cause, so that in a few days more an 'organization' may be anticipated scarcely less formidable than that which marked the years preceding the great concession of 1829.[80]

The pastoral letter, Clarendon told Russell, caused Murray much pain, but he was convinced that the bill was injurious to his Church.[81] Yet Murray remained in friendly contact with Clarendon. Cullen, in a bitter mood, complained to Smith that 'The archbishop of Dublin, however, still defends him [Clarendon]. . . . At first the viceroy was decided on opposing the law—then he was ready to resign rather than to consent. So said the archbishop.'[82] Although it could be said that Murray was anxious to retain the initiative, his reaction was dictated by his concern for the Church and was a genuine protest against a real grievance. Murray's action received further support when the bishops held a special meeting in Murray's house in Dublin on 25 and 26 February and all twenty-seven of them signed a petition to parliament and addresses to the queen, the pope, and the Irish people.[83] In addition to the grievances listed by Murray, they claimed that the thrust of the bill was 'to separate the faithful from the Supreme Head of the Church' and the priesthood from the people.

The terms of the bill caused another significant protest. The Catholic members of the Irish bar, *en masse*, now took the unusual step of issuing a solemn protest against the bill, denouncing it as retrogressive and penal and as creating difficulties for charitable trusts. It was conceived, they complained, in a spirit of hostility to Catholicism and was calculated to revive old animosities.[84] A shaken Clarendon immediately wrote to the home secretary. 'Such a meeting of the Roman Catholic Bar is important,' he warned, 'for many of its members are highly respectable and in general abstain from politics and are as much attached to the British

---

[80] *Times*, 24 Feb. 1851.

[81] Clarendon to Russell, Clarendon to Grey, 22 Feb. 1851, Clarendon Papers, Letterbook 6.

[82] Cullen to Smith, 29–30 July 1851, Smith Papers, StPA. Bernard Smith (1812–92), vice-rector of Irish College (1850–5); joined Benedictine monastery of St Paul-Outside-the-Walls (1857); rector of Sant'Anselmo, Rome (1868); Roman agent for many Irish, English, American, and Australian bishops and religious orders; titular abbot.

[83] *Nation*, 1 Mar. 1851.   [84] Ibid.

connection as the best Protestants.'[85] Some of the ablest Catholic laymen were members of the Irish bar and they had played a notable role in the campaign for Catholic emancipation. Catholic anger also surfaced within government ranks. Redington again spoke of resigning. Richard More O'Ferrall, a leading Irish Whig, did take that step, resigned the governorship of Malta, and joined the Tories. Meetings to protest against the 'penal law' were held all over the country, in Meath, Armagh, Limerick, Cork, Cavan, Louth, Down, and Westmeath, and were attended by both clergy and local Catholic gentry.

The government also lost the support of Shrewsbury. His incredulity on reading Russell's letter gave way to fury and, despite Clarendon's attempts to mollify him, he had 'fired a Pamphlet of a hundred and twenty pages' at Russell which Clarendon described as 'spiteful enough'.[86] The terms of the bill angered him further. He complained to Lord Arundel that 'Much as the Irish deserve severe repression, and even punishment . . . [the bill's attempt] to destroy their Ancient Hierarchy . . . is an act of mad, and fanatical, and vengeful Persecution.' Examining Russell's criticism of the synod he denied that 'the Thurles address [is] open to . . . Johnny's animadversions. I see no Communism in it.' Finally, Shrewsbury complained that 'it is a hard case that *we* [the English Catholics] are to be sacrificed, who have done no wrong to any one and yet the Cardinal in his answer to the Armagh address, speaks as if the Irish were sacrificed to us!!!'[87] His view that the English Catholics were suffering because of Irish misdoings was not shared by the Irish Catholics. They believed that they were being penalized for the pomposity of Wiseman and the petulance of Russell. Shrewsbury, however, had for long been sharply critical of Irish Catholic 'excesses'.[88]

The most effective challenge to the new measure, however, came from within parliament itself. Already, on 8 February, Edward Stanley had noted in his diary that so great was the indignation of the Irish members, that they were ready to join the Tories in turning out Russell, adding 'From us, no other course was expected: nor did the measure originate with us, though it will have

---

[85] Clarendon to Grey, 22 Feb. 1851, Clarendon Papers, Letterbook 6.
[86] Clarendon to Bedford, 3 Feb. 1851, ibid., Box 80.
[87] Shrewsbury to Arundel, 2 Mar. 1851, Arundel Castle Archives, MS c. 489.
[88] Shrewsbury to MacHale, *Morning Chronicle*, 4 Jan. 1848.

our support, nor is it so much the Bill itself, as the introductory speech, which has provoked their enmity.'[89] Although the Irish members rarely acted together, they now mounted a spirited and persistent attack on the bill at first individually and then as a body. The bill had the effect of banding them together into a party. The initiative was taken by George Henry Moore, MP for Mayo, with the encouragement of Dr Gray, of the *Freeman's Journal*, to adopt a policy of voting against the government on all issues.[90] Soon most of the Irish Liberals and Catholics followed suit. An important side-development was the persistent lobbying by Irish constituents to persuade members to follow this line. An alarmed Somerville, the chief secretary and member for Drogheda, reported to Russell a demand from his constituents and supporters to resign and avowed that 'there are names attached to that document which nothing short of what the parties think a religious obligation, could have detached from my interest'.[91] The group of members increased and included men of talent such as 'the pocket O'Connell', John Sadleir, John Reynolds, and William Keogh. Mockingly referred to by their opponents as 'the Pope's Brass Band', they called themselves 'the Irish Brigade' and the name stuck. They developed successful tactics challenging every stage of the bill in lengthy speeches and, then, by refusing to support the government even on issues to which they were not opposed, they significantly reduced its majorities. The main thrust of the Brigade's case against the bill was that it was penal and, in its application to Ireland, constituted regressive legislation. How, they asked, could a government which had addressed the Irish bishops by their titles and given them precedence over peers of the realm now make the assumption of titles a penal offence? Others questioned why Catholic Ireland should pay for the mistakes of Cardinal Wiseman in England. It was now apparent, as Grey admitted to Clarendon early in the session, that 'The real difficulty in the whole case is Ireland.'[92]

One way out of this dilemma would be to exempt Ireland from

[89] Stanley's journal, 8 Feb. 1851, cited in Vincent, *Disraeli and the Conservative Party*, 39.

[90] J. H. Whyte, *The Independent Irish Party, 1850–9* (1958) is the major work on this group. George Henry Moore (1811–70), Mayo landowner. John Gray (1816–75), part-owner and editor of *Freeman's Journal*.

[91] Somerville to Russell, 4 Mar. 1851, Russell Papers, PRO 30/22/9B.

[92] Grey to Clarendon, 11 Feb. 1851, Clarendon Papers, Box 15.

the scope of the act, which would then merely forbid the assumption of new titles in England. Lewis and Minto strongly urged this course of action and Redington, whose resignation Russell and Clarendon wanted at all costs to avert, also supported it. Clarendon, however, advised George Grey against it and begged him to persuade Delane not to advocate it in *The Times*. Unless the same law was passed for Ireland as for Britain, he told him 'it would be virtually repealing the Union'. Despite the major difficulties foreseen on all sides and the different history of religion in Ireland, Whig dogma demanded that Irish Catholics be submitted to the same legal constrictions as English Catholics. Russell then came up with the idea that the law be differently administered in Ireland. By early March, however, Clarendon began to waver in his opposition to the exempting of Ireland because 'the excitement is of such a formidable character'.[93] George Grey, however, opposed exemption and Russell supported him.[94] Grey's task in parliament was not easy. He had to explain Minto's failure, when official government emissary to Rome, to follow up intimations by Pius IX and others that the appointment of an English hierarchy was imminent. He had also to defend both Clarendon's involvement in the Nicholson letter and the titles given to the Catholic bishops on the queen's entrée list. This was later attributed to a mistake by the overworked gentleman usher.[95] A few weeks later, however, when Inglis wanted to move for a copy of the *Dublin Gazette* of 7 August 1849 which contained the entrée, Clarendon begged George Grey not to let him have the supplement of 8 August, for it contained more explicit acknowledgement of territorial titles: 'the address of the Roman Catholic Bishop and clergy of Cork [which] as Inglis and Co know nothing about it they may as well remain in ignorance'.[96] It was clear that Clarendon had approved of the recognition given to the Irish bishops and the overworked gentleman usher was no more than an excuse. Contradictions were showing in Clarendon's policies, and George Grey appeared more than a little impatient with him. His insistence in 1846 on

[93] Clarendon to Russell, 5 Mar. 1851, ibid., Letterbook 6.

[94] Russell to the queen, 4 Mar. 1851, Royal Archives RA C46, cited in Prest, *Russell*, 329.

[95] *Hansard*, cxiv. 348–55, 10 Feb. 1851.

[96] G. Grey to Clarendon, 15 Apr. 1851, Clarendon Papers, Box 15; Clarendon to Grey, 16 Apr. 1851, ibid., Letterbook 6.

recognizing the bishops' titles, despite Lord Grey's misgivings, and his secret negotiation on the colleges with Nicholson were now contributing to the embarrassment of the government. More importantly, despite his assertion that when the bill was in preparation he kept roaring out 'whatever you do remember Ireland!', this is precisely what was not done. When the bill was introduced, Clarendon complained that he had not been informed of the details, but this was only when Redington pointed out the havoc that clauses two and three would create in Ireland. As the vice-regal post from Westminster arrived within two days, it is strange that he did not insist on seeing the text of a bill so important to Ireland and which had an immediate and catastrophic effect on the government's standing in Ireland.

Whig popularity in Ireland certainly plummeted. Clarendon complained that the bill 'has lowered Whig popularity twenty fathoms deep and we shall not live to see it dug up again'.[97] Supported by most of the radicals and the Peelite leaders, the Irish members fought the bill tenaciously. Their withdrawal of support for the government on all issues meant that the administration quickly came under pressure. 'The fate of the Government is trembling in the balance,' Somerville wrote to Clarendon on 13 February, 'and it depends upon the extent of the Irish defection.'[98] Within a few weeks of the introduction of the bill a parliamentary crisis occurred, which the Irish exploited. When Locke King brought up his annual motion on county and borough franchises, many Liberals, disappointed with the budget, stayed away. The Irish now defected *en masse*. The result was an unanticipated defeat for the government and Russell, to general surprise, resigned. 'The Pope has killed us', wrote Somerville to Clarendon, while Sir John Gray, editor of the nationalist *Freeman's Journal*, rejoiced that 'the Irish vote has done it'.[99]

Some ministers, including apparently Clarendon, were relieved to be rid of the responsibility of the bill. The government's resignation, however, gave Russell an excellent opportunity for strengthening his position by bringing leading Peelites into a new government, a move strongly favoured by both the queen and

[97] Clarendon to Russell, 23 Feb. 1851, ibid., Letterbook 6.
[98] Somerville to Clarendon, 13 Feb. 1851, ibid., Box 28.
[99] Whyte, *Irish Party*, 22; Somerville to Clarendon, 25 Feb. 1851, Clarendon Papers, Box 28.

Prince Albert. The Ecclesiastical Titles Bill proved an insurmountable obstacle, for when Russell contacted the leading Peelites, Graham and Aberdeen, they refused to join the government on the grounds that they could not accept the bill's provisions. In a bitter mood the philanthropist Lord Ashley asked: 'Who could now assert that the Pope has no power in England? He has put out one Administration and now prevents the formation of another.'[100] After a week of crisis, during which all attempts at forming a new administration failed, a weakened Whig government resumed power—in the words of *The Times* like the Indian fakirs who bury themselves for a week and come out exhausted but alive.[101] They had to take up again the Ecclesiastical Titles Bill. Somerville and Redington mounted a sustained campaign to have the second and third clauses dropped. Somerville pleaded that if this were not done the resulting 'permanent estrangement from us of the moderate Roman Catholic party would be a great misfortune and would render doubly difficult the task of governing Ireland'. Against those who saw the opposition of the Irish members as purely factious, he argued 'that the opposition [of the Irish Brigade in parliament] is only really formidable because backed by the general opinion and encouragement of the country'.[102] Redington canvassed the ministers and politicians in London and was astonished at their ignorance of the true state of affairs. 'I find', he told Clarendon, 'that like Lord John they had not an idea how the Ecclesiastical Titles Bill would work [in Ireland] and those who now see are not surprised at *our* [the Catholics'] feeling.'[103] He saw George Grey and Fox Maule, both of whom he found unsympathetic. Fox Maule, he believed, 'really prefers gratifying Scotch bigotry to the pacification of Ireland'.[104] On the other hand, the influential Lansdowne was well disposed, as was Carlisle. Russell, unwilling to increase Irish discontent, and influenced by the criticism made by Aberdeen and Graham, convinced the cabinet that the offending clauses must go:

The cabinet . . . have come to the unanimous resolution to omit all the clauses but the first which prohibits the titles. This decision may make the

---

[100] Cited in A. Briggs, *1851* (1951), 11.   [101] Cited in Prest, *Russell*, 329.

[102] Somerville to Russell, 4 Mar. 1851, Russell Papers, PRO 30/22/9B.

[103] Redington to Clarendon, 28 Feb. 1851, Clarendon Papers, Box 25.

[104] Redington to Clarendon, 4 Mar. 1851, ibid.

high Protestants indifferent to the fate of the Bill and they may join in throwing it out. But I prefer this alternative to the continued agitation in Ireland.[105]

Although taken under pressure, this decision shows Russell rising to a higher level of statesmanship, as he prepared to back down rather than exacerbate the situation in Ireland. The episode also illustrates how decisions affecting Ireland, as Redington discovered, were taken with insufficient knowledge of the consequences for Ireland. The omission of the clauses pleased Clarendon who remarked that clauses two and three were not worth a civil war.[106] George Grey, in a speech that appeared to contradict the changes he was introducing, announced the dropping of the two clauses. As Somerville remarked, 'Sir George had to eat humble pie'.[107] The excision of the more penal clauses did little to ease the progress of the bill, for the Catholics would not accept any penal bill and the excision angered the ultra-Protestants. An element of farce entered the discussion. An opponent of the bill, George Smyth, MP for Canterbury, called it *Much Ado About Nothing* and described it as 'a sham bill, of sham pains and sham penalties, against a sham aggression'.[108] Sir Robert Inglis compared it to 'the play of *Hamlet* with the character of Hamlet omitted' and complained that 'whereas previously it had been a milk-and-water measure now the government had succeeded in extracting all the milk'.[109] *Punch* had previously portrayed Russell as little Jack the Giant Killer, pluckily entering the arena to fight the Roman giant, Wiseman; now it caricatured him as the boy who chalked 'No Popery' on Wiseman's door and then ran away. With everyone dissatisfied, opposition and frustration made the progress of the bill slow and tedious. Little other parliamentary business was done during the whole session. Greville complained that

we have plunged ourselves into a situation of embarrassment, which leaves us no power of advancing or receding without danger or disgrace. Our Government, and especially its chief, have gone on from one fault and

---

[105] Russell to Clarendon, 5 Mar. 1851, ibid., Box 44.
[106] Clarendon to Russell, 7 Mar. 1851, ibid., Letterbook 6.
[107] Somerville to Clarendon, 7 Mar. 1851, ibid., Box 28.
[108] *Hansard*, cxv. 441, 24 Mar. 1851.
[109] *Hansard*, cxiv. 1141, 7 Mar. 1851.

blunder to another. . . . Their concessions are treated with rage and indignation on one side, and with scorn and contempt on the other.[110]

Even Delane of *The Times*, who bore responsibility for kindling the controversy in the first place, when questioned by Aberdeen replied: 'My Lord, I entreat you never to mention that subject to me, for I am heartily ashamed of it.' The government also felt that things had gone awry. Somerville described it all as 'a sad business'.[111] Lord Grey acknowledged that 'the papal bill is a mess in every way'.[112] Both Lansdowne and Wood, whose handling of the economy did the government little service, confided to Derby that things were going ill, and that 'their [the government's] time had expired'.[113] Russell admitted to Clarendon that 'things have been looking dark and gloomy for some days' and expressed his fear that Henry Drummond, MP for West Surrey, might succeed in having the excised clauses restored.[114] This news appalled Clarendon, who threatened to resign if this happened.[115] The religious question was poisoning all others, he noted. 'Luckily', he added, 'there is no O'Connell to move the masses.' Still he feared that 'the priests are making political capital of the Bill and are recovering much of the influence which I hoped they had lost forever'.[116] The worst was yet to come. On 20 March Charles Newdegate (the ultra-Protestant member for North Warwickshire) and Drummond delivered speeches in parliament so offensive to Catholics that they caused uproar. Drummond alleged that Catholic convents 'have ever been either prisons or brothels' and asked Catholics if they thought they could bring over here with impunity 'a cargo of blinking statues, of bleeding pictures, of liquefying blood, and the Virgin Mary's milk?'[117] So outraged were the

---

[110] Greville, *Memoirs*, 10 Mar. 1851, vi. 401.

[111] Somerville to Clarendon, 7 Mar. 1851, Clarendon Papers, Box 28.

[112] Lord Grey to Clarendon, 10 Mar. 1851, ibid., Box 41.

[113] Stanley's journal, 12 Mar. 1851, cited in Vincent, *Disraeli and the Conservative Party*, 54.

[114] Russell to Clarendon, 11 Mar. 1851, Clarendon Papers, Letterbook 6. Henry Drummond (1786–1860), a founder of the Irvingites; MP for West Surrey (1847–60).

[115] Clarendon to Russell, 13 Mar. 1851, Clarendon Papers, Letterbook 6.

[116] Clarendon to G. Grey, 1 Apr. 1851, ibid.; Clarendon to Russell, 28 Mar. 1851, ibid.

[117] *Hansard*, cxv. 267–80, 20 Mar. 1851. Charles Newdegate (1816–87), MP for N. Warwickshire (1843–85).

Catholic members that Edward Stanley feared that actual violence would have followed: 'many Irishmen rose from their seats, calling and gesticulating . . . Drummond sat near the Irish benches: whereon fearing lest he should be openly insulted, three or four friends crossed the House and took their seats also near him.'[118] A shaken Somerville reported back to Clarendon: 'You will have seen what a sad turn the debate took last night—really I am beginning to think that it would have been better to endure anything rather than give rise to these unhappy debates and religious discussions.'[119] Lord Clanricarde, the postmaster-general, recounted that Arundel refrained with difficulty from using the fists he visibly clenched. Then in a revealing statement Clanricarde added: 'The Romans, however, should be told that if they put their Church so forward the practices thereof will be plainly expounded, and the main question is whether Drummond's assertions were true.'[120] Such a statement bore out the truth of Newman's insistence that Protestant suspicion of Catholicism was deeply embedded. Graham took the floor immediately after Drummond and made a telling and dignified speech against the bill, pausing only momentarily to dismiss Drummond's insults.[121]

Opposed by the Irish, the Peelites, and the Radicals on the one hand, and criticized by the more Protestant members on the other, Russell was now driven to appeal for help to his political rival, Stanley. Edward Stanley reported in his journal for 21 March that 'My Father showed me a letter from Lord John, entreating aid to carry the Papal Bill, lest it should slip through our fingers, and then Cardinal Wiseman may toss up his hat for joy.' Stanley, believing its loss after being introduced would be a great evil, promised that the Protectionists would support it.[122] Russell was assured that the bill would pass, but amendments flowed in mainly from the ultra-Protestants. By now, however, the government, so brave at the beginning of the session, would have been happy to get away with the minimum; even the irritable Clarendon who

[118] Stanley's journal, 20 Mar. 1851, cited in Vincent, *Disraeli and the Conservative Party*, 57–8.

[119] Somerville to Clarendon, 21 Mar. 1851, Clarendon Papers, Box 28.

[120] Clanricarde to Clarendon, 23 Mar. 1851, ibid., Box 9.

[121] *Tablet*, 20 Mar. 1851; *Hansard*, cxv. 278, 20 Mar. 1851.

[122] Stanley's journal, 21 Mar. 1851, cited in Vincent, *Disraeli and the Conservative Party*, 58; Russell to Stanley, 21 Mar. 1851, Derby Papers, Box 130; cf. Prest, *Russell*, 329.

applauded when Lord Campbell had spoken of trampling the cardinal's hat underfoot, now advised Russell 'to stick to your resolution of only tapping the Cardinal's hat gently'. The reason was obvious: 'we cannot afford to do more if we care about keeping things tolerably quiet in Ireland.'[123] The whole bench of Irish bishops petitioned the queen on the injustice that was being done to them. Wiseman wanted them to come *en bloc* to London to present their petition but Murray, to avoid embarrassing the government, forestalled him by sending the petition on to Sir George Grey.[124]

Ireland remained the sticking-point. Minto and Clarendon both warned Russell of the danger of dealing similarly with both countries, because 'from the assumption that England and Ireland must fare alike, you are harnessing two horses to your carriage which will pull in opposite directions and upset the coach'. Russell could only agree that 'the great difficulty is to make what is suitable for England fit Ireland'.[125] Yet Ireland might not have proved such an obstacle were it not for the Brigade's skill in embarrassing the government. The government, hoping that fear of Tory rule would frighten them into line, was not unhappy at some ultra-Protestant amendments being put forward. Russell believed that the way to deal with the fractious Irish members was the Bo-Peep policy. 'Leave 'em alone and they'll come home, And bring their tails behind 'em', he wrote amusedly to Clarendon who, equally convinced, passed the comment on to Bedford.[126] They misjudged the determination of their opponents, for the threats made no impression whatever on Cullen or the Brigade. Before long Clarendon had to admit that 'the samples of Stanley's policy which their [Tory] amendments afford have not had the effect I expected. They have increased Roman Catholic bitterness against England, but they have not abated the previous ill-will towards the Whig Government.'[127]

As the bill slowly edged towards the end of its second reading,

[123] Clarendon to Russell, 24 Apr. 1851, Clarendon Papers, Letterbook 7.
[124] George Grey to Clarendon, 3 Mar. 1851, ibid., Box 15.
[125] Minto to Russell, 19 Apr. 1851, Russell Papers, PRO 30/22/9C; Clarendon to Russell, 25 Apr. 1851, Clarendon Papers, Letterbook 7; Russell to Clarendon, 24 Apr. 1851, ibid., Box 44.
[126] Russell to Clarendon, 21 Apr. 1851, Clarendon Papers, Box 44; Clarendon to Bedford, 27 Apr. 1851, ibid., Box 80.
[127] Clarendon to Russell, 25 Apr. 1851, ibid., Letterbook 7.

another powerful voice was raised against it. Gladstone, in a speech that lasted two hours, produced all the most persuasive reasons for rejecting the penal legislation. He was listened to, according to Lewis, with unbroken attention. For Ireland he could foresee nothing but evil effects from the bill, for it would undermine and weaken the authority of the law. On purely practical grounds, too, he saw it as a blunder:

When you opened the Colleges ... last year, there was much said of the division of feelings among the Roman Catholic laity ... I hear nothing said of that division of feeling now, because you have contrived to band together the whole Roman Catholic body of England and Ireland against you, whether in respect of the Colleges or to the appointment of Dr Cullen, and you have contrived to unite the Roman Catholic body in a greater degree, almost than is upon record.

Underscoring the contradiction, he recalled Russell's fine speech supporting the Maynooth Grant in 1845 and asked:

Would any man who heard the noble Lord deliver these impressive sentiments have believed that the strife with regard to religious liberty was to be revived not only with a greater acerbity in ... 1851, but that his was to be the head that was to wear the helmet and his was to be the hand to grasp the spear?[128]

Gladstone's criticisms left a deep impression and the question he raised was never answered for, even in his memoirs, Russell never satisfactorily explained the contradiction between his lifelong campaign for religious liberty and his sponsorship of the Titles bill. Perhaps it was the result of a distinction Russell drew between Catholics and 'Popery'; it was when Catholicism set itself up with legal structures, a 'Roman system', that his ancestral 'no-popery' surfaced. This may be the meaning of the distinction he made to Clarendon: 'A missionary Establishment is clearly directed to its own communion: a fixed Roman Catholic Establishment by the decrees of the Council of Trent extends to all baptized persons.'[129] Whatever his motives, he devoted much of his life to achieving complete freedom for Catholics while retaining a deep elemental distrust of and aversion to Romanism. The synod of

---

[128] *Hansard*, cxv. 592, 25 Mar. 1851; Lewis to Clarendon, 26 Mar. 1851, Clarendon Papers, c. 530.
[129] Russell to Clarendon, 9 Dec. 1850, Clarendon Papers, Box 26.

Thurles and Cullen's utterances were for him further instances of aggressive 'popery'.

The smear of 'mummeries' and the introduction of the law made Catholics close ranks. It gave a boost to Ultramontanism, for it united Irish Catholics behind Cullen and English Catholics behind Wiseman, both men of Ultramontane tendencies, and brought together the interests of the two leading Catholic prelates in the United Kingdom. Nevertheless, despite Gladstone's speech, the bill passed its second reading on 27 March with a majority of 438 to 95. The Irish Brigade kept up pressure and April and May proved as trying for the government as February and March. Clarendon complained that the 'impudence of these gentlemen renders them perfectly callous to public opinion', but their proceedings were popular in Ireland and foreshadowed the Irish parliamentary party of the later 1870s and its deliberate obstructionist tactics. 'Again the Irish party wasted the entire night', commented Lord Edward Stanley on 15 May.[130] 'The night closed with another Irish row', reported Somerville wearily on 20 May.[131] The prominent Liberal Quaker, John Bright, who had opposed the Maynooth Grant, made one of his fiercest speeches against the Titles Bill, underlining the evil consequences for Ireland of such a retrograde action. The members of parliament, he added, could see clearly:

that the course in which the noble Lord has been so recklessly dragging us ... had separated Ireland from this country, had withdrawn her national sympathies from us, and done an amount of mischief which the legislation of the next ten years could not entirely, if at all, abate. The noble Lord had drawn up an indictment against eight millions of his countrymen; he had increased the power of the Pope over the Roman Catholics for he had drawn closer the bonds between them and their Church and the head of their Church.[132]

Russell, Bright claimed, had a party among the ecclesiastics of the Church of Rome but he had destroyed it. It would be difficult to dispute his assessment. As the bill proceeded painfully, more than one person applied the lines of Pope to it: 'The Ecclesiastical Titles Bill dragged its slow length along amidst repeated debates

---

[130] Stanley's journal, 15 May 1851, cited in Vincent, *Disraeli and the Conservative Party*, 65.

[131] Somerville to Clarendon, 20 May 1851, Clarendon Papers, Box 28.

[132] *Hansard*, cxvi. 927, 12 May 1851.

and votes but with slow progress.'[133] On 16 June Spooner, supported by Inglis and Newdegate, moved that the vote on miscellaneous estimates be reduced by the sum appropriated to Maynooth College. To the surprise of many the motion was defeated by the slenderest of margins—121 votes to 119. Murray and the Maynooth staff were alarmed and the government hoped that the scare would force Catholics to tone down their opposition. It had no effect on Cullen, who was displeased that Maynooth was dependent on a government grant.

On 27 June Sir Frederick Thesiger, member for Abingdon, proposed amendments designed to make the bill more penal by broadening the application of the declaratory clause to all rescripts and by giving the power to prosecute to any individual.[134] The government, confident that the Irish would also oppose this further aggravation of the bill, prepared to resist the amendments. To its chagrin the Irish deliberately walked out, leaving the government to be defeated and to accept a bill more penal than it wanted.

The committee stage passed on 27 June and the third reading on 4 July, the majority this time being 263 to 46—the Irish members having again left in a body. A reluctant Lansdowne introduced it into the House of Lords, but he was unhappy with the bill especially as amended by Thesiger for, he complained to Russell, since the amendment would entail mischief in Ireland 'I must speak and protest sharply against it.'[135] There was no Irish Brigade in the Lords and the bill's passage there was easy, despite the spirited opposition of Aberdeen, St Germans, who had been chief secretary in Peel's government, and Monteagle. Many of the lords solemnly recorded their objections to it after it had been enacted. It received the royal assent on 1 August, six months after it had been introduced.

While a weary parliament was debating in Westminster a penal religious bill, Londoners and six million foreigners were crowding into the Crystal Palace to see the Great Exhibition—a superb embodiment of the age of work, peace, and progress. *Punch* wittily showed Russell's gloomy shipwrecked cabinet on their drifting

---

[133] *Tablet*, 17 May 1851; Lewis to Clarendon, 20 May 1851, Clarendon Papers, c. 530.

[134] Sir Frederick Thesiger (1794–1878), 1st Baron Chelmsford; Conservative MP (1840–58); attorney-general (1845–6).

[135] Lansdowne to Russell, 5 July 1851, Russell Papers, PRO 30/22/9D.

raft, from which had been jettisoned measures of all sorts—Ecclesiastical Titles, Suffrage, Income Tax Adjustment—hailing with relief and delight the appearance on the horizon of the steamship 'Great Exhibition'.[136] An amused Greville, who appreciated the accuracy of the cartoon, remarked that the attractions of the Exhibition, by acting well upon public and parliament, had 'saved' the government.[137]

The Act had finally been carried, but at enormous cost. It had exacerbated feelings in both England and Ireland, taken up most of the parliamentary session, and occasioned emotional scenes in the House of Commons. It had enfeebled the administration and prevented the formation of a strong new government supported by Aberdeen and Graham. It had fatally weakened the Whigs' position in parliament. For Russell, even more than for his party, it was an unmitigated disaster. The brief moment of popular acclaim after the publication of the Durham letter evaporated. The long struggle to get the bill passed, the changes introduced in the bill, and its other vicissitudes frustrated parliament and lost him popularity in the house. His own cabinet colleagues, already restless at his leadership, blamed him for his unilateral action, and his ability to lead was further eroded. Unwittingly, too, he had also fanned religious controversy and cast a shadow over the work of a lifetime. The confidence of the Roman *Curia* in Whig benevolence was confounded. Ever since the Lichfield House compact in 1835 the Whigs had counted on Irish support in parliament. From faithful allies, Irish members were transformed overnight into bitter and persistent antagonists, and, once they had co-ordinated their tactics, the defeat of a weakened government was only a matter of time.

Accounts of the papal aggression concentrate on the Durham letter. Russell's behaviour three months later in introducing the Ecclesiastical Titles bill has attracted less attention. Yet it is, if anything, more puzzling. Russell's impulsiveness in blurting out his petulance, as Greville called it, was seen as extenuating his outburst in the letter. Murray made allowances for initial reaction and encouraged his people to rely on the English sense of fair play once this spontaneous outburst was over. Russell, however, had a full three months before introducing the bill, during which

---

[136] *Punch*, 1851, xx. 237, vi. 415.
[137] Greville, *Memoirs*, 8 June 1851.

Clarendon and others had alerted him to the shock and hurt it caused to Catholics. Yet, despite this ample interval, he produced, in February 1851, a quite severe, indeed a penal, bill. Other formulae were open to him, as Aberdeen pointed out and as he himself accepted later in his *Recollections*. He compounded the injury by justifying his bill in a speech that switched the focus from England to Ireland and constituted an attack on the Irish bishops in their corporate capacity at their synod. The reaction of moderate Irish Catholics was one of consternation. Murray's pained letter to Graham made it clear that the bill as formulated would impede the normal functioning of his Church; Clarendon's Irish advisers and the conservative Irish Bar protested equally strongly. An alarmed Redington crossed to London where he found the explanation of the blunder: neither Russell nor the ministers had any idea of how the bill would work in Ireland! As so often before, and most recently during the Famine itself, ignorance of the situation on the ground led to avoidable mistakes.

The shock liberal Irish Catholics sustained from the letter, the bill, and Russell's speech, which indicated that the state was not merely Protestant but anti-Catholic, was not readily forgotten. Russell had destroyed the position of that section of Irish Catholics, including eminent men like Murray who, especially since the Whig administration of the 1830s, had supported the government for decades, pleaded its good will at Rome, and worked for all-round conciliation with England. Conversely, as Gladstone and Bright intimated, it had given an unexpected boost to Ultramontanism, as English and Irish Catholics closed ranks in the face of what they saw as Whig aggression. The episode brought into focus the tensions between Liberalism and Ultramontanism, 'Whiggery' and 'popery', which the uneasy alliance of O'Connell with the Whigs had masked. Ultramontanism, in the ascendant in Rome since Pius IX's return, and engaged in a duel with Liberal Catholicism in France and other European countries, would find strong backing from Irish and English Catholic bishops in the decades ahead.

9

The Queen's Colleges or the Catholic University?

'Education . . . is the field selected by the ultramontanes for battle with the State and to beat them would be a social, political, religious and lasting triumph.'

(Clarendon to George Cornewall Lewis, 28 Nov. 1851)

'The battle there [in Ireland] will be what it was in Oxford twenty years ago. . . . It is very wonderful—Keble, Pusey, Maurice, Sewell, etc., who have been able to do so little against Liberalism in Oxford will be renewing the fight, although not in their persons, in Ireland.'

(Newman to Mrs William Froude, 14 Oct. 1851)

While anger at the Ecclesiastical Titles Bill had united English and Irish Catholics, both laity and clergy, it had not brought unity to the Irish bishops. The question of the Queen's Colleges still sharply divided them. Murray remained calmly, if not obstinately, convinced of the value of the colleges despite the shock of the Titles bill. His long and excellent record as pastor and administrator for forty years gave him a high standing within and without his own Church. As Bishop Murphy of Cloyne, a supporter of Cullen, ruefully commented, 'there is a prestige about the name and act of *Dr Murray* in this country, that will for a while counteract and even neutralise the beneficent recommendation of *Pio Nono*!!!'[1] Although opposed by the other three archbishops, he retained the support of almost half the bishops. Many influential priests in Maynooth College and elsewhere took the same line. Middle-class Catholics welcomed the inexpensive university education offered by the Queen's Colleges. This was true not merely in Dublin where Catholics, many of them Whigs, were closer to the influence of

[1] Murphy to Cullen, Mar. 1851, Cullen Papers, AB4, DDA.

government, but also in Cork, the second city of Ireland, with a population of over 100,000. Cork Catholics had been among the first to organize and press for university education and they were pleased with the offer of a college for their city.

Their bishop, too, William Delaney, influenced perhaps by the opinions of the laity, sided with Murray in his support for the colleges. The situation in Galway was not altogether dissimilar, for its leading citizens, pleased to be chosen as a centre for the western college in preference to Limerick, were anxious to retain it. Its bishop, Laurence O'Donnell, was the first to break ranks within the Connacht hierarchy, despite continuous pressure from MacHale.

Opposing those who accepted the Queen's Colleges was a zealous group of bishops and priests who had distrusted the scheme from the start as dangerous to the faith and morals of Catholic youth. Despite Clarendon's modifications they remained suspicious. The appointment in August 1849 of sixty professors, only seven of whom were Catholic, did nothing to dispel their suspicions. To protect his new university, Clarendon had decided that the degrees of the Queen's University would be open only to the constituent colleges in order to exclude Catholics attending a Catholic university.[2]

It was to Cullen that the leadership of the anti-college party had switched from the first days of the synod of Thurles. Cullen was as dedicated a churchman as Murray, but while Murray accepted the existing establishment in Church and state and was content to work with the government as long as the Church could carry out its mission, Cullen regarded the Established Church as an unjust imposition, and the state as a hostile confessional one, whose every concession had to be scrutinized with care. When the colleges question first surfaced in 1845 Cullen, unlike MacHale or Slattery, was not content to criticize the scheme, but had suggested the setting up of a Catholic university.[3] The achievement of Belgian Catholics in establishing a university in Louvain after the revolution of 1830 impressed him, and he had followed closely Montalembert's successful campaign for the right of French

---

[2] Clarendon to Monteagle, 10, 21 May 1849, Monteagle Papers, NLI; T. W. Moody and J. C. Beckett, *Queen's, Belfast, 1845–1949; The History of A University* (1959), i. 73.

[3] Vote of Mgr. Paolo Cullen, 31 Jan. 1846, *Acta* (1846), vol. 209, fos. 274–84, PFA.

Catholics to establish their own schools and university faculties. Propaganda approved his suggestion of a Catholic university and, in three rescripts, urged it on the bishops. With Cullen's unexpected return to Ireland as archbishop of Armagh, the main burden of making a reality of this vision fell on him.

The beginnings proved difficult. At the first meeting of the university committee, held on 17 October 1850, Murray and his vicar-general, Walter Meyler, expressed no confidence in the scheme and refused to contribute to it.[4] Murray attended no further meetings. 'The opposition of Dublin puts us in a very critical state', Cullen told Kirby, but though he frequently complained to Kirby and to Bernard Smith, vice-rector of the Irish College, that Murray was keeping many back, he added determinedly 'we shall get on without him and in despite of him'.[5] Money was the problem and so desperate was he for funds that he tried in vain to persuade Propaganda to be allowed to divert the subscriptions raised by the Society for the Propagation of the Faith to the support of the university.[6] To make any real progress towards a Catholic university, it was essential that the Queen's Colleges be removed as a viable option for Catholics, and so the next step was to have Rome approve as soon as possible the decrees of the synod of Thurles, for that would effectively prevent Catholics from attending them. To this end he and his friends in Rome, Tobias Kirby and Bernard Smith, respectively new rector and vice-rector of the Irish college, bent all their efforts, lobbying cardinals and officials. Russell's Durham letter proved a godsend to Cullen, who used it to unmask government hostility to his Church. During the controversy Murray and Cullen reacted differently. Murray deplored the measure and hoped it would not be passed. Cullen believed that instead of doing harm it would do good, indeed, was already doing so.[7] It had united Irish and English Catholics, he told Smith, and had rallied the faithful, including the Irish members who fought like lions and, after every defeat, rose to fight again. Commenting

---

[4] Cullen to Kirby, 18 Oct. 1850, Kirby Papers, ICAR; cf. E. Larkin, *The Making of the Roman Catholic Church in Ireland, 1850–1860*, (1980), 49; F. McGrath, *Newman's University: Idea and Reality* (1951), 96–102.

[5] Cullen to Smith, 24 Dec. 1850, Smith Papers, StPA.

[6] The Society for the Propagation of the Faith was founded in Lyons by Pauline Jaricot in 1822 to organize support for Catholic foreign missions.

[7] Cullen to Smith, 3 Feb. 1851, Smith Papers, StPA.

on the shrill no-popery sentiments expressed in the House of Commons, he declared that the constituent assembly that sat in the Campidoglio in Rome in 1849 did not act with a worse spirit than parliament; some members were every bit as bad as the 'Roman ruffians'. If the law were passed, and he expected it would be, it would be trampled underfoot in Ireland and happy would be the lot of any bishop imprisoned under it. While he was willing to face any consequences from the state with equanimity, he needed Roman approval of the synod's decrees to end the uncertainty among Catholics, rally the waverers, and unite the bishops on an agreed programme. It would also secure his position as leader within the Church.[8] His only fear was that Rome would lose its nerve. His warning was unequivocal: Rome should not compromise, nor think of trading off a reduction in the penal bill in exchange for a free hand for the government in Ireland. 'All the pope must do is to concede nothing. The English government must yield to him.' When Roman approval of the decrees tarried, he voiced his fears of government interference to Kirby. 'It seems certain that every effort will be made to persuade the Holy See to sacrifice Ireland in order to bring to an end the threats against Catholics in England.' The lord lieutenant, he believed, had already written to Lord Shrewsbury and to Prince Doria along those lines, and the supporters of the colleges claimed that the no-popery campaign had so pressurized the pope that he would not now dare issue another document hostile to the government.[9]

Cullen's suspicions of Shrewsbury were justified. Despite his anger with Russell, Shrewsbury was again involved, neatly shifting the blame for the no-popery campaign from Wiseman and Russell to his old enemies, MacHale and the Irish priests. Writing to Lord Arundel from Palermo, he made clear his perception of the origin of what he disparagingly called 'Johnny's penal code':

That these Colleges have done it all is quite clear . . . it was the long-continued, violent, systematic meddling in civil affairs, and outrageous abuse and opposition to the Government on the part of the Irish faction of the Clergy that has worn out their patience and determined them to take the matter into their own hands. The Cardinal's Hat and the archbishopric of Westminster have been the pretext.[10]

---

[8] Cullen to Smith, 12 May 1851, ibid.
[9] Cullen to Kirby, 18 Mar. 1851, ibid.
[10] Shrewsbury to Arundel, 2 Mar. 1851, Arundel Castle Archives, MS c489.

Although Shrewsbury overemphasized the importance of the Irish dimension in Russell's reaction, his linking of the Ecclesiastical Titles Bill with Roman condemnation of the colleges had occurred to others. Greville suggested it to Bowyer in November 1850. Now again a Scottish priest at Rome, James Hamilton, made a similar suggestion to Minto. Hamilton had reminded Minto that he had raised the matter of the re-establishment of the hierarchy with him when Minto was in Rome, and was surprised that Minto had paid no attention to it.[11] Hamilton, having accepted Minto's limp explanation that he thought he was referring only to a new archbishop of Westminster and not to a new hierarchy, warned Minto that the pope would not make any spontaneous gesture for he is 'unfortunately ... at this moment in the hands of a party who are most exasperated against England. He is surrounded by Irishmen of the most rabid opinions.' Hamilton advised the government to take a strong line on the aggression issue, 'for to have been defeated in England will be a sufficient reason for the Pope to withdraw all his favour from those who may have advised the late Bull, and amongst those are most of the opponents of the Colleges'.[12] Whom Hamilton had in mind when he alleged in December 1850 that the pope was surrounded by Irishmen of rabid opinion is not certain, but it was probably Kirby and Smith, who, however, would not have been involved in the establishment of the English hierarchy.

Despite Shrewsbury and Hamilton, the government trusted more in official representatives. Richard Lalor Sheil, who as an Irishman and a Catholic was well versed in Irish affairs, arrived in Florence in January 1851, with the task of seeing what could be done in Rome on Irish government policies. Sheil soon reported that William Petre, an English Catholic and unofficial British agent at Rome, had raised the colleges question with Cardinal Antonelli, secretary of state, pointing out to him that the majority against the colleges was only 13 to 12. Antonelli replied that it was nevertheless a

---

[11] Hamilton to Minto, 23 Oct. 1850, Russell Papers, PRO 30/22/8F; Minto to Hamilton, 14 Dec. 1851, ibid. Hamilton, a former MP who had converted to Catholicism, busied himself with the question of the restoration of diplomatic relations. Some Catholics suspected that he was being used by the government. D. Gwynn, *Father Luigi Gentili and his Mission, 1801–1848* (1948), 226–7, 235–7.

[12] Hamilton to Minto, 28 Dec. 1850, Russell Papers, PRO 30/22/9A.

majority and returned later to point out to Petre that the majority was 14 to 11. Both Antonelli and Fransoni promised that the *Curia* would not come lightly to a decision on the synod. After discussions with the papal *chargé d'affaires* at Florence and with Petre, Sheil came to the conclusion that the Ecclesiastical Titles bill would be the best lever to change papal policy on the colleges, and suggested seeking the support of Rafaele Fornari, the influential nuncio in Paris.[13] Palmerston duly informed Normanby, ambassador in Paris, but nothing appears to have come of it, and Russell's suggestions that more lines of communication be opened with Rome met with little response from Palmerston.[14] By May Sheil believed he had made some progress in preventing a hostile decision on the colleges by impressing on Rome its need of England's friendship to balance growing Austrian dominance in Tuscany.[15] Within a few weeks, before this move could bear fruit, Sheil had died. His death was a blow to the government. It would be difficult, at a time when the debate on the Ecclesiastical Titles Bill was at its most acrimonious stage, to find competent and respectable Irish Catholics to replace him.

Sheil, Shrewsbury, and the government used Murray in their attempts to influence Rome, but Murray's influence there was waning. Rome was irritated at the leaking of the proceedings of the synod to the press. When Kirby translated the anonymous memorandum detailing events at the synod, Barnabò, secretary of Propaganda, wrote an angry letter to Murray.[16] A courageous Murray replied that he hoped that the pope would not endanger religion and cause schism among Catholics by confirming the synod's decrees. Rome was not impressed and Kirby recounted an astonishing interview in which the pope, in the presence of Miles Gaffney, the dean of Maynooth College, and Kirby, berated Murray's conduct:

---

[13] Sheil to Foreign Office, 18 Mar. 1851, PRO FO 79/149, cited in M. Buschkühl, *Great Britain and the Holy See* (1982), 188–9. Giacomo Antonelli (1806–76), prosecretary of state (1848–52); secretary of state (1852–76).

[14] Larkin, *Making of the Church*, 74–81. Normanby indicated that he and Fornari had been let down (presumably by Palmerston) in a previous *démarche* and that the nuncio was unwilling to compromise himself again.

[15] Sheil to Russell, 7 May 1851, Russell Papers, PRO 30/22/9C.

[16] Barnabò to Murray, 7 Oct. 1850, Murray Papers, DDA; Clarendon to Russell, 3 Nov. 1850, Clarendon Papers, Letterbook 6. Alessandro Barnabò, secretary to Propaganda, later cardinal prefect. He was a constant supporter of Cullen.

His Holiness asked [Gaffney] whether he was in Ireland at the celebration of the Synod, and then quickly passed on to speak of the late disedification given in the newspapers. He reprobated in the strongest and most indignant terms the conduct of a certain archbishop, whose name he did not even suppress; and after many most severe remarks, characterized his conduct as truly scandalous: *c'était un vrai scandale* . . . the tone and language of the Holy Father awed me in the extreme. I can never forget it.[17]

Kirby, who though naïve in some ways was a reliable witness, had every reason to be awed. It was unusual for the pope to castigate a senior archbishop who had served the Church so well for over half a century. To do so in the presence of two priests, one of whom was a subject of Murray, added to the extraordinary nature of the act. Kirby's account is borne out by Shrewsbury who was also amazed at the pope's criticism of Murray:

what had most hurt him was the *Protest* made by Dr Murray in the Public Papers immediately after the closing of the Synod. He said, 'Having just signed the Decrees as passed by unanimity . . . it was too bad to protest immediately against them and to proclaim the differences in the Synod to the world.'

Shrewsbury attempted to defend Murray, but he was taken aback by the pope's reaction. ' "Yes," says the Holy Father, "he professes to submit but yet ever tries to divert the Holy See from its decisions." ' Pius did not want the Church's private differences made public and expected Murray to accept Rome's decisions without question.[18] Another incident gave Murray's opponents further cause to complain of him to Rome. The university committee had set aside Sunday, 16 March, for a nationwide St Patrick's Day collection at the church doors. Philip Dowley, provincial superior of the Irish Vincentian Fathers, reported to Kirby a revealing conversation between senior clerics of the Dublin diocese:

---

[17] Kirby to MacHale, 2 Nov. 1850, cited in B. O'Reilly, *John MacHale Archbishop of Tuam: His Life, Times and Correspondence* (1890), ii. 243–5; Miles Gaffney (1798–1861), dean of students, Maynooth College (1834–55); joined the Jesuits (1855).

[18] This was not the only occasion, however, in which Pius, irritated at what he interpreted as disobedience, scolded a senior cleric. G. Martina, *Pio IX, 1846–1850* (1974), 555–7, recounts his sharp reprimand to Cardinal Guidi during the First Vatican Council.

Yesterday the vicar-general, Dr Yore, asked the Archbishop what was to be done on Patrick's Day. He boldly and strongly declared that 'he would have nothing to do with such a Collection'. . . . Hamilton said 'none should be *here*' [in Marlborough Street Church] and Meyler *the same* for *Westland Row* . . . I should add that the A[rch]B[ishop] added that He would not *prevent* it i.e. *Collection*.[19]

Canon Peter Cooper, one of the secretaries of the university committee and a curate in Murray's parish in Marlborough Street, now publicly announced that a collection was to be made. Astonished and annoyed, Murray took the unusual step of writing to the *Freeman's Journal*, categorically denying that he gave any order for a collection.[20] He gave Hamilton, his administrator, a measured explanation of his decision:

I quite applaud the zeal of those who have the means of giving effect to their charitable wishes, and who voluntarily subscribe, in the hope of obtaining the establishment of an institution so useful. But in the present impoverished conditions of our city, while our charitable institutions of prime necessity are, as you know well, languishing for want of adequate support, while the very rent which is due for your parochial house has not . . . from the decayed state of the parish been fully collected, I could not bring myself to call on the poor labourer and the struggling shopkeeper for a collection at their entrance into their place of worship for the establishment of an institution, which many think of doubtful possibility, and which, if attainable, ought, they think, to be procured by other means. I would much prefer, that those . . . who wish to subscribe . . . would . . . deposit their contributions with you . . .

With his usual tolerance, Murray added that 'each parish priest, however, keeping in view the state of his parish, will act in this case as his own judgement will direct'.[21] Hamilton placed an advertisement in the *Freeman's Journal* to say that 'there is no authority

---

[19] Philip Dowley (1789–1864), dean at Maynooth College (1816–34); founding member and later provincial superior of the Irish Vincentians. William Yore (1781–1865), vicar-general of the Dublin diocese, founder of many educational and charitable institutions, including the asylums for the deaf and dumb, and for the blind. Walter Meyler (1784–1864), parish priest of Saint Andrews, Westland Row, vicar-general and dean of the Dublin chapter. John Hamilton (*c*.1800–62), archdeacon of the Dublin diocese and administrator of Marlborough Street church of Saint Mary's. Much of the day-to-day administration of the diocese fell to him. Marlborough Street church, which served as the cathedral for Dublin, and Westland Row church, were the archbishop's mensal churches.

[20] *Freeman's Journal*, 12 Mar. 1851.   [21] Ibid.

for any other Door-collection of the Metropolitan Church on Sunday . . . than the usual Door-collection devoted to Church purposes'.[22] An angry Cooper replied on the following day, blaming the archbishop and Ennis.[23] This was another unseemly public row. Cooper who, not for the first time, had deliberately acted against the wishes of his archbishop, was at fault. Murray's lack of commitment to the university scheme is evident, yet he was right in claiming that university education in either the Catholic University or a Queen's College was out of the reach of the poor and lower middle class of Marlborough Street parish. Still, by departing from the line taken by his episcopal brethren and letting the dispute get into public print, Murray gave his opponents another occasion to criticize him. Cullen denounced him to Kirby, knowing that it would be passed on to higher authority.[24] To Cullen's annoyance, three bishops of his own province, Browne of Kilmore, Denvir of Down and Connor, and Blake of Dromore, refused to take up a collection for the university on the grounds that they had other heavy demands, Blake reiterating his conviction that a full-scale university was unrealizable for want of money.[25] Cullen was not to be shaken from his purpose. To his great joy, Rome approved the synod's decisions on 28 April.[26] As this decision was tantamount to a renewed rejection of the colleges, Cullen could now turn his attention to the university question. The university committee, agreed on by the synod of Thurles, consisted of eight bishops; but he got little support from them. If MacHale proved awkward, Murray absented himself. The St Patrick's Day collection, however, proved a success and brought in £22,840; other monies also began to come in.[27] America contributed £4,735 and England £3,100 in 1851 alone.[28] Cullen now contemplated broadening the scheme. The new university, he decided, would not be solely for Ireland as the Louvain one was for Belgium. Instead it would be a great Catholic university for all the Empire. While the rector was to be a priest, the vice-rector should be a layman. For

---

[22] Ibid. 13 Mar. 1851.   [23] Ibid. 14 Mar. 1851.
[24] Cullen to Kirby, 18 Mar. 1851, Smith Papers, StPA.
[25] Denvir to Cullen, 11 Jan. 1851; Browne to Cullen, 13 Jan. 1851; Blake to Cullen, 11 Jan. 1851, Cullen Papers, Section 39/2, File I, DDA.
[26] Cullen to Smith, 12 May, 1 June 1851, Smith Papers, StPA.
[27] McGrath, *Newman's University*, 102.
[28] Cullen to Kirby, 18 Mar. 1851, Smith Papers, StPA.

the key post of rector he decided that they must consider an Englishman, 'for one of the Oxford converts gives it a better name and the English have been generous'. On 15 April, following the advice of Robert Whitty, Wiseman's vicar-general, he wrote to Newman, now a priest of the Oratory at Birmingham, seeking his advice on the university. At the same time he invited him to give a set of lectures in Dublin against 'mixed education', by which was meant undenominational or neutral education.[29] A delighted Newman replied that there was nothing in which he was more interested than Irish education, and sent Cullen both the names of possible staff members and a sketch of how he envisaged the university.[30] Cullen was impressed, and shortly afterwards, in what was a momentous decision, resolved to try to obtain Newman as president of the university.[31] Cooper had earlier proposed this step, suggesting that a word from the Holy See would be enough to secure his services.[32] Cullen, fearing that Newman or his community in Birmingham Oratory might refuse, now decided to follow that advice and asked Smith to have Barnabò bring the influence of Rome to bear on Newman to accept the office of president. Since, he avowed, 'we have no one in Ireland comparable to him', he must be 'at the head of the affair'.[33] Turning to his advantage the unusual unity between English and Irish Catholics which the Ecclesiastical Titles Act had created, he travelled to London to set up a committee for the Catholic University.[34] Then he went on to Birmingham and delightedly reported to Smith that 'Newman himself has no difficulty about coming over to join us, so Rome's intervention will not be necessary'. Smith, however, had moved already in Rome, for within a few weeks Newman got word that Pius IX signified his pleasure at his acceptance, though Newman revealed later that he did not need the Pope's express wish 'to induce me to take part in the establishment'.[35] Enthused with the prospect of a Catholic university, he told his friend and fellow

---

[29] Newman, Memorandum, sect. 1, cited in McGrath, *Newman's University*, 104–11.

[30] Newman to Cullen, 16, 28 Apr., 1 May 1851, Cullen Papers, DDA.

[31] Cullen to Smith, 28 June 1851, Smith Papers, StPA.

[32] Cooper to Cullen, 13 Apr. 1850, Cullen Papers, Section 39/1, File III, DDA.

[33] Ibid.   [34] Cullen to Smith, 12 July 1851, Smith Papers, StPA.

[35] Newman to J. S. Northcote, 7 Apr. 1872, cited in C. S. Dessain and T. Gornall (eds.), *The Letters and Diaries of John Henry Newman*, xxvi (1975), 58. J. Spencer Northcote (1821–1907), president of Oscott College.

convert, Thomas William Allies, former fellow of Wadham College, Oxford, that 'It will be the Catholic University of the English tongue for the whole world.'[36] Newman saw it as a renewal of his lifelong struggle against Liberalism.

The battle there [in Ireland] will be what it was in Oxford twenty years ago. Curious too that there I shall be opposed by the Whigs, having Lord Clarendon instead of Lord Melbourne, that Whately will be there in propria persona, and that while I found my tools breaking under me in Oxford, . . . I am renewing the struggle in Dublin, with the Catholic Church to support me. It is very wonderful—Keble, Pusey, Maurice, Sewell, etc. who have been able to do so little against Liberalism in Oxford, will be renewing the fight, alas not in their persons, in Ireland.[37]

Given the surging Irish nationalism that O'Connell and the *Nation* had created, Cullen was showing vision and courage in inviting Newman. It was a bold step for an Irish nationalist of Cullen's stamp and he knew it would meet opposition in many quarters—MacHale and the Irish, who would want an Irish president, the Birmingham Oratory, which would be reluctant to lose its founder and superior, and Rome, cautious about advancing untried converts to such senior positions. By securing as president one of the most outstanding scholars of the day, however, instead of some little-known Irish cleric, he was ensuring that the new venture would be one that would command all-round respect. For most bishops, in so far as they had a clear idea of what was involved, the Catholic University was merely a rejoinder to the Queen's Colleges. Newman, however, saw it as Oxford in Ireland where the battles against theological liberalism could be fought and won. Both he and Cullen envisaged it as a Catholic college for the English-speaking world. Cullen's vision and Newman's enthusiasm were transforming the whole venture. Plans were being laid, courses considered, and staff recruited. On 1 October, Newman and Allies came to Ireland to consider sites and other arrangements. They visited Slattery in Thurles and Cullen in Drogheda, though they failed to meet Murray in Dublin. By the end of 1851, the idea of a Catholic university, which a year earlier had appeared chimerical, had become a distinct and attractive possibility.

---

[36] Newman to Allies, 20 Apr. 1851, in C. S. Dessain and V. F. Blehl (eds.), *Letters and Diaries of John Henry Newman*, xiv (1963), 262.

[37] Newman to Mrs William Froude, 14 Oct. 1851, in Dessain and Blehl, *Letters and Diaries*, xiv. 389–90.

By that time, too, an ominous development had taken place that boded ill for relations between the government and the Catholic Church and set them on a direct collision course. The resentment among Catholics about the Ecclesiastical Titles Bill had led to the holding of simultaneous protest meetings on 11 May 1851 throughout the country and the drawing up of petitions to parliament. The meetings gave unstinted praise to the Irish Brigade for the vigour with which they opposed the government, and, thus encouraged, the members of the Brigade decided to establish a permanent organization to protect Catholic interests. On 19 August this body, which called itself the Catholic Defence Association, held a meeting at the Rotundo in Dublin which brought together Catholics not merely from Ireland but from England and Scotland. Beside the Irish MPs, seven Irish bishops (including three archbishops), an English bishop, a Scottish bishop, and two other bishops were present. Other bishops, including Wiseman, Thomas Brown of Newport and Menevia, Andrew Carruthers of eastern Scotland, William Morris, retired vicar-apostolic of Mauritius, and Lords Arundel and Kenmare sent messages of support. Cullen was invited to attend and accepted, as he told Smith, 'to detach Ireland from the Whigs and from Palmerston's and Clarendon's policies'.[38] His acceptance was to have important consequences, for the Defence Association provided him with a ready-made instrument to promote his ideas, and brought him to the centre of the political stage. He took the chair and made a moderate but firm speech thanking Aberdeen and Graham for their parliamentary support, praising the work of the Brigade, and pointing to the achievement of the Liberal Catholics in France where Falloux, Dupanloup, and Montalembert had won important concessions in the Falloux law of 1850. The Association, he hoped, would 'cement firmly the union of all Catholics of the empire'. Demanding equal rights for Catholics, he laid down the primary aims of the Association as the protection of the poor from 'a heartless proselytism', whether in workhouses or in schools, and the provision of Catholic schools and a Catholic university. This speech by Cullen contains the elements of his programme over the next quarter of a century: religious equality, Catholic education, the elimination of proselytism, and the unity of Catholics throughout the Empire.

[38] Cullen to Smith, 22 Aug. 1851, Smith Papers, StPA.

If any one aspect predominated it was the war against proselytism. 'I hope', he wrote, 'it [the Defence Association] will put an end to proselytism and to evil schools—this is the principal good I expect from it.'[39]

If Cullen claimed in his speech and in his letters to Rome that his motives were religious, others took a different view. The part he took at the meeting gained him prominence with nationalists of all hues, and the nationalist press enthusiastically reflected that newly won popularity.[40] The *Nation* saw the meeting as recalling O'Connell's campaign for emancipation:

The Meeting of Tuesday . . . carries back the recollection at a bound of 22 years to the great days of the Catholic Association. . . . Not in the greatest days of that great Association was there, we do believe, any so magnificent a public demonstration as this. The Primate in the chair—the prelates on the platform—the 'Brigade'—the crowd of wealthy and eminent Catholics from all the ends of the island. . . . Before us lie the Resolutions of the Meeting unflinchingly subscribed, 'Paul, Archbishop of Armagh, Primate of all Ireland'. Whatever comes of it, the law is now broken, and will be *broken usque ad finem*—and not broken, it should be marked, in a bull, or by letters of ordination, or any peculiarly spiritual act, but in a public political meeting of Catholics. . . . The Catholics had not spoken as a Catholic body for 20 years.[41]

The London press, however, took a different line. The *Morning Chronicle* declared that 'the challenge . . . is fair, plain and decided', for the meeting had calmly and deliberately set at nought the provisions of the Ecclesiastical Titles Bill. 'The game', it added, 'must be played out.' Like the *Nation*, the *Morning Chronicle* was also struck by the similarity between the Catholic Defence Association and the great Catholic Association which O'Connell had forged to win Emancipation. 'The . . . government has now to confront difficulties, perplexities, and dangers as far superior to those presented by the Catholic Association of other days as the men engaged in the present movement, excel . . . the demagogues of the past.'[42] *The Times* angrily presented the issue as a contest for supreme authority between the British state and the Church of Rome. The government, it insisted, must take up the challenge:

---

[39] Cullen to Smith, 7 Oct. 1851, ibid.; see, too, Cullen to Smith, 22 Aug., 21, 22 Oct., 14 Nov. 1851, ibid.
[40] *Freeman's Journal*, 20 Aug. 1851; *Nation*, 23 Aug. 1851; *Tablet*, 23 Aug. 1851.
[41] *Nation*, 23 Aug. 1851.   [42] *Morning Chronicle*, 22 Aug. 1851.

[T]he menace with which we are threatened ... will vest the power of decision ... not in the Queen, Lords, and Commons of our constitution but in the priestly demagogues of the Irish Rotundo. It is not a mere question of titles or privileges but a contest for supreme authority. If the 'Catholic Defence Association' can dictate a recantation to the English people on such a point as this, they can do so on any point which may be raised ... In self-defence, therefore we must take our stand, and maintain our rights. ... the voice that spoke last autumn, throughout the length and breadth of England, will not be silenced at the bidding of an Italian monk. ... Dr Cullen has thrown down the glove. ... The people of England ... will see that this law is obeyed ... .[43]

Punch published a cartoon depicting a bloated Cullen bestriding Ireland from the north to the south brandishing aloft the fiery cross of religious war.[44] The meeting enraged the government. Hatchell, the attorney-general, considered that if Cullen was moved to the chair as archbishop of Armagh he could be prosecuted, but Somerville and Redington were inclined 'to keep the sword in the scabbard till an English case arises'.[45] Others were equally angry. Protestants, led by Thresham Gregg, the founder of the Protestant Operatives' Association, held a counter-demonstration in the Rotundo and attempted to force the government to act. The queen, Bedford told Clarendon, was indignant and wanted active measures against the bishops.[46] Sorely tempted though he was, Russell decided to follow Redington's and Somerville's advice, expressing the hope, however, that Cullen might yet furnish the government with sufficient evidence to convict him of contravening the Relief Act. 'In that case', he declared determinedly, 'we cannot leave his glove on the ground.'[47] It was an empty threat and nothing was done. Cullen, while believing a prosecution possible, remained unmoved and went on to denounce as an instrument for proselytizing the government's new model school for trainee teachers in Drogheda. This again drew the ire of the press on him. As he told Smith, 'they would have eaten me alive if they could'.[48]

When the Defence Association came to an understanding with

[43] *Times*, 22 Aug. 1851.   [44] *Punch*, Sept. 1851.
[45] Somerville to Clarendon, 15, 20, 24, 29 Aug. 1851, Clarendon Papers, Box 28; Redington to Cullen, 30 Aug. 1851, ibid., Box 44.
[46] Bedford to Clarendon, 27 Aug. 1851, ibid., Box 5.
[47] Russell to Clarendon, 2 Oct. 1851, ibid., Box 44.
[48] Cullen to Smith, 20 Sept. 1851, Smith Papers, StPA.

the Tenant League, all was set for the formation of an Independent Irish Party in parliament. Within a few months, however, the Association had run into trouble.[49] In December, Henry Wilberforce, a younger brother of Robert, who had preceded him into the Catholic Church, was voted in as secretary, an appointment which pleased English Catholics but annoyed leading members of the Brigade. They protested that 'the defence of the Catholic people of Ireland and of their national character and position' was a primary object in the foundation of the Association and so the secretary should be Irish. Wilberforce, they claimed, was wholly ignorant of the feelings, habits, and politics of the Irish people.[50] Although they were supported by MacHale, the protesters found no public backing except in the columns of the *Nation*, and many of them withdrew from the Association. Cullen, who had been ill when the meeting took place, took a conciliatory line, but pointed out that from the foundation of the Association all Catholics of the United Kingdom were to constitute one body without distinction of country. Religion rather than nationality was the criterion.[51] More than ever the Association began to express the preoccupations of Cullen, and at its meeting on 29 January 1852 it dealt almost exclusively with proselytism.[52] Claiming that 'there is a systematic attempt to seduce the Catholic poor from their faith by means of bribery and corruption', it alleged that proselytism was most active where the sufferings of the poor were greatest. It complained, too, of attempts to get Catholic children to attend Protestant schools. The fight against proselytism was now as high on the Association's agenda as Cullen wanted.

Underlying the controversy about the appointment of Wilberforce was another issue. Should the Association be just Catholic, or Irish and Catholic? The Brigade, Duffy, and others wanted Irish concerns, such as evictions and emigration, kept to the fore, for they believed that the threat to religious freedom was over, and wanted an end to unnecessary celebrations of the heroic stand against the Ecclesiastical Titles Bill. A more fundamental danger threatened the Irish race—that of its very survival:

---

[49] The most complete account of the Catholic Defence Association is in Larkin, *Making of the Church*, ch. 4.

[50] *Nation*, 20 Dec. 1851. Henry Wilberforce (1807–73), son of William Wilberforce, the philanthropist, and brother of the bishop of Oxford.

[51] Ibid.   [52] *Catholic Directory 1853*, 315.

while the independence of the Church has been apostrophised and vindicated, the Church itself, the Catholic Church of Ireland, has been vanish-
ing before the landlord and the tax-gatherer.... Week after week, the
banquet and the *Io triumpho*. Week after week, the eviction and the
Exodus.[53]

There was reason for the concern, and the term exodus was not
misplaced. The census commissioners calculated that in the nine
months from April to December no fewer than 205,000 people
had emigrated.[54] A combination of famine deaths and emigration
caused whole villages to disappear. English and Scottish farmers
moved in.[55] *Punch* quipped that:

The old Irish cry of 'Ireland for the Irish' will soon be ... heard no more;
for if emigration keeps up its present enormous rate, there will soon not
be a single Irishman in Ireland, and the cry must be changed to 'Ireland
for the English'.[56]

The Times predicted that 'in a few years more a Celtic Irishman
will be as rare in Connemara as is the Red Indian on the shores
of Manhattan'.[57] For the Association to go on about threats to
religious freedom when the existence of the people was so threatened indicated a certain blindness. The attitude of the clergy to
emigration was mixed. They were as bewildered by the extent of
the catastrophe as their people. At first, most opposed emigration.
Faced, however, with the spectacle of continuing deaths, increasing evictions, and degrading misery, some of the staunchest opponents of emigration came to accept it as a necessity. That militant
Catholic and nationalist, James Maher, parish priest of Graigue,
had been totally opposed to emigration but now declared that
he would rather see his people 'alive in Illinois than rotting in
Ireland'.[58] Archdeacon O'Sullivan's evidence in 1849 before the

---

[53] *Nation*, 8 Dec. 1851.

[54] W. E. Vaughan, *Irish Historical Statistics: Population 1821–1971* (1978), 250;
O. MacDonagh, 'Irish Emigration to the United States of America and the British
Colonies during the Famine', in R. D. Edwards and T. D. Williams (eds.), *The Great
Famine: Studies in Irish History, 1845–1852* (1956), 388.

[55] Emigration in the period 1845–1850 totalled 1.2 million. J. S. Donnelly, 'Excess
Mortality and Emigration', in W. E. Vaughan (ed.), *A New History of Ireland*
(1989), v. 353.

[56] *Punch*, 21 (1851), 167.   [57] Cited in Sullivan, *New Ireland* (1909), 566.

[58] *Freeman's Journal*, 2 May 1849; *Nation*, 8 Dec. 1849, cited in O. MacDonagh,
'The Irish Catholic Clergy and Emigration during the Great Famine', *Irish Historical Studies*, 5 (1946–7), 298–9.

select committee on the poor laws is a moving testimony of the dilemma facing a pastor deeply committed to his people. Though he hated, he said, with all his soul the loss of the best blood of Ireland, circumstances had forced him to advise every man to emigrate because he believed that every man must place his own life and happiness, and the lives and happiness of those who depended on him, before other loyalties. His parishioners again and again begged him to accompany them to America, but he could not bring himself to go.[59] Cullen also deplored emigration but saw it as inevitable. 'Everyone', Cullen told James More O'Ferrall in the spring of 1851, 'must deplore the sad circumstances which compel the inhabitants of this fine country to emigrate ... from their cherished fatherland, and it would seem to be most desirable that means should be devised to keep them at home.'[60] By late 1851, however, horrified at the scale of the exodus, which was around 5,500 a week, priests joined nationalists in deploring the haemorrhage. At the end of December one priest, writing in support of the *Nation*'s plea that the survival of the people should receive priority, declared that 'the vital, the real Catholic question for Ireland now is, how to preserve the remnant of the Irish people'.[61] A concerned Cullen relayed to Barnabò in Rome the extent of the loss:

here in Ireland our woes continue or rather continue growing. Emigration is extraordinary; more than five thousand people leave every week for America and entire areas of country are left abandoned. . . . Already the population has decreased by two million in a few years and if emigration continues the loss will shortly be doubled.[62]

The clergy, generally, were grieved to see people forced to leave their country, and it was with sadness that Bishop Moriarty commented despondently some years later: 'the exodus of the people bids fair to solve all questions. They are all going.'[63] To a Church weakened and dispirited by the Famine and under threat from

[59] *Third Report of the Select Committee, Commons, on Poor Laws, Ireland*, PP 1849, xv, pt. i, 235–9, cited in MacDonagh, 'Clergy and emigration', 295.
[60] Cullen to O'Ferrall, 4 Apr. 1851; cf. 31 July 1850, both cited in P. Mac Suibhne, *Paul Cullen and his Contemporaries, with their letters* (1961–77), ii. 75, 54.
[61] A Munster Priest, 23 Dec. 1851, *Nation*, 27 Dec. 1851.
[62] Cullen to Barnabò, 10 Oct. 1851, Mac Suibhne, *Cullen*, iii. 104.
[63] Moriarty to Kirby, 1 May 1864, Kirby Papers, ICAR.

Evangelical missions, the mass emigration of their parishioners was more than a financial blow. Depressed by the tragedy of families divided or uprooted and whole communities dispersed, the clergy also feared for the spiritual welfare of the emigrants. The priests, *The Times* remarked, who had formerly derided the Established Church for preaching to empty churches, would soon face the same dilemma. Clarendon was equally unsympathetic. 'Priests and patriots howl over the "Exodus" ', he reported to Lewis, 'but the departure of thousands of papist Celts must be a blessing to the country they quit. . . . Some English and Scots settlers have arrived and . . . they encourage others to come.'[64]

The departure of many thousands of Irish Catholics and the political disarray in which he found his Catholic opponents were a source of hope to Clarendon when, with the vexatious Ecclesiastical Titles Act finally disposed of, he returned to Ireland at the end of October. The Catholics' political unity which the Ecclesiastical Titles Bill had established was fast crumbling, he told Lewis, for the Defence Association was a dead failure. 'Those who take active part in it are quarrelling among themselves', he commented gleefully, 'those who do not, are ashamed of it.' Convinced of the superiority of modern and liberal ideas over what he perceived as the outdated and obscurantist outlook of Cullen, he prepared to meet the challenge from that quarter with confidence. The contest would be a straightforward struggle between Ultramontanism as incarnated in Cullen's outlook and policies, and Liberalism as advanced by the government. The battleground, he believed, would be the colleges, where he hoped that some judicious improvements would gain their acceptance by the Catholics.[65] He had dropped his earlier dislike of the scheme, for he believed that they were capable of producing durable benefits.[66] In May, he had raised again the question of the deans of residence, repeating his request that they be paid as part of the colleges scheme but, with parliament absorbed by the Ecclesiastical Titles Bill and enraged at the Irish Brigade's obstruction tactics, Russell believed it was not the time to look for grants for Catholic purposes.[67] By autumn Clarendon was noting with satisfaction that 'the Priests no longer

---

[64] Clarendon to Lewis, 31 Oct. 1851, Clarendon Papers, c. 532/2.
[65] Ibid.   [66] Clarendon to Monteagle, 2 May 1850, Monteagle Papers, NLI.
[67] Clarendon to Russell, 16 May, 20 June 1851, Clarendon Papers, Letterbook 7; Russell to Clarendon, 20 May, 22 June 1851, ibid., Box 44.

exercise the same influence over the people', which was 'one of the many good results of Education which much alarms the ultramontane party and should encourage us in strenuous efforts to rescue the people from their ignorance'. Now was the time, he believed, to crush Irish Ultramontanism, and the education issue would be the weapon. Cullen had overplayed his hand, he was convinced. 'The ultramontane policy of Cullen is producing schism in the Church', he confided to Lewis, 'and his crusade against education elicits the national feeling in its favour and if this is liberally met by the Government we shall beat the *parti prêtre* on the field they themselves have chosen for battle.'[68] Clarendon began to take Cullen's Catholic University more seriously when Redington reported that 'Newman, W. Allies and other Oxford converts had come over by arrangement between Cullen and Wiseman' to help the new venture. When Redington reported how MacHale 'broke out violently against the invasion of Saxons', Clarendon was pleased.[69] Again he sought press support and again, in November, *The Times* published articles in favour of his policy. Appealing to Reeve to continue that support, he explained the situation as it appeared to him:

the Pope has made us a valuable present in Dr Cullen who is so ignorant of Ireland and so fanatical in his Ultramontanism that he is producing schism in the Church and disgust among the Laity. His crusade against education has evoked a strong national feeling in its favour and his Catholic University begins to excite fears for Maynooth which extend to every village as there is not a Peasant who does not hope to be the father of a Priest but it is said that when the University is now launched Cullen is to be a Cardinal and hence his alacrity.

Clarendon had some justification in claiming that Cullen was ignorant of Ireland, and undoubtedly the new archbishop acted in a way that to some Catholics was both naïve and highhanded.[70] Clarendon's claim, however, that the peasants in every village were concerned about Maynooth was not credible; potatoes to stave off famine, rent to avoid eviction, or remittances to pay the fare to

---

[68] Clarendon to Lewis, 31 Oct. 1851, ibid., c. 532/2.

[69] Redington to Clarendon, 6 Oct. 1851, ibid., Box 25.

[70] Archdeacon O'Sullivan's diary contains many such criticisms of Cullen. Patrick Murray of Maynooth commented later that Cullen came with 'very strong views which he often put forward in very strong forms'. Diary, 25 Oct. 1878, Maynooth College Library.

America were their main concerns.[71] It was true that the competing claims of the Catholic University and Maynooth College were causing concern to Murray, who was still prepared to fight for his view on these issues. Lest his banning of the St Patrick's Day collection for the Catholic University be misunderstood, Murray decided to contact Fransoni, the cardinal secretary of Propaganda, who knew him longer and better than either Pius IX or Barnabò. He assured the cardinal that he was anxious to do all he could to establish a Catholic university, but explained that many good Catholics did not think it feasible. He publicly praised the zeal of those who contributed to it, he told Fransoni, but warned against asking too much of the suffering poor.[72] This attempt to forestall criticism failed, however, for Roman patience with Murray's stubborn defence of the colleges scheme was coming to an end. On 28 September, Fr. Ignatius Spencer, the Passionist preacher, who knew and admired Murray, warned him that it was widely held in Rome that he was opposing the decrees against the Queen's Colleges and that the pope was embarrassed and annoyed.[73] To this Murray made a dignified reply professing his continual submission to papal wishes, which Fr. Ignatius brought to the pope's attention.[74]

Before any reaction came from Rome, events had taken an important turn in Dublin. On 12 November the bishops' committee on the university had appointed Newman rector; he accepted at once. Clarendon reported that Cullen sent Murray 'an offensive letter' urging him to support the Catholic University and not to oppose the wishes of the pope but that Murray had replied that, while he would always obey the pope, the university scheme was foolish and uncalled for and would endanger Maynooth College.[75] This initiated a debate on the merits of the proposed university and of Maynooth. Already, in May, when an irritated parliament appeared to threaten the Maynooth Grant, Cullen brushed the threat aside. 'Tell them [in Rome]', he told Smith, 'that it is feint attack. It is the interest of the government to support and enrich that establishment—as yet they have not been able to pervert its spirit but

---

[71] Cf. Kerr, *Peel, Priests, and Politics* (1982), 238–48.

[72] Murray to Fransoni, 19 Mar. 1851, Murray Papers, DDA.

[73] Father Ignatius to Murray, 28 Sept. 1851, ibid.; Fr. Ignatius, a Passionist priest, was the Hon. George Spencer, brother of John Spencer Althorp, Viscount Althorp and 3rd Earl Spencer.

[74] Murray to Father Ignatius, 13 Oct. 1851, Murray Papers, DDA.

[75] Clarendon to Russell, 11 Nov. 1851, Clarendon Papers, Letterbook 7.

with time they will do so.'[76] There was more substance to the fear concerning Maynooth than Cullen allowed. From Maynooth Edmund O'Reilly had warned Cullen that he dared not give open support to the proposed Catholic university because the no-popery feeling in England might force the withdrawal of the Maynooth Grant.[77] In February 1853 Richard Spooner's hostile motion on Maynooth was supported by 164 members. Cullen, however, viewed Maynooth with a jaundiced eye, for he feared that the government, by endowing it so munificently, would eventually control it and through it control the Church. Furthermore, he believed some of its professors were tainted with Gallicanism and had not followed papal directions on the question of the Queen's Colleges. When Cullen expressed some of these reservations, Murray was shocked, and, in reasoned but firm tones, defended Maynooth:

Were Your Grace's opinion regarding Maynooth to be made known to the Catholics of Ireland, it would, I am sure, be heard with astonishment and dismay. The difficulty of paying, in the impoverished state of the Country, for the permanent support of five hundred Clerical Students would at once rise up in every mind. Were I, without manifest necessity, to imperil that magnificent Establishment it would cost me many a bitter pang of conscience and I would tremble at the thought of going to judgment with such a weight upon my soul.[78]

Cullen's arguments calling for public and parliamentary agitation and the establishment of a university did not convince him. How would the Catholics of Ireland judge of the 'relative value of our National Seminary and the chance of a Catholic University?'. To Murray it was shadow or substance, the 'chance' of a Catholic university or the reality of the national seminary. For him, and, he believed, for 'the Catholics of Ireland' the national seminary was the priority.[79] To continue the training of 500 priests for the Irish mission was vital. In answer to Cullen's hint that by opposing the project for a Catholic university he was disobeying the pope, Murray retorted vigorously. 'The Pope', he wrote, 'has expressed the satisfaction He would feel at finding a Catholic University established in Ireland if such a blessing could be procured. So

[76] Cullen to Smith, 23 June 1851, Smith Papers, StPA.
[77] O'Reilly to Cullen, 14 Feb. 1851, Cullen Papers, 39/2, DDA.
[78] Murray to Cullen, 15 Nov. 1851, Cullen Papers, Section 39/2, File I, DDA.
[79] Murray to Cullen, 22, 25 Nov. 1851, ibid.

would we all.' It was, however, a 'fruitless attempt' which, since it was in open defiance of the government, would bring 'a heavy calamity' on the Church, such as the withdrawal of the Maynooth Grant. When Cullen put to him the text of St John of being of one mind and one heart, Murray retorted by reminding him of the difference of opinion between St Paul and St Peter. 'We differ', he told Cullen, 'as ever has been the case in the Church on matters of mere prudence.' Despite agreeing to differ, Murray indicated his willingness to enforce the decrees of the synod, whether as a result of Fr. Ignatius' letter or of the exchange with Cullen.[80] This exchange cleared the air, and Murray and Cullen met. Apparently, they reached an agreement, because a number of bishops wrote to Cullen delighted that unity had been restored.[81]

Meanwhile Clarendon, heartened by Murray's spirited defence, decided not to leave Ireland after all, believing that victory over Cullen was within his grasp. As he geared himself for the struggle, he described it in terms reminiscent of the struggle within the French Church—the Ultramontanes against the state over education. 'I am prodigiously interested about education', he told Lewis, 'which is the field selected by the Ultramontanes for battle with the State and to beat them would be a social, political, religious and lasting triumph and so I dont mind staying till Easter tho' the Dublin season makes a big hole in my pocket.'[82] Russell, undaunted by the controversy over the Ecclesiastical Titles Bill, was also prepared to renew his efforts. He had decided to try again at Rome with a new mission. His remarks to Clarendon are an indication that the special mission he had discussed with Wiseman fifteen months earlier would have had a significant Irish dimension:

Bulwer is to go to Florence with a . . . special mission to Rome. We have been twice assured by the Pope that he has no objection to receive a special mission . . . I shall be very glad to receive some hints from you on this subject.

Clarendon's reply was to tell Bulwer 'that the Catholic University is an act of political hostility against the system of education

---

[80] Ignatius to Cullen, 6 May 1852, Cullen Papers, 325/2/64, DDA.

[81] Cantwell to Cullen, 1 Dec. 1851; McNally to Cullen, 3 Dec. 1851; Murphy to Cullen, 15 Dec. 1851, Cullen Papers, Section 39/2, File I, DDA.

[82] Clarendon to Lewis, 28 Nov. 1851, Clarendon Papers, c. 532/2.

established by the State'.[83] However, before either Bulwer's diplomatic offensive in Rome could get under way or Clarendon could be asked to make the financial sacrifice he was willing to make in order to win the colleges dispute, nemesis overtook Clarendon. He had used the press, without too much scruple, to further his views. Now what he had least expected came to pass.

Shortly after his assumption of office, Clarendon had engaged James Birch, the proprietor of a political journal, the *World*, to use his paper to support the government. Clarendon paid him both from his private purse and from the secret service fund. Two years later Birch, an indifferent journalist, who had spent time in jail on embezzlement charges, claimed that the amount was insufficient and asked for £4,700 more. 'I put the case in Monahan's hands', Clarendon explained to Wood, the tight-fisted chancellor of the exchequer, 'and, as he said that counsel would have a right to extort from the witnesses whether the money given had come from public sources, together with all manner of disagreeable and inconvenient information compromising to the Government, he strongly advised me to buy the fellow off, and I was actually obliged to pay him £2,000!' The affair, however, was not to end there. Birch now made similar demands on Somerville, the chief secretary. Somerville refused to pay up and Birch brought him to court in December 1851. The sensation of the day was when Clarendon was called as witness and had to go into the witness box and admit that he had paid Birch £1,700 for expenses and a further £2,000 to buy him off. The amounts were substantial. All parties, nationalists and Orangemen, Young Irelanders and Tories, made the most of the spectacle of the viceroy admitting in court that he paid Birch monies, and the *Nation*, the *Dublin University Magazine*, and the *Quarterly Review* took Clarendon to task. The *Quarterly* commented sharply:

His shameful conduct to Lord Roden; his correspondence with the Pope and Dr Murray; his hypocrisy . . . his disreputable connexion with *The World*, makes it impossible that he can any longer continue to misrule this country. . . . [His] administration has been highly praised by a portion of the press which these recent discoveries have satisfactorily explained. When a politician discusses his own acts in the pages of a newspaper,

[83] Russell to Clarendon, 27 Nov. 1851, ibid., Box 50; Clarendon to Russell, 29 Nov. 1851, ibid. Letterbook 7.

he is likely to view them somewhat in a favourable light. . . . The English reader may fully comprehend . . . Clarendon's conduct, by considering what the opinion . . . would have been if Lord John Russell had been detected and exposed as a contributor of political articles to the pages of the *Satirist.*[84]

It was altogether an unfortunate episode for Clarendon. Although Somerville won his case, the prestige of the lord lieutenancy was damaged, and when Clarendon thought the matter at rest, Lord Naas decided to raise it in the House of Commons, a move which Clarendon ascribed to Stanley, now Lord Derby, still smarting at his defeat on the Dolly's Brae affair. He complained to Russell how unfortunate he was 'that Birch was such a villain and that I must bear the brunt of that which all Governments more or less have done'. By now Clarendon had become thoroughly disillusioned. To his sister, Theresa, with whom he was on intimate terms, he bared his feelings:

they [ambition, self-confidence, zeal for public service, capability for good and successful efforts] have been smothered in this country where a residence of five years, nearly, has produced a contempt for human nature in general, and political life in particular that I cannot get over. You have no idea what my depression of spirits and disgust of public life amount to.[85]

His comments may indicate a certain moodiness, but they also arise from the difficulties he had encountered as viceroy which were exacerbated by this new embarrassment which he had brought on himself. To his credit Russell strongly and successfully defended Clarendon's Irish policy in the House of Commons. The following day, however, a crisis overtook Russell himself.

Palmerston's unilateral action in approving Louis Napoléon's *coup d'état* on 2 December 1851 created a serious disagreement between the court and Palmerston which was but the latest in a series. Russell, tired of the continual scrapes in which Palmerston's *frondeur*-like actions were involving the government, decided to finish the affair suddenly. He asked for Palmerston's explanation

---

[84] 'Clarendon', *Quarterly Review*, 86 (1851), 148, 156–7. *The Satirist or Monthly Meteor*, became involved with Whig politicians when it published some of the party secrets in 1810. It was regarded as a scurrilous paper.
[85] Clarendon to Theresa Cornewell Lewis, n.d. [Jan. 1852], cited in G. Villiers, *A Vanished Victorian, Being the Life of George Villiers, Fourth Earl of Clarendon* (1938), 205.

and, finding it unsatisfactory, had the queen dismiss him from the foreign secretaryship. He offered the post to Clarendon, but either Clarendon refused or, for fear of offending Palmerston, couched his reply in such guarded and indefinite language that led Russell to give it instead to Granville. Clarendon's refusal surprised Greville, who thought it pusillanimous. It would have enabled Clarendon to quit Ireland in an honourable manner, he believed, for 'in no other way could he have left his present post, just after the recent trial of Birch v. Somerville, and this trial with its disclosures must render it particularly irksome to him to stay there'.[86] Having filled the vacant ministry, the weakened government struggled on. Palmerston bided his time for revenge. It was not long in coming. On 21 February, the day after the government defeated Naas's motion against Clarendon, Palmerston gave Russell his 'tit for tat', defeating him on the Militia bill. Lord John's administration resigned. Carlisle, as John Prest remarks, delivered its funeral oration:

So ends the Administration . . . but the body had become too weak for dignified existence. Many causes have co-operated . . . above all the Ecclesiastical Titles Bill . . . on that occasion I thought it [the administration] was not true to the cause of religious liberty, and I have always been inclined to question the vote against the Irish Disturbance Bill upon which it was originally founded.[87]

Just as Russell had come to power on an Irish issue, so it was another issue closely connected with Ireland, the Ecclesiastical Titles Act, that had fatally weakened his government and brought about its collapse.

At the same time as Russell left office, dramatic developments also took place within the Irish Catholic Church. Father Ignatius' letter to Murray was an inspired one for, on 21 November, Pius IX wrote directly to the archbishop. A postal error sent the papal letter first to Lublin in Poland, and it did not reach Murray in Dublin until January 1852. While expressing his pleasure at Murray's letter to Father Ignatius and the proof it gave of his fidelity to the Holy See, Pius added:

it is still our earnest wish . . . that they [the decrees] be observed most studiously . . . as the preservation of Catholic Doctrine is the object they

---

[86] Greville, *Memoirs*, 24 Dec. 1851, vi. 436.
[87] Morpeth's diary, 21 Feb. 1852, cited in Prest, *Russell*, 341.

have in view. And than such an object, nothing . . . can . . . be more sacred in our eyes. We cannot dissemble that it was to us a subject of no small regret to hear of the occurrences which . . . took place after the termination of the Synod of Thurles . . . its transactions having been publicly divulged, notwithstanding our earnest recommendation that silence on those matters should be most carefully observed.[88]

He also asked Murray to strive with all his might to erect the Catholic University. Despite its praise of Murray's piety, this letter was a reproof. Murray replied forthwith, explaining that he and his colleagues had been convinced 'that . . . it were safer far to tolerate these colleges, though not unattended with danger, . . . than to repudiate them utterly'. He assured the pope, however, that as soon as 'the Holy See gave utterance to a different opinion . . . at once I announced it as our duty to conform ourselves with all possible submission'. The bishops were influenced only by their zeal for religion, he said, but to decline obedience to the chair of St Peter never once entered their hearts. As for the pope's request to exert himself vigorously to give effect to the decree on the colleges, Murray pointed out that none of the new colleges was in his own province of Dublin.[89] It was a sober letter accepting the decision of the Holy See but defending his and his fellow bishops' actions. Of the Catholic University he said nothing, but whether by design or oversight, or because he regarded his acceptance of the decree as an indication of his readiness to support it, is not clear. One element that emerged in his letter was his determination to defend those other bishops who had followed his line of action. This dignified defence was to be Murray's final effort. If he had succeeded on the earlier issues of the national schools and the Charitable Bequests Act, he had lost on the colleges. The Eglinton clause, the Durham letter, and the Ecclesiastical Titles Act had destroyed the claim of government goodwill towards the Church which had formed the core of Murray's case for co-operating with the administration. All the Roman cards were stacked against him, the pope as well as Propaganda, and he was no match for Cullen, Kirby, and Smith.

On 24 February, three weeks after writing the letter and days after the fall of the ministry, the aged, but still very lucid, Murray,

---

[88] Pius IX to Murray, 21 Nov. 1851, Murray Papers, DDA.
[89] Murray to Pius IX, 31 Jan. 1852, Larkin, *Making of the Church*, 128–92.

on the point of celebrating mass, was seized with total paralysis. Sir Philip Crampton, the doctor attending him, hastened out to Lord Clarendon, now packing his bags at the viceregal lodge, to tell him. Crampton reported that when Clarendon heard the news he wept. ' "So he ought", said Dr Meyler, "for Dr Murray loved him, and stood by him to the last".' Cooper, who conveyed this account to Cullen, vouched for its authenticity.[90] Murray died on 26 February. He was 82 years old. Father Laurence Forde, Cullen's master of ceremonies at Thurles, remarked piously: 'Let us pray God to have mercy on a great and good bishop whatever may have been his errors of judgement.' Kirby, whom Murray in a moment of irritation had described as 'a pious fool', told Smith that when he heard the news of the archbishop's death he remembered with fear 'what I understood Monsignor Barnabò once to say, namely, that it is a grave thing to bear about one's person a curse of the Pope. . . . May the Almighty receive his soul in Peace. As he was, at least in other days not distant, very kind to the [Irish] College, get a High Mass sung for his eternal repose.'[91]

So passed from the scene a bishop who had been a central figure in the Irish Church during the first half of the nineteenth century. He constituted a link with the later penal epoch and with the rebellion of 1798. At the historic meeting on the veto in 1808 he had played a significant part, and was chosen as the bishops' representative to put to the pope the Irish bishops' opposition to it. His pastoral work and his reputation lived on after him. Gentle, yet far-seeing, he was revered by his colleagues and clergy. His prudence had been remarked on by many observers. Towards the end of his life he showed a tenacity in clinging to his views that bordered on stubbornness and irritated fellow bishops, including the pope. It was his relationship with the government, where he was suspected of being too trusting and compliant, that was at the root of the dissension. According to Slattery this was 'the *fons et origo mali*'.[92]

The Whig policies towards Irish Catholics had finally run their

---

[90] Cooper to Cullen, 24 Feb. 1852, Murray Papers, personal. Sir Philip Crampton (1777–1858), surgeon at the Meath Hospital and surgeon in ordinary to the queen.

[91] Cited in Larkin, *Making of the Church*, 140.

[92] Slattery to Cullen, 18 Feb. 1851, Cullen Papers, 39/2/44, DDA. Scarcely any letters documenting his contact with the government remain in Murray's papers in DDA.

course by the spring of 1852. The Queen's Colleges, in particular, had received a setback. The approval of the Catholic Church, in doubt since 1845, had finally been denied them, and their strongest supporter among the bishops was dead. Clarendon, who had made the promotion of the colleges central to his policy, had also left the scene. On the other hand, a Catholic university had now become feasible. The death of Murray removed a major obstacle, and even Newman, who had been far removed from the controversies, believed that Murray's disapproval was 'so undisguised that the University could hardly have been commenced in Dublin during his lifetime'.[93] The Church had opted against integration into the state system and had set up a parallel Catholic system. How the two rival systems would compete remained to be seen.

With the fall of Russell's government, the departure of Clarendon, and the death of Murray, relations between the Irish Catholic Church and the British government entered a new phase. Leadership passed into more conservative hands. In government, Derby, regarded by Irish Catholics since the 1830s as a bitter enemy, became prime minister, Eglinton, whose amendment of the Diplomatic Relations Act had rendered it unacceptable to the pope, replaced Clarendon as lord lieutenant, and Naas, a moderate conservative, who had humiliated Clarendon in the Birch affair, replaced Somerville as chief secretary. The death of Murray left the way open for Cullen to carry through his reforms, his ambitious educational schemes, and his Ultramontane policies. It would also enable him to consolidate his hold over the Irish Church.

---

[93] Newman, Memorandum, sect. 7, cited in McGrath, *Newman's University*, 140.

10
Success and Failure?
Whigs and Ultramontanes

February 1852, which saw the end of the government of Russell and Clarendon, also saw the end of Murray's long reign as archbishop of Dublin. In the aftermath of a bishop's death, interest focuses less on the obsequies than on the succession, and this was especially true after Murray's. Whoever succeeded him in the diocese of Dublin, the richest and most important see in Ireland, situated in the country's political capital, would be of fundamental importance for both the Church and the government. The Dublin priests met, and after the usual behind-the-scenes speculation and manœuvring, the result of the 51 votes cast could not be more decisive. Of the three names placed in the usual order of *dignus*, *dignior*, *dignissimus*, Laurence Dunne, parish priest of Castledermot, got 8 votes, Dean Meyler 9 votes, and Paul Cullen 23. Many of the more important parish priests voted for Cullen including, surprisingly, Ennis. It was an extraordinary vote of confidence. When, following normal procedure, the bishops of the province examined the list, they also recommended Cullen though perhaps without great warmth. Rome was only too pleased to confirm the appointment without delay and, on 3 May, Paul Cullen became archbishop of Dublin. Cullen was also made perpetual Apostolic Delegate, which confirmed him as the head of the Irish church.[1] His appointment meant that the leader of the 'moderate' or pro-government bishops had been replaced in the most important see in the land by the leader of the 'intransigents'. The vote of the Dublin clergy had silenced those who had criticized him as an unwanted intruder imposed by Pius IX on the Irish Church. If he could win such support in the stronghold of his erstwhile most tenacious opponent it was evident that he was highly esteemed not just in

---

[1] An important unpublished study is C. O. Carroll, 'Paul Cullen' (Ph.D. thesis, 1993).

Rome but in Ireland. There was a further satisfactory sequel for him shortly afterwards. When the Armagh priests met to select a successor to Cullen in the see of Armagh, they selected Joseph Dixon, professor of scripture at Maynooth. Cullen had no hesitation in recommending Dixon, who remained one of his warmest supporters until his death in 1866. A few months later one of MacHale's allies, O'Higgins of Ardagh, died and Cullen had John Kilduff appointed in his place. Cullen was now on the crest of a wave. The synod had gone the way he wanted, its decrees were approved, and the colleges were condemned. He was at the centre of power in Dublin and far better placed than in Armagh to forward his plans to reform the Church on Roman lines and give it decisive leadership. His great rival Murray was dead. More bishops favourable to his reforming policies were being appointed and the trend was set to quicken. Contrary to the expectations of critics he had successfully launched the Catholic University and secured Newman as its rector.

From his arrival in Ireland his first concern had been Protestant missionary activity, and he preached throughout the diocese of Armagh against the mixed schools—'*scuole cattive*', or evil schools, as he called them.[2] The open proselytism of the Evangelicals, and what he saw as the covert proselytism of the Liberals and their mixed schools, were alike anathema to him. He moved quickly and determinedly to make the national schools more acceptable to Catholics. Realizing that the great weakness of Catholic education lay neither in the university nor in the primary schools but in the absence of intermediate schools, he built up, with the help of the religious orders, a secondary school system that provided secondary education for Irish Catholics for over a century. Already, in his first year in Ireland, despite indifferent health, he had engaged on a strenuous pastoral programme. The fact that he had spent all his adult life in Rome and that in Ireland he would have been familiar only with the east and south-east of the country lends added interest to his first reports on the northern see of Armagh. Within a short time he had visited all his diocese, confirming almost a thousand children and giving six hundred more First Communion. Among those confirmed were ten converts; twenty others had converted during the visit. He was surprised to observe that the children

---

[2] Cullen to Smith, 10 Sept. 1851, Smith Papers, StPA.

knew their catechism so well: the poorest, who had not even shoes to their feet, were able to respond marvellously on all the mysteries of the faith and were better instructed than children in Italy. He arranged a retreat for sixty priests in Armagh, 'the first', he said, 'ever given in this diocese since the days of Elizabeth'.[3] Rather provocatively, in June 1851 he organized a Corpus Christi procession in Drogheda, to the fury of many Protestants. 'We must restore good old Catholic practices', he remarked to Smith.[4] The cathedral city, Armagh, caused him concern, for he found the schools in a miserable state and the church in ruins with neither vestments nor sacred vessels for mass. His attempts to bring in the Sacred Heart sisters was frustrated, for he could get no site for a convent; the city, he said, belonged to the Protestants.[5] Nevertheless, in a long letter to the pope in November 1851 he described the people of his diocese as excellent Catholics and totally loyal despite twenty years of well-financed proselytism. They needed better schools and instruction. Since the landlords, almost all Protestant, would not give an inch of ground for a priest's house, many priests had to live in inns. This meant that they lived far apart and often at some distance from the church. Their ministry was impaired and study was impossible.

Cullen's remarks about the priests are worth comparing with those of Archdeacon O'Sullivan, who gives the most complete account available of clerical life. He was the constant companion of Bishop Egan in his visits to the parishes and was well thought of by the priests, whom he knew well. He commented freely on them in his diary. He found a few who were too exacting in their demands for money. This was usually due to the expenses they incurred through involvement in politics or attempts to better their families, both of which activities O'Sullivan saw as a 'curse' in clerical life. He mentioned some who lacked good sense, were lazy, or drank to excess. In two cases he recorded rumours of a moral lapse. Many were not well off, some sought richer parishes, and occasionally discord arose between them. The vast majority, however, were good-living, zealous pastors. The bishop, whose diligence and good sense O'Sullivan admired, was severe with those who did not catechize properly and strict on deviant priests.[6]

---

[3] Cullen to Smith, 29–30 July 1851, ibid.
[4] Cullen to Smith, 23 June 1851, ibid.
[5] Cullen to Smith, 12 May 1851, ibid.
[6] O'Sullivan, diary, 21 July 1851; 15, 16, 18, 22 Aug. 1852; 28 July 1855.

It was neither the state of the laity nor of the priests that worried Cullen, he told the Pope, but that of the twenty-six bishops of the Irish Church. Many of the bishops were old and ill, but the dioceses were so poor that they could not support a coadjutor. The provision of reforming bishops was the key to progress, and bishops, he warned, would have to be chosen with great care. In September 1851 he wrote first to Barnabò, with whom he appears to have been particularly friendly, and later to Fransoni. In these letters he scrutinized mercilessly the performance of the bishops of his own province and that of Tuam. McGettigan of Raphoe, he warned, 'once came to this city [Drogheda] in a state of inebriation and then spoke without much judgment'. Denvir of Down and Connor, he alleged, 'has not visited his parishes for seven years, and then he has only four priests in the city of Belfast where there are at least fifty thousand Catholics who repeatedly complain to me of their state of neglect'. Going on to the province of Tuam, he said the bishop of Achonry had been very ill for three or four years 'and I believe also a little mentally ill at all times'. French, the bishop of Kilmacduagh, old, ill, and scrupulous, he complained 'has not visited his diocese in fifteen years'. Of the bishop of Galway, O'Donnell, he complained that he was 'old and inactive' and that his diocese had many apostates, including four hundred in the parish of Oughterard alone. O'Higgins of Ardagh, he said, 'shuts himself up in his house for months at a time, and receives no one. . . . I believe he allows himself to be conquered by wine and his diocese is much neglected.'[7]

Many of his accusations were well founded, as for instance his criticism of the situation in Belfast where four priests for a Catholic population of 30,000–40,000 was totally inadequate.[8] His accusations against O'Higgins were probably accurate. He was scrupulously fair in his assessment of the good work done by Blake of Dromore, who had opposed him at the synod, and praised McNally and Cantwell who, although they had supported him, were more associated with MacHale. Nevertheless, these letters constitute a devastating, even pitiless, assessment of fellow bishops. He had

---

[7] Cullen to Fransoni, 28 Sept. 1851, *Scritture riferite nei congressi, Irlanda*, vol. xxx, fo. 712, PFA; E. Larkin, *The Making of the Roman Catholic Church in Ireland, 1850–1860* (1980), 149–51; V. A. McClelland, *English Roman Catholics and Higher Education* (1973), 89–90. According to the 1861 census, the Catholic population of Belfast in 1861 was 41,406.

[8] A. Macaulay, *Patrick Dorian: Bishop of Down and Connor, 1865–1885* (1987), 87–8.

learned much about the Irish Church while agent of the Irish bishops at Rome and later during the synod of Thurles in 1850, yet some of his information was second-hand, especially that concerning the province of Tuam. Whether he was well enough informed to make sweeping judgements on his fellow bishops after a little over a year in Ireland is doubtful. A few years later he sent Rome unfavourable reports on the province of Cashel, which annoyed the Cashel bishops. O'Sullivan complained derisively:

Such is the mode in which Dr Cullen hopes to advance the cause in Ireland, to alienate not only every Bishop individually but the whole Bishops of a Province collectively. . . . Bravo, brave Cullen, . . . Snub them all in the round. Take it for granted there is not a pious, nor a zealous, nor an active Bishop in the Church but yourself or some of your choosing.[9]

Cullen was severe in his dealings with Murray, to whom he referred as the '*vecchio*', or old man, whose demise he awaited with impatience. He complained continually that Murray was standing in the way of the progress of the Catholic university project, which was indeed true, and of being under the influence of Clarendon, Bellew, and the government, which was less certain. When Murray went to the lord lieutenant's reception during the controversy over the Ecclesiastical Titles Act, he scoffingly reported to Smith that 'yesterday he was alone in his glory—not another bishop turned up'. Some felt his criticisms had overstepped the mark and, later, Patrick Murray, the Maynooth professor, in a bitter mood over Cullen's unceremonious dressing-down of the divinity staff at Maynooth, complained that Cullen had worried the archbishop to his death.[10] Others, including his colleagues, were critical of the authority he assumed over the Church. Leahy, who was a close friend of Slattery and was to succeed him as archbishop, spoke of 'the deep dissatisfaction of the Prelates, caused by their seeing one person but lately come among them, and having but little experience of things here, set at nought the feelings and the opinion, and the authority of his Brethren in the Episcopacy'.[11] For Cullen it was less personal power than what he saw as the good of his Church. He was wholeheartedly a man of the Church and unrelentingly

---

[9] O'Sullivan, diary, 10 Mar. 1854.
[10] Murray to Duffy, 12 Feb. 1855. This letter is preserved with Murray's diary in Maynooth College Library.
[11] Leahy to Slattery, May 1854, Leahy Papers, CDA.

singleminded in promoting its welfare. If a bishop or priest performed his duties well he supported him; if he stood out against the programme and reforms which Cullen believed necessary, he wanted him out of the way. Episcopal disunity was a major problem. Writing to Pius IX on 31 January 1852, Cullen explained:

The dissensions among the prelates that existed for about twenty years have done great harm. Matters have been conducted in the spirit of party, and it seems to me that when new bishops will be chosen, those who will recommend them should have more regard for their opinions on certain controversial points, that here stamp them as true ecclesiastics.[12]

Bishops in sympathy with Cullen's views were appointed. Apart from Dixon and Kilduff, William Keane was appointed first to Ross in 1850 and then promoted to Cloyne in 1857. John McEvilly succeeded to Galway in 1858 and, then in 1878, was forced on an outraged MacHale as his coadjutor in Tuam, with the right to succession! Cullen was determined to unite the bishops in a common programme under his leadership, and a powerful instrument came almost fortuitously to hand. This was the new structure of the bishops' meeting. After the synod of Thurles there was no return to the older form of meeting. Nor was there to be a regular annual meeting. From then on it was Cullen who decided when a meeting was opportune and proposed it to Rome. Rome then determined who was to convoke and preside at the meeting and laid down its agenda and procedure. This meant that control lay with Cullen; it was who, in effect, determined when a meeting was necessary, set its agenda, and, as Apostolic Delegate, presided over it. Since, however, Rome officially called the meeting, Cullen's authority benefited from the sanction of the Holy See. In vain did the bishops seek a return to the annual meetings with their less formal structure. Cullen advised against it, and Rome agreed with him.[13] The new-style meetings gave Cullen the opportunity to establish uniformity among the bishops along his own orthodox lines. The parliamentary style of the earlier meetings gave way to synodical procedure. In the older system the agenda had been drawn up without any reference to Rome and decisions were rarely

---

[12] Cullen to Pius IX, 31 Jan. 1852, *Scritture riferite nei congressi, Irlanda*, vol. xxxi, fos. 78–81, PFA; Larkin, *Making of the Church*, 135.

[13] S. Cannon, 'Irish Episcopal Meetings, 1788–1882', *Annuarium Historiae Conciliorum*, 13 (1981), 371–83.

communicated to Rome. From now on Rome controlled the agenda and ratified the decisions. Up to then an individual bishop had not felt bound by the decisions of the meetings and could abstain or absent himself; now he was bound to accept them. As Cullen told Rome, the government, too well informed of the dissension at the meetings, had been able to use them to its own ends.[14] Now, however, the bishops were bound by the collective decisions, and the proceedings were kept secret so the government could no longer interfere. The radical change in the style of the bishops' meetings remodelled the manner in which the Irish Church was governed, gave far more power to Cullen, so facilitating his reform plans, and was a powerful boost to Ultramontanism.

The introduction of Ultramontanism into Ireland is credited to Cullen. To assess this claim an understanding of Ultramontanism and of the outlook of the pre-Famine Church is necessary. Rejection of state control, a centralization of power in Rome, and devoted loyalty to the pope were characteristics of nineteenth-century Ultramontanism. Cullen was, indeed, an ardent and able promoter of the Church's freedom from state interference, but the bishops generally, and the supporters of MacHale and Slattery in particular, had always defended the Church's freedom.[15] Irish Catholics over the centuries had proved their loyalty to Rome: with no Louis XIV or Joseph II to defend or to exaggerate the claims of a national Church, the oppressed Irish Church looked to the pope as the centre of unity. It was true that the bishops professed obedience to papal injunctions and yet on occasion ignored them. This occurred only when they were convinced that they knew the local scene better and had reason to fear government intrigue. Their correspondence showed an intense loyalty to the pope. Murray again and again expressed his willingness to accept papal decisions even when he disagreed with them, and Stanley remarked of him: 'let any occasion arise on which he [Murray] can support the Pope against the King, and he will do so to the uttermost.'[16]

Gallicanism as it existed in France never flourished among the

---

[14] *Acta* (1854), vol. 218, fo. 342, PFA; Cannon, 'Irish Episcopal Meetings', 379.

[15] In the eighteenth-century controversy on Jansenism, the Irish College in Paris where most Irish priests trained took the orthodox papal line.

[16] Gladstone's memorandum, 9 Dec. 1837, BL Add. MSS 44777, fos. 40–51, cited in W. E. Gladstone, *Prime Ministers' Papers*, ed. J. Brooke and M. Sorensen (1972), ii. 88.

Irish bishops, whose priorities were in any case pastoral, not theological. Bishop Doyle's replies to a parliamentary committee in 1825
did reveal Gallican tendencies, but he was exceptional and anxious to present his Church, so often accused of double loyalties,
in the most favourable light. The French professors of theology at
Maynooth, Louis Delahogue and François Anglade, would have
taken the obligatory Gallican oath on their appointment to a seminary in pre-revolutionary France and probably taught Gallicanism.
It is unlikely that the other professors were committed to Gallican
ideas. The evidence of Edmund O'Reilly is interesting. He had
been a student at Maynooth before going to study at the Irish
College in Rome. When he returned to Maynooth as professor in
1839 he was agreeably surprised to be able to inform Kirby in
Rome that Gallicanism in Maynooth was almost dead: 'the papal
infallibility is not looked on in any odious light, and is certainly
inclined to by several of the professors.'[17] In 1853 Thomas Furlong, one of the professors and later bishop of Ferns, told the
Royal Commission that since the 1820s 'a more decided bias
prevails in favour of the infallibility of the Pope and his authority
in spiritual matters'.[18] Another professor, Patrick Murray, taught
papal infallibility in his textbooks published between 1860 and
1866.

French Liberal Catholics gave a powerful impulse to Ultramontanism, and Irish Catholicism had much in common with Liberal
Catholicism. Increased attachment to the pope was a phenomenon
common to all Catholic countries, and during the second half of
the century pilgrimages to Rome, press reports, and photographs
had made Pius IX better known than any pope before him. As his
political misfortunes increased, he became the centre of an extraordinary popular affection among Catholics. Centralization in Rome

---

[17] O'Reilly to Kirby, 23 July 1839, Kirby Papers, ICA.

[18] *Report of Her Majesty's Commissioners appointed to inquire into the Management and Government of the College of Maynooth ... PP 1854–5*, Minutes of
Evidence, xxii. 100. Thomas Furlong (1802–75), professor of rhetoric at Maynooth
(1834–45); professor of sacred scripture (1854); bishop of Ferns (1857); he was
one of the inopportunists at the Vatican Council. P. Corish, 'Gallicanism at
Maynooth: Archbishop Cullen and the Royal Visitation of 1853', in A. Cosgrove
and D. McCartney (eds.), *Studies in Irish History, presented to R. Dudley Edwards*
(1979), 176–89. A set of notebooks preserved in St John's College, Waterford,
shows that Gerald Molloy, professor of theology (1857–79), taught infallibility as
the better theological opinion. Phelan Notebooks, Waterford College Archive. I am
grateful to Dr Thomas Marsh for this reference.

was a key element in Ultramontanism and, apart from protests in sections of the French and German Churches, it was welcomed throughout most of the Catholic Church as providing support against the power of the state and making for more unity and efficiency. There were other Ultramontanes in Ireland before Cullen, one of the most influential of whom was Frederick Lucas, the convert editor of the *Tablet*. To be Ultramontane was to be progressive and in line with the leadership given by Rome. Cullen proved an enthusiastic and efficient promoter of Ultramontanism in Ireland. No doubt his Ultramontanism was more thoroughgoing than that of his fellow bishops and the small section of the laity interested in such matters, but he found the soil already prepared. Even without him, Ultramontanism would have come to Ireland as it came to the western Church in general.[19]

Ultramontanism led to a growth of Roman devotional practices and liturgy and Cullen is credited with spearheading a devotional revolution.[20] In a pioneering article Emmet Larkin claimed that:

Cullen not only reformed the Irish Church, but, what was perhaps even more important, in the process of reforming that church he spearheaded the consolidation of a devotional revolution. The great mass of the Irish people became practising Catholics, which they have uniquely and essentially remained both at home and abroad to the present day.[21]

Much of the continuing debate about pre-Famine devotional life centred around attendance at Sunday mass, since David Miller's deductions from the Report of the Commissioners of Public Instruction in 1834 indicated that in rural Ireland attendance was low, particularly in Irish-speaking areas.[22] In early decades of the nineteenth century, many of the devotions that marked twentieth-century Catholicism were either absent or less widespread. The cluster of beliefs and practices that constituted the religion of the

[19] J. F. Supple, 'Ultramontanism in Yorkshire, 1850–1900', *Recusant History*, 17 (1984–5), 274–86.

[20] The debate on Emmet Larkin's thesis of a Devotional Revolution in nineteenth-century Ireland is still proving fruitful after twenty years: D. Miller, S. Connolly, D. J. Keenan, and P. Corish have all contributed substantially. The best recent summary and critical evaluation is T. G. McGrath, 'The Tridentine Evolution of Modern Irish Catholicism, 1563–1962: A Re-examination of the "Devotional Revolution" Thesis', in R. O. Muirí (ed.), *Irish Church History Today*, Cumann Seanchais Ard Mhacha Seminar, 10 Mar. 1990 (1991), 84–99.

[21] E. Larkin, 'The Devotional Revolution in Ireland, 1850–1875', *American Historical Review*, 87 (1972), 625.

[22] D. W. Miller, 'Irish Catholicism and the Great Famine', *Journal of Social History*, 9/1 (1975), 81–98.

poorer peasants, in addition to such central Catholic devotions as the sacraments, the rosary, fasting, and daily prayers, also included devotions connected with patterns, pilgrimages, holy wells, wakes, and charms.[23] Many of these came under attack, as a reforming Church opposed them as either superstitious or providing the occasion for insobriety, immorality, or other abuses. The Famine dealt them a devastating blow, for it bore heaviest on the labouring and cottier classes. Thenceforth, religious practices became more 'orthodox' and the quickening pace at which this took place wrought a rapid change in Irish devotional life. If, however, this thesis of a devotional 'revolution' implies that previous to 1850 the Irish were 'non-practising Catholics, if indeed they were Catholic at all', one must enter a caveat.[24] The reasons for the low attendance at Sunday mass were many, and the extensive use of mass stations must be taken more into account. An indication of the Church's attitude on the matter may be deduced from the form which the bishop required the parish priest to fill in before episcopal visitation. The form, which detailed the essential information the bishop required, did not ask about Sunday mass, but whether the Paschal duty had been fulfilled. The energetic reforming Bishop Kinsella told Tocqueville: 'It is nearly unknown in the towns and still less in the country that a Catholic fails to make his Easter communion'; neither he nor Tocqueville mentioned Sunday mass.[25] Easter communion, rather than regular Sunday mass attendance with the difficulties that such attendance involved, was probably regarded as the criterion of a practising Catholic.

The visitation reports—available for the dioceses of Dublin and Cashel—and the bishops' reports to Rome, while revealing neglect in certain areas, indicate that the clergy were satisfied with Paschal practice.[26] The diaries of priests—O'Sullivan in Kerry and O'Carroll in Tipperary—also give a favourable impression of the people's

---

[23] S. J. Connolly, *Priests and People in Pre-Famine Ireland, 1780–1850* (1982), 74–218; id., *Religion and Society in Nineteenth-Century Ireland* (1985), 45–60.

[24] Larkin, 'Devotional Revolution', 651; D. A. Kerr, 'Under the Union Flag: The Catholic Church in Ireland, 1800–1870', in *Ireland after the Union* (1989), 37–9.

[25] A. de Tocqueville, *Journey in Ireland, July–August, 1835*, ed. E. Larkin (1990), 64.

[26] For an examination of some of those reports see Kerr, *Peel, Priests, and Politics* (1982), 45–7; id., 'Under the Union Flag', 37–9. Not untypically, the parish priest of Lattin, Co. Tipperary, reported that '[T]here are some who do not approach the Sacraments but they are so few I believe it is not necessary to take any notice of them.' James Hanley to Slattery, 6–7 Aug. 1846, Slattery Papers, CDA.

faith. O'Sullivan, who was deeply concerned at the proselytism in Kerry, complained that the faithful were poorly instructed, but did not fault their piety. O'Carroll often spent four or more hours hearing confessions in his parish, and during parts of the year went daily to a 'station' where mass was celebrated for all the people of the neighbourhood.[27] John Forrest, parish priest of Castlemartyr, County Cork, told Kirby that he regularly spent ten hours in the confessional.[28] In his many letters to Kirby, and to Propaganda, Cullen was critical of bishops and, occasionally, of priests, but did not complain of a lack of faith or devotion among the people, although he often commented on their miserable state. Father Ignatius, who preached extensively in Ireland, believed that the people were devout and saw his task as 'the banishment of three great vices—cursing, company-keeping, and intemperance—and the practice of daily meditation, with a frequent approach to the sacraments'.[29] The vices which the Redemptorist missioners tried to heal were local feuding, intemperance, wakes, and American wakes.[30] Tocqueville questioned two bishops closely on the virtues and faults of the people. Kinsella replied: 'These people have all the divine virtues. They have the faith. No one is a better Christian than the Irishman. Their morals are pure. Their crimes are rarely premeditated. But they lack the civil virtues. They are without foresight, without prudence.' Bishop Nolan told Tocqueville that they were gentle, polite, hospitable, and of pure morals. They could not, however, resist drinking to excess, and acts of violence were frequent.[31] Taking into account marked regional differences, the indications from the increasing, if still meagre, evidence is that both observers and pastors believed that the people were devout.[32] They were intemperate, however, and could be violent. They were not always well instructed; O'Sullivan's remarks on this were

---

[27] O'Carroll of Clonoulty mentions in his diary going to stations as often as four times a week. Diary, 7, 8, 9, 12, 13, 14, 15 Jan.; 8, 9, 10, 11, 12, 13 Mar. 1846, CDA. The stations survived Roman disapproval after 1850, for bishops argued successfully that they fulfilled a useful purpose.

[28] Forrest to Kirby, 5 June 1848, Kirby Papers, ICA, cited in P. O'Dwyer, 'John Francis Spratt, O. Carm., 1796–1871' (Ph.D. thesis, 1968), fo. 18. The ten hours were probably on Saturday.

[29] Pius a Spiritu Santo, *Life of Father Ignatius of St Paul, Passionist* (1866), 449–52, 464–8.

[30] R. Gallagher and B. McConvery (eds.), *History and Conscience: Studies in Honour of Seán O'Riordan, CSsR* (1989), 287–8. An American wake was a celebration on the eve of an exile's departure for America.

[31] Larkin (ed.), *Tocqueville*, 62–3, 41.   [32] Kerr, *Peel*, 44–51.

re-echoed over a decade later by the parish priest of Goleen, West Cork, who found that few of his parishioners 'can do more than say their beads'.[33] Here, too, regional differences were great; in much of Leinster, parts of Munster, and in the towns the situation was more favourable than elsewhere.

The key area of the inner faith or spiritual life of the community is difficult to assess, but devotions and practice constitute the outward expression of this life. Important developments in Catholic devotional life took place in the nineteenth century and at a quickening pace. Some devotions associated with Ultramontanism had been common in the cities and towns before 1850 and, even in the countryside, popular devotion to the Blessed Virgin, and particularly the family Rosary, was deep-rooted. Increasingly, Catholics absorbed Roman and continental devotions: retreats, missions, the Quarant'Ore, devotions to the Virgin. The French Church, too, whose influence was pervasive, shifted from the austere theocentric religion of the Age of Reason to a warmer Christocentric and Marian religion, with its emphasis on the mercy of Christ and the intercession of Mary and the saints. The most popular nineteenth-century French devotion was the cult of the Sacred Heart of Jesus, and soon a gaudy Italian lithograph of the Sacred Heart took an honoured place in every Irish Catholic home to become the stereotyped symbol of an Irish Catholic's religion.[34] The liturgy became increasingly Roman, but since the Irish Church had no developed liturgy of its own this romanization simply filled a void. The same was probably true of other forms of worship: Catholics were catching up with nineteenth-century devotions which were adapted to their more modern life style. It was a modernization willingly accepted rather than a forceful conversion to 'Ultramontanism', and went hand-in-hand with the abandonment of the Irish language. There was loss as well as gain in this modernization. Although popular religion had some practices which official religion regarded as bordering on the superstitious—holy wells, patterns—it also contained a rich and age-old oral tradition of prayers, religious poetry, and narrative.[35] Enshrined in the native Gaelic culture, this

---

[33] O'Dwyer, 'Spratt', fo. 21.

[34] *The Messenger of the Sacred Heart* was soon selling more copies than any other monthly in the country.

[35] P. Ó Fiannachta (ed.), *Léachtaí Cholm Cille VII: Ár nDúchas Creidimh* (1970); D. Ó Laoghaire, *Ár bPaidreacha Dúchais* (1975); E. de Waal, *A World Made Whole: Rediscovering the Celtic Tradition* (1991).

spiritual tradition suffered enormously from the Famine and slowly retreated in the face of the modernization of Ireland.

Among the main agents of the devotional change were the religious orders. To combat proselytism the synod of Thurles had urged missions in the parishes. The mission was one of the most successful methods devised by the counter-Reformation Church to awaken and deepen the faith of its followers, and it was widely employed as part of the Catholic revival of nineteenth-century Europe. The mission, similar in some ways to Evangelical revival meetings, lasted from four to eight weeks, during which the missioners preached on the Four Last Things, inviting the congregation to repent, fast, and receive the sacraments of Penance and Eucharist. Missions were new to Ireland. The first was given by the Congregation of the Mission, or Vincentian Fathers, at Athy, County Kildare, in 1842. Then in 1846 Pigot and O'Connell, alarmed at the success of proselytism in west Kerry, persuaded Bishop Egan to invite the Vincentians to preach a mission in Dingle to strengthen the faith of the people. Since more missions were needed, Cardinal Wiseman recommended setting up a house for Passionist and Redemptorist priests in Ireland. Before long Passionists and Rosminians from England and Italy, Oblates and Marists from France, and Redemptorists from Austria, the Netherlands, and Belgium came to Ireland. They included famous preachers and missioners: Luigi Gentili, Moses Furlong, the Oxford convert William Lockhart, Joseph Prost from Austria, and Vladimir Pecherin, a convert from Orthodoxy and ex-professor of Greek at Moscow University.[36] The missioners encountered initial opposition from some local parochial clergy, but by 1869 Cullen was able to tell the Powis Commission on national education that almost every parish in Ireland had experienced a mission.[37] They made a significant

[36] Wiseman to Cullen, 19 Oct. 1851, Cullen Papers, Section 39/2, File II, DDA; Anon., *Missions in Ireland: especially with reference to the Proselytizing Movement showing the marvellous Devotedness of the Irish to the Faith of their Fathers*, by one of the missioners (1855). J. Sharp, *Reapers of the Harvest: the Redemptorists in Great Britain and Ireland, 1843–1898* (1989). Pecherin was charged with burning a Protestant bible with consequent inflaming of passions. He was acquitted of the charge.

[37] J. H. Murphy, 'The Role of Vincentian Parish Missions in the "Irish Counter-Reformation" of the Mid-Nineteenth Century', *Irish Historical Studies*, 24 (1984), 152–71; M. Baily, 'The Parish Mission Apostolate of the Redemptorists in Ireland, 1851–1898', in R. Gallagher and B. McConvery (ed.), *History and Conscience* (1989), 274–96.

impact on the religious life of the people, and the devotional changes of the second half of the century owe much to them. The missioners brought practices associated with the towns, or in use by their mother houses on the continent, into every parish in the land. It was they who promoted Ultramontanism at a popular level. They weeded out what they saw as abuses, encouraged a frequent approach to the sacraments, and confirmed Catholics in their faith. They also won back many whom the zealous missioners of the Irish Church Society had gained for Protestantism.

Although the changes in Irish Catholicism bore some relation to the conflict between Ultramontanism and Gallicanism in France, the differences were probably greater. Gallicanism had no deep roots in Ireland and, on the contrary, the soil was well prepared for a more Roman and continental style of churchmanship. For Cullen, Ultramontanism was simply modern, progressive, and orthodox Catholicism. Accused of propagating it, he remarked humorously to Kirby:

The Catholics and Protestants here are strangely at a loss to know what Ultramontanism is. They think it is some horrid monster. Scully the MP for Cork, went down to Maynooth a short time ago and spent a whole day there getting himself instructed on the nature of Ultramontanism. What lessons he received I know not, but I think the people and all the real Catholics are Ultramontanes.[38]

His assessment was substantially accurate. Cullen simply took for granted that the Ultramontane Church he had grown up with in Rome was the ideal Church, and promoted it with untiring zeal. As always during its history, the Church needed not only updating but reforming. In post-Famine Ireland, the energy and single-mindedness of Cullen, using Ultramontanism to its fullest advantage, brought about more quickly reforms already commenced before the Famine. Other factors helped. The dominance of the tenant farmers (the class from which the clergy drew most support), the improving ratio of priests to people, and the influx of new religious orders to give missions and provide education all combined to give more control to the clergy, to strengthen the Church's institutions and to bring about a revived devotional life among the faithful.

The bitter struggle for souls was a conspicuous feature of Ireland

---

[38] Cullen to Kirby, 30 Nov. 1852, Kirby Papers, ICA.

in this period. In 1851 a mounting concern about proselytism is evident from the growing correspondence between the bishops on the subject. Both Catholics and Protestants now matched each other in their uncompromising approach to conversion or proselytism. Cullen is accused of being most responsible for the sharp sectarianism of the day, but it existed long before he returned to Ireland. The Second Reformation itself, which in the 1820s had launched the Protestant 'crusade', was no more than an important landmark in the history of religious antagonism. Cullen detested what he perceived as proselytism, but such repugnance was common to all Catholics. Earlier, Bishop Doyle of Kildare and Leighlin, normally fair-minded and ecumenical, became vitriolic in his denunciations of the missionary activities of the Second Reformation, and that pillar of moderation, Archbishop Murray, was one of many bishops to applaud him.[39] MacHale and his clergy harassed preachers and converts of the missionary societies. For Cullen, countering Protestant proselytism was a priority and his hatred of it is crucial to an understanding of his policy in his early years in Ireland. Behind all his campaigns for Catholic education or for reform of the clergy and bishops, behind his involvement in the Catholic Defence Association, lay this anxiety to protect the faith of Catholics from the inroads of Protestantism or infidelity.[40] O'Sullivan rightly accused him of causing Rome 'to charge all the Bishops and Priests of Munster with inactivity and indifference to Souperism and obliged them to hold a synod to meet the evil'.[41] Catholic detestation of what they perceived as proselytism was not new, but Cullen brought to the conflict a determined leadership. In his early years, Cullen was so inflexible in his attitude to Protestantism that in 1856 he expressed concern when he learned that the new bishop of Kerry, David Moriarty, had publicly subscribed to a Protestant orphan society.[42] It was only when the 1861 census

[39] T. G. McGrath, 'Politics, Interdenominational Relations and Education in the Public Ministry of James Doyle, O.S.A., Bishop of Kildare and Leighlin, 1819–1834', Ph.D. thesis, 1992, fos. 159–237; T. G. McGrath, 'Interdenominational Relations in Pre-famine Tipperary', in W. Nolan and T. G. McGrath (eds.), *Tipperary: History and Society; Inter-disciplinary Essays on the History of an Irish County* (1985), 257–85; D. Bowen, *The Protestant Crusade in Ireland, 1800–1870* (1978), 83–123, 310; S. J. Connolly, 'Mass Politics and Sectarian Conflict, 1823–30', in W. E. Vaughan (ed.), *A New History of Ireland* (1989), v. 77–84.

[40] McGrath, 'Doyle', fos. 203, 212–37.   [41] Diary, 10 Mar. 1854.

[42] Cullen to Kirby, 21 Aug. 1856, Kirby Papers, ICA.

made it clear that the Protestant crusade was far from achieving its aim of converting the population to Protestantism that the struggle between Protestants and Catholics began to subside. Politically Cullen was a nationalist and an erstwhile ardent O'Connellite. Yet, in the 1850s, he was pragmatically prepared to accept the *fait accompli* of the Union, and to work within it to further Catholicism in Ireland and throughout the English-speaking world. Cullen was certainly a formidable bishop. Single-minded and energetic, he commanded respect among the ablest of the Irish clergy, who valued his ability and his genuine reforming zeal. His courage and vigilance also generated fear. He had scorned the Ecclesiastical Titles Act, claiming that, instead of injuring the Catholics, it would only unite them, and he declared his readiness to go to prison for his defiance of it. He had welcomed Derby's government, maintaining that the open hostility of the Tories was preferable to the hidden hostility of Palmerston, Clarendon, and Russell. 'Here in Ireland', he told Smith, 'our efforts are directed to the establishment of a party that is neither Whig nor Tory but Catholic and Irish.'[43] Cullen took for granted the identification of Irish and Catholic.[44]

On the question of the Catholic University, Cullen's brain-child and a main source of division between the two bishops, time was to show that Murray was right: a full-blown Catholic university was not practicable.[45] In the state of Ireland, wracked by famine and drained by emigration, the scheme was illusory. When Newman came to organize it, Laurence Renehan and Charles Russell, president and vice-president of Maynooth College, and John Curtis, provincial superior of the Jesuits, were pessimistic about the chances of success.[46] The new institution had to depend on subscription for its support and compete with the well-endowed Queen's Colleges for students and many believed, as Curtis told Newman, that 'the class of youths *did not exist* in Ireland who would come to the University'.[47] The Catholic gentry and the Catholic Bar, most of whom were whig in outlook and dependent on the government

[43] Cullen to Smith, 13 May 1852, Smith Papers, StPA.
[44] J. H. Whyte, *The Independent Irish Party 1850–9* (1958), 82–93.
[45] Denvir to Cullen, 11 Jan. 1851; Browne to Cullen, 13 Jan. 1851; Blake to Cullen, 11 Jan. 1851, Cullen Papers, Section 39/2, File I, DDA.
[46] F. McGrath, *Newman's University: Idea and Reality* (1951), 251–2, 261–6.
[47] Newman's journal, 8 Feb. 1853, cited in McGrath, *Newman's University*, 251.

for patronage, shared this disbelief.[48] Furthermore, since it was started largely in reaction to the government scheme, the state refused to grant it a charter. With the exception of the Medical School it proved a costly failure. Murray proved to be the realist, Cullen the impractical dreamer.

One of Cullen's greatest assets was the high regard he enjoyed in Rome. In 1853 Richard Lyons, attaché to the British Legation at Florence, in a series of reports to the Foreign Office, revealed how highly he was valued and the reasons for it:

Archbishop Cullen appears to be highly esteemed here; his learning is much thought of; and his strong ultramontane and exclusive religious views are in themselves a strong recommendation to him, especially with the reigning Pope. The Archbishop is represented here as strongly disapproving the turbulent and factious conduct of many of the Irish . . . clergy and, although extremely uncompromising on religious points, still, is conscientiously desirous . . . to confine his Clergy, as much as possible to the peaceful discharge of their Ecclesiastical Duties.[49]

There was much truth in his assessment, as Cullen's future policies were to show. Cardinal Antonelli, the secretary of state, told Lyons that 'Dr Cullen, from his long residence here, was probably better acquainted with the principles and sentiments of the Holy See, and less influenced by local feelings than the generality of the Irish . . . Bishops'.[50] Soon Rome sought his views not merely on the Irish church but on the appointment of bishops throughout the empire. Cullen had many battles yet to fight, but he was on course to mould public attitudes and the policies of the Irish Church of the second half of the nineteenth century and beyond it. The future lay with him and his Ultramontanism. Although he mellowed with years and later expressed open admiration for Gladstone and his Irish policies, the younger Cullen was intransigent and intolerant of any opposition or lack of zeal for the Church as he had known it in Rome. The pastoral care Murray had lavished on the metropolitan diocese made it possible for him to build solidly for the

---

[48] M. J. Barry to Cullen, 23 Mar. 1850, Cullen Papers, Section 39/1, File VIII, DDA.

[49] Lyons to Scarlett, 27 Aug. 1853, PRO, FO 79/168 cited in M. Buschkühl, *Great Britain and the Holy See* (1982), 194. Richard Lyons (1817–87), appointed to Florence (1853); later secretary of the British Legation at Florence. Peter Scarlett (1804–81), secretary of the Legation at Florence (1844–55).

[50] Lyons to Scarlett, 15 Oct. 1853, PRO, FO 79/169.

future. The Dublin diocese was to retain Cullen's structure until well into the twentieth century.

The Irish record of Lord John Russell needs reviewing. History has not been kind to Russell. He had played a major role in bringing in the first Reform bill, yet Grey, as his senior, overshadowed him; he had hoped to close his career with the second Reform bill, but it fell to Derby and Disraeli to carry it. Russell's failure in Ireland was particularly tragic, for he was the first prime minister to make justice for Ireland central to his political programme. No prime minister with the same commitment to Irish reconciliation or with such a broad band of reform measures would come on the scene until Gladstone in 1868. Not all of Russell's initiatives were well advised or took sufficient account of the complex nature of Irish life, particularly its religious divisions, but, up to his fall from office in 1852, he placed Irish questions among his priorities. His ambition was the assimilation of Irish Catholics which, he was convinced, was in the highest interest of the peoples of both islands. For close on twenty years he preached 'justice for Ireland'. Even the scourge of famine, he hoped, could work out to advantage, for it would enable a sympathetic England to cement the bonds of the Union through its generosity to a starving Ireland. The achievement of 'a golden age for Ireland' was a main reason for wanting the premiership in 1846. His loosely worked-out plans envisaged a policy of even-handed enforcement of justice, concurrent endowment of the three religions, and the substitution of insolvent landowners, most of whom were Protestant, by merchants, most of whom would be Catholic. Finally, he would eliminate the last vestiges of difference between the two countries by abolishing the lord lieutenancy, and place Irishmen on the same level in every way with their English, Welsh, and Scottish fellow subjects. The time seemed ripe: Bessborough was committed to his policy, O'Connell was well disposed, and the Catholic clergy, whose conciliation formed an essential element in Russell's plan, would follow his lead. The possibilities for Ireland, as Russell told Bessborough, were never greater. A major step towards the final conciliation of the Catholic Irish was possible.

Administratively, Russell was able to achieve some improvements immediately. Catholics had received a greater share in patronage: Redington, Sheil, Monahan, Bellew, Pigot, and More O'Ferrall all received government offices, and the repeal magistrates were

restored to office. Clarendon could boast to Sir George Grey in
1851 that Catholics had received half the important positions in
the Irish administration, something unheard of since the seventeenth century.[51] Although he cut the relief expenditure, Russell
showed himself more sympathetic of famine victims than his cabinet or civil servants and was outraged by the evictions. He tried
to be even-handed in his approach to Irish problems and accepted
coercive measures only as a last resort, insisting, with limited success, that they be accompanied by positive conciliatory measures.
In the spring of 1848 he warned a sorely-tempted Clarendon not
to pack the jury, and was unwilling to have the Young Ireland
leaders executed. His Encumbered Estates Act achieved some good,
for it eliminated the weaker landlord.

Yet by the time he left office in 1852 little of the substantial
programme he had dreamed about had been achieved. His six-
year administration had seen a million or more Irish people die of
famine or famine-related disease, while his government appeared
unable, or unwilling, to put the finance and effort into relief that
would have saved hundreds of thousands of lives.[52] Another
million fled the country. Helplessly, he had watched evictions grow
to proportions never equalled. A pathetic rebellion had broken
out, the first for 45 years, and if Russell did not behave vindic-
tively towards the leaders, his government, which had so indignantly denounced the jury-packing in the trial of O'Connell in
1844, had descended to similar practices in 1848. His great plan
of endowing the Church of the majority collapsed. The Queen's
Colleges failed to win the support of the Catholic Church which
was necessary for their success. Despite Russell's joy at coming to
power on an Irish issue, and his conviction that the regeneration
of Ireland was reserved for him, his ambitious plans for perman-
ently reconciling the two islands came to nought. After 1848 most,
though not all, Irish Catholics were resigned to membership of the
United Kingdom, but the collapse of the Repeal movement was
the result of O'Connell's death and the Famine and not of Russell's
policies of conciliation. By 1852 Irish Catholics, the reconciliation
of whom was at the heart of Russell's reforms, were more united
in their hostility to the government than at any period since 1829.

[51] Clarendon to Grey, 17 Feb. 1851, Clarendon Papers, Letterbook 6.
[52] Estimates of 'excess mortality' vary. See J. S. Donnelly, 'Excess Mortality and
Emigration', in Vaughan, *New History*, v. 350–2.

A Catholic Defence Association had been set up and, together with a Tenant Right League, was beginning to exercise power in parliament. In England, serious rioting took place between Irish Catholics and English Protestants in Stockport. In parliament, after stormy sectarian debates, a commission was set up to investigate the alleged disloyalty of Maynooth College. Catholic Ireland had not been assimilated.

A satisfactory explanation of Russell's failure involves many elements. The deaths, early in his administration, of O'Connell and Bessborough deprived him of allies who knew the Irish scene well. The ever-present Famine cast its shadow over all areas of Irish life, darkening and distorting it. Apart from soaking up money, time, and energy that could have been spent on the more lasting reforms that Russell hoped to effect, it brought mass deaths and emigration and then led to a chain reaction of rural unrest, evictions, assassinations, recriminations, and, finally, rebellion. These events, perceived differently in England and Ireland, deepened the alienation between English public opinion and Irish Catholics.

Russell's precarious position in parliament was not unconnected with this hostility. He became prime minister without an effective majority, and in the elections of 1847 the ultra-Protestants, enraged by Peel's Maynooth Grant of 1845, secured the election of many of their supporters. In the new parliament ultra-Protestants and Voluntarists were hostile to any endowment of the Catholic Church and radicals were opposed to bailing out Irish landlords. Together they limited Russell's freedom of action on Irish questions. Peel's tragic death in July 1850 further weakened the parliamentary support Russell needed for his Irish reforms.

Difficulties in Britain were compounded by difficulties in Ireland from the bishops, particularly MacHale, Slattery, and Cullen. MacHale, who had a difficult temperament, opposed anything that threatened what he saw as the cultural and religious identity of the people. With Slattery and Cullen he feared that state education would erode the values of Irish Catholics, and particularly their faith. Most bishops feared government influence in the affairs of the Church and the loss of popular confidence in the clergy which endowment would bring. Their distrust was the normal wariness of a Catholic Church dealing with a Protestant government in the wake of centuries of confrontation, which had been renewed by allegations of clerical connivance at assassination, and by Minto's negotiations in Rome. The Ecclesiastical Titles Act destroyed what trust remained. To make matters worse, increased Protestant missionary activity frightened and angered the bishops. Personal problems complicated Russell's difficult ministry. Already by 1848 Greville, noting that Russell was a great failure, had told Clarendon that his own ill-health, and that of his wife, had not helped.[53] According to Russell's grandson, Bertrand Russell, the domination of his second wife 'made him vacillating, with unfortunate political results'.[54]

Russell's major failing, however, was one of government. Clarendon was right to be grieved 'beyond expression to see that Lord John ... [was] ... not master in his own Cabinet', for if Russell was weak in parliament, his weakness in cabinet was more damaging. John Prest points out that his shyness and stiffness told against him, that he scorned the arts by which a leader wins the affections of a party, and that he lacked the authority to dominate a cabinet. His choice of ministers, many of whom were Irish landowners, was partly to blame, for very few of them supported his Irish policy, particularly when it involved expense. Russell could not control his own cabinet; if he wished to escape from the shadow of Palmerston he had to rely on Lansdowne, who was also an Irish landowner. Wood, briefed by Trevelyan, wanted to spend as little as possible on Ireland, and Russell allowed his policy wide scope. The failure to cope adequately with the Famine and its baneful consequences eroded Russell's image as the champion of 'justice for Ireland'. Faced with opposition both from within in the cabinet and from without in parliamentary and public opinion, Russell hesitated where, perhaps, a Gladstone might have soldiered on. Vacillation was the characteristic weakness of the administration. After his failure to go ahead with the endowment plan, his reluctance to take on opposition in cabinet and parliament meant that he had nothing substantial to offer Ireland. He lost credibility all round.

The final blow to Russell's Irish policies, however, was largely of his own making when, for once, he identified himself with the prejudices of the press and of public opinion in the 'no-popery' cry of 1850. The Durham letter, with its description of the religious rites of the people he was trying to reconcile as 'the mummeries

---

[53] Greville to Clarendon, 23 Jan. 1848, Clarendon Papers, c. 521.
[54] J. Prest, *Lord John Russell* (1972), pp. xvi, 181–2.

of superstition', and their doctrines as 'enslaving the mind', made his position difficult. With three months to rethink the matter, he introduced a bill which was penal in its effects on the Irish Church and damaged irretrievably his relations with Irish Catholics. His hard-hitting speech introducing the bill brought the Irish dimension, which had been absent, to the centre-stage. It was a key mistake. It distressed the government's great supporter among the bishops, Archbishop Murray, and caused him to come out sharply against it and to turn to Graham and Aberdeen for support. As Gladstone and Bright commented, Russell had united all Catholics against him, moderates and Ultramontanes, Liberals and nationalists, opponents and supporters of the colleges, English and Irish alike. The temporary defeat of his government in February 1851, its permanent weakening following that crisis and its final defeat in February 1852, were largely due to the Ecclesiastical Titles Act. It prevented a much-needed alliance with the Peelite leaders and robbed him of Irish support on which he had been able to count ever since the Lichfield House compact. Irish Catholic leaders were willing to welcome back 'Scorpion Stanley', as nationalists called Lord Derby, whose unconcealed dislike for Ireland they preferred to the betrayal of 'False Little John'.

In attempting to understand Russell's action, his religious outlook must be taken into account. His sense of justice and his Foxite tradition made him strive to gain fair treatment for Irish Catholics, but he remained devoutly Protestant and as intensely anti-Roman as many nineteenth-century statesmen and his own seventeenth-century ancestors, whose stance he emulated. The sympathy which he felt for a downtrodden people and his espousal of religious freedom clashed with his fear of Catholic, and particularly priestly, pretensions to power, which he thought he detected in Wiseman's pastoral and in the anathemas of Thurles. O'Connell was right when he spoke of Russell's conscientious abhorrence of popery, particularly of Irish popery.[55] This dislike, which extended to Tractarianism, comes through in his diary in 1833 and is still evident in his *Recollections and Suggestions* of 1875, where he speaks disparagingly of the Roman Church's 'preposterous pretensions and its ultramontane doctrines' and denounces its 'sensual or symbolical

---

[55] O'Connell to Buller, n.d. [Jan. 1844], cited in S. Walpole, *The Life of Lord John Russell* (1889), i. 385–6.

worship' as 'a shocking profanation'.[56] Russell's problem was how to give Catholics equal status and, at the same time, resist the power and pretensions of popery as he saw it. In the Hampden affair, the Durham letter, and his speech introducing the Ecclesiastical Titles Bill, his animosity to their religion surfaced and dismayed Catholic bishops.

Clarendon's Irish career proved just as disappointing. Like Russell, he was genuinely interested in Irish reforms and hoped for the eventual assimilation of Irish Catholics into the United Kingdom. On the important issue of the land, he had tried to obtain a fair Landlord and Tenant bill and had worked to improve the Encumbered Estates Act. Within some months of arriving in Ireland, learning of the horrors of the Famine, he had reversed his earlier *laissez-faire* stance and pleaded incessantly for more generous relief. Like Russell, he was anxious to work in harmony with the Irish bishops and made a promising start in his contacts with Murray, MacHale, and Nicholson. The Mahon affair and its repercussions, particularly the denunciations of the clergy in the press and in parliament together with Propaganda's reproach to the Irish clergy in January 1848, destroyed that initiative.

Yet at the risk of alienating powerful interests he insisted on justice in the Dolly's Brae affair. On the colleges question he had been genuinely committed to finding a compromise solution that would satisfy the bishops. The lead up to the 1848 rebellion was a frightening episode for Clarendon and may well have been a turning-point in his attitude to Irish affairs, for he felt let down in England and in Ireland. Russell refused his plea for a Coercion bill as long as he could; Irish priests, alienated by famine mismanagement and parliamentary denunciations, appeared ready to bless the revolution. As he grappled with sedition, there was little support forthcoming, except that of an embarrassing kind, from Orangemen. In May 1848 Clarendon told Cornewall Lewis: 'the Catholics almost to a man, I grieve to say, have behaved like cowards and traitors and it is clear that in any real danger we have only the Protestants to rely upon. However this must not be said.'[57] This charge is no doubt an exaggeration, but it was at this point that Greville detected a change in his attitude:

---

[56] J. Russell, *Recollections and Suggestions, 1813–73* (1875), 267, 345–56, 375–9, 263.

[57] Clarendon to Lewis, 8 May 1848, Clarendon Papers, c. 532/1.

Lord Barrington asked me if it was true that . . . he [Clarendon] was now convinced Ireland could only be governed in connection with and by the support of the Orangemen. I told him there was . . . much exaggeration in this, but some truth.[58]

His decisive action quashed the rebellion and left the way open for Russell's great plan. Although Clarendon was initially in favour of the main element in the plan—the payment of the clergy —when the scheme came up he appears to have given it less than full support. His own solution to the Irish problem was quite thorough-going: emigration, or 'depletion' as he called it, and colonization. 'I would sweep Connacht clean', he confided to Reeve, 'and turn in upon it new men and English money just as one would to Australia or any freshly discovered Colony—the nearer one can get to that the more probable will be the solution of the "Irish Problem".'[59] Whether this radical solution of the 'Irish problem' pleased Reeve is uncertain, but for Clarendon, the chief governor of the country, to say that he would sweep clean the province of Connacht—which had some two million inhabitants —was remarkable.

After Cullen's arrival, Clarendon's criticism switched to the faults of the Roman religion. The synod of Thurles sharpened his dislike of what he saw as fanaticism; the bishops at Thurles were 'mummers', Cullen 'the devil incarnate', Catholic laity 'supine'. On papal aggression Clarendon's role was ambivalent. On the one hand, he deplored the awkward position in which Russell's Durham letter had placed him in relation to Irish Catholics, especially supporters such as Redington and Murray. On the other, he fuelled Russell's anti-Catholicism as he berated 'Rome's daring attempt to establish the Roman Catholic yoke in Ireland'. When the Ecclesiastical Titles Bill was passing through parliament, Greville remarked that it was 'not a little remarkable what a strong anti-Papist Clarendon is. He writes to me in that sense, but not so vehemently as he does to others.'[60] The baseness of Catholicism now became a constant theme in his letters. On more than one occasion, he told Fr. Ignatius, who had been with him at Cambridge, that he would shed the last

---

[58] C. C. F. Greville, *The Greville Memoirs: A Journal of the Reign of Queen Victoria*, ed. H. Reeve (1903), 18 June 1848, vi. 79–80.

[59] Clarendon to Reeve, 21 Aug. 1848, Clarendon Papers, c. 534.

[60] Greville, *Memoirs*, 26 Nov. 1850, vi. 380.

drop of his blood to prevent its progress.[61] After one of his outbursts against Catholicism, Greville retorted sharply:

> I dare say the character you give of the Roman Catholic religion is quite
> correct, but what then? The logical conclusion from such premises would
> be that such a religion ought to be exterminated, and if Cromwell had
> ruled Ireland long enough to rid Ireland of popery, it would have been
> a fortunate thing. But, as it is, one third of the people of these islands are
> Roman Catholics.[62]

Clarendon complained that the pope had not followed the system of canonical election but had directly appointed Cullen. Greville
smartly turned the criticism on its head, pointing out that it was
this system of canonical election that the pope was being faulted
for introducing into England.[63] Greville was right, but he did not
succeed in mollifying Clarendon. Even after he left Ireland, Clarendon remained bitter. The sting of disappointment at the difficulties
he had encountered and the failure of his plans, particularly the
last battle with Cullen over the colleges, remained. Some months
later he commented with savage sarcasm:

> I dont know of anything even in Ireland, which is saying a great deal, so
> audacious and iniquitous as the opposition made to these Colleges simply
> because the Romans were not allowed to have the management of the
> funds and to make a lay Maynooth *à l'instar* of the clerical College which
> has answered so well for the training of peasants into illiterate, bigoted,
> disloyal priests.[64]

Given Clarendon's own violent criticism of the colleges as Graham's foolish experiment, this comment is surprising; it is equally
so given his sympathetic accounts in 1847 of both the priests and
Maynooth College. Many priests were, indeed, either hostile to
England or ambivalent in their attitude and felt so threatened by
proselytism as to view Protestantism with sharply increasing
hostility. Clarendon's picture of them, however, as a bigoted,
disloyal, illiterate, peasant priesthood was overdrawn. It is more
of a commentary on Clarendon than on the Roman clergy. His
mind was inflamed against Ireland, which, as Greville remarked,

---

[61] Pius a Spiritu Santo, *Father Ignatius*, 407.
[62] Greville to Clarendon, 19 Dec. 1850, Clarendon Papers, c. 522.
[63] Ibid.   [64] Clarendon to Reeve, 20 Oct. 1852, ibid., c. 534.

'is odd in so practical a man'.[65] Some fickleness of character may be to blame, but the main explanation probably lies in his disappointment at his lack of success as lord lieutenant. His had been a most difficult viceroyalty. In 1850 he drew up a list of what he called some of the 'unusual difficulties' he had encountered: agrarian outrage, landlord shooting, revolution, state trials, the queen's visit, Orangemen.[66] To this list, he added the great tragedy that cast its black shadow over all the government's efforts: 'famine, destitution, and discontent ... augmented every difficulty of my position since the hour I arrived'.[67] He did not exaggerate the enormous difficulties he faced. Further trials in the shape of Cullen, the synod of Thurles, the Ecclesiastical Titles Bill, and the Birch scandal awaited him.

Some blame for his failure attached to himself. His approach was that of a well-meaning nineteenth-century Liberal who failed to grasp the complexities of the Irish situation. He was an alarmist, and his constant appeals for coercive powers rattled and unnerved Russell, and left him less room to propose positive measures. He tucked himself away in Dublin Castle or the viceregal lodge, often in dread of immediate and bloody insurrection. His work habits—he often did not rise until after midday—did not help. He attributed unworthy motives to all who took a different line from him, and this propensity to disparage the people he came to govern as 'lying, blustering, dishonest' inhibited him from understanding them.[68] Given Clarendon's position as the head of the Irish administration it would have been wiser for him if his outlook had been less contemptuous. Colleagues believed that he was an inveterate intriguer and he certainly was manipulative in his use of the press.[69] The revelation of his relationship with Birch damaged his standing as lord lieutenant. When he left Ireland a few weeks later not only was he thoroughly disillusioned but he was distrusted by Orangemen and Nationalists, Protestants and Catholics.

It is difficult not to feel that older underlying factors were also at work in the failure of both Russell and Clarendon. Distrust had long existed between England and the Irish Catholics. If Russell

[65] Greville, *Memoirs*, 26 Nov. 1850, vi. 380.
[66] Clarendon to Russell, 20 Mar. 1850, Clarendon Papers, Box 80.
[67] Ibid.   [68] Clarendon to Reeve, 21 Aug. 1848, ibid., c. 534.
[69] K. Bourne, *Palmerston: The Early Years, 1784–1841* (1982), 473–4.

had a fundamental, ancestral dislike of 'popery' in all its shapes and Clarendon was willing, as he assured Fr. Ignatius, to shed his blood to prevent the success of Catholic religion, many Irish Catholics harboured an old antagonism towards England which nurtured exaggerated suspicions. A few months after leaving Ireland that sympathetic and perceptive observer, Newman, reflecting on his Irish experience, wrote: 'one sentiment of hatred against the oppressor "manet alta mente repostum". The wrongs which England has inflicted are faithfully remembered; her services are viewed with incredulity or resentment.'[70]

For a moment of history British public opinion had been profoundly moved by the horrendous suffering of famine-stricken Ireland, and a wave of sympathy swept the country. This sympathy could well have proved the occasion for creating a true union between the two countries. It was not to be. Peel had been the Joseph who warded off the worst effects of the first year of the Famine, but it is doubtful whether Peel or Russell could have prevented Black '47. By the end of 1847 what trust had grown up between the two countries was fast disappearing. The denunciations of the priests as instigators of agrarian murders shocked Irish Catholics, many of whom, moreover, were beginning to see government incompetence or callousness as the cause of the appalling death-toll. The bishops interpreted those attacks and British moves in Rome, as an attempt to manipulate their Church. From England, however, events in Ireland were perceived differently. In language that was almost emotional, Clarendon put the case as seen from the other side of Saint George's channel:

I know of nothing . . . comparable to the demonstration in favour of Ireland by England two years ago. It was not the enormous amount of money subscribed, but the spirit of brotherly love and true human kindness, with which it was given. From the Queen down to the private soldier and the lowest and most suffering operative, every class contributed cheerfully and unsolicited—it was felt to be a labour of love . . . why is all this love turned into bitterness . . . ? The manner in which it has been received, . . . and the attempts to shake off English rule. . . . The great body of the Catholic clergy promoting all this . . .[71]

[70] *Rambler*, May 1859, repr. in J. H. Newman, *Historical Sketches* (1872; repr. 1970), 257–60.
[71] Clarendon to Monteagle, 20 Feb. 1849, Monteagle Papers, NLI.

A frustrated Clarendon was making a case for his own bitterness and attempting to explain to Monteagle, who was critical of government efforts, why the government had no new initiative in 1849. His criticism of the misuse to which relief aid had been put and the curses it had provoked was unsubstantiated. The claim that 'the great body' of the clergy promoted rebellion was exaggerated. Yet Clarendon represented accurately enough British exasperation with Irish affairs. Russell, faced with all-round reluctance to give money for Irish measures, had come to a similar conclusion a few months earlier. *Punch* in its pitiless cartoons and *The Times* in its biting editorials made the same point. Relations between the British ruling class and Irish Catholics were back on the traditional track of mutual hostility.

Towards the end of the famine period, the sharp rise in religious tension made the situation more difficult. The Evangelical missions, the dubious methods of a minority of missioners, and their loudly trumpeted successes generated alarm and antagonism. As if on cue, Paul Cullen, the unrelenting adversary of any compromise in religious matters, took over as leader of uncompromising Catholicism. The Ecclesiastical Titles Act electrified an already highly charged religious atmosphere.

The effects of this Act were felt in Ireland for some considerable time. It sharpened the hostility of Irish Catholics not merely towards Protestantism, but towards the British connection. The ill-feeling was by no means confined to the clergy, for the laity also took offence at the abuse of their religion in press and parliament and at what they believed would be the effects of the Act. Sixteen years after its passage, the able and well-informed David Moriarty, bishop of Kerry and the most convinced unionist on the bench, told a select committee on ecclesiastical titles that 'it is one of the good effects of that evil [the Ecclesiastical Titles Act] that our authority is increased . . . by the antagonism which exists between the people and the Government'. While expressing his deep regret for this antagonism, he made the remarkable assertion, that 'we [the bishops] can state with the greatest possible certainty that if the Emperor of Russia, or the Emperor of China, or the Grand Turk, made a successful occupation of Ireland tomorrow, the great mass of the lower orders would joyfully transfer their allegiance to either of those worthies'. When an astonished member of the committee questioned him as to whether he did really think so, Moriarty replied 'I am certain of it.'[72]

Sir Colman O'Loghlen, judge-advocate-general, maintained that the Act materially affected subsequent elections: John Fitzpatrick and Richard Bellew, members for Cork and Louth respectively, both lost their seats. Redington tried two or three constituencies, only to be defeated. When the general election came in the summer of 1852, the religious dimension was more to the fore than ever before and the clergy were prominent at the elections. The combination of this religious motive with the tenants' rights issue gave a striking electoral success to the recently established Independent Irish Party, which returned with a pledged membership of forty-two in the new parliament.[73] The 1852 election marked the zenith of the political influence of the clergy.[74]

The Famine cast a longer shadow. The attitude to what was gradually, but in the end widely, perceived as the government's failure to relieve the people effectively was to prove significant for the future. During the disaster Hughes, MacHale, Slattery, and Cullen, and some other exasperated clergy, had blamed the appallingly high level of famine deaths on the government's bungling or indifference. This cry was muted during the crisis and scarcely raised in its immediate aftermath. Many in Ireland blotted out the Famine as something best forgotten. By 1860, however, Mitchel had given it the sharp and bitter note that found a resonance among Irish exiles abroad and many Irish nationalists at home: 'The Almighty, indeed, sent the potato blight, but the English created the Famine.' Jaundiced though his interpretation was, such a perception of the Famine and its repercussions was to have a far-reaching impact on relations between Britain and Irish Catholics throughout the English-speaking world.

This was an age when the majority of people in Britain and

---

[72] *Report of the Select Committee of the House of Lords on Ecclesiastical Titles in Great Britain and Ireland, together with the Proceedings of the Committee, Minutes of Evidence and Appendix, PP 1867–8,* viii. 281, 76–7. David Moriarty (1814–77). Moriarty spoke in the aftermath of the Fenian outbreak during which he had taken a strong anti-Fenian stand, warning the organizers from the pulpit that 'Hell is not hot enough, nor eternity long enough' to punish them. Nationalists neither forgot nor forgave his remarks.

[73] R. V. Comerford, 'Churchmen, Tenants, and Independent Opposition, 1850–56', in W. E. Vaughan (ed.), *New History,* v. 405.

[74] Whyte, *Independent Irish Party,* 81.

Ireland were passionately concerned about religion which, in 1851, ranked far higher in the public mind than any other subject until the Great Exhibition provided a distraction.[75] Yet, despite the concentration on disputes over titles and liturgies, papal bulls and penal laws, more important problems were emerging in England for the Established Church and Christians in general. German rationalist scholarship and Darwinian evolutionism were beginning to present challenges which appeared to threaten the basis of Christian revelation. Charles J. Blomfield, bishop of London, in his charge on 2 November 1850 condemning the papal aggression, perceptively remarked 'we have more to apprehend from the theology of Germany than from that of Rome'.[76] The year the Ecclesiastical Titles Bill was passed, the first complete religious census was taken in England, and had unmistakable messages for all Christian denominations. As Protestant and Catholic Churches vied for the souls of the Irish migrants in London's east end, the dechristianizing effects of urbanization were becoming painfully obvious.

In Ireland, however, a process of evangelization was taking place as both Protestants and Catholics devoted time and resources to missionary endeavour. More priests, brothers, and nuns became available for evangelization, and devotional practice increased. Paradoxically, in this post-Famine, or mid-Victorian, era nationalist Ireland accepted more readily the permanence of the Union. The Famine had affected its self-confidence and appeared to show that self-government, which most now thought impossible to achieve, would not solve the country's social and economic problems. The 1848 rebellion, born of frustration at the Famine, had, indeed, left a hankering among a minority for independence which European national movements would encourage. Emigrants would often look back in anger to what they came to regard as their enforced expulsion from their native land. But both Young Irelanders and emigrants were, as yet, on the fringes of the political scene. If most Irish Catholics accepted the Union their attitude was a pragmatic acceptance of the political reality; few embraced it enthusiastically. Cullen, and most churchmen too, accepted that self-government was not feasible nor, perhaps, desirable. Nevertheless, as R. V.

[75] A. Briggs, *1851* (1951), 9–13.
[76] A *Charge Delivered to the Clergy of London* (1850).

Comerford has perceptively remarked, 'a "nationalist" Catholic identity was the largest political fact of Irish political life in the mid-nineteenth century'.[77] This identity persisted whether or not self-government was the aim. Within the United Kingdom, Irish Catholics had their own separate agenda. Religion's role was central to this refusal to identify fully with England. The decay of Irish culture, especially the language, had accelerated under the hammer blows of famine and emigration, but religion remained their essential badge of identity. Irish Catholics still felt themselves different from other subjects of the queen, and at the heart of that difference lay their attachment to the Catholic religion. As Irish Catholics they still nourished the grievance of inequality in a land which they regarded as their own and where they constituted the overwhelming majority. The presence of a privileged minority church, a wealthy Protestant landowning class, and a Protestant government all nourished their sense of a separate and different identity. For many, reaction to the Protestant missions sharpened the sense of separateness from England and nourished the identity of 'Catholic' and 'Irishness'. Within ten years of the 1848 rebellion, John Blake Dillon, the leading Young Irelander in Ireland and co-founder with Davis and Duffy of the *Nation*, could declare publicly: 'I, an Irish nationalist, know, and the enemies of Irish nationality also know it, that the cause of the Irish Catholic Church and the cause of the Irish Catholic people are one and indivisible.'[78] No permanent peace had been achieved, as Russell hoped, between Catholics and Protestants, and the quarrel over proselytism spilled into demands for inquiries into Maynooth College and Catholic convents. To those domestic issues was added, before long, conflict over the temporal power of the pope.

The energetic and reforming Cullen pressed for the disestablishment of the Anglican Church, accepting as its price the abolition of endowment for all religions. To achieve it he was prepared to ally himself with the Liberal party in which Russell, as well as Gladstone, was a leading member. In his early years in Ireland Cullen was angered by Murray's co-operation with government and contemptuous of his attendance at the viceregal levées. Now he found himself co-operating with the Liberal government and

---

[77] R. V. Comerford, *The Fenians in Context: Irish Politics and Society 1848–82* (1985), 31.
[78] Cited in B. O'Cathaoir, *John Blake Dillon, Young Irelander* (1990), 151.

exulting in the precedence accorded him as cardinal at the lord lieutenant's dinner to honour the Prince of Wales in 1868. 'How things have changed', he wrote to Kirby.[79] The times had certainly changed, and Cullen had changed with them. Disraeli, mindful of Liberal support for the overthrow of the temporal power of the pope, commented sardonically:

I understand that he [Cardinal Cullen] is a distinguished member of the Liberal party. Whether His Eminence is of opinion that the progress of Liberal opinions under his powerful influence has operated generally in favour of the fortunes of the Holy Father, is a question which I will not ask; but which I think Cardinal Cullen, in his solitude must sometimes have asked himself.[80]

Over a period of twenty years Cullen, who, fearful of revolutionaries, accepted the political *status quo* of the Union and yet remained nationalist in outlook, pursued a policy of demanding equal status for the Irish Catholics rather than concessions. In the Liberal party, Gladstone, in many ways the authentic successor to both Peel and Russell, was to try again to achieve what they had attempted in vain. Dependent, however, on the voluntarists in England, he favoured levelling down rather than levelling up the religions of Ireland. When proposing disestablishment in 1869, Gladstone told the House of Commons:

while we are altering this particular provision of the Act of Union, we are confirming its general purport and substance, and labouring, to the best of our humble ability, to give it those roots which unfortunately it has never yet adequately struck in the heart and affections of the people.[81]

To give the Union roots in the hearts and affections of the people had been the underlying issue in the 1840s, for it was the Union itself that was on trial in the administrations of both Peel and Russell even if they did not express it in such explicit terms. Neither of them managed to carry through policies which would bring Irish Catholics to a whole-hearted acceptance of the Union. For Peel it was the backlash of the Tory party that unnerved him. Russell's more ambitious programme was overshadowed by the Famine and, faced with a reluctant treasury, a recalcitrant cabinet,

[79] Cullen to Kirby, 18 Apr. 1868, Kirby Papers, ICA.
[80] *Hansard*, cxc. 1776, 16 Mar. 1868.
[81] *Hansard*, cxciv. 412, 1 Mar. 1869.

a precarious parliamentary majority, and hostile public opinion, his leadership faltered, and in the no-popery uproar he rashly antagonized his Irish allies. Yet the importance of his contribution, often overlooked, cannot be denied. He had played a major part in putting 'justice for Ireland' on the agenda of politicians and parties, and had striven for that equality of religions which Cullen and Gladstone hoped to achieve in the Disestablishment Act of 1870. Even then he argued for Catholic endowment. Although Gladstone could not accept this concurrent endowment of both Churches, he paid him a well-earned tribute, assuring him that the Disestablishment Act was 'really founded upon principles of which you were the expositor long ago'.[82]

It would be ironic, however, if Cullen and Gladstone, two deeply religious Christian leaders, found that only by following a secular path could they achieve an even-handed treatment for Irish Catholics that would be acceptable throughout a United Kingdom where religion still remained important. Through their co-operation, the establishment of the Anglican Church in Ireland, which many had long condemned as the weakest link in the Union, would be removed. Whether this radical move would win over Irish Catholics to a full acceptance of the Union was another question.

---

[82] Gladstone to Russell, 24 Mar. 1870, BL, Add. MSS 44538, fos. 217–20, cited in Prest, *Russell*, 419.

Bibliography

A. MANUSCRIPT COLLECTIONS

I. IRELAND

CAVAN

Kilmore Diocesan Archives

Browne Papers:

Papers of James Browne (1786–1866), bishop of Kilmore.

DUBLIN

Dublin Diocesan Archives

Cullen Papers:

Papers of Cardinal Paul Cullen (1803–78), archbishop of Dublin. The papers in these archives deal almost exclusively with the period after 1852.

Hamilton Papers:

Papers of John Hamilton (*c*.1800–62), archdeacon of Dublin.

Maynooth College File:

Documents for the years 1796–1849.

Meetings of the Irish Bishops 1826–49:

A handwritten volume containing a record of the meetings and the resolutions of the bishops.

Murray Papers:

Correspondence etc. of Daniel Murray (1768–1852), archbishop of Dublin.

Nicholson Papers:

Correspondence of Francis Nicholson (1803–55), coadjutor bishop of Corfu.

National Library of Ireland

Monteagle Papers:

Correspondence and papers of Thomas Spring Rice, 1st Baron Monteagle (1790–1866).

Society of Saint Vincent de Paul, Cabra Road

Returns of the Society of Saint Vincent de Paul.

Royal Irish Academy

Halliday Pamphlets:

Pamphlets relating to Ireland.

KILLARNEY, CO. KERRY

Kerry Diocesan Archives

Diary of John O'Sullivan, parish priest of Kenmare (1839–74). Consulted on copy of text as established by Revd James Hanley and Revd John McKenna, made available to me by Dr Kieran O'Shea.

MAYNOOTH, CO. KILDARE

Archives of St Patrick's College, Maynooth

Journal of the Board of Trustees

Renehan Papers:

Correspondence etc. of Dr Laurence Renehan (1797–1857), president of Maynooth College, 1845–57.

MONAGHAN, CO. MONAGHAN

Clogher Diocesan Archives

McNally Papers:

Correspondence etc. of Dr Charles McNally (1787–1864), bishop of Clogher.

THURLES, CO. TIPPERARY

Cashel Diocesan Archives

Leahy Papers:

Correspondence etc. of Patrick Leahy (1806–75), archbishop of Cashel, 1857–75.

Slattery Papers:

Correspondence etc. of Dr Michael Slattery (1783–1857), archbishop of Cashel, 1834–57.

The papers of Leahy and Slattery were consulted on microfilm. Stencilled calendars, drawn up by Dr Mark Tierney, provided a comprehensive guide.

Diary of Thomas O'Carroll (1810–65) curate in Clonoulty, County Tipperary, 1846–52. Consulted on xerox supplied by Dr Mark Tierney.

II. ENGLAND

DURHAM

University of Durham, Department of Palaeography and Diplomatic
Earl Grey Papers:
Papers of Henry Grey, 3rd earl Grey (1802–94).

LEEDS

Leeds Diocesan Archives

Briggs Papers:
Papers of John Briggs (1788–1861), vicar apostolic of the Northern district
(1836–40), vicar apostolic of the Yorkshire district (1840–50), bishop of
Beverley (1850–61).

LONDON

British Library, Additional Manuscripts

Broughton Papers:
Correspondence of John Cam Hobhouse, Baron Broughton (1786–1869).

Public Record Office

Russell Papers:
Correspondence of Lord John Russell, 1st Earl Russell (1792–1878).
Home Office Papers

University of London

Brougham Papers:
Correspondence of Henry Brougham, 1st Baron Brougham and Vaux
(1778–1868).

NETHERBY (Cumberland)

Graham Papers:
Papers of Sir James Graham (1792–1861). Consulted on microfilm in the
Bodleian and the National Library of Ireland.

NOTTINGHAM

Nottingham University Library

Newcastle Papers:
Papers of Henry Pelham Pelham-Clinton, earl of Lincoln (1811–64).
Consulted on microfilm in the National Library of Ireland.

OXFORD

Bodleian Library

Clarendon Papers:

Papers of George William Frederick Villiers, 4th earl of Clarendon (1800–70). The Letterbooks and Boxes are in the Clarendon Irish Deposit and constitute a source of prime importance.

The Queen's College

Derby Papers:

Papers of Edward George Geoffrey Smith Stanley, 14th earl of Derby (1799–1869). Through the kindness of Lord Blake, I was able to consult this collection at the Queen's College, Oxford.

III. ROME

Archives of the Congregation for the Evangelization of Peoples, or Propaganda Fide

Acta Sacrae Congregationis, or *Acta Congregationum Generalium,* normally referred to as *Acta,* are the minutes of the monthly meeting of cardinals and other members of the Congregation. They give the decisions of the Congregation and reflect its main activities.

Lettere e Decreti (1849).

Scritture Riferite nei Congressi, Irlanda.

Archives of the Pontifical Irish College, via dei SS Quattro

Cullen Papers:

Correspondence of Cardinal Paul Cullen (1803–78).

Kirby Papers:

Correspondence of Archbishop Tobias Kirby (1804–95).

Archives of Saint Paul-Outside-the-Walls

Smith Papers:

Correspondence of Abbot Bernard Smith (1812–92).

B. PARLIAMENTARY DEBATES AND PAPERS

Eighth Report of the Commissioners of Irish Education: Roman Catholic College of Maynooth, PP 1826–7, xiii.

Hansard's Parliamentary Debates, third series (1830–91).

Report of Her Majesty's Commission appointed to inquire into the Progress and Condition of the Queen's Colleges at Belfast, Cork and Galway, PP 1857–8, xxi.

Report of Her Majesty's Commissioners appointed to inquire into the Management and Government of the College of Maynooth . . . PP 1854–5, xxii.

Report of the Select Committee of the House of Lords on Ecclesiastical Titles in Great Britain and Ireland, together with the Proceedings of the Committee, Minutes of Evidence and Appendix, PP 1867–8, viii.

Reports and Minutes of Evidence of the Select Committee, Lords, on Irish Poor Laws, PP 1849, xvi.

Reports from the Select Committee appointed to inquire into the State of Ireland . . . PP 1825, viii.

Royal Commission on University Education in Ireland, Second Report, PP 1902, xxii.

Third Report of the Select Committee, Commons, on Poor Laws, Ireland, PP 1849, xv.

C. CONTEMPORARY NEWSPAPERS AND JOURNALS

L'Ami de la Religion
Dublin Gazette
Dublin University Magazine
Edinburgh Review
Freeman's Journal
Le Correspondant: receuil périodique de religion, philosophie, politique, sciences, littérature, beaux-arts
Limerick Reporter
Morning Chronicle
Nation
Northern Whig
Protestant Penny Journal
Punch
Quarterly Review
Rambler
Revue des deux mondes
Tablet
The Times

D. CONTEMPORARY PAMPHLETS, WORKS, ETC.

[ANON.], *Missions in Ireland: Especially with Reference to the Proselytizing Movement Showing the marvellous Devotedness of the Irish to the Faith of their Fathers*, by one of the missioners (Dublin, 1855).

BEAUMONT, G. DE, *L'Irlande sociale, politique et religieuse*, 2 vols. (7th edn., Paris, 1863).

BICKERSTETH, R., *Ireland*, a lecture to the YMCA, on 6 Jan. 1852 (1852), cited by D. N. HEMPTON, 'Bickersteth, Bishop of Ripon: The Episcopate of a Mid-Victorian Evangelical', in G. PARSONS (ed.), *Religion in Victorian Britain*, iv: *Interpretations* (Manchester, 1988).

BLOMFIELD, C. J., *A Charge Delivered to the Clergy of London* (London, 1850).

Brevi Rilievi sopra il Sistema d'Insegnamento Misto che si cerca di stabilire in Irlanda nei collegi così detti della Regina (Rome, 1848).

Bulletin de la Société de Saint-Vincent-de-Paul, i: *1848–9* (Paris, 1854).

[BUTT, I.], 'Ireland Under Lord Clarendon', *Dublin University Magazine*, 39 (1853), 377–83.

[CROKER, J. W.], 'Lord Clarendon and the Orange Institution', *Quarterly Review*, 86 (Dec. 1849), 228–94.

CROLLY, G., *Disputationes Theologiae de Justitia et Jure ad Normam Juris Municipalis Britannici et Hibernici Conformatae*, 3 vols. (Dublin, 1877).

CULLEN, P., *A Letter to the Catholic Clergy of the Archdiocese of Armagh* (Dublin, 1850).

Decreta Synodi Plenariae Episcoporum Hiberniae Apud Thurles Habitae Anno MDCCCL (Dublin, 1851).

DOHENY, M., *The Felon's Track, or History of the Attempted Outbreak in Ireland, Embracing the Leading Events in the Irish Struggle from the Year 1843 to the Close of 1848* (New York, 1849; repr. Dublin, 1951).

Government Patronage of Popery: The Pope and the Irish Colleges. Address of the Dublin Branch of the Evangelical Alliance to the Protestants of the British Empire (Dublin, 1848).

GREVILLE, C., *Past and Present Policy of England Towards Ireland* (London, 1845).

HUGHES, J., *A Lecture on the Antecedent Causes of the Irish Famine in 1847 delivered . . . by the Right Rev. John Hughes, D.D., Bishop of New York at the Broadway Tabernacle, March 20th 1847* (New York, 1847).

LEWIS, G. C., *On Local Disturbances in Ireland and the Irish Church Question* (London, 1836).

MILL, JOHN STUART, 'England and Ireland 1868', in J. M. ROBSON (ed.), *Essays on England, Ireland and the Empire* (Toronto, 1992).

MURRAY, P., *Essays Chiefly Theological*, iv (Dublin, 1852).

NEWMAN, J. H., *Lectures on the Present Position of Catholics in England Addressed to the Brothers of the Oratory in the Summer of 1851* (London, 1851).

—— *Historical Sketches* (London, 1872; repr. 1970).

Report of the British Association for the Relief of the Extreme Distress of Ireland and Scotland . . . (London, 1849).

Report of the Proceedings of the General Famine Relief Committee of the Royal Exchange, from 3 May to 3 September 1849 (1849).

Report of the Proceedings of the Society of Saint Vincent de Paul in Ireland during the Year 1848 (Dublin, n.d.).

The Roman Catholic Question: A Copious series of Important Documents, of Permanent Historical Interest, on the Re-establishment of the Catholic Hierarchy in England, 1851 (London, 1851).

[SAVRY, M. W.], 'Relief of Irish Distress', *Edinburgh Review*, 89 (1849), 189–266.

—— 'Lord Clarendon's Administration', *Edinburgh Review*, 93 (1851), 208–303.

SENIOR, N. W., *Journals, Conversations and Essays Relating to Ireland*, 2 vols. (London, 1865).

—— *On National Property and on the Prospects of the Present Administration and of their Successors* (London, 1835).

The Synodical Address of the Fathers of the National Council of Thurles to their Beloved Flock, the People of Ireland (Dublin, 1850).

TALBOT, JOHN, earl of Shrewsbury, *Letter to Lord John Russell, Containing Strictures on his Letter to the Bishop of Durham* (London, 1850).

Transactions of the Central Relief Committee of the Society of Friends during the Famine in Ireland in 1846 and 1847 (Dublin, 1852).

TREVELYAN, C., 'The Irish Crisis', *Edinburgh Review*, 87 (1848), 229–320.

E. COLLECTIONS OF PRINTED CORRESPONDENCE, MEMOIRS, DIARIES, AND BIOGRAPHIES

ATKINSON, S., *Mary Aikenhead: Her Life, Her Work, and Her Friends . . .* (Dublin, 1879).

CROLLY, G., *The Life of the Most Rev. Dr Crolly* (Dublin, 1851).

DAUNT, W. J. O'NEILL, *A Life Spent for Ireland: Selections from the Journal of W. J. O'Neill Daunt . . .* (London, 1896).

FITZGERALD, P., *Personal Recollections of the Insurrection at Ballingarry in July 1848* (Dublin, 1861).

—— *A Narrative of the Proceedings of the Confederates of '48 . . .* (Dublin, 1868).

FITZPATRICK, W. J., *The Life, Times and Correspondence of the Right Rev. Dr. Doyle, Bishop of Kildare and Leighlin*, 2 vols. (Dublin, 1861).

GLADSTONE, W. E., *Prime Ministers' Papers*, ed. J. BROOKE and M. SORENSEN, 2 vols. (London, 1972).

GOOCH, G. P. (ed.), *The Later Correspondence of Lord John Russell, 1840–1876* (London, 1925).

GREVILLE, C. C. F., *The Greville Memoirs: A Journal of the Reign of Queen Victoria*, ed. H. Reeve, 8 vols. (London, 1903).

JOHNSTON, J., *A Tour in Ireland, with Meditations and Reflexions*, 2 vols. (London, 1844).

KOHL, J. G., *Ireland: Dublin, the Shannon, Limerick . . .* (London, 1843).

LAWLESS, VALENTINE, Second Viscount Cloncurry, *Personal Recollections of the Life and Times, with Extracts from the Correspondence of Valentine, Lord Cloncurry* (Dublin, 1849).

McCullagh, W. T., *Memoirs of Richard Lalor Sheil* (London, 1855).

MacDermot, B., *The Irish Catholic Petition of 1805* (Dublin, 1993).

McGee, T. D., *A Life of Rt Rev Edward Maginn, Coadjutor Bishop of Derry, with Selections from his Correspondence* (New York, 1857).

MacHale, J., *Letters* (Dublin, 1847).

Meagher, W., *Notices on the Life and Character of His Grace, Most Reverend Daniel Murray, late Archbishop of Dublin . . . with Historical and Biographical Notes* (Dublin, 1853).

Mitchel, J., *Jail Journal* (New York, 1854; repr. Dublin, 1921).

Montalembert, C. de, *Journal Intime Inédit*, ed. L. Le Guillou and N. Roger-Taillade, 2 vols. (Paris, 1990).

Moran, P. F. (ed.), *The Letters of Rev. James Maher . . . on Religious Subjects . . .* (Dublin, 1877).

Morley, J., *The Life of William Ewart Gladstone*, 2 vols. (London, 1905).

Murray, D., *Sermons of the late Most Rev. Daniel Murray, Archbishop of Dublin* (Dublin, 1859).

Newman, J. H., *The Letters and Diaries of John Henry Newman*, ed. C. S. Dessain *et al.*, vols. i–vi (Oxford, 1978–84); vols. xi–xxii (London, 1961–72); vols. xxiii–xxxxi (Oxford, 1973–7).

O'Connell, M. R. (ed.), *The Correspondence of Daniel O'Connell*, 8 vols. (Shannon and Dublin, 1972–80).

O'Sullivan, W. K., *University Education in Ireland: A Letter to Sir John Dalberg Acton, Bart., M.P.* (Dublin, 1860).

Pius a Spiritu Santo, *Life of Father Ignatius of St. Paul, Passionist (the Hon. & Rev. George Spencer, Compiled Chiefly from his Autobiography, Journal and Letters)* (Dublin, 1866).

Russell, J., *Recollections and Suggestions, 1813–73* (London, 1875).

Russell, R. (ed.), *Early Correspondence of Lord John Russell, 1805–1840*, 2 vols. (London, 1913).

Smith, E., *The Irish Journals of Elizabeth Smith, 1840–1850: A Selection*, ed. D. Thomson with M. McGusty (Oxford, 1980).

Tocqueville, A. de, *Journeys to England and Ireland*, ed. J. P. Mayer (London, 1958).

——*Journey in Ireland, July–August, 1835*, ed. E. Larkin (Dublin, 1990).

Ventura, G., *The Funeral Oration on Daniel O'Connell Delivered at Rome on the 28th June, 1847, . . .* (Dublin, 1847).

Whately, R., *The Right Use of National Afflictions, being a Charge Delivered . . . on 19 and 22 Sept. 1848* (Dublin, 1848).

F.   SECONDARY SOURCES

(i)   UNPUBLISHED WORKS

Acheson, A. R., 'The Evangelicals in the Church of Ireland, 1784–1859' (Queen's Univ. of Belfast, Ph.D. thesis, 1968).

CULLEN, B., 'Thomas L. Synnott: Famine Relief Secretary and Dublin Prison Governor' (unpub. study in possession of author).

DREYER, F. A., 'The Russell Administration 1846–1852' (Univ. of St Andrews, Ph.D. thesis, 1962).

GALOGLY, D., 'Background of Kilmore Priests' (paper in author's possession).

GRAY, P. H., 'British Politics and the Irish Land Question, 1843–1850' (Univ. of Cambridge, Ph.D. thesis, 1992).

HATTON, H. E., ' "The Largest Amount of Good"; Quaker Relief in Ireland' (Toronto Univ., Ph.D. thesis, 1989).

LIECHTY, J., 'Irish Evangelicalism, Trinity College Dublin, and the Mission of the Church of Ireland at the End of the Eighteenth Century' (National Univ. of Ireland, Ph.D. thesis, 1987).

McGRATH, T. G., 'Politics, Interdenominational Relations and Education in the Public Ministry of James Doyle, O.S.A., Bishop of Kildare and Leighlin, 1819–1834' (Hull Univ., Ph.D. thesis, 1992).

MONTAGU, R. J., 'Relief and Reconstruction in Ireland, 1845–9: A study in Public Policy during the Great Famine' (Univ. of Oxford, D.Phil. thesis, 1976).

O'DONOGHUE, P., 'The Catholic Church and Ireland in an Age of Revolution and Rebellion, 1782–1803' (National Univ. of Ireland, Ph.D. thesis, 1975).

O'DWYER, P., 'John Francis Spratt, O. Carm., 1796–1871' (Pontificia Università Gregoriana, Rome, doctoral thesis 1968).

PRUNTY, J. L., 'The Geography of Poverty, Dublin 1850–1900: The Social Mission of the Church, with Particular Reference to Margaret Aylward and Co-workers' (National Univ. of Ireland, Ph.D. thesis, 1992).

(*ii*) PUBLISHED WORKS

AHERN, J., 'The Plenary Synod of Thurles', *Irish Ecclesiastical Record*, 5th ser. lxxv (1951), 385–403; lxxviii (1952), 1–20.

AKENSON, D. H., *A Protestant in Purgatory: Richard Whately, Archbishop of Dublin* (Hamden, Conn., 1981).

ALTER, P., 'O'Connell and German Politics', in M. R. O'CONNELL (ed.), *Daniel O'Connell: Political Pioneer* (Dublin, 1991), 110–17.

ARNSTEIN, W. L., *Protestant versus Catholic in Mid-Victorian England: Mr Newdegate and the Nuns* (Colombia, 1982).

BAILY, M., 'The Parish Mission Apostolate of the Redemptorists in Ireland, 1851–1898', in R. GALLAGHER and B. McCONVERY (eds.), *History and Conscience* (Dublin, 1989).

BARRY, P. C., 'The Legislation of the Synod of Thurles, 1850', *Irish Theological Quarterly*, 26 (1959), 131–66.

—— 'The National Synod of Thurles, 1850: Contemporary Accounts', *Irish Ecclesiastical Record*, 5th ser. lxxxvi (1956), 73–82.

BATTERSBY, W. J., *The Complete Catholic Directory, Almanac and Registry* (Dublin, 1848–53).

BLAKE, R., *Disraeli* (London, 1969).

BOLSTER, E., *A History of the Diocese of Cork, from the Penal Era to the Famine* (Cork, 1989).

BOSSY, J., *The English Catholic Community, 1570–1850* (London, 1975).

BOURKE, A., 'Apologia for a Dead Civil Servant: In the Service of Russell', *Irish Times*, 6 May 1977.

—— '*The Visitation of God*'? *The Potato and the Great Irish Famine*, ed. J. HILL and C. Ó GRÁDA (Dublin, 1993).

BOURKE, U. J., *The Life and Times of the Most Rev. John MacHale, Archbishop of Tuam and Metropolitan* (Dublin, 1882).

BOURNE, K., *Palmerston: The Early Years, 1784–1841* (London, 1982).

BOWEN, D., *Souperism: Myth or Reality? A Study of Catholics and Protestants during the Great Famine* (Cork, 1970).

—— *The Protestant Crusade in Ireland, 1800–1870* (Dublin, 1978).

—— *Paul Cardinal Cullen and the Shaping of Modern Irish Catholicism* (Dublin, 1983).

BOYCE, D. G., *Ireland 1828–1923: From Ascendancy to Democracy* (Oxford, 1992).

BRENT, R., *Liberal Anglican Politics: Whiggery, Religion, and Reform, 1830–1841* (Oxford, 1987).

BRIGGS, A., *1851* (London, 1951).

—— *Victorian People: A Reassessment of Persons and Themes* (Chicago, 1972).

BRODERICK, J., *The Holy See and the Repeal Movement 1829–1847* (Rome, 1951).

BUSCHKÜHL, M., *Great Britain and the Holy See* (Dublin, 1982).

CANNON, S., 'Irish Episcopal Meetings, 1788–1882', *Annuarium Historiae Conciliorum*, 13 (1981), 270–421.

CHADWICK, O., *The Victorian Church*, 2 vols. (London, 1966).

CLARK, S., and DONNELLY, J. S., *Irish Peasants: Violence and Political Unrest 1780–1914* (Dublin, 1983).

COEN, M., 'Gleanings—The Famine in Galway', *Connaught Tribune*, 14, 21, 28 Mar.; 4, 11, 18, 25 Apr.; 9, 16 May 1975.

COMERFORD, R. V., *The Fenians in Context: Irish Politics and Society 1848–82* (Dublin, 1985).

—— 'Churchmen, Tenants, and Independent Opposition, 1850–56', in W. E. VAUGHAN (ed.), *A New History of Ireland, v: Ireland under the Union, I, 1801–70* (Oxford, 1989), 396–414.

CONDON, K., *The Missionary College of All Hallows, 1824–1891* (Dublin, 1986).

CONNELL, K. H., *Irish Peasant Society: Four Historical Essays* (Oxford, 1986).

CONNOLLY, S. J., *Priests and People in Pre-Famine Ireland, 1780–1845* (Dublin, 1982).

—— *Religion and Society in Nineteenth-Century Ireland* (Dundalk, 1985).

COOKE, C., and KEITH, B., *British Historical Facts, 1830–1900* (London, 1984).

—— and PAXTON, J., *European Political Facts 1848–1918* (London, 1978).

CORBETT, T. P., *Ireland Sends India a Noble Prelate* (Calcutta, 1955).

CORISH, P., 'Cardinal Cullen and Archbishop MacHale', *Irish Ecclesiastical Record*, 5th ser. xci (1959), 393–408.

—— 'Cardinal Cullen and the National Association of Ireland', *Reportorium Novum*, iii (1962), 13–16.

—— 'Gallicanism at Maynooth: Archbishop Cullen and the Royal Visitation of 1853', in A. COSGROVE and D. MCCARTNEY (eds.), *Studies in Irish History, presented to R. Dudley Edwards* (Dublin, 1979), 176–89.

—— 'The Radical Face of Paul Cardinal Cullen', in id. (ed.), *Radicals, Rebels and Establishments* (Belfast, 1984), 171–84.

CORISH, P. J., *The Irish Catholic Experience: A Historical Survey* (Dublin, 1985).

COSTA, E., 'Da O'Connell a Pio IX: Un Capitolo del Cristianesimo Sociale del P. Gioacchino Ventura (1847)', in L. MORABITO (ed.), *Daniel O'Connell: Atti del Convegno di Studi nel 140° Anniversario della Morte* (Genoa, 1990), 93–115.

COSTELLO, N., *John MacHale, Archbishop of Tuam* (Dublin, 1939).

COULON, P., and BRASSEUR, P., *Libermann 1802–1852: Une pensée et une mystique missionnaires* (Paris, 1988).

COULTER, J. A., 'The Political Theory of Dr Edward Maginn, Bishop of Derry, 1846–9', *Irish Ecclesiastical Record*, 5th ser. xcviii (1962), 104–13.

CRAWFORD, E. M. (ed.), *Famine: The Irish Experience, 900–1900: Subsistence Crises and Famines in Ireland* (Edinburgh, 1989).

CUNNINGHAM, T. P., 'The Great Famine in County Cavan', *Breifne*, journal of Cumann Seanchais Bhreifne [Breifne Historical Society], 2 (1965), 413–37.

—— 'Church Reorganization', in P. J. CORISH (ed.), *A History of Irish Catholicism* (Dublin, 1970), vol. v, no. 7.

CURATO, F., *Gran Bretagna e Italia nei documenti della missione Minto*, 2 vols. (Rome, 1970).

CURRAN, M. J., 'The Correspondence of Abbot Smith, O.S.B.', *Reportorium Novum*, i (1955), 243–4.

DALY, M. E., *The Famine in Ireland* (Dundalk, 1986).

DASENT, A. I., *John Thadeus Delane, Editor of 'The Times': His Life and Correspondence*, 2 vols. (London, 1908).

DAVIS, R., *The Young Ireland Movement* (Dublin, 1987).

DE RUGGIERO, L., 'Inghilterra e Stato Pontificio nel Primo Triennio del

Pontificato di Pio IX', *Archivio della Società romana di Storia patria*, lxxvi (1953), 51–172.

DE WAAL, E., *A World Made Whole: Rediscovering the Celtic Tradition* (London, 1991).

DONLON, B., 'The Mahon Murder Trials', *County Roscommon Historical and Archaeological Journal*, 1 (1986), 31–2.

DONNELLY, J. S., 'Famine and Government Response, 1845–6', 'Production, Prices, and Exports, 1846–51', 'The Administration of Relief, 1846–7', 'The Soup Kitchens', 'The Administration of Relief, 1847–51', 'Landlords and Tenants', 'Excess Mortality and Emigration', 'A Famine in Irish Politics', all in W. E. VAUGHAN (ed.), *A New History of Ireland*, v: *Ireland under the Union, I, 1801–70* (Oxford, 1989), 272–371.

DREYER, F. A., 'The Whigs and the Political Crisis of 1845', *English Historical Review*, 80 (1965), 514–37.

DUFFY, C. G., *Four Years of Irish History* (London, 1883).

—— *Young Ireland: A Fragment of Irish History* (Dublin, 1884).

—— *The League of North and South, 1850–54: An Episode in Irish History, 1850–1854* (London, 1886).

EDWARDS, R. D., and WILLIAMS, T. D. (eds.), *The Great Famine: Studies in Irish History, 1845–1852* (Dublin, 1956).

FLAXMAN, R., *A Woman Styled Bold* (London, 1991).

FORBES, H. A. C., and LEE, H., *Massachusetts Help to Ireland during the Great Famine* (Milton, Mass., 1967).

FOSTER, R. E., *Modern Ireland 1600–1972* (London, 1988).

GALLAGHER, R., and McCONVERY, B. (eds.), *History and Conscience: Studies in Honour of Seán O'Riordan CSsR* (Dublin, 1989).

GASH, N., *Sir Robert Peel: The Life of Sir Robert Peel after 1830* (London, 1972).

GILLEY, S., *Newman and his Age* (London, 1990).

GRANT, J., 'The Great Famine and the Poor Law in Ulster: The Rate-in-Aid Issue of 1849', *Irish Historical Studies*, 27 (1970), 634–52.

GRAY, R., *Cardinal Manning: A Biography* (London, 1985).

GROGAN, G. F., *The Noblest Agitator: Daniel O'Connell and the German Catholic Movement, 1830–50* (Dublin, 1991).

GWYNN, D., 'Father Kenyon and Young Ireland', *Irish Ecclesiastical Record*, 5th ser. lxxi (1949), 226–46, 508–32.

—— *Young Ireland and 1848* (Cork, 1949).

—— *Father Luigi Gentili and his Mission (1801–1848)* (Dublin, 1951).

HAMELL, P. J., *Maynooth Students and Ordinations Index, 1795–1895* (Maynooth, 1982).

HART, J., 'Sir Charles Trevelyan at the Treasury', *English Historical Review*, 75 (1960), 92–110.

[HAYDEN], A., *Footprints of Father Theobald, O.F.M. CAP: Apostle of Temperance* (Dublin, 1947).

HEALY, J., *Maynooth College: Its Centenary History* (Dublin, 1895).

HEMPTON, D., and HILL, M., *Evangelical Protestantism in Ulster Society, 1740–1890* (London and New York, 1992).

HEPBURN, A. C., 'The Catholic Community of Belfast, 1850–1940', in M. ENGMAN (ed.), *Ethnic Identity in Urban Europe* (Aldershot and New York, 1992), 39–70.

HERNON, J. M., 'A Victorian Cromwell: Sir Charles Trevelyan, the Famine and the Age of Improvement', *Eire-Ireland*, 22/3 (1987), 15–29.

HICKEY, J., and DOHERTY, J. E., *A Dictionary of Irish History since 1800* (Dublin, 1980).

HILL, J. R., 'Nationalism and the Catholic Church in the 1840s: Views of Dublin Repealers', *Irish Historical Studies*, 19 (1975), 371–95.

HILTON, B., *The Age of Atonement: The Influence of Evangelicalism on Social and Economic Thought, 1785–1865* (Oxford, 1988).

HOGAN, E. M., *The Irish Missionary Movement: A Historical Survey, 1830–1980* (Dublin, 1990).

HOLMES, J. D., *More Roman than Rome: English Catholicism in the Nineteenth Century* (London, 1978).

HOPPEN, K. T., 'National Politics and Local Realities in Mid-Nineteenth-Century Ireland', in A. COSGROVE and D. MCCARTNEY (eds.), *Studies in Irish History, Presented to R. Dudley Edwards* (Dublin, 1979).

—— *Elections, Politics, and Society in Ireland 1832–1885* (Oxford, 1984).

—— *Ireland since 1800: Conflict and Conformity* (London, 1989).

HURST, M., *Maria Edgeworth and the Public Scene: Intellect, Fine Feeling and Landlordism in the Age of Reform* (London, 1969).

HYNES, E., 'The Great Hunger and Irish Catholicism', *Societas*, 8 (1978), 137–56.

KEENAN, D., *The Catholic Church in Nineteenth-Century Ireland: A Sociological Study* (Dublin, 1983).

KELLY, J., 'The Catholic Church in the Diocese of Ardagh, 1650–1870', in R. GILLESPIE and G. MORAN (eds.), *Longford: Essays in County History* (Dublin, 1991).

KENNEDY, B. A., 'The Tenant Right Agitation in Ulster, 1845–50', *Bulletin of the Irish Committee for Historical Sciences*, 34 (1944), 2–5.

KERR, D. A., *Peel, Priests, and Politics: Sir Robert Peel's Administration and the Roman Catholic Church in Ireland, 1841–1846* (Oxford, 1982).

—— 'Under the Union Flag: The Catholic Church in Ireland, 1800–1870', in R. BLAKE (ed.), *Ireland after the Union* (London, 1989).

—— 'Religion, State and Ethnic Identity', and 'Government and Roman Catholics in Ireland', in id. (ed.), *Religion, State and Ethnic Groups* (London and New York, 1992).

KIERSE, S., *The Famine Years in the Parish of Killaloe, 1845–1851* (Killaloe, 1984).

KLAUS, R. J., *The Pope, the Protestants, and the Irish: Papal Aggression and Anti-Catholicism in Mid-nineteenth Century England* (New York and London, 1987).

—— 'The Devotional Revolution in Ireland, 1850–1875', *American Historical Review*, 87 (1972), 625.

LARKIN, E., 'The Quarrel among the Catholic Hierarchy over the National System of Education in Ireland, 1838–41', in R. BROWNE, J. ROSCELLI, and R. LOFTUS (eds.), *The Celtic Cross: Studies in Irish Culture and Literature* (New York, 1964), 121–46.

—— *The Making of the Roman Catholic Church in Ireland, 1850–1860* (Chapel Hill, 1980).

—— *The Historical Dimensions of Irish Catholicism* (New York, 1981).

—— *The Consolidation of the Roman Catholic Church in Ireland, 1860–1870* (Chapel Hill, 1987).

LEE, J., *The Modernisation of Irish Society, 1848–1918* (Dublin, 1973).

LEETHAM, C. L., *Luigi Gentili: a Sower for the Second Spring* (London, 1965).

LEIGHTON, C. D. A., 'Gallicanism and the Veto Controversy: Church, State and Catholic Community in Early Nineteenth-Century Ireland', in R. V. COMERFORD, M. CULLEN, J. R. HILL, and C. LENNON (eds.), *Religion, Conflict and Coexistence in Ireland: Essays Presented to Monsignor Patrick J. Corish* (Dublin, 1990).

LEVY, S. L., *Nassau W. Senior 1790–1864: Critical Essayist, Classical Economist, and Adviser of Governments* (Newton Abbot, 1970).

LIMOUZIN, R., and LEFLON, J., *Mgr Denys-Auguste Affre, archevêque de Paris, 1793–1848* (Paris, 1971).

MACAULAY, A., 'Dr Cullen's Appointment to Armagh, 1849', *Seanchas Ard Mhacha*, 10 (1980–1), 3–36.

—— *Patrick Dorian, Bishop of Down and Connor, 1865–1885* (Dublin, 1987).

—— 'William Crolly, Archbishop of Armagh 1835–49', *Seanchas Ard Mhacha*, 14 (1990), 1–19.

MCCLELLAND, V. A., *English Roman Catholics and Higher Education* (Oxford, 1973).

MACDERMOT, B., *The Irish Catholic Petition of 1805* (Dublin, 1993).

MACDONAGH, O., 'The Irish Catholic Clergy and Emigration during the Great Famine', *Irish Historical Studies*, 5 (1946–7), 287–302.

—— 'The Politicization of the Irish Catholic Bishops, 1800–1850', *Historical Journal*, 18 (1974), 37–53.

—— *O'Connell: The Life of Daniel O'Connell, 1775–1848* (London, 1991).

MCGRATH, F., *Newman's University: Idea and Reality* (Dublin, 1951).

MCGRATH, T. G., 'Interdenominational Relations in Pre-Famine Tipperary', in W. NOLAN and T. G. MCGRATH (eds.), *Tipperary: History and*

Society; Inter-disciplinary Essays on the History of an Irish County (Dublin, 1985).

McGRATH, T. G., 'The Tridentine Evolution of Modern Irish Catholicism 1563–1962: A Re-examination of the "Devotional Revolution" Thesis', in R. O'MUIRÍ (ed.), *Irish Church History Today*, Cumann Seanchais Ard Mhaca seminar, 10 Mar. 1990 (Armagh, 1991).

MACHIN, G. I. T., *Politics and the Churches in Great Britain 1832–1868* (Oxford, 1977).

MACINTYRE, A. D., *The Liberator: Daniel O'Connell and the Irish Party, 1830–1847* (London, 1965).

MACKIERNAN, F. J., *Diocese of Kilmore: Bishops and Priests, 1136–1988* (Cavan, 1990).

McREDMOND, L., *Thrown Among Strangers: John Henry Newman in Ireland* (Dublin, 1990).

MAC SUIBHNE, P., *Paul Cullen and his Contemporaries, with their Letters*, 5 vols. (Naas, 1961–77).

MAJOR, S. H., 'The *Nonconformist* and the Roman Catholic Church', *Recusant History*, 19 (1988–9), 183–97.

MANDLER, P., *Aristocratic Government in the Age of Reform: Whigs and Liberals 1830–1852* (Oxford, 1990).

MARTIN, T., *Life of H.R.H. the Prince Consort*, 5 vols. (London, 1879).

MARTINA, G., *Pio IX, 1846–1850* (Rome, 1974).

MAXWELL, C. E., *The Stranger in Ireland, from the Reign of Elizabeth to the Great Famine* (London, 1954).

MAXWELL, H. E., *The Life and Letters of George William Frederick, Fourth Earl of Clarendon*, 2 vols. (London, 1913).

MILLER, D. W., 'Irish Catholicism and the Great Famine', *Journal of Social History*, 9/1 (1975), 81–98.

MOKYR, J., *Why Ireland Starved: A Quantitative and Analytical History of the Irish Economy, 1800–1850* (London, 1983).

MONAHAN, J., *Records Relating to the Diocese of Ardagh and Clonmacnoise* (Dublin, 1886).

MOODY, T. W., and BECKETT, J. C., *Queen's, Belfast, 1845–1949: The History of a University*, 2 vols. (London, 1959).

—— MARTIN, F. X., and BYRNE, F. J. (eds.), *A New History of Ireland: A Chronology of Irish History to 1976* (Oxford, 1982).

MOORE, J. R., *Religion in Victorian Britain*, iii: *Sources* (Manchester, 1988).

MORLEY, T., ' "The Arcana of that Great Machine": Politicians and *The Times* in the Later 1840s', *History*, 73 (1988), 38–54.

MURPHY, I., 'Primary Education', in P. J. CORISH (ed.), *A History of Irish Catholicism* (Dublin, 1970), v. 1–52.

—— *The Diocese of Killaloe, 1800–1850* (Dublin, 1992).

MURPHY, J. H., 'The Role of Vincentian Parish Missions in the "Irish

Counter-Reformation" of the Mid-Nineteenth Century', *Irish Historical Studies*, 24 (1984), 152–71.

MURRAY, P., 'State Endowment of the Catholic Church in Ireland', in id. (ed.), *The Irish Annual Miscellany*, 4 vols. (Dublin, 1850).

NEWMAN, J., *Maynooth and Victorian Ireland* (Galway, 1983).

NEWSINGER, J., 'Revolution and Catholicism in Ireland, 1848–1923', *European Studies Review*, 9 (1979), 457–80.

NÍ CHEANNAIN, ÁINE (ed.), *Leon an Iarthair: Aistí ar Sheán Mac Héil, Ardeaspag Thuama, 1834–1881* (Dublin, 1983).

NORMAN, E. R., *The Catholic Church and Ireland in the Age of Rebellion, 1859–1873* (London, 1965).

—— *Anti-Catholicism in Victorian England* (Cambridge, 1968).

NOWLAN, K. B., 'The Political Background', in R. D. EDWARDS and T. D. WILLIAMS (eds.), *The Great Famine* (Dublin, 1956).

—— *The Politics of Repeal: A Study in the Relations between Great Britain and Ireland, 1841–50* (London, 1965).

O'BRIEN, R. B., *Fifty Years of Concessions to Ireland*, 2 vols. (London, 1883–5).

—— *The Great Famine in Ireland and a Retrospect of the Fifty Years 1845–92* (London, 1896).

O'CATHAOIR, B., *John Blake Dillon, Young Irelander* (Dublin, 1990).

O'CONNELL, M. R., 'John O'Connell and the Great Famine', *Irish Historical Studies*, 25 (1986), 138–43.

Ó FIANNACHTA, P. (ed.), *Léachtaí Cholm Cille VII: Ár nDúchas Creidimh* (Maigh Nuad, 1970).

Ó GRÁDA, C., *Ireland before and after the Famine: Explorations in Economic History, 1800–1925* (London, 1988).

—— *The Great Irish Famine* (London, 1989).

—— '"For Irishmen to Forget?" Recent Research on the Great Irish Famine', in A. HÄKKINEN (ed.), *Just a Sack of Potatoes? Crisis Experiences in European Societies, Past and Present* (Helsinki, 1992), 17–52.

Ó LAOGHAIRE, D., *Ár bPaidreacha Dúchais* (Dublin, 1975).

OLIEN, D. D., *Morpeth: A Victorian Public Career* (Washington, 1963).

O'MAHONY, C., *The Viceroys of Ireland* (London, 1912).

O'NEILL, T. P., 'Sidelights on Souperism', *Irish Ecclesiastical Record*, 5th ser. lxxi (1949), 50–64.

—— 'The Society of Friends and the Great Famine', *Studies*, 39 (1950), 203–13.

—— 'The Catholic Clergy and the Great Famine', *Reportorium Novum*, i (1956), 461–9.

—— 'The Organisation and Administration of Relief, 1845–52', in R. D. EDWARDS and T. D. WILLIAMS (eds.), *The Great Famine* (Dublin, 1956).

O'REILLY, B., *John MacHale, Archbishop of Tuam: His Life, Times and Correspondence*, 2 vols. (New York, 1890).

O'ROURKE, J., *The History of the Great Irish Famine of 1847 with Notices of Earlier Irish Famines* (3rd edn., Dublin, 1902).

O'SHEA, J., *Priest, Politics and Society in Post-Famine Ireland: A Study of County Tipperary, 1850–1891* (Dublin, 1983).

PARRY, J. P., *Democracy and Religion: Gladstone and the Liberal Party, 1867–1875* (Cambridge, 1989).

PARSONS, G., *Religion in Victorian Britain*, iv: *Interpretations* (Manchester, 1988).

PATTISON, R., *The Great Dissent: John Henry Newman and the Liberal Heresy* (Oxford, 1991).

PAUL, H., *A History of Modern England*, 5 vols. (London, 1904–6).

PAZ, D. G., 'Another Look at Lord John Russell and the Papal Aggression, 1850', *The Historian*, 45 (1982–3), 47–64.

—— *Priesthoods and Apostasies of Pierce Connelly: A Study of Victorian Conversion and Anti-Catholicism* (New York, 1986).

PREST, J., *Lord John Russell* (London, 1972).

PURCELL, M., 'Sidelights on the Dublin Diocesan Archives', *Archivium Hibernicum*, xxxvi (1981), 44–50.

RAFFERTY, O. J., 'Nicholas Wiseman, Ecclesiastical Politics and Anglo-Irish Relations', *Recusant History*, 30 (1993), 381–400.

RALLS, W., 'The Papal Aggression of 1850: A Study in Victorian Anti-Catholicism', *Church History*, 43 (1974), 242–56.

REYNOLDS, J. A., *The Catholic Emancipation Crisis in Ireland* (Yale, 1954).

SCHIEFEN, R. J., *Nicholas Wiseman and the Transformation of English Catholicism* (Sheperdstown, 1984).

SHARP, J., *Reapers of the Harvest: the Redemptorists in Great Britain and Ireland, 1843–1898* (Dublin, 1989).

SHEEHY, D., 'Archbishop Murray of Dublin and the Great Famine in Mayo', *Cathair na Mart* [journal of the Westport Historical Society], 11 (1991), 118–28.

STEELE, E. D., 'Cardinal Cullen and Irish Nationality', *Irish Historical Studies*, 19 (1975), 239–60.

—— 'Gladstone, Irish Violence, and Conciliation', in A. COSGROVE and D. MCCARTNEY (eds.), *Studies in Irish History, presented to R. Dudley Edwards* (Dublin, 1979).

STERN, D., *Histoire de la Révolution de 1848* (Paris, 1985).

SULLIVAN, A. M., *New Ireland* (London, 1909).

SUPPLE, J. F., 'Ultramontanism in Yorkshire, 1850–1900', *Recusant History*, 17 (1984–5), 274–86.

SWIFT, R., and GILLEY, S., *The Irish in the Victorian City* (London, 1985).

—— *The Irish in Britain, 1815–1939* (London, 1989).

TOWNSHEND, C., *Political Violence in Ireland: Government and Resistance since 1848* (Oxford, 1983).

USSHER, J. M., *Father Fahy: A Biography of Anthony Dominic Fahy, O.P., Irish Missionary in Argentina, 1805–1871* (Buenos Aires, 1951).

VAUGHAN, W. E., *Landlords and Tenants in Ireland, 1848–1904* (Dublin, 1984).

—— (ed.), *A New History of Ireland*, v: *Ireland under the Union, I, 1801–70* (Oxford, 1989).

—— and FITZPATRICK, A. J., *Irish Historical Statistics: Population 1821–1971* (Dublin, 1978).

VILLIERS, G. J. T. H., *A Vanished Victorian, Being the Life of George Villiers, Fourth Earl of Clarendon* (London, 1938).

VINCENT, J. (ed.), *Disraeli and the Conservative Party: Journals and Memoirs of Edward Henry, Lord Stanley 1849–1869* (Hassocks, Sussex, 1978).

WALPOLE, S., *The Life of Lord John Russell*, 2 vols. (London, 1889; repr. 1969).

WARD, B., *The Sequel to Catholic Emancipation*, ii: *1840–1850* (London, 1915).

WHELAN, I., 'Edward Nangle and the Achill Mission 1832–54', in R. GILLESPIE and G. MORAN (eds.), *A Various County: Essays in Mayo History, 1500–1900* (Westport, Conn., 1987).

WHYTE, J. H., *The Independent Irish Party, 1850–9* (Oxford, 1958).

—— 'The Influence of the Catholic Clergy on Elections in Nineteenth-Century Ireland', *English Historical Review*, 75 (1960), 239–44.

WIGHAM, M. J., *The Irish Quakers: A Short History of the Religious Society of Friends in Ireland* (Dublin, 1992).

WILLIAMS, T. D., 'O'Connell's Impact on Europe', in K. B. NOWLAN and M. R. O'CONNELL (eds.), *Daniel O'Connell: Portrait of a Radical* (Dublin, 1984).

WILSON, A., *Blessed Dominic Barberi: Supernaturalized Briton* (London, 1967).

WOLFFE, J., *The Protestant Crusade in Great Britain, 1829–1860* (Oxford, 1991).

WOODHAM-SMITH, C., *The Great Hunger: Ireland 1845–9* (London, 1962).

Index